# *Sowing Good Seeds*

# *Sowing Good Seeds*

## THE NORTHWEST SUFFRAGE CAMPAIGNS OF SUSAN B. ANTHONY

G. THOMAS EDWARDS

*Oregon Historical Society Press*

Designed and produced by the Oregon Historical Society Press.

Library of Congress Cataloging-in-Publication Data

Edwards, G. Thomas.
Sowing good seeds.

Bibliography: p.
Includes index.
1. Women—Suffrage—Oregon—History. 2. Anthony, Susan B. (Susan Brownell), 1820-1906. I. Title.
JK1911.07E39 1989 324.6'23'09795 89-8824
ISBN 0-87595-192-9

The paper used in this publication meets the minimum requirements of American National Standard for Information Sciences—Permanence of Paper for Printed Library Materials, ANSI Z39.48-1984.



Oregon Historical Society Press
1230 SW Park
Portland, Oregon 97205



Printed in the United States of America.

*Dedicated to five family members*
*from four generations*
*who taught me much*
*about the female experience*

Clara Cheska
Marie McMullen
Alyce Tuttle
Nannette Edwards
Stephanie Edwards

# Contents

Susan B. Anthony, 1871. (Nebraska State Historical Society)

# Foreword

ONE OF THE WAYS that the photographs of Susan B. Anthony fail to do her justice is that they never reveal her adventurous nature. They show a sharp-chinned woman whose moral determination seems evident, but there is little sign of the curiosity about people and places, the unpretentious, natural manner and general warmth that is evident in her letters and the accounts of those who knew her. By drawing on her letters and diary entries, on the papers of Oregon suffragist Abigail Scott Duniway, and on a wealth of press reports to tell the story of Susan B. Anthony's visits to the Northwest in 1871, 1896, and 1905, G. Thomas Edwards captures this outgoing nature, this adventurous spirit.

The story of Susan B. Anthony in the Northwest begins at a turning point in her long career. When she started working for woman's rights in upstate New York shortly after she met Elizabeth Cady Stanton in 1851, her work remained mainly in the Northeast for the next fifteen years. Though many woman's rights organizations had formed in other states, Anthony's first extensive campaign outside New York did not take place until 1867 when she and Stanton went to Kansas. Then in 1871 Anthony and Stanton made their first trip west. They went to San Francisco to begin a California lecture tour, and when Stanton decided to return east to attend to family affairs, Anthony accepted an invitation to go to Oregon.

She had gone on her own to new places before but never into such unfamiliar territory. Just after her arrival in Portland, she wrote to

Stanton on 10 September 1871. At the age of fifty-one her excitement over the adventure was youthful, her usual anxiety about speaking countered by a new confidence:

> I've been & gone & done it—Announced at close of my second lecture Friday night—(& it was a grand success—not quite so crowded, by a splendid audience of best people—& they sat spell-bound my hour & thirty minutes through my best & closest argument on 14 & 15 amendment—) that I would address the Ladies Alone on social questions & the Proposition to *License* Proposition [she meant to write 'prostitution' for there were such proposals afoot]—I was *afraid* the women would not come that I threw open doors—free admission—and 400 came—. . . Oh If I can only hold my own & my audience tomorrow night!! Guess I can—will—I haven't had a minute of sleepy good for nothing feeling here—I think it is the climate—perfectly lovely—smoky from forest fires all around—but just warm enough—& my hotel window opens on to the beautiful Willamette River. . . .[1]

She was out of Stanton's shadow. G. Thomas Edwards' vivid account of Anthony's 1871 trip with its travel by river and over corduroy roads throughout Oregon and up to Washington Territory and Victoria, British Columbia, makes clear that this woman was coming into her prime, coping well with the physical hardships of travel and learning—painfully—to cope with derisive audiences and insolent reporters.

Edwards' book contributes to the much needed history of local suffrage movements. Who supported woman suffrage and who opposed it is still a live question. At the time of Susan B. Anthony's death in 1906 only four states had granted full suffrage to women—Colorado, Idaho, Wyoming and Utah—and two of those, Wyoming and Utah, had had equal suffrage as territories. Anthony had lobbied Congress to protect suffrage in Wyoming and Utah when their statehoods were up for approval. But of the state campaigns in which she herself worked, grassroots work that was long and tiring, none succeeded, whether haphazardly organized and meagrely funded as in South Dakota or superbly organized and well-heeled as in California. The 1893 Colorado and 1896 Idaho successes were probably anomalous: in Idaho there was

Mormon support to supplement the Populist support in both states, and in neither case was there the usual opposition from liquor interests.

Anthony and Stanton had always seen poor and working women as their natural constituents but in state campaigns found themselves caught between the immigrant vote and the anti-immigrant temperance vote. A letter from Anthony to fellow worker Olympia Brown during the South Dakota campaign of 1890 describes the problem:

> It is the most difficult sort of campaign—the strongest argument to win the Prohibition men to vote for W.S. is the very strongest one to drive from us the high license men—so the strongest testimony showing how all women's voting will lessen the ratio of the foreign vote & of the Catholic vote is just the worst thing—in fact wholly estops all hope of winning the foreign born men's vote—& the Catholic vote. We are between two distracting dilemmas at every step—so I try to keep my talk on general principles—the bettering of women's chances for work & wages, tyranny of taxation &c &c But it is hardly possible to say anything that will not hurt somebody—so each of us must be governed by our own true inwardness—as to what & how to present our claims.[2]

Anthony tried to keep the suffrage movement distinct from the much bigger temperance movement, but the support of the Woman's Christian Temperance Union, which brought thousands to endorse suffrage, could not be disavowed and, as Abigail Scott Duniway feared, may have become a liability. By the turn of the century woman suffrage seemed to find its support among the "respectable" people, and thus Duniway favored the quiet approach of appealing only to those respectable sorts who occupied positions of influence, the tactic known as the "still hunt."

But despite the defeats, the women laid the groundwork for later success. The burgeoning of women's groups formed after the Civil War taught women how to organize and how to deal with politicians and the press. The 1910 ratification of suffrage in the state of Washington marked the start of a wave of successful statewide efforts in the West. Although these victories were followed elsewhere only in New York (1917) and Michigan (1918), many other states had partial suffrage for women. These local campaigns, including the unsuccessful ones, formed the networks of support needed for congressional passage of the constitutional amendment granting women the vote. It would be a new generation of women who combined the old organization's tactics of town-by-town lecturing with massive public demonstrations formed of coalitions of working-class women and the wealthy that would see the final success of the cause. In 1918, following impressive achievements by women's organizations during World War I, the amendment nearly passed both houses of Congress, did so the following year, and final ratification of the now Nineteenth Amendment was announced on 26 August 1920.

The movement gained the respectability it needed for political success through the idea that women would improve the morals of society—an idea many still have today and many doubt, and an idea that Anthony herself wavered on. The Nineteenth Amendment did not bring women equality nor would their voting remedy society's ills. But they had gained a status, a recognition, that would allow a new view of themselves and make future gains possible. And Susan B. Anthony's role in creating this new recognition was to keep the idea alive, keep the movement going for over fifty years, and in her own person set an example of self-reliance and independence.

When Anthony first arrived in Oregon, people associated the movement with free love and sexual promiscuity, but by the time she came for her last visit in 1905, when the National American Woman Suffrage Association held its convention in Portland, she was a saintly figure for whom the respectable citizenry held grand dinners. She was eighty-five then, in good health, and her own health symbolized for people the lingering viability of the cause. What made this extraordinary change in public opinion possible is the subject of Edwards' fascinating study.

Patricia G. Holland Co-Editor,
*The Papers of Elizabeth Cady Stanton and Susan B. Anthony*
University of Massachusetts at Amherst

# *Acknowledgements*

A HISTORICAL STUDY that has lasted as long as this one means that the author compiles a large debt of gratitude to numerous institutions and individuals. Whitman College provided me with a sabbatical and financial assistance through its Aid to Scholarship and Instructional Development Committee. In either public presentations, classes, or private conversations, members of the college community have listened to me talk about Susan B. Anthony and they have responded with ideas, bibliography, and encouragement. Whitman's history department has long been supportive; undoubtedly, its members have heard more about Anthony and her co-workers than they wanted. Three department members—Donald King, David Schmitz, and the late Robert Whitner—read some or all of the chapters in various stages of development. Although the college does not have graduate students to assist faculty, it does have competent undergraduates. These loyal and efficient individuals have equaled graduate students in their resourcefulness and dependability, especially in helping read newspapers on microfilm. Mary Beth Haynes, Suzanne Gunther, Evan McFadden, Greg Thomas, Minor Lile, Laurie Johnson, Tia Kolbaba, Cindy Hillis, Kim McKaig, Michelle Staley, and Amber Olsen have carried out various tasks. Lisa May and Arlene Weible have long been involved with the research and checking citations. Dana Bell gave the manuscript a close reading.

The school's librarians have provided research assistance, inter-library loan materials, and other services. I am especially indebted to Marilyn Sparks and Larry Dodd.

Several secretaries have managed to read my handwriting and to meet unfair deadlines. Robbie Skiles, Charlotte Pauly, Jeanette Herrera, Dottie Wissenback, and Shirley Muse have all typed on this manuscript.

My indebtedness, of course, extends far beyond the Whitman campus. I have been the beneficiary of institutions and individuals from one coast to the other. The following libraries and librarians were important: the University of Washington (Carla Rickerson and Glenda Pearson), the University of Oregon, the Seattle Public Library (Jean Coberly), the Multnomah County, the Washington State Historical Society, the Washington State Library (Jeanne Engerman), the Oregon Historical Society (Peggy Haines), Provincial Archives of British Columbia, the Library of Congress, and the Huntington Library, which generously allowed me to use the Jean Carr collection, Susan B. Anthony Memorial collection, the Clara Colby collection, Elizabeth Morrison Harbert papers, Ida Harper papers, and Caroline Maria Severance papers. Thanks also to the Schlesinger Library, Radcliffe College, for permission to use the diary of Mary S. Anthony.

A variety of historians shared their expertise. Dr. Patricia Holland wrote the foreword, shared important primary materials, answered questions, and critiqued the manuscript. Carlos Schwantes and Eckard Toy provided ideas about women and other groups in regional history. The late Martin Schmitt critiqued an early chapter and Carol Zabilski provided encouragement and expertise as I sought elusive footnotes completing these drafts. David Duniway generously permitted me to use his collection of Abigail Scott Duniway papers, and he related events in the life of his famous grandmother. Beverly Beeton, who also has an interest in Anthony's work in the West, co-authored an article. Judy Austin, T.A. Larson, Bruce Taylor Hamilton, Liz Buehler, Lee Nash and Ross Woodbridge assisted in various ways.

My editor, Adair Law, patiently prepared various "final drafts" and supplied materials and ideas.

My family has been involved in this project from its start. My son Randall and my daughter Stephanie have talked with me about most of the ideas and many of the facts that are in these pages. My wife Nannette has been the most important supporter over these many years. She has gone on many research trips that reduced family vacation time, she has written out or xeroxed hundreds of documents, she has listened to me analyze the Pacific Northwest's suffrage movement, and she has given the manuscript a keen reading. She has cheerfully allowed another woman, Susan B. Anthony, to be a part of our lives.

The subject of this study enlisted dozens of regional volunteers to advance her reform. I learned from Anthony's example and also put capable volunteers to work. My deepest thanks to all of them for helping me make this book.

# *Introduction*

IN THE TWENTIETH CENTURY Susan B. Anthony's reputation has had peaks and valleys. At the time of her death in 1906 many citizens considered her to be an extraordinary American woman. Henry B. Blackwell, one of her esteemed allies, provided such an interpretation: "Miss Anthony had qualities of leadership such as are possessed by few women or men. With rare devotion and unflinching tenacity of purpose, she has identified herself for years with the suffrage movement. . . . Her name will always be identified with this greatest of all political reforms."[1] Anthony's name was often invoked as the fight for female suffrage continued to be a major issue. In 1920 the Nineteenth Amendment granted woman suffrage; some called this law the Anthony Amendment in recognition of her hard labor to bring this reform into reality.

In the next half century, Americans, who generally have short historical memories, gave too little attention to Anthony and the other suffragists. The nation followed the lives of contemporary women, including the accomplishments of Amelia Earhart, the politics of Eleanor Roosevelt, the work of "Rosie the Riveter," and the marriages of Hollywood stars. But Susan B. Anthony had not been completely forgotten: in 1933 a poll co-sponsored by the *Ladies' Home Journal* ranked her as the fifth greatest female leader in American history, the government issued a three-cent Anthony postage stamp in 1936 to commemorate the sixteenth anniversary of the ratification of the Nineteenth Amendment and offered a fifty-cent stamp with her likeness in 1955.[2] In 1937, an early and influential proponent of woman's history, Mary R. Beard, called Anthony "a peaceful warrior" who deserved immortality because her long political battle for her sex helped bring democracy to the nation. Until the 1970s high school and college American history textbooks—the barometers of public opinion about the past—gave scant attention to famous or ordinary women. Therefore, the goals as well as the tactics of Anthony and her allies dropped from our collective memory.

In the late 1970s, the entire nation again became aware of Anthony. In 1978, after some polling and much deliberation, Congress created a new $1.00 coin bearing her likeness. Diverse groups lobbied for this measure. The president of the Daughters of the American Revolution called the suffragist leader "a pioneer worker for women's rights," especially for the voting privilege.[3] At the other end of the ideological spectrum, the president of the National Organization of Women endorsed Anthony because, "We need a real role model of females of this country"; furthermore, "she was not only a leader for women's rights but was a leader for justice and democracy. Her writings . . . are comparable to Thomas Jefferson's." Members of Congress also lauded the long-time reformer; one stated that she and Benjamin Franklin held unique places in American history.

The passage of the Susan B. Anthony Silver Coin Act seemed to be popular in the Pacific Northwest. The Portland *Oregonian* judged that "this great pioneer in human rights richly . . . deserves the honor." The newspaper, like many individuals, wondered if the current generation "actually knows who she was."[4] The American Association of University Women helped reestablish Anthony's reputation when in 1981 its members in an informal poll chose her as the nation's outstanding woman. But by the mid-1980s, her fame had again faded—in part because the new coin, which was easily confused with the quarter, disappeared from circulation. Perhaps her decline in popularity is proved when a distinguished historian, John A. Garraty, failed in 1989 to cite her in his compilation, 1001 *Things Everyone Should Know About American History.*

This book is not an attempt to provide a modern biography of Anthony, including her lasting influence in the eighty years since her death. It is, however, intended to show how her reform work in Oregon, Washington, and Idaho in three campaigns—1871, 1896, and 1905—sowed "good seed" for the woman's suffrage movement.

Anthony understood the general history of Pacific Northwest reform and helped shape its course. The region had not been significantly affected by the reform ferment that was such a vital part of the national American life from 1815 to 1860. Because of their remote location, small population, and the arduous demands of establishing farms, homes and other institutions, Oregon and Washington pioneers were much less influenced by the apostles of societal change than were their families and friends in the Northeast and Midwest. The powerful and divisive abolitionist movement altered many Northern lives, but those in the Pacific Northwest largely only read about it.

But during the nineteenth century there were other types of reformers scattered from Eugene to Seattle. Some immigrants who had participated in the vast eastern reform chorus sought to establish western ones, especially in the Willamette Valley. Reform-minded folks generally pushed—as did their eastern counterparts—for a variety of causes at once. Those favoring change generally advocated one special reform but gave time to others as well. Frontier reformers expressed a desire to save their new communities from the flaws embedded in the older social fabric. Thus these small groups championed better schools, safer medicine, the establishment of cooperatives, the creation of temperance societies and liquor laws, and improved conditions and opportunities for women.

During the last three decades of the nineteenth century the two most important regional reform movements were for woman's suffrage and temperance. Oregon, Washington, and Idaho women played an important role in both; furthermore, they received national-level instruction from Anthony about suffrage and from Frances Willard of the Women's Christian Temperance Union (WCTU) about temperance. Both famous national leaders came to the region, where they taught reform, won adherents, and organized supporters. The struggle for equal suffrage in Pacific Northwest states was a long one, lasting from 1871 to 1912. Unlike the other reforms it was led by women, who necessarily had to become politicians so as to win support from legislators and voters. The WCTU, of course, was also led by women, but it enjoyed more male support, including the Prohibition Party.

At times an impressive number of women and men in the suffrage ranks vigorously pursued their cause. Sometimes only a few soldiered. At both the national and the regional level it proved difficult to maintain enthusiasm for the fight when victories were few, defeats were frustrating, and apathy was so commonplace. It was often necessary for Anthony, Abigail Scott Duniway, and allies to arouse interest among regional reformers as well as politicians.

For a half century the Pacific Northwest had followed eastern reform practices. This changed during the Progressive period when the region assumed a national leadership role. From the turn of the century to the First World War, journalists, politicians, reformers, and others hailed the region for its liberal measures. Scholars have pointed out that Woodrow Wilson applauded the reformatory work of William S. U'Ren in Oregon; Anthony also appreciated U'Ren's work in establishing the initiative and referendum and the Pacific Northwest's reformatory spirit. It seemed to her that because of liberal male leadership the states in the nation's far corner were ready to adopt woman suffrage. In other words, in the early 1900s the reform-minded Far West might now switch its traditional role and actually teach the East by its example of enfranchising women.

Anthony played a significant role in this long reform history. In 1871 she made her first campaign to the region, teaching woman's rights—especially equal suffrage—and reform tactics. She recruited extensively for her cause. Historian Ellen Carol DuBois has recently concluded that "the demand for woman suffrage attracted many women—especially writers, physicians, and other pioneering professionals—who had never before identified themselves with women's rights."[5] Anthony's suffrage work in the Pacific Northwest substantiates this generalization, for such women built and directed the state and local suffrage groups.

During her initial visit Anthony prepared Abigail Scott Duniway to be the regional suffragist leader. For years she aided and encouraged her pupil. A reform-minded, combative, witty, and political individual, Duniway in 1871 established the *New Northwest*, a Portland newspaper that spoke for woman's rights. An unusual frontier woman, Duniway attracted considerable attention in her own lifetime, and in recent years she has been the subject of several biographies, including a delightful one for children, *Ladies Were Not Expected,* by Dorothy Nafus Morrison. Her effort on behalf of her sex in Oregon, Washington, and Idaho was essential, but there were other effective regional suffragists—especially Emma Smith DeVoe—who also came under Anthony's influence. Like U'Ren, DeVoe moved into the region and became a leading reformer. Though drab in comparison with Duniway, this steady worker and skilled politician fought for the cause in all three Pacific Northwest states, especially in Washington.

Other easterners besides Anthony plunged into the regional suffrage battles during the Progressive period. The National American Woman Suffrage Association (NAWSA) responded to the calls of Anthony and its other leaders by sending organizers, lecturers, and money in to Pacific Northwest referenda elections. In these contests voters decided whether the state constitution should be amended so that women would have equal voting rights. Anthony defended the participation of eastern women in western suffrage fights on the grounds that her national lieutenants had the required experience, ability, and political tactics. To the great leader's way of thinking the same political tactics should be employed by reform soldiers on battlefields from one coast to the other. Local women and men often resented this imposition of an outside agenda, complaining about the rift in the ranks that occurred after the eastern women dominated western referenda fights.

In the 1890s Anthony became disappointed with the independent direction of Duniway's leadership. Thus, the mentor successfully challenged the pupil for power in Idaho and Oregon. The internal politics of the regional suffrage movement are hazy, but it is clear that reformers disagreed among themselves as well as with antisuffragists. The public that sometimes learned about this infighting may have compared it with the dissentions within the two major political parties, which led to such internal splits in the 1890s over the gold issue and in the Progressive period over liberal political reforms.

At the time that Congress honored Anthony in 1978, I had just researched her initial western visit in 1871. Although I was not an authority on her full life—and am still not—I understood that she and Duniway had launched the regional suffrage movement. Seeking details about the first American woman to appear on a coin, Northwest journalists—who had only recently learned the most rudimentary facts about the outstanding suffragist—asked me for details about Anthony's work, especially in Oregon and Washington. For once I had a "relevant" research topic. During my brief moment in the media sun, I compared the long suffrage struggle with the then current battle over the Equal Rights Amendment (ERA). In both the 1870s and in the 1970s, some individuals heatedly debated the proposition that giving women more rights would necessitate giving them the concurrent responsibility of compulsory military service. This was too much for Senator Sam Ervin. The North Carolinian warned that with the ERA "daughters of America" would be drafted and sent into combat "to be slaughtered or maimed by the bayonets, the bombs, the bullets, the grenades, the mines, the napalm, the poison gas and the shells of the enemy."[6] But such a terrible prospect could be avoided, Ervin asserted, because women on the whole did not want the ERA. This same sweeping generalization had been made by antisuffragists who thundered that women did not want the ballot. Anthony's informal polling in lecture halls one hundred years earlier indicated otherwise.

The defeat of the ERA in several state legislatures prompted its advocates to reappraise the tactics that they had employed in their lengthy and frustrating campaign. Proponents of equal suffrage had also agonized and disagreed over the tactics practiced in state referenda elections. For over a century those pushing for woman's rights have responded to a negative state vote in the same way as other defeated politicians. They studied state election returns, reconsidered their organizational structure, thought about the message that they and their opponents had carried to voters, criticized the leadership of opponents openly and their own leadership privately. The results of this evaluation shaped the types of campaign that both nineteenth and twentieth century woman's rights advocates adopted for their next political contests.

While there were many similarities between the crusades for suffrage and for the ERA, there were several important differences. One of these was the fact that the earlier group of reformers had more appreciation for the nation's rich reform tradition. They put their struggle into historical context, recalling the reform activity of William Lloyd Garrison, the Grimke Sisters, Lucy Blackwell, Horace Greeley, and numerous others. Anthony, for example, insisted that Elizabeth Cady Stanton's early speeches for women were for that time—the middle of the nineteenth century—"far more revolutionary than was the Declaration of Independence. . . . There had been other rebellions against the rule of kings and nobles; men from time immemorial have been accustomed to protest against injustice; but for women to take such action was without a precedent and the most daring innovation in all history." She reminded that those women who battled for reform "were not sustained even by those of their own sex" and that they "imperiled their reputation and subjected themselves to mental and spiritual crucifixion."[7] Alice Paul was another tested woman's rights veteran who sought to convince the ERA recruits to keep an eye on the past as well as on the future. In 1970 she observed: "I don't see any lack of continuity in the fight. It's been one long struggle."[8] A few years later Midge Mackenzie, a historian, film producer, and author of *Shoulder to Shoulder*, complained about the generational difference, concluding that modern feminists waged their contest "in a historical vacuum." She urged women to "repossess the true dignity of our history" in their ongoing struggle for total equality.[9]

The need for historical perspective has seemed obvious, whether in meetings advocating reform or the status quo. Those opposed to reform can argue that change does not always produce beneficial results; the prohibition movement is an example. Agitators, like other types of politicians pushing legislation, have been guilty of excessive rhetoric; but it is the reformers themselves who are best served by putting reform into historical perspective. One such failure to do so occurred during the National Women's Political Caucus held in Portland in August 1987, which, like the 1905 National American Woman Suffrage Association Convention in Portland, planned several days "of strategizing and old-fashioned politicking." About 800 feminists came to discuss the organization's general mission—"women's participation in political and public life."[10] According to press reports their workshops were conducted in precisely such a historical vacuum as had earlier disturbed Mackenzie. Apparently the delegates made no issue of the fact that the suffragists had long ago been concerned about the involvement of women in political and public life. These early reformers did not see the ballot as an end in itself, but as a necessary first step if women were to ever possess equal rights. If women voted they could protect themselves from unfair laws and acquire significant political power. Delegates at the 1987 caucus discussed a variety of critical issues, including child care, education, pay equity, and the appointment of women to public office without placing them in their proper perspective within the long and appealing reform tradition.

This disregard of the past is in stark contrast to the 1905 NAWSA convention in Portland. Its speakers found inspiration in history and referred to the Declaration of Independence, the Constitution, the

Seneca Falls convention, the abolitionist and other reform movements, state suffrage battles, and the commitment and dedication of those who had first sought to expand the rights of American women. The words, deeds, and photographs of these predecessors inspired them. These delegates saw themselves as the new ranks in an old and honorable battle for societal improvement.

There are, of course, contemporary men and women who appreciate this continuity. In the past twenty years journalists, scholars, professors, and activists have made the public aware of the richness of America's reform tradition. The findings of many scholars now working in women's history have made it clear that societal stumps have deep and entangled roots that earlier generations have first sought to dig up. Surely dictums about the use of history in bringing about woman's rights—full equality between the sexes—relate as much to reformers as to policymakers.

*Sowing Good Seeds*

# ONE

# *A Peaceful Warrior*

A FIFTY-ONE-YEAR-OLD PASSENGER aboard the steamer *Idaho* was lonely, anxious, and seasick. On this her first sea voyage and furthest journey from home, Susan Brownell Anthony found the strength to scribble in her diary about her miserable surroundings on the week-long trip. The diarist described herself as "sick as death midst these most sickening sounds and smells"; nauseated men and women groaned, children vomited and cried, and fathers scolded.[1] Bound from San Francisco to Portland in August 1871, she endured at least one sleepless night, worrying that the ship would lose its lengthy battle with the churning sea and that she would soon join her father, who had departed from this world in 1862. But finally she became well enough to dine on gruel, crackers, tomatoes, and tea and to urge her agenda of reforms, including woman suffrage and the termination of prostitution, on a male passenger. For twenty years Anthony had been an energetic and resourceful fighter for various reforms; this long experience had taught her that physical discomfort and mental anguish were more often than not a reformer's lot. She accepted it all as a part of a determined fight for her sex. Improved health, however, failed to end her dread of the reception Portland editors would give the initial lecture of her planned Northwest campaign.

Born in 1820 in Massachusetts and reared in New York, Susan was the second of eight children. Her Quaker father, Daniel, greatly influenced her life. Intelligent, independent, energetic, and compassionate, he advocated a variety of reforms, including temperance, abolition, and

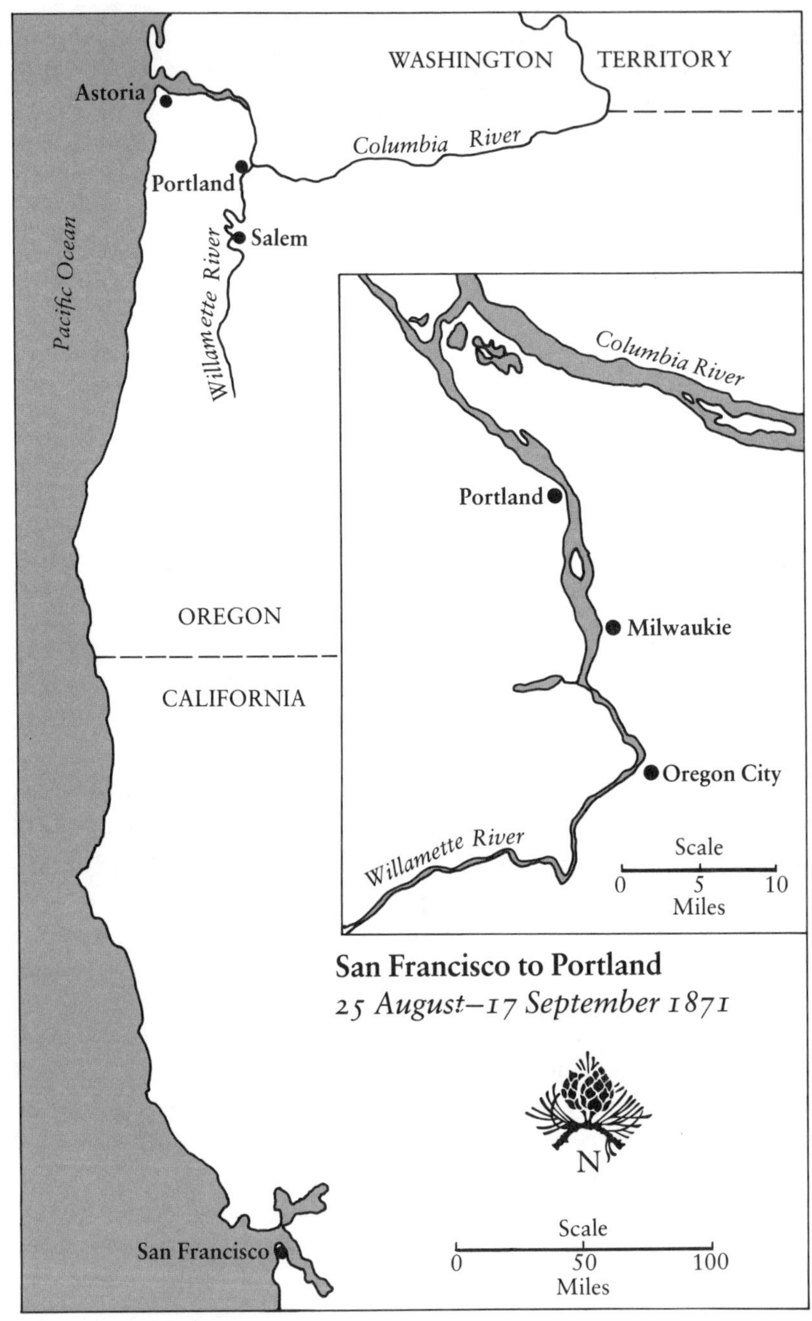


**San Francisco to Portland**
*25 August–17 September 1871*

woman suffrage. Daniel and his wife, Lucy Read Anthony, maintained that women must be able to vote if they were to help effect such reforms. He brought notable reformers into their home, where the children heard them plead their causes. Susan's mother also supported her children and reform; even in her middle years, Susan could always depend upon Lucy to understand and relieve the fatigue and frustration that resulted from her battle for societal change. These high-minded parents were in large part responsible for the fact that their children were achievers and supporters of one another. Susan wished that other families were as close as her own. She also believed that if more men had shared her father's respect for women, then it would not be necessary to wage the exhausting suffrage fight that by the time of this campaign of 1871, had continued unabated since the Seneca Falls Convention in 1848.

The parents made the financial sacrifice necessary to educate Susan at a Quaker boarding school. Like so many other intelligent young women of her time, Susan, because of pressing family obligations, became a school teacher. But she was in that minority that fought against unequal pay for females and male domination of the profession. She eventually wearied of teaching and turned her ambitions toward large-scale societal reforms. A close friend explained that "the multiplication table and spelling book no longer enchained her thoughts; larger questions began to fill her mind."[2]

It has been argued that the 1850s was Lincoln's period of preparation for greatness; this decade was similarly important to Anthony. In these years both leaders learned much about politics and society as they sought to realize political change. In her quest to influence politicians, Anthony worked in partnership with a stimulating co-worker. In 1851 she became acquainted with Elizabeth Cady Stanton; they soon formed a remarkable team. Five years older than Susan, Elizabeth was born in New York to Margaret Livingston Cady and Daniel Cady and enjoyed a superior education. Her father was a judge; through him she became well acquainted with legal and constitutional history. In 1840 she married a fellow abolitionist, Henry Stanton. In 1848 she was the person most responsible for the Seneca Falls Convention and its famous declaration. Convinced that men's legal control over women was tyrannical, Stanton insisted that the situation would not change until women enjoyed political equality with men. And, as she argued to Anthony and many others, equality could not be won without woman's suffrage.

In the 1850s Stanton and Anthony worked together in the temperance, abolition, and woman's rights movements. They neatly blended their outstanding talents: Stanton was a theorist, writer, and speaker; Anthony was a researcher and organizer. Stanton had seven children; Anthony, who never married, helped supervise them so that their mother could have more time for reform work. Stanton explained that she and Anthony maintained a close friendship despite the fact that they "hotly contended whenever we have differed." They agreed not to publicize their disagreements and that they would, "like husband and wife . . . have no differences in public."[3]

The two women often emphasized different goals for the woman's movement, and their close association inevitably led to friction. These famous activists often disagreed with each other; it was a testament to the character of each that they were able to maintain a meaningful friendship through fifty years of the frustrations and exhilarations of reform activity.

From the time she first came into the public eye to the present day, there has always been considerable curiosity about the fact that Susan remained single. Her most recent biographer explains that she met only a few men who "measured up to her intellect or her standards, which even at an early age, made an unequal relationship incomprehensible to her."[4] At some point in her thirties she married her work. Stanton reminded that Frances Willard and Clara Barton had also made the same decision and concluded: "All honor to the noble women who have devoted earnest lives to the intellectual and moral needs of mankind!"[5] Once when Stanton had lost touch with Anthony she asked: "Are you dead or married?"[6] In the 1880s, if not earlier, her admirers maintained that all of the major suffragists were wives and that Anthony, who was the notable exception, was actually "a mother to all womanhood."

In the 1850s the two leaders also agreed upon the principal goals of the woman's rights movement: that married women should control their own wages, that mothers should have joint guardianship over their children, that women should have broader inheritance rights, and that women should have the franchise. As Stanton had predicted, both men and women perceived equal suffrage as the most threatening of the movement's proposed reforms; the vast majority of Americans did not believe that women required the same economic and political options as men. Many foes argued that women were already represented in politics through the votes cast by husbands and sons. Others warned that women would be debased if they participated in politics. According to one scholar, "The early feminists' dual allegiance—to radical abolition, which rejected the corruption of politics, and women's rights, which demanded access to it—also posed a liability."[7] Stanton, Anthony, and other female activists found it difficult to convince the public that women should emerge from their private spheres of domesticity into a full participation in public life.

In the 1850s Anthony and Stanton waged an energetic campaign for woman's rights in New York. Anthony stumped the state before audiences large and small, winning both new recruits to the movement and the stinging censure of New York newspaper editors. On the eve of the Civil War, Anthony, Stanton, and their many allies had convinced the New York legislature to enact the Married Women's Property Act, which was the nation's "most comprehensive piece of women's rights legislation."[8] Through lectures, conventions, petitions, writings, and personal solicitations New York women had won a great victory.

The Civil War and Reconstruction periods had a tremendous impact on the woman's movement. Although suffragists had no formal state or national organizations or officers at this time, they continued to attract recruits and build unity through their annual conventions and publications. In many states feminists also enjoyed the support of abolitionists and their organizations, whose cause the feminists reciprocally promoted. During the war women activists supported the Union, principally through a patriotic organization, the Women's National Loyal League. At the end of this costly war, these activists stressed anew the need for woman's suffrage, both as a necessary foundation on which to attain other needed reforms and in a logical and timely linkage to one of the major issues of Reconstruction, black suffrage. Many reformers urged a universal suffrage, arguing that blacks and women were both entitled to the franchise. To achieve this goal, Stanton, Anthony, and others in 1866 formed a new organization, the Equal Rights Association. Working at the federal level for the first time, women activists petitioned and lobbied Congress. In 1866 the new organization opposed the Fourteenth Amendment (adopted in 1868). In establishing the citizenship of black Americans, the amendment succeeded in ensuring blacks the franchise, but it simultaneously excluded women from the same right through the explicit introduction of the word "male" into the

Constitution. Radical Republicans and Abolitionists—including those who had long favored female suffrage—supported the Amendment before Congress, arguing that the public was not ready for universal suffrage and that blacks needed the ballot more than women. The Equal Rights Association split over the universal suffrage idea with Anthony, Stanton and others waging an 1867 campaign for universal suffrage in Kansas. The campaign proved unsuccessful. Stanton and Anthony thus concluded that they and like-minded associates must seek to achieve woman suffrage without depending on the aid of males with Abolitionist or Radical antecedents. As historian Ellen DuBois concludes, these militant women "began to build women's rights into something it had never been before, a movement which gained its power primarily from the support of women rather than from the aid of other reformers."[9] Because they felt betrayed by former male allies, militant women added to their agenda a distrust of male leadership of the woman's reform organizations.

Stanton approved of Theodore Tilton's 1868 assessment of her and Anthony: "I know of no two more pertinacious incendiaries in the whole country. Nor will they themselves deny the charge. In fact this noise-making twain are the two sticks of a drum, keeping up what Daniel Webster called 'The rub-a-dub of agitation.'"[10] In the late 1860s, the two agitators, using the reform techniques they had employed in New York in the 1850s, stumped the Midwest in search of recruits. They also established in New York the *Revolution*, a weekly newspaper. It provided them a vehicle for disseminating their controversial ideas, including the improvement of the conditions of women workers, divorce reform, and the suffrage. They also joined in the fight against the Fifteenth Amendment (adopted in 1870), which was written, as was the Fourteenth, to guarantee rights to blacks, but not to women. In 1869 advocates of woman's rights split into two groups. Moderates formed the American Woman Suffrage Association (AWSA or American). Led by such able leaders as Julia Ward Howe, Lucy Stone, and Henry Blackwell, and by the writers of the *Woman's Journal*, a weekly journal, this organization sought to win suffrage victories in the state legislatures. In 1869 radical women, led by Stanton and Anthony countered with the National Woman Suffrage Association (NWSA or National), which championed a broader agenda of reforms for the improvement of the social, economic, and political condition of women. In Congress it lobbied for a

Sixteenth Amendment that would enfranchise them. The National served another purpose in that it provided Anthony with "a field for her particular political genius. She was a consummate organization builder and dedicated herself to creating an enduring feminist organization."[11] In 1870, however, Anthony suffered a setback when it became necessary to sell the debt-ridden *Revolution*, which had been instrumental in publicizing the National's views. She was determined to pay the debt—a daunting $10,000—a goal achieved after many years of struggle.

Early in 1871 leaders of the National adopted a new tactic for overcoming the obstacle of the detested Reconstruction Amendments. A radical and controversial figure, Victoria Woodhull, in the first appearance of a woman before a Congressional committee, argued an interpretation of the Fourteenth and Fifteenth Amendments that gave women, as citizens, the right to vote. Anthony and Stanton agreed with this so-called "New Departure argument." In 1871 and 1872 they urged women everywhere to exercise a right of citizenship by attempting to vote. If their votes were denied, the National leaders anticipated that a Supreme Court decision would be forced and rule in favor of woman suffrage. In time Woodhull became a problem for the National. Woodhull's radical writings in her newspaper (*Woodhull and Claflin's Weekly*) and her lectures on various platforms for free love provoked a major crisis in the suffrage association and between Anthony and Stanton.

But the bitter struggle in the National group over "the Woodhull" was in the future. In 1871 Anthony was far more interested in stumping for the woman's movement than in evaluating or restraining Woodhull. In that year Anthony campaigned more extensively than ever before—she delivered about 170 speeches during 13,000 miles of travel from one coast to the other.[12] She chose to make an intensive effort in the Pacific Northwest, where she estimated that she traveled 2,000 miles and delivered 60 talks. No reformer had ever stumped the region as thoroughly as this suffragist leader.

Anthony's effort was extremely significant to the growth of the region's woman suffrage movement and a study of the three months she labored in Oregon and Washington reveals much about the campaigner and the region's attitudes toward her and its own frontier women.

Anthony undertook her arduous work in the Pacific Northwest still suffering from what she considered to be an unusually abusive attack on her campaign by San Francisco editors. In 1871 she and Stanton had traveled by rail to the Pacific coast. They had made this trip for a variety of reasons: to resolve their personal disagreements, to visit with the recently enfranchised women in both Wyoming and Utah territories, to explore Yosemite, and to campaign for woman's rights in California. The notable women promoted their organization against the rival and more conservative American Woman Suffrage Association (according to Horace Greeley, the essential difference between the two groups was that the American pleaded and the National threatened); solicited signatures for suffrage petitions addressed to Congress; and were paid to lecture on such topics as suffrage, prostitution ("the social evil"), the double standard, male-dominated marriages ("man marriages"), and divorce. Their work was fairly well received until 12 July 1871 when the two reformers visited the San Francisco jail cell of Laura D. Fair, who had murdered her lover. That evening Anthony lectured on the subject, "The Power of the Ballot," and boldly proclaimed: "If all men had protected all women as they would have their own wives and daughters protected, you would have no Laura Fair in your jail tonight."[13] Outraged by this charge, San Francisco editors accused the speaker of condoning Fair's action. The fury of the press prompted her to cancel additional San Francisco speeches and to restrict her campaigning to a few nearby towns. In her diary Anthony expressed her dismay at "the shadow of the newspapers being over me every moment," and her hurt: "I never was so dreadfully cut down."[14]

While in California, Stanton and Anthony received earnest invitations from Portlanders, especially from a local newspaper editor, Abigail Scott Duniway, whose *New Northwest*, launched in May 1871, championed ideas similar to those of the two eastern reformers. These requests to campaign in the Pacific Northwest provided Anthony with an opportunity to rebound from her frustrating California setback. Stanton declined these appeals and returned to resume her domestic duties in New Jersey.

California suffragists had encouraged Portlanders to list inducements that would attract the two suffrage leaders. Thus the correspondents wrote of good travel conditions, including a railroad in the Willamette Valley, steamboats on the Columbia, and comfortable hotels. But such enticements were probably not crucial to Anthony's decision. In frontier Kansas in 1867 and across the Midwest in 1871, she had encountered fatiguing transportation, uncomfortable lodging, and unappetizing meals.

She fully expected such discomforts in frontier Oregon and Washington. Dedicated to the advancement of women, Anthony would travel wherever she might promote her cause. She accepted the request because she believed that she would accomplish more in the Pacific Northwest than in California. But there was another compelling reason for her acceptance. She needed to sell lecture tickets in order to reduce the $10,000 debt that she had incurred from 1868 to 1870 while managing the *Revolution.*

From the pleas of Oregonians and recommendations of Californians, the suffragist leader learned that there was considerable interest in the Pacific Northwest in the status of women and that she would be heartily welcomed. She was probably reassured that the regional press would not be as hostile to her as the one in San Francisco. The Portland *Oregonian* was the only regional newspaper to criticize the invitation to the feminists and it denounced Stanton, not Anthony.[15]

Although those who urged the leaders to campaign in Oregon overstated the popularity of woman's rights, there was reason to believe that a lecture tour would succeed. Anthony could expect to receive support in Portland, especially from Duniway's newspaper and from the Pioneer Society, an organization that began—according to the Portland *Herald*—with "but three or four gentle creatures" and after six months numbered seventeen suffragists.

But Portlanders were not the only ones who praised national suffragists. Throughout the Northwest, especially in the region's two capitals—Olympia and Salem—men and women gathered and discussed ways to attain woman suffrage. The fact that women had been enfranchised in Wyoming and Utah territories encouraged Pacific Northwest suffragists, who offered to publicize Anthony's visit, arrange her transportation, and provide her housing and meals.

There were other indications, besides the willingness of suffragists to aid her campaign, of the region's receptiveness. One of the few newspapers in the nation devoted to woman's advancement, Duniway's controversial *New Northwest* had stimulated readers to discuss woman suffrage, marriage, divorce, and the general social and economic conditions of frontier women. Outraged at the power men exercised over women through laws and customs, Duniway advocated that societal change could come only after the enfranchisement of women—convictions that were likely influenced by reading Stanton and Anthony's views in the *Revolution*. While she sought broad support among both sexes for her reform, Duniway especially undertook to convert those who influenced public opinion—editors, ministers, and politicians. The editor proclaimed lofty goals which she hoped would entice supporters:

> [T]he object of the woman movement is to elevate all humanity; to make the world better, purer and happier; to make woman, who is by nature and association the best friend of man, his political equal, and that thereby both may receive the equal benefit of the laws by which both are equally governed. The object of the movement is to abolish the indulgence of men and women in the sins of adultery, intemperance, war, infanticide, murder, obscenity, profanity and injustice of every description.[16]

Duniway reassured her readers that woman suffrage would not "inaugurate a state of morals that will unsex women, revolutionize society . . . [or] turn connubial bliss into bitterness."

Both favorable and unfavorable editorial and reader responses to the ideas promulgated in the *New Northwest* publicized the suffrage question. The most persistent criticism voiced against the editor and other suffragists was that their arguments opposed Biblical teaching. A McMinnville minister expressed such fears in evaluating suffrage:

> Should husband and wife vote alike, it will effect nothing, and can work no reform. If they vote on different sides, as they doubtless will in some cases, will it not create family broils? I should not seriously object to old maids and old widows voting. I would, however, with Paul, advise young widows to marry, and then they will have one to represent them.[17]

A clergyman in Eugene, James Henderson—he had served a term as Oregon's Congressman and been counted among Radical Republicans—disagreed: "I regard the sexes as equal in intellectual ability and natural rights, and equally in need of governmental protection; consequently equally entitled to a choice in their representation."[18] Though Henderson doubted that marriages would be undermined by enfranchising wives, he warned that he would oppose the reform if it would "transpose the natural order of things . . . and place the women at the anvil and the plow, and the men at patching, darning, and nursing the babies." Because of his position he anticipated that "the little one-horse editors all over the country will begin to level their pop-guns at me" and defiantly stated: "let them fire their paper bullets to their heart's content." Despite his brave talk, however, the clergyman refused to be a target as he became silent in the battle over suffrage.

While readers mulled over the conflicting opinions of the clergy, they joined other settlers discussing the newspaper coverage given to three unusual female characters—the convicted murderer Laura Fair of San Francisco, the free love advocate Victoria Woodhull of New York City, and Minnie Myrtle Miller of Portland, who had been deserted by her husband, poet Joaquin Miller.[19] These three figures, and the women's issues they brought to public debate, would be of varying importance in Anthony's Pacific Northwest campaign. Fair's sensational trial was no longer appealing. A seasoned campaigner, Anthony realized that defense of a prostitute convicted of murder would win few adherents to the cause of woman's rights. Although she rarely mentioned Fair, Anthony publicly applauded and sympathized with Minnie Myrtle Miller, who, in turn, supported Anthony and played a leading role in regional suffrage fights. The individual who increasingly created the most problems for Anthony and Pacific Northwest suffragists actually lived on the other side of the continent. Several Oregon and Washington editors quoted suffragist Victoria Woodhull's unconventional political, economic, and social opinions—especially her endorsement of free love—from her newspaper, *Woodhull and Claflin's Weekly*—and denounced Anthony for endorsing the radical editor's legal opinions. Dismayed by Anthony's success in raising interest in woman's rights, these anti-suffrage regional editors attempted to discredit the movement by associating it with Woodhull's obnoxious ideas. In public Anthony steered clear of the radical editor. She understood that her detractors waited to catch her defending the unconventional feminist. In private conversations the campaigner cautioned western suffragists to be wary of the accusations editors made about Woodhull; she ventured further to praise the radical's appearance in Congress and the importance of her New Departure argument.

Discussion of women's issues had also been fomented, shortly before Anthony's arrival, when two California lecturers spoke in many Pacific

Northwest communities about the desirability of giving women the ballot. Carrie F. Young, editor of the *Woman's Pacific Coast Journal*, lectured on health reform and temperance, assuring audiences that her sex would vote to end intemperance. Much more vocal in support of suffrage, Mrs. Laura de Force Gordon—Duniway called her "a female Patrick Henry"—spoke on subjects such as "What Good will Result from Woman Suffrage?" During her tour Gordon received a nomination to the California Senate; this made her a most unusual visitor, but it also shortened her itinerary as she hurried home to campaign. Both Young and Gordon drew good audiences and stimulated diverse newspaper responses; Duniway congratulated her fellow editors for being candid and fair. Antisuffragist editor, Beriah Brown, discounted Gordon's ideas but found her attractive: she "enjoys the advantages of a graceful figure, a prepossessing face, a pleasing address, a musical voice, and a maddening wealth of curls; all of which is in decided contrast to the physical features of the earlier evangels of this new dispensation."[20] While we cannot know how many men and women were attracted to the woman suffrage movement as a result of the agitation during the summer of 1871, it is safe to assume that Duniway, who was not only ambitious but optimistic as well, might have overestimated their number. In July 1870 she had invited Stanton or Anthony to come and promote the movement. By August 1871 she believed that the time was even riper for a national leader to drum up Pacific Northwest support. She knew that her reform needed publicity, converts, and local organizations that would pressure regional politicians to enact laws on behalf of women.

From her wobbly-legged arrival in Portland on 31 August until her first lecture scheduled on 6 September, Anthony recuperated from her ocean voyage in the city's best hotel, the St. Charles, where she noted: "Everything rolling as on shipboard." She did more than rest. The campaigner wrote her family that she took "time to get my head straightened, and, I hope, my line of argument"; and she became acquainted with several Portlanders.[21] Her first and most influential caller was Abigail Scott Duniway. During their initial meeting, the two ladies studied each other and quickly reached a business arrangement: Duniway would serve as tour manager and receive half the gross receipts of ticket sales. Anthony was eager to be free from travel details, looked forward to Duniway's companionship, and sought the chance to teach her the tactics employed by eastern agitators since the 1850s. She very much wanted to secure a suffrage leader in this remote area, and the Portland editor was the obvious choice.

Duniway immediately outlined an extensive campaign route that would take the New Yorker to nearly all the region's important towns and many of the villages. To reach a maximum number of listeners, the lecture tour was divided into four parts: a railroad journey up the east side of the Willamette Valley to Salem; a steamboat and stagecoach trip to The Dalles and Walla Walla; a return trip to the Willamette Valley, including communities west of the Willamette River and the popular Oregon State Fair in Salem; and finally, a swing around Puget Sound with a visit to Victoria, British Columbia. The campaign would culminate in a final address in Portland, which among other things, would show that Portland supported its distinguished guest, even if San Francisco had not. Duniway also proposed a trip by steamer to Kalama and Vancouver. The two activists decided that Anthony, who emphatically declared that she would not repeat her miserable ocean voyage, could appear before other Oregon audiences south of Albany on her overland return to California. Undoubtedly the two planners considered and rejected a campaign into Idaho Territory, the third part of the Pacific Northwest. Both women knew that in January 1871 the Idaho House had narrowly rejected a bill that would have enfranchised women.[22] But Idaho was remote and underpopulated. It seemed much wiser for Anthony to concentrate on western Oregon and Washington where there was a better opportunity to lecture, teach, organize, and earn money. Duniway would not stump in Idaho until 1876; Anthony never appeared in the state until after it granted women equal suffrage, twenty years later in 1896.

Anthony and Duniway discussed other important subjects besides the logistics of the lecture tour. The visitor asked numerous questions about Duniway's life, the status of frontier women, the attitudes of the region's opinion makers—editors, ministers, and politicians—and the region's response to the *New Northwest* and to the recent visit by California suffragists. In a public letter to the New York *Revolution*, Anthony provided the following biography of her tour manager:

> Mrs. Duniway is a sprightly, intelligent young woman, filling the office of wife and mother to the full requirement of the law, having five sons and one daughter. She has been successful as a

> farmer's wife, school-teacher, music-teacher, public speaker, milliner, dressmaker and housekeeper. . . . Her newspaper is sprightly, vigorous and prosperous; her three oldest sons—boys from sixteen to ten—set the type . . . her daughter [is] a fine musician . . . her husband [Ben]—a sensible man—is proud that his wife possesses brains and self-respect to use them.[23]

There were other important facts that were necessary to round out this sketch. Abigail had been born in Illinois in 1834; in 1852 her father moved their family to Oregon. Her mother had opposed the trip and died of cholera on the Oregon Trail. Abigail, who always remembered her mother's dutifulness and death, became interested in the status of frontier women, wrote a novel, published accounts in local newspapers, followed Civil War politics, and moved from Lafayette to Albany after her husband lost his farm to creditors. In 1869 she had her sixth and last child. Besides fulfilling the traditional role of wife and mother, she had through her writing, teaching, and successful millinery business become a most versatile and noted local figure. Some praised her for going beyond the traditional frontier woman's domestic sphere; others denounced her. Duniway had been an early subscriber to Stanton and Anthony's *Revolution*; probably this publication had led her to join the National Woman Suffrage Association, where she was listed as a member of its Executive Committee. (She was probably displeased to read that her name was given as "A. Jane Dunning.") In 1870 the activist visited California, met with suffrage leaders, and was impressed with San Francisco editor Emily Pitts Stevens' *Pioneer*—a newspaper which fostered the woman's movement and inspired Duniway to launch a similar weekly in Portland. In 1871 the Duniway family moved to Portland; on 5 May she started the *New Northwest*. The Pacific Northwest's woman's movement can be dated from the founding of her newspaper—a lively addition to the region's journalism.

Duniway and Anthony often talked about the prospects for suffrage victories in California, Oregon, and Washington. Both could assess the climate of reform in California from recent visits and correspondence and probably each concluded that suffragists had a better chance for success in the Pacific Northwest. In California despite the fact that the San Francisco *Pioneer* promoted woman's rights, that some editors (especially J.J. Owens of the San Jose *Mercury*) supported woman's suffrage, and that some talented suffrage leaders (especially Laura de Force Gordon) won converts through an impressive state suffrage convention in early 1871—feminists faced powerful resistance. Reporters from San Francisco's principal four dailies had delighted in ridiculing and disparaging delegates at that convention. These major publications, joined by editors, ministers, and politicians throughout the state, were formidable opponents. Anthony was painfully aware of the San Francisco press' power and the unsympathetic climate that it created in California for their reforms. She must have concluded that the current battle for equal suffrage in that state would be as arduous as those being waged simultaneously in Illinois and Ohio.

Chastened by years of the frustrating realities of campaign work, the veteran was still less sanguine about a suffragist victory in Oregon and Washington than was the neophyte. The positive response to her newspaper—particularly the reasonable response from the influential *Oregonian*—fed Duniway's optimism. Further both women expressed delight over the fact that in two underpopulated territories—Wyoming in 1869 and Utah in 1870—women were granted voting rights. Duniway explained to Anthony that in Washington Territory a few women had actually voted under provisions of a territorial law. The two feminists assumed that it would be easier to win in the Pacific Northwest than in California because there was more opposition in California and because Oregon and Washington had much smaller populations. The Wyoming example seemed to teach that reformers might be more successful in reaching and convincing a sparsely populated state or territory. With women playing a vital role in the frontier's development it seemed that men might recognize this fact and pass the necessary voting laws.

Painfully aware that organized suffragists had not persuaded a single state to enfranchise women, Anthony realized from her recent visit that women in Wyoming and Utah Territories received the ballot because of particular local conditions. Suffering no illusions, the activist thought less in terms of an immediate victory on the Pacific Coast than of laying the groundwork through her upcoming campaign around the Pacific Northwest for an eventual triumph. She would need to publicize her reform, recruit local leaders, establish suffrage organizations, and link regional women with those in the national movement. Her experience led her to assume that once the public accepted the notion of equal suffrage then legislators would enact the necessary laws. Fully aware that her campaign would arouse a hostile reaction from those fearful of her message, the Easterner anticipated difficulty in the Far West. Her work in Kansas in 1867 and in California in 1871 demonstrated that female and male attitudes about woman suffrage were about the same in the West as those she had long experienced in the East. Clearly immigrants brought to their new western homes their traditional ideas about women—encrusted eastern attitudes had not been washed away in fresh western streams. Anthony had not encountered a prevailingly liberal attitude toward equal suffrage in the West, and she even feared that woman suffrage might soon be terminated in Wyoming Territory. Surely if the campaigner had encountered a more sympathetic attitude in the West—she traveled from the Missouri River Valley to the Pacific Coast—she would have praised the frontier for its progressive outlook in her speeches and letters. But she saw no fundamental differences between east and west; thus her campaign message to western audiences was similar to that delivered to eastern listeners. Although some historians have assumed that westerners were more sympathetic to the idea of equal suffrage than were easterners—the fact that most of the suffragist victories prior to the passage of the Nineteenth Amendment in 1920 were primarily in the western states supports such a notion—evidence from the early 1870s does not bear out such a conclusion. In the summer of 1871 California had demonstrated its resistance to Anthony's appeals; in the fall rejection would come from Oregon and Washington. Although Anthony and Duniway would win friends to their cause, their efforts aroused the majority of regional opinion makers to speak against them. In a pattern that would by now be familiar to Anthony, fearful editors, sensing that suffrage reformers threatened the status quo, generally responded with emotional criticism and ridicule, not with factual or reasoned rebuttal. She had developed the ability to cope with such hostility—the fact that she did not become a "man-hater" after all her frustrations with male reformers, politicians, ministers, and editors reflects her humanity—but Duniway, who had less experience and a more combative disposition, often lashed out at detractors.

# TWO

# *Educating the Teacher*

SUSAN B. ANTHONY'S FIRST DAYS in Portland included more than wide-ranging talks with Abigail Scott Duniway. She granted an interview to a newspaperman, received callers, toured the city, wrote letters, enjoyed the liberal sermon of Rev. Thomas L. Eliot at the Unitarian Church, and attended a reception at his home—where the two liberals exchanged ideas about social reform and initiated a long, fruitful friendship. She also perfected her first lecture.

From conversations in Portland parlors, Anthony fully understood that most residents did not consider woman suffrage to be crucial. Interested in learning as much as possible about the lives of these frontier women and men, the seasoned traveler and politician asked numerous questions to discover what issues were vital to them. In Portland—as throughout the region—residents boasted to her of the Pacific Northwest's scenic beauty, including the snow-capped peaks of the Cascades (one authority urged tourists to see Mt. Rainier and Mt. Hood in early summer before forest fire smoke screened the view), the waterfalls of the Columbia Gorge, and the lush forests of Puget Sound. Many boasted about the region's economic potential. Duniway predicted: "right here in our midst, in the next hundred years . . . prodigies of labor and improvement will be achieved without a parallel in the world's history."

In the frontier period, as well as in our own time, everyone had an opinion about the Pacific Northwest's weather. Some were "afflicted with a chronic growl" owing to the rain.[1] One politician, like many of his fellows, was defensive: "The rains are frequent but generally light, often not sufficient to wet the clothing during an entire day's exposure." On the other hand a journalist fleeing foul weather moaned that the storm "makes the world look like a dreary waste, and makes one feel as if there was nothing worth living for."[2] Settlers frequently made favorable comparisons of their mild climate to eastern snow storms and California drought. Anthony, who had recently traveled through California's parched lands also concluded that Oregon and Washington enjoyed a better climate.

As obvious as the region's pleasing climate and beauty was its lack of population; residents everywhere considered this a major liability. The 1870 census gave Oregon a population of 91,000 and Washington Territory 24,000. With about 9,000 inhabitants in 1871, Portland was not only the region's largest city, it was also the economic and cultural center of the Pacific Northwest. Portland was properly a frontier city only in a geographical sense, for it had most of the social and cultural attributes of urban centers in older regions. Even travelers from the region's competing trading centers envied Portland and acknowledged that it was more like eastern cities than other frontier towns. The city was—or would soon be—as its dwellers crowed, as dominant in the Pacific Northwest as Chicago was in the Old Northwest. An Olympia editor concluded: "Probably no town of its population was ever relatively more important and airy than Portland."[3] There were other important towns in the vast Pacific Northwest. Salem was a substantial political and economic center, whose population of 3,000 made it the region's second largest city. The three largest towns in Washington were Walla Walla (1,500), Olympia (1,300), and Seattle (1,200). The composition of this small population created a further problem. Historian Ray A. Billington has generalized that "on virtually all frontiers that had reached the agricultural stage men outnumbered women only in slight degree."[4] The Pacific Northwest was a clear exception, for men outnumbered women by about a two to one margin creating a great shortage of marriageable women. Residents hoped to attract marriageable females and families, so as to help tame the land and build a civilization.

Speculation was as powerful an impulse on this frontier as on others: the prospect of a railroad in Puget Sound and the existing one in the Willamette Valley increased the value of land in these areas and residents hoped to make spectacular profits from the sale of surplus lots. Landholders wanted potential immigrants to learn of the opportunities awaiting them in the nation's far corner and must have agreed with the Northern Pacific Railroad's promotional literature. In selling its extensive Pacific Northwest holdings in 1872, the company cautioned that "thrift and success will not follow idleness, chicken-heartedness, changeableness, corner-grocery lounging, bad management and drinking habits."[5] The railroad advised:

> Washington Territory and Oregon are not a Garden of Eden—neither is Kansas, California, Pennsylvania nor New York—but those who go to the New Northwest expecting to find a noble country and climate, where hard work, frugality, courage and honest endeavor are tolerably sure to be rewarded with comfort and competence, and yet expecting to meet the annoyances and obstacles common to all countries—will not be disappointed.

In addition to the problem of underpopulation, considerable attention was paid to agriculture, industry, railroads, investments, and current affairs. Anthony, like all other visitors to the region, consistently heard frontier folk glowingly describe the potential of nearby resources. They saw the prospect of a boundlessly abundant future. Undoubtedly the campaigner repeated some of these sentiments on the rostrum and in private parlor conversations. As a politician she knew it was important to acknowledge local aspirations.

In most regional trading centers—the exceptions being those towns on Puget Sound where fir and cedar lumber were of prime concern—the production of wheat, its movement to markets, and its market price were vital to growers and urban dwellers. While other grains, fruits (some called Oregon "the land of red apples"), vegetables, and livestock were important, farmers in the Willamette and Walla Walla valleys raised wheat as their staple crop. They and Portlanders expressed pleasure with the fact that Great Britain was beginning to import their wheat, but some argued that flour would be a more profitable export. This absorbing interest in wheat meant that oats—a neglected crop, locally—had to be imported. Thus the *Oregonian* complained about a primitive economy: stating that the region was still in its "Cayuse period."[6]

Anthony cast an appreciative eye—developed as manager of her father's farm—upon the products of the region's farmers, praising them for the quality of their wheat, fruit, and wool. She seemed less interested in such economic activities as fishing, sawmilling, mining, and manufacturing. The packing of Columbia River salmon—a fifty-pound fish could be purchased on the river for fifty cents—for domestic and international markets was making good profits and growing in importance. Sawmills bordering Puget Sound produced lumber, piling, and lath. Backed by San Francisco money, new and expanded mills sent products in their own ships to San Francisco or more distant ports as part of the international lumber trade. Mining in such places as southern Oregon was a steady, if not a spectacular, endeavor. Cattlemen in eastern Oregon and southeastern Washington enjoyed good profits from the movement of animals over the Snoqualmie Pass to the Puget Sound Basin or by sending them down the Columbia River to Portland and other markets. A booster of The Dalles challenged: "If there is any legitimate business on the Pacific Coast that can beat cattle raising for money making, we don't know it."[7]

The major towns as well as villages such as Roseburg, Jacksonville, Lafayette, and The Dalles were primarily agricultural trading centers. Merchants in these places not only solicited local customers but also competed for the patronage of the surrounding countryside. Most of the manufactured goods sold in the region came by sea from San Francisco to Portland, where they were reshipped to outlying frontier merchants at wholesale prices or put on the local retail market. Promoters predicted that if Oregon and Washington could attract money there would be a great increase in regional manufacturing. Anthony and other visitors often heard enthusiastic businessmen state that such capital would mean the development of a varied economy and of the region's abundant natural resources, including iron and coal. Some Portlanders surmised that if the city had more manufacturers then unemployed, troublesome boys would turn to useful trades. In discussions about money, frontier merchants emphatically informed newcomers that they conducted business in gold coin and hooted away attempts to pay in paper money.

Anthony would see evidence that despite the region's geographical remoteness, it was not involved only in its own problems, but took a keen interest in distant affairs. Traveler Frances Fuller Victor reported in 1872 that the men and women of this remote land were "full of the intellectuality of the nineteenth century."[8] Because of the telegraph, the Associated Press, the availability of local newspapers, the circulation of eastern publications, the public libraries, the schools, and visitors from other regions, residents of the Pacific Northwest were well aware of those events, movements, and characters familiar to more densely populated parts of the nation. Eastern fashions and fads had adherents on the distant frontier. In 1871, the period's roller-skating rage reached Portland, where a large rink opened. Spectators came "to see the skaters kiss the floor and make grimaces" and "to study character," including "the rude . . . fellow who whirls by upsetting every person," and "the lady-killer," whose "movements . . . show that he is a physical and intellectual nonentity."[9]

But sports, fashions, and fads were less important to regional leaders than the current controversial political and economic issues. Portland businessmen and lawyers were as well aware of national controversies and economic opportunities in a growing industrial society as were their counterparts in Chicago or San Francisco. In fact, a Portland merchant, Republican Senator Henry Corbett, became embroiled in the disagreement over the nation's money problems and the heated debate over anti-Chinese legislation. Oregon's other senator, George Williams, was an important Radical Republican who left office in 1871; early the next year he became Grant's Attorney General and continued his involvement in national politics. Unhampered by the isolation of Portland, Federal District Judge Matthew P. Deady, wrote significant opinions on troublesome issues and earned a regional, if not national, reputation. Newspaper editors in the region, like their urban counterparts, easily pontificated on national affairs, confident that their access to important national news was as complete as was any editor's in the East. An Oregon female even soldiered at the national level in the fight over woman suffrage. Emma L. Corbett, the young wife of Senator Corbett, was among the leaders of an antisuffragist group in the nation's capitol—many of the group's members were married to ranking military men and politicians—that petitioned Congress to reject the appeals of Stanton, Anthony, and their allies.

Anthony and Duniway generally favored Republicans, but they knew both Senator Corbett and ex-Senator Williams were unsympathetic to their cause and considered it useless to talk politics with them. Williams rationalized that Congress would grant women the vote whenever the majority of people favored it, but he made no effort to bring about such a grass roots attitudinal change. Corbett advocated hiring women as governmental clerks because they would perform capable work for less pay than men. Rankled by Mrs. Corbett's negativism and her zealous attempts to harvest antisuffragist signatures, Duniway in 1872 worked to prevent Senator Corbett's reelection. She accused his wife of attempting "to rivet the political chains on women whose husbands do not hold public office."

The fact that residents, especially editors and lawyers, expended numerous hours discussing or practicing politics failed to surprise Anthony, for this was the norm in every section of the country she had visited. In this distant region, as elsewhere, politics—referred to as a "filthy pool"—was one of the most colorful and controversial arenas of public activity. Politicians had an unsavory reputation; on election days drunken men and their obscene language discouraged women from approaching polling places, where losers complained that votes were bought. In 1871 neither of the two major parties monopolized the region; the Republicans enjoyed supremacy in Washington Territory and the Democrats controlled Oregon. In both Oregon and Washington intra-party factions often fought each other as bitterly as they did the opposition party.

Newspaper editors generally championed a major party and fueled political fights by damning or praising politicians at all levels. In Portland, Eugene, Olympia, Roseburg, Salem, and Walla Walla political editors hurled insults at each other as well; these verbal battles brought a measure of excitement and entertainment to dreary towns and farms. Today's males have replaced politics with televised football, receiving about the same degree of pleasure from these athletic contests that an earlier generation derived from exciting political fights. Despite the time spent with late nineteenth century politics or with modern football, it is hard to see that either was or is very important to the lives of most males except as entertainment. The Oregon style of journalism that has been defined as "a species of storm-and-stress composition, strong chiefly in invective" came under criticism but still had its practitioners.[10] In 1871 editors in Roseburg, Salem, and Walla Walla fell from shots or blows because of their slashing denunciations of townsmen.

An observer of American politics from one coast to the other, Anthony knew that honest citizens everywhere denounced the scandal and intrigue rampant in the national government as well as on state and local levels. They nodded agreement with the Philadelphia *Press*: "Money is the universal motor of the civilization of this day. It runs all institutions, religions and reforms." President Grant's reputation had been tarnished early in his administration by the Black Friday gold scandal, by an unsavory attempt to annex Santo Domingo, and by his shameless removal of honest cabinet members. In 1871 politics proved to be interesting indeed: the New York *Times* exposed the fraudulent practices of William "Boss" Tweed, Grant was forced to form a Civil Service Commission with a mandate to prescribe rules that would bring better men into government work, and in 1871 Congress passed a Ku Klux Klan Act to protect black voting rights.

Only Portland was large enough to provide conditions wholly conducive to the political "boss" systems emerging elsewhere in the nation. Oregon did experience its share of the political scandals and devious business practices that were alarming Americans across the country. In Salem Republican Secretary of State Samuel E. May was caught appropriating state funds, and Ben Holladay brought the Gilded Age and full-blown Grantism to Oregon. Following a successful career in stage-coaching, he came to Portland in 1868 seeking to control the Oregon Central Railroad and its lucrative land grant. He bribed the Oregon legislature (some compared his techniques with those of the wealthy men who had often bought off the New York legislature), lived lavishly in Portland, and in various ways shocked prudent frontier men and women. Called the "Money King" by opponents, Holladay purchased large amounts of Portland real estate, controlled Willamette Valley railroads and steamboats, operated the Portland street railroads, owned Pacific Coast steamboats, and erected mills and wharves. He established a newspaper, the Portland *Bulletin*, to ensure himself a favorable and influential public voice.

Many Pacific Northwest residents voiced opinions about Holladay's enormous economic and political influence. Some Oregonians praised him for building railroads and for developing the state. There were heated arguments over whether he would go to Salem and buy a United States Senate seat in 1872. Oregon pioneer Jesse Applegate, whose political ethics came from a different age, concluded that Holladay "has formed a low estimate of the integrity of men generally . . . mainly he is right."[11] A critic in Kalama, Washington warned about Holladay's transportation monopoly in an editorial entitled, "Oregon is Bottled," and argued that "with the exceptions of Paraguay and Utah, no other community in America has been so completely harnessed to the uses and behests of the 'one-man power' as . . . Oregon."[12] Anthony made some general criticisms of the state of American politics, but she had come to the region not to warn about Holladay's tyranny—his type was all too familiar to her—but to denounce male domination, which was entrenched and more complete than that exercised by the "Money King."

Anthony, like every other newcomer to the region, heard endless talk about railroads—either recently constructed or proposed. Everywhere promoters insisted that the obvious solution to the problems of underdevelopment and underpopulation was a railroad network that would link the region to the rest of the nation and tie local communities together. Because of its isolation, promoters argued, their potentially rich region lagged behind California and the Missouri Valley.

In 1871 there was already rail service from Portland down the Willamette Valley to Eugene and around obstructions in the Columbia River, and considerable excitement about a promising new railroad development. Jay Cooke's Northern Pacific—the most powerful corporation in the area—had in May employed Chinese laborers on the western end of its transcontinental route. They slashed a route from Kalama on the Columbia River towards Puget Sound. Some insisted that Kalama, the Northern Pacific's raw village on the Columbia, would take river trade away from Portland. One Kalama booster argued that the town would become "to the up-river cities and towns of the Columbia as the city of New York is to the flourishing cities on the Hudson."[13] Portlanders hooted at such a prediction, but even some of its notable citizens speculated in Kalama's corner lots. There was frantic speculation and competition northward as well because towns and villages ringing the Sound hoped to become the terminus of the Northern Pacific. Here Pacific Northwest promoters carried maps of proposed rail lines to large public or small private meetings. One Oregon group sought to link Portland, La Grande, and other Oregon towns with the Central Pacific in Utah; rivals desired to build from Eugene across Oregon to Winnemucca on the Central Pacific. Promoters also advanced more modest railroad projects; the most promising in 1871 was urged by Walla Wallans seeking funds to build a thirty-mile road linking their town with its river port, Wallula. All across the Pacific Northwest settlers hoped to end their dependence upon stagecoaches and freight wagons and the horrible travel conditions to which Anthony would be introduced: choking dust, sticking mud, and teeth-jolting corduroy roads. She, like residents, would measure the duress of a trip by the amount of stagecoaching required to the nearest railhead.

Settlers quickly alerted Anthony to those societal problems that attracted both serious thought and emotional outbursts in the region. These included crime (a Seattle editor sympathized with victims but rationalized that robbery occurred everywhere and was "a sure indication of activity and progress in our midst"), the effectiveness of public schools (then, as now, there was a search for a practical curriculum), the vices of boys (one editor, complaining that local boys smoked pipes and cigars, urged parents to caution sons about tobacco, and quoted a physician who warned of "nicotine poison"), and the reliability of patent medicine and physicians. (Could one trust the reports that Dr. Aborn the successful Oculist, Aurist, Catarrh, Throat and Lung Physician of San Francisco "has been effecting some wonderful cures" in Portland?)[14]

While there was some talk of improving politics and schools, the two leading reform movements in 1871 were the emerging woman suffrage agitation and the old issue of temperance. There was a connection, temperance folk argued, between whiskey and crime. Foes of whiskey liked to compare the number of churches with the number of saloons, pointing to Eugene where there were fifteen saloons making drunkards and only six churches teaching Christian living. A Portland reporter "estimated that 38,000 drinks of the various spirituous and malt liquors quench the thirst of our population each day. This would be about four drinks to every man, woman and child in the city."[15] Clergymen, temperance newspapers in Albany and Olympia, church newspapers in Portland, Good Templar lodges in various towns, and emotional temperance conventions fought for victory over King Alcohol and his retinue of saloonkeepers, political allies, fawning adherents, and disgraceful drunks.

While the victims of alcohol were a traditional societal concern, Anthony sought information about victims of political, social, and economic injustices. The visitor interviewed some of Portland's working women. Ever since she became acquainted with the female workers in her father's mills, she had been interested in the pay, working conditions, and opinions of women employed outside of their homes. She assumed that middle-class working women on both coasts would support her suffragist arguments. A city with only a few manufacturing plants, Portland did not offer many jobs to either skilled or unskilled female workers. The 1870 federal census shows that most of the city's women, even those from low income households, were housekeepers, working at home for their families. In Portland, as in other cities, wage-earning women generally served as domestics, but some were teachers, seamstresses, assistants in their husbands' businesses, or prostitutes. Anthony patiently explained to audiences everywhere that some women needed to earn wages outside of the home. "I perfectly agree," she explained, "that women should be married. The real fact of life is that women have to support themselves." The reformer continued by adding that such wage earners must receive decent pay. Historian Ellen DuBois has neatly summarized Anthony's judgments:

> What she wanted for working women, for all women, was at once obvious in its justice, and revolutionary in its implication for the relations between men and women: "to give them a chance to earn an honest living . . . not merely a pittance, enough to keep body and soul together . . . and have houses and homes of their own, and make them just as independent as anybody in the country."[16]

Anthony and Duniway particularly discussed the status of seamstresses. The New Yorker had stated that "women . . . are stitching with their needles at starving prices."[17] From her experience as a seamstress and from correspondence with those practicing this trade, Duniway well understood the occupation. In need of money and work that could be done at home, many Northwest women, like those in the Northeast, sought sewing jobs, which were plentiful, as the stylish dresses required skilled seamstresses. But sewing machines were common, and severe competition drove down wages. She stated that dressmaking was highly competitive because "there are many married women in this city who are nominally supported by husbands who are in such straitened circumstances that they are compelled to do dressmaking or plain sewing at starvation prices to earn a little needed spending money to keep up outside appearances." There was, she explained, a second problem: many ladies "who hire dresses . . . made are so unreasonable in their demands that it is very rasping to a sensitive temperament to endure their moods and notions." Thus Duniway urged women not to become milliners or dressmakers; she advised them to "learn photography, bookkeeping, clerking . . . or some other of the thousand light and easy occupations which are now monopolized by men who were out of their 'sphere.'" The editor advised females to raise fruits and vegetables, for market gardening was "far more remunerative than needlework."[18]

The inability of seamstresses and other working women to make fair wages was a problem familiar to Anthony. But in Portland she soon became better informed about another societal concern that she had first encountered in California—the Chinese minority. Chinese contributed to the Pacific Northwest's economy as railroad construction workers, miners, cannery workers, operators of laundries, unskilled workers, and domestics. Duniway urged overworked frontier women to hire a "Chinaman," for "they make faithful servants."[19] Victims of racial prejudice, this minority suffered some physical and extensive verbal abuse. In regional editorial offices, parlors, and streets there was considerable discussion about their cleanliness, morality, reliability, and future. Many predicted that large numbers of Chinese would move into the region and create a variety of problems because of cultural differences. A Portland editor believed "that all efforts to teach Pacific coast Indians, or Chinese, the social and religious duties and obligations that white people respect, is nothing less than 'love's labor lost.'"[20] In 1871 newspapers gave more space to the Chinese than to another minority, the Indian. However, there was continuing complaint that Indians could never be civilized and that they squandered valuable land. Some residents predicted that these natives were dying out; an Olympian explained that the Indians were

> in reality but human weeds, vegetable men, occupying the earth in its primitive form, as it were in trust until a superior race supplants them. Were they exterminated by the Caucasians with fire, sword and famine, philanthropists could then have some foundation for the censure of the latter, but such not being the case they must lay the blame on nature.[21]

The regional press carried stories about Indian reservations but tended to publicize those Indians who illegally left their camps and came to town, where they foraged, begged, awoke sleepers with their "bacchanalian celebrations," and under the influence of whiskey, seemed likely to ignite dangerous urban fires. The Northern Pacific Railroad felt it necessary to assure potential home seekers that the Pacific Northwest's Indians had "long since abandoned all thought of hostility to the whites, and have mostly adopted civilized customs and habits of industry." The Indians were actually "an advantage" because in some places they were "the main reliance for hired help."[22] With peace on the frontiers, urban dwellers, especially some politicians, warned about the Chinese minority settled in their midst, not the Indian minority on their border.

In summary Anthony acquired considerable politically useful information during her first week in Portland and in subsequent months. She mastered regional facts and used them in her lectures, which often began with references to existing local conditions and the promising future. The reformer's interest in Oregon and Washington was genuine, and it helped to win her a hearing.

Anthony always inquired about the local newspapers. To her way of thinking editors were extremely important because they shaped and reflected public opinion. She had the *Revolution* and other eastern journals forwarded and avidly read and clipped local newspapers for her scrapbook, including Portland's three handsome and combative dailies. Republican Harvey Scott edited the *Oregonian*; Burrell Taylor, a newcomer from Missouri, edited the *Herald*; and veteran newspaperman James O'Meara edited the *Bulletin* on behalf of Ben Holladay.

During discussions of her family, Duniway talked about her younger brother, Harvey Scott. He had crossed the plains with his family, fought in the Yakima Indian war, had been well educated—as the first graduate of Pacific University, and had become editor of Portland's leading daily newspaper, the *Oregonian*. A self-made man, Scott was the most able of the regional editors; he was well grounded in classical literature and American history. He considered editors to be teachers, and he provided readers with instruction in political, economic and social matters.

Abigail was both proud and envious of her brother's attainments, including his powerful role in the Republican Party, but was not yet completely certain what he thought about woman's rights. A man of enormous certitude, Scott would react strongly one way or the other to Anthony's message. Abigail nervously awaited his editorials.

The major newspapers noted the campaigner's arrival; the *Oregonian* commented: "We presume she will tell this public soon how much below the brute creation man is, and discourse some of her pet hobbies in true feminine style." Although Scott did not interview Anthony, he knew that his readers were curious about her appearance and provided a description: "She is an elderly maiden lady, quite different in appearance from the vinegar-faced virago whom we had been led to look for from the representations of the San Francisco papers."[23]

J. Mortimer Murphy, a reporter for the *Herald* who had been with the New York *World*, realized that the controversial visitor, one of the most famous individuals to have visited Oregon, was an excellent subject for a story and interviewed her. He began with a description of her appearance:

> She is above the medium height, and, we should judge, about forty-five or fifty years of age . . . guessing a lady's years is a difficult matter to a man, and we are not sure of our guess. The face is somewhat broad and angular, the forehead of a good height, quite broad and well rounded at the temples, the hair is of a dark brown, but is freely sprinkled with the gray: the eyes are a grayish blue, and the face is strongly marked with lines of thought. The entire contour of the face and head indicates that she possesses the characteristics of her father, and inherits his strength of mind. She was dressed in a robe of black silk, and wore a black and white checked shawl carelessly thrown over the shoulders.[24]

In his long account, Murphy praised Anthony for being fluent, concise, and logical—"in contradistinction to the sex in general, she does not depend on mere assertions but gives proofs to carry conviction." Most of his questions related to woman suffrage, and Anthony explained that she battled for this reform because she wanted "justice for all." The visitor insisted that the ballot would make women "more self-reliant, and better able to earn a livelihood, as she would have the same privileges as man, and, besides, it belonged to her, if she were the equal of man." If a woman voted, Anthony generalized, "it would give her more self-esteem and abate her love of approbation, which was her most prominent characteristic." Although she argued that women wanted to participate in government, she did not predict that they could improve the present form of government. Woman suffrage was, she explained, "but an experiment and the improvement which she could accomplish was thus far merely theoretical. If she could not better it she was responsible for the evils she might introduce, and would bear her share of the odium and burthen as well as man." According to Murphy, the reformer shifted course in the interview, asserting that if women could not improve the republican form of government then some other form should be tried. Apparently Murphy believed it unnecessary to comment upon this bold idea because he fully anticipated that his readers would easily fault her logic and reject her radicalism.

Anthony also addressed another important topic: the opportunity for females to enter prestigious professions. "As it was now," she complained, "woman was debarred from many professions in which she could acquire distinction as well as man." To make her point she declared that women should be allowed to seek election as superintendent of schools. The reporter "asserted that there was not one woman of a hundred who was competent to fill the position, and even if she were, that her ambition would be to get married." Anthony quickly responded that if there was only one qualified for the position she should have the right to obtain it.

The newspaperman's interest in her—as well as that demonstrated by other Portlanders—helped the campaigner to regain some of the confidence she had lost at the hands of San Francisco editors. She wrote her mother:

> I miss Mrs. Stanton, still I cannot but enjoy the feeling that the people call on me, and the fact that I have an opportunity to sharpen my wits a little by answering questions doing the chatting, instead of merely sitting a lay figure and listening to the brilliant scintillations as they emanate from her never-exhausted magazine. There is no alternative—whoever goes into a parlor or before an audience with that woman does it at the cost of a fearful overshadowing, a price which I have paid for the last ten years, and that cheerfully, because I felt that our cause was most profited by her being seen and heard, and my best work was making the way clear for her.[25]

But the suffragist couldn't shake her fear and anxiety about newspapermen. Anthony wrote Stanton about her troubled state of mind: "I am awaiting my Wednesday night execution with fear and trembling such as I never before dreamed of, but to the rack I must go, though another San Francisco torture be in store for me."[26] In her diary Anthony confided: "Never dreaded, trembled so at prospect before—fear of the Press skinning me alive again."[27]

Editors also anticipated her first lecture. The *Bulletin*, for example, urged: "Let her have a rousing audience, and let us show the maiden that the 'wicked men' are not afraid of her."[28]

A large number of Portlanders would attend her first talk at Oro Fino Hall. Although they did not suspect her apprehension, they understood that something special was going to happen in town.

Susan B. Anthony in 1848. She was working as a school teacher. As a young woman, she enjoyed colorful clothing, but as she became more involved with suffrage work she made the decision to wear black garments because she wanted people to concentrate on what she was saying rather than on what she was wearing. (University of Rochester Collections)

Susan B. Anthony, 1871. C. Mosher, photographer. (OHS neg. OrHi 64966)

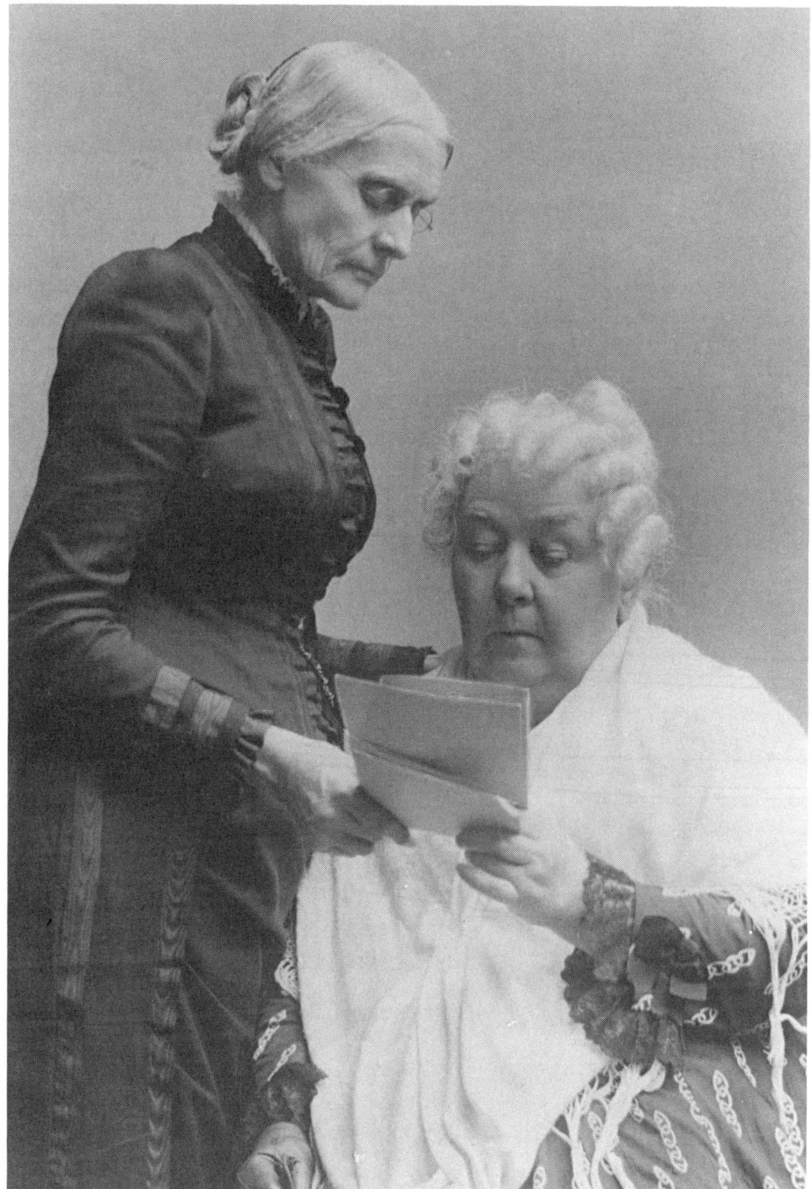

Susan B. Anthony and Elizabeth Cady Stanton in the later years of their partnership. (Library of Congress)

Abigail Scott Duniway and her newspaper the *New Northwest*. (OHS neg. OrHi 37312.

Victoria Woodhull. Bradley & Rulofson photographers. (Sophia Smith Collection, Smith College)

Dr. Bethenia Owens-Adair. (OHS neg. OrHi 4062)

St. Charles Hotel, Susan B. Anthony's residence on her first tour to Portland. (OHS neg. OrHi 12045)

The Dalles, Oregon in 1864. (OHS neg. OrHi 5345-A)

The Dalles Congregational Church, where Susan B. Anthony spoke on her 1871 tour. (OHS neg. OrHi 4062)

# THREE
# *Urban Campaigns*

OPERATED BY SALOONKEEPERS, Oro Fino Hall, a popular building near the Willamette River, was often booked by theatricals and lecturers. Duniway, who had arranged for its use, arrived early and commented on the heavy traffic in front of the wooden structure. Hacks, phaetons, and other vehicles jammed the street; a large crowd of well dressed men and women elbowed into the hall. Latecomers could not gain admittance. Men with fashionable hay-colored moustaches and muttonchop whiskers wore black attire. Women able to afford chic blonde wigs (which could cost as much as $150) mixed with other ladies who had bleached their hair. According to one observer, "The latest style for wearing the hair is in braids, or free as the bounding wave," which gave young ladies "a very romantic appearance."[1] Portland ladies sported dresses with sweeping trains—as stylish as those worn to public events by eastern women. Anthony, however, dressed conservatively; an eastern friend explained: "All female vanities she rigorously discarded—no hoop, train, bustle, . . . powder, paint, rouge, patches, no nonsense of any sort."[2] The speaker wanted listeners to concentrate on her ideas, not her clothing.

Clara Duniway opened the meeting with a rendition of the suffrage campaign song, "Wait for the Turn of the Tide," written by her mother. Abigail introduced the speaker and recalled the exciting occasion:

> I went in fear and trembling before a cold, curious and critical crowd, half bent with weariness resulting from long, contin-

> uous mental and physical overwork, and said in a faltering voice, "The movement that arose in the East nearly twenty years ago, to demand Equal Rights for Women, and appeared, at first, as a shadow not larger than a woman's hand, has grown and spread from the Atlantic Coast, till it pauses tonight in farthest Oregon, almost in hearing of the Pacific Ocean. Keeping ahead of that shadow is the illustrious visitor, who illuminates it wherever she goes with the freedom spirit of her devotion. This distinguished visitor is my world renowned coadjutor, Susan B. Anthony of Everywhere, who will now address you."[3]

In her first lecture, "Power of the Ballot," Anthony, overcoming her fear, elaborated on the arguments summarized in her *Herald* interview. She insisted that a woman must have the vote so as "to protect her wages, her person and property."[4] The speaker, according to Duniway, reminded listeners of the "transitory period from the negroes' emancipation to the time of their enfranchisement" and asserted,

> negroes' heads were as curly, their heels as long and skulls as thick as they were before, but politicians no longer harped these things upon the stump, and the reason was because the negroes, now having *votes*, are respected by politicians, and consequently receive protection in their rights.

Anthony argued that Irish- and German-Americans without the suffrage "would be as badly abused by men in power as the negroes once had been," and that "Woman, armed with the ballot, would be respected because of the power she would thereby possess." To demonstrate that, despite the arguments of antisuffragists, men did not already protect women, she told about saving "a young and unsophisticated girl from the clutches of a posse of ribald young fellows, before the . . . eyes of a number of gentlemanly appearing men, who had looked on and watched their nefarious designs without once raising their arms or voices to protect her."

In her diary, she summarized: "audience splendid. Made clear statements of argument—but was not free as I could wish. Take an hour and 20 minutes . . . with hope I wait the morning papers."[5] In a letter to Stanton, she elaborated on her emotions:

> The first fire is passed. I send you the *Bulletin* and *Oregonian* notices. I have not seen the Democratic paper—the *Herald*—but am told it says Miss Anthony failed to interest her audience. Not a person stirred save when I made them laugh. . . . Last night I made the San Francisco speech, but was not nearly so free and easy in the brain-working; still I got my points clearly stated. The wet blanket is now somewhat off. I hope to present the fact of our right to vote under these amendments with a great deal more freedom. . . . I want to tell you that with my gray silk I wore a pink bow at my throat and a narrow pink ribbon in my hair! Mrs. Duniway is delighted, so you see my tide is turning a little from that terrible, killing experience. . . . it is a comfort to get a little outside assurance again.[6]

Despite the fact that the dailies had encouraged readers to hear the noted visitor—the *Oregonian* admitted that she had received "frequent mention the last few years"—none of their editors attended. They probably ignored this speech because they had read versions of it in their San Francisco newspaper exchanges and because they did not want to publicize the agitator. For whatever reason, the Portland newspapers gave scant report of her performance. A brief account in the *Bulletin* mentioned a large, appreciative, and "intelligent" audience.[7] "Her remarks were listened to with an interest which betokened that she was making a marked impression upon her hearers, very few of whom, perhaps ever before listened to a woman lecture about Woman's Rights." Noting that she spoke bluntly about the need for woman suffrage, the reporter interpreted her words:

> Miss Anthony takes the ground of appealing to the selfish nature of mankind to gain her points for suffrage and power, and after twenty years of moral appeal, having exhausted that kind of logic, throws persuasiveness and scolding to the dogs, so to speak, and is now open for an interview with any set of politicians or political party with whom a trade can be made of "present power" for "future votes" when women shall be enfranchised.

Scott of the *Oregonian* neither heard the lecture nor sent a reporter but simply wrote that he had "learned that Miss Anthony is a fluent and argumentative speaker and well sustains the cause she advocates."[8] The *Herald*, placing its notice under its amusement column, dismissed her effort as but "a resume of the usual assertions concerning the rights of woman, assertions which apparently received but little sympathy from the auditors."[9]

Two Portland weeklies responded to her initial effort. Isaac Dillon, editor of the Methodist *Pacific Christian Advocate*, concluded:

> Miss Anthony's appearance was not particularly in her favor, nor did she aim at the least show of eloquence; but in her presentation of facts, she was clear, forcible and logical. So much so, that she secured the unbroken attention and commanded the respect of her large audience, although a portion doubtless did not sympathize with her movement.[10]

Pleased with her famous co-worker's efforts, Duniway delayed her newspaper's analysis for a week. She then informed her readers that the lecture hall "was literally packed with calm, dispassionate and interested listeners, whom the speaker held spell-bound. . . . Susan's fund of anecdote, incident and argument is inexhaustible."[11]

Advertised as the campaigner's last lecture in Portland, the second speech, held on 8 September at Oro Fino Hall, included an introduction by Duniway and suitable songs performed by professional musicians. Portland's dailies took a greater interest in this speech because newspapermen knew that she would address the challenging "New Departure" argument: that the Constitution, properly interpreted, already granted women the right to vote.

The three dailies acknowledged that the speaker had a large and intelligent audience. Both the *Oregonian* and the *Bulletin* praised her delivery; the latter explained:

> In appearance Miss Anthony is tall, bony and ungraceful, and before commencing to speak her face is expressionless; yet, when warmed up with her subject her countenance becomes fairly illuminated with intelligence. . . . She makes no pretension to high oratorical powers. . . . Her style is forcible and argumentative. She contents herself with facts—presenting

> them in plain language; resting her case upon these, unaided by sophistry and the blinding influence of oratory.[12]

None of the dailies published a complete account of the speech; the *Bulletin* and the *Oregonian*, however, carried useful reports. Scott, who apparently attended this lecture, wrote both a summarized and a more detailed article. According to his account, Anthony, after reading from the Declaration of Independence, the Constitution, and some state constitutions, emphasized "that none of them recognized any peculiar class or portion of the people as the source from which power is derived. . . . None of them make any distinctions invidious to women as a constituent portion of the people."[13] She cited decisions of the Supreme Court, including the Dred Scott case, "which sustained the conclusion that women are citizens," reminded her listeners that the Fourteenth Amendment declared that all persons born or naturalized in the United States are citizens, and read definitions of the word "citizen" from several dictionaries to show that citizens inherently possessed the right to vote. "If, then," Anthony ruled, "every person born or naturalized in the United States is a citizen, and a citizen is one who has the right to vote, it follows incontrovertibly that women have the right to vote unless it be held that a woman is not a person." The Fifteenth Amendment, the reformer explained, prevented the federal and state governments from denying or abridging the right of suffrage. The speaker blamed the condition of women on existing legal restrictions (the *Bulletin* quoted her as arguing: "women are no more or less than slaves") and, as an example of local oppression, asserted that if Oregon women held offices in a society it could not be incorporated.

Returning to the evening's major topic, she insisted that it was unnecessary to amend the Constitution so that women might vote; it was only necessary to give it a broader interpretation. To force such an interpretation, Anthony predicted, women in several parts of the country would soon try to vote. If turned away they would seek redress in the courts. The lecturer urged female listeners to join their sisters across the nation in this struggle for suffrage and also to refuse to pay taxes until they were able to elect their own representatives. She emphasized that her recent visits to Wyoming and Utah had demonstrated that woman suffrage there had been "highly beneficial to the state of morals, temperance, schools, etc."

Sometime during the speech she expressed a desire to hold another meeting so she could debate or answer objections raised on the floor or mailed to her hotel. Anthony counted on opinion makers, especially lawyers, judges, editors, and ministers, to enter into debate with her by raising questions. She fully realized that Oregon's antisuffragist senators, Corbett and Williams, would shun her; they preferred to join owner Ben Holladay's party for a ride on his Oregon and California Railroad to view a new bridge near Harrisburg. But she might have hoped for a reaction from two important judges. Stephen J. Field, associate justice of the United States Supreme Court, was visiting from his California home and staying at the same hotel as Anthony. Field was hosted by Judge Deady and entertained by Holladay. It is somewhat surprising that Deady neglected to attend one of her Portland meetings; he would later shun her in Albany and Salem as well. Deady, who frequently heard popular entertainers and lecturers, shared Anthony's interest in the Fourteenth Amendment. He was studying a case, *McKay v. Campbell*, in which he would rule that the amendment's provisions for citizenship extended to Indians and foreign born. Local lawyers also refused to comment upon Anthony's legal argument. Perhaps they agreed with the Albany *Register* correspondent who predicted that any attempt by a Portland lawyer to rebut it "would be about as sensible as the effort to dig down Mount Hood." No one at the lecture informed the speaker that Oregonians had protested the passage of the two Reconstruction amendments. Ten months prior to Anthony's arrival, the Oregon legislature passed a resolution rejecting the Fifteenth Amendment, partly because Congress "by means of an arbitrary majority of votes acquired by the power of the bayonet has sought to force" it upon the states.

The *Herald*'s sketchy report virtually ignored her constitutional interpretations and concentrated only on the political aspects of the speech, including Anthony's frank opinion that women would support whichever political party would secure them the vote.[14] The writer, who underscored the political opportunism of Ben Butler ("the great Sardine"), heartily agreed with the lecturer for stating that Butler, who had switched from the Democratic to the Republican Party, hoped to reap a political harvest from supporting woman suffrage. "Her closing argument," the reporter sarcastically wrote, "was to convince the skeptical that woman would bring the millennium sooner than expected if she could only have the opportunity for voting for Jones or Smith when they aspired for an office."

Editor Duniway praised the speech—"a masterly argument"—and rejoiced: "many who listened to her logical, womanly words went to their homes with new ideas as to the rights of women in our Government."[15] Satisfied with the summaries of the argument carried in the dailies, Duniway published them rather than writing her own. She briefly reiterated, however, Anthony's exhortation to Portland women to try to vote and, if denied, to initiate a court case.

On Saturday, 9 September, Anthony, who was "shivering over next lecture to women alone," spoke on prostitution—the "Social Evil"—to about four hundred "very earnest and interested" members of her sex.[16] They paid no admission fee but were asked for donations. Anthony thought that the twenty dollars was "splendid for women" and over one hundred of them signed a petition demanding the right to vote. The speaker heatedly denounced licensed prostitution in this and other regional speeches. There was, of course, much public curiosity about this restricted talk; the best summary, written by the pseudonymous "Mated," appeared in the *Oregonian*:

> As I did not detect any "reporters" in the hall I deem it my duty to tell our brothers something about the lecture, as I know they are half crazy with curiosity, not to say anxiety over it. The speaker talked eloquently, using chaste and dignified expressions which would have spoiled no gentleman to hear. She urged upon women the necessity of marrying pure and noble men, showing very clearly how the iniquities of fathers are visited upon children. She was particularly severe upon those women who degraded themselves by marrying merely for a support; argued that the social evil was the legitimate result of women's pecuniary dependence, and that this dependence was the result of her irresponsible position. She said that legislation would not suppress the social evil; that license laws did not repress intemperance, neither could they efface prostitution from society. She argued that the ballot would give woman the right to own her own person, and this would be her safeguard against the social evil, because no woman follows such a life from choice. A petition urging Congress to pass a declaratory

> act pronouncing women voters under the Fourteenth and Fifteenth Amendments, received about one hundred signatures. A liberal collection was taken up for the lecturer, who says that the women thereby proved that the Portland ladies had money and were willing to use it.[17]

The *Herald* carried a flippant account, providing this sarcastic description of the audience:

> Some were tall, many medium, several short, some were pretty, a few passable, and many ugly as a mud fence; several looked intelligent, others inquisitive and prying, and several as if they were going just to hear the lectures without caring much for her assertions. The majority of the auditors were married ladies, but not a few maidens, rejoicing in single blessedness, went to list[en] to the oracle recount the horrors of the social evil—an evil which they knew nothing about, and about which it would be better they did not even hear.[18]

Although Anthony probably got the idea for a frank talk restricted to women from Stanton, she did not discuss some of the more personal issues often raised by her co-worker, such as liberal divorce laws and a wife's right to control sexual intercourse.[19] Perhaps Anthony did not think that a Portland audience would want a single lady to discuss these controversial topics.

The diary entries for the two days between her private talk and her third public lecture are missing, but newspaper accounts help to fill the gap. She spent the afternoons receiving callers and visiting about the city. Aware that Portland's seamstresses received inadequate pay for their tiring work and thus could not attend her talks, Anthony visited tailor shops, distributing free lecture tickets. The owner of one establishment told her that the male employees worked as hard as the females and that they might also like to attend her next lecture. Anthony instructed Duniway to distribute tickets to them as well.

On Sunday the campaigner reported to the New York *Revolution*: "There is something lovely in this Oregon climate beyond any I have yet known on either side of the Rocky mountains. . . . I am surprised at the size of this city, and the evidences of business and solid wealth all about."[20] She expressed an interest in the condition of another minority:

> John Chinaman too is here, cooking, washing and ironing, quiet and meek-looking as in San Francisco. The Republicans of this coast, like the Democrats, talk and resolve against him for political effect, merely to cater to the ignorant voters of their party. . . . Their pretense that the Chinaman may not become a citizen of the United States, precisely the same as an African, German, or Irishman, is matched only by their denial of citizenship to the women of the entire nation. Under the old regime it was the negro with whom we had to make common cause in our demand for the practical recognition of our right to representation. In snatching the black man from our side, the Republicans, out of pure sympathy doubtless, lest we should be without any "male" compeer in our degradation, leave the innocent Chinaman to comfort and console us. Are we not most unreasonable in our dissatisfaction with the company our fathers and brothers constitutionally rank with us—idiots, lunatics, convicts, Chinamen?

At her third public appearance, Anthony answered questions and objections about woman suffrage. Prior to this meeting at Oro Fino Hall on 11 September, she had solicited questions and objections; in a note to the *Oregonian* she requested that they be sent to her ahead of time or voiced in the hall so "that I may thus have opportunity to at least try to brush away every cobweb of prejudice from every brain present."[21]

For the third time the reformer faced a packed house. The *Oregonian* said that the audience included "very many of the first men and women of the city," who listened to her answer questions for 2 1/2 hours—these questions had been submitted to her and published in advance of the meeting. Undoubtedly this was Anthony's most lively, amusing, and controversial talk. Impressed with her performance editor Scott wrote, "We think she answered most of the questions more nearly satisfactorily than had been anticipated, and made a really good argument in favor of woman suffrage—certainly the best we ever heard." The other dailies and the *New Northwest* published somewhat different summaries—they varied in length and analysis—of the meeting.[22]

One question was inevitably asked: "Is the Bible against the ballot?" Anthony reminded the crowd that the Bible had been used against scientists and reformers; moreover, it had been used to justify slavery. She believed that "the injunction of the Bible upon women to submit themselves to their husbands had no more rightful force than that which exhorted servants to be obedient to their master, or that which advised wine for the stomach's sake. Duniway gave a blunter report of the speaker's answer: "The time is speedily coming when such scriptures as 'wives submit'. . . . will be cast aside as obsolete."

To the question, "Don't husbands represent their wives?" the lecturer pointed out that widows lacked representation and that the 300,000 drunkards and 150,000 liquor dealers in the country could not act for women. "No individual," Anthony insisted, "can represent another, as that other would do for himself or herself." She rejected the allied and popular argument that decent women were represented in their influence over male voters: "So far as women now influence men in public life, courtesans exert more power than the combined numbers of all the virtuous and pure women;" moreover, "a female lobbyist will control the vote of a Congressman with half a million constituents."

In meeting the common objection that the ballot would degrade women, the reformer raised some stimulating points: "Women would be as refined and pure with power as without it"; "Good, pure and noble women meet vile men every day; they hold the most intimate family relations with them, being their wives, sisters, daughters." Anthony, as she often did, countered with her own question: "Will woman's meeting vile men on the place of equal powers to control circumstances, make her more the victim of their lusts and tyrannies than now?" The speaker judged, "The ballot would not degrade, but elevate woman morally, intellectually, and therefore, socially."

Anthony asked, "Who will take care of the babies?" and answered that fashionable ladies attending watering places, balls, and parties felt no qualms in entrusting their children to "ignorant hirelings." At the same time widows and the wives of drunkards were compelled to leave their children so as to earn a livelihood. "Let woman have her proper share of the means to live, of the government offices, places of profit and trust, equal wages with men, and she will be able to provide for the proper care of her children."

Anthony responded to the query, "Did women want to vote?" Although this question brought a variety of responses from one coast to the other, the speaker ruled that women found politics interesting, desired to vote, and had time to be a housewife, voter, and officeholder. She added a story. Horace Greeley had instructed suffragists that the country did not need more voters; it needed 60,000 cooks. Anthony agreed with the need for the cooks, but, noting that well-paid male ones monopolized the trade, she cleverly deducted, "as women as a class do not like to cook, they must learn to do something else."

"If women voted," many people asked, "would it not create family discord and divorce?" The speaker maintained that the ballot and equal rights would actually improve marriages. The franchise "would lift woman out of the necessity under which so many now live, of marrying just to secure a home." If men and women were equal before the law "there will then be more marrying for love, less for money, and fewer divorces." She recommended that one way to ease domestic strife was for the husband to give his spouse a "political bone." At about this point Anthony asked and answered a related question about who would lead a family if the wife voted. She bluntly explained: "Brains will always rule, whether in the head of man or woman."

The speaker predicted the impact of woman suffrage, stressing that females would employ the ballot so as to improve society. They would vote against legalized prostitution and intemperance. Women would be, she promised, a force for morality and decency.

Anthony voiced interesting responses to the argument that if women voted they must also fight. Despite the fact that he had avoided Civil War military service, Horace Greeley advanced such a view. The speaker brought laughter by telling that she had informed Greeley that "every woman would be perfectly willing to take the ballot and bullet together, and to fight just as he had done during the war." She denied the premise that there was a connection between the ballot and bullet—"half of the men who vote never smelt gunpowder"—recalled that women could do valuable work as noncombatants, saw no objection to women who wanted to soldier, and assured that when women voted they would always attempt to resolve difficulties short of war.

Anthony dismissed as a "silly bugbear" the objection that "woman suffrage would tend to free love." She must have stirred her audience by insisting that most women were virtuous and most men were "loose in their morals." Although Portland editors ignored or agreed with this judgment, other community leaders, including an Oregon City minister and a Salem newspaperman, bristled over her provocative generalization.

The reformer denied the popular assertion that women did not want to vote. Why, she asked, do men put the words "white males" into their constitutions? To her way of thinking men knew that women wanted to vote so they prevented this by restricting the vote to themselves. She used an analogy: "Men don't fence a corn field because the pigs don't want the corn, but because they, themselves do." Anthony then predicted that women would use the ballot to improve society—they would vote against legalized prostitution and intemperance. Women would be, she promised, a powerful force for morality and decency. To support her premise that her sex wanted to vote, the speaker asked the women in the audience if they favored the franchise. Many answered yes and no one voted no.

In answer to the objection that the advocates of the cause would support any political party that would offer them the franchise, "thus practically declaring the movement to be of a single idea—woman suffrage," Anthony reminded her audience that revolutionaries, abolitionists, and Unionists had all accomplished much by supporting a single idea. She asserted that "the trouble with a good many people is to have even one idea." The speaker chided men for voting a straight party ticket and stressed: "All that the women want in this movement is to know neither Democrats nor Republicans; to know nobody unless pledged to woman suffrage. There is no question now pending, so important as the disfranchisement of half the people."

At the conclusion of this final lecture, Portland editors evaluated the impact of her three speaking engagements. The *Bulletin*'s O'Meara, who admitted that he had attended only the middle portion of the third lecture, based his summary on that part he had heard. The editor granted that "she presented her views in very captivating manner and supported her deductions and pressed her conclusions with a fair amount of cleverness and a good deal of *popular* attractiveness, her premises were not sound, and her reasoning was neither consistent nor logical," especially on the subject of woman suffrage and free love.[23] After praising the reformer as a "good, thoroughly well-disposed apostle of what she believes to be a noble and most important cause," O'Meara criticized her. "After a tolerably fair hearing of her doctrines and arguments we fully and frankly express our opinion of them in general terms by saying they are mischievous and revolutionary in a social way." He warned that the adoption of her doctrines would "bring about division in homes, anarchy in families, and chaos in society in general."

The Methodist newspaper, the *Pacific Christian Advocate*, denounced the reformer for other reasons.[24] Editor Dillon acknowledged that Anthony's second lecture was a convincing argument that woman had the legal right to vote and would use her voting power to correct evil. But he expressed surprise and anxiety to hear her "express utter disregard, if not supreme contempt for any Bible teaching, which came between her and the ends she aimed at." She admitted, Dillon continued, "that wives were commanded to obey their husbands; but boldly declared that it was not the wife's duty to obey her husband, any more than it was the husband's duty to obey the wife." The Methodist leader asserted that the reformer favored easy divorce laws and cried: "We express our abhorrence of all such teachings, fully believing that, if carried to their legitimate results, they will be alike destructive of all virtue, order, decency and government, in either Church or State."

In the next week's issue, Dillon resumed his attack, stating that Anthony, like spiritualists and infidels, wanted to "relax the bands of matrimony, so as to increase the facilities for divorce to an extent that, for all practical purposes, abolishes the institution of marriage and in its stead introduces free-love, which is only another name for licentiousness."[25] Fearful that marriages would be made only for convenience—"legalized prostitution"—Dillon charged that the reformer taught that the wife was free from her husband's control; thus "this would simply confer on her the independent enjoyment of the rights and privileges of a kept-mistress, at the cost of surrendering her claim to the honored position of wife, and to its endearing appellation and character." When the wife controlled her own property, he contended, it weakened a marriage; and he reminded that Christ had taught that adultery was the only grounds for divorce.

The *Oregonian*'s Scott provided a stimulating editorial analyzing the lecturer's premises, avoiding the emotionalism that often characterized the writing of his competitors. He began by noting that while the suffrage movement was well known in the East, it had only recently been introduced in the West.[26] Scott then stressed his central argument:

> Whether those who are making a speciality of it shall be disappointed or not in securing the suffrage for woman, it is tolerably clear that they will be disappointed in the results to flow from it, in case they gain it. What occurs to us most plainly in the present state of the discussion is that much more is expected from the suffrage for woman than can possibly be gained by it.

Advocates of woman suffrage, he asserted, saw the ballot "as the sovereign cure for all injustice to women; as the great and sure agent of complete social reform; as the be-all of human progress, and the end-all of perplexing social problems." Continuing to discredit Anthony's expediency arguments, he predicted: "Some important changes and results it may produce, but it will not change human nature, do away with injustice, abolish utterly social evils, greatly purify the body politic, or materially change the conditions of our political and social life."

Scott scoffed at the notion that the suffrage would protect women from the brutality of their husbands, rejected the prediction that the suffrage would increase the amount paid for woman's labor, denied that the ballot would "make any material change in the relative duties and employments of men and women," predicted that "bad women will vote with the good; and, what is more, the bad will exert far more influence in proportion to their numbers," and asserted that "human nature in men and women is very much the same." He concluded by restating his central theme: when women voted it would not end "fraud, corruption, vice, and injustice."

Scott refuted the accusation that if women voted it would damage society: "These alarmists are as extravagant in their notions as those optimists who advocate woman suffrage in the belief that it will prove a remedy for [the] greatest political and social evils." If women voted there would be, he prophesied, "Neither a deluge of woes nor a millennium of felicity."

Scott announced his position: "As an individual we shall probably vote for woman suffrage when the question is presented, and we shall do so because we see no serious objection to it, and because we feel that it is necessary to do so in order to satisfy the arguments of those who insist on woman's right to vote." In his judgment there was merit in the suffragist's arguments that women paid taxes and should vote and that the constitutional amendments enfranchised women.

Abigail rejoiced over her brother's editorial. She generalized that the *Oregonian* "comes boldly out for Woman Suffrage. Bravo!"[27] Editor O'Meara, however, was irked with Scott's conclusions, including the implication that he was an alarmist. In a lengthy editorial, "Woman Suffrage Considered," he rationalized that his decision to give the issue more attention rested upon the belief that journalists should respond to subjects agitating the public.[28] This was precisely what Anthony hoped to attain. Noting that there had recently been much local interest in woman suffrage, he judged that the campaigner, "as one of the most conspicuous and ablest agitators and champions" of woman's rights deserved more credit than Duniway in creating "temporary prominence" of the subject. The more he deliberated upon the enfranchisement of women, O'Meara explained, the more convinced he was that it would "introduce fresh disorder into the politics of the country, to create mischiefs not easily to be corrected or composed, and to produce such a condition of things in the home circle and in society generally as will result in very lamentable consequence."

O'Meara asserted that such conclusions did not make him an alarmist; he insisted that his opinions were those voiced by the majority since the beginning of history. He then denounced Scott for predicting that women's votes would not change the status quo; such an argument, to O'Meara's way of thinking, ignored the undue influence that bad women would have on politics.

Having disposed of Scott, O'Meara continued his generalized attack on the woman suffrage movement. He maintained that no "truly great . . . public men" had supported it but that "a number of *politicians*, and *enthusiasts* in modern*isms*, and others who seek notoriety because they cannot win true fame, have expressed themselves favorably on the subject, but we think this fact injures more than it improves the matter." The editor ruled that nine out of ten women did not want to vote—apparently he disregarded the poll that Anthony took at her lecture—and that very few clergymen endorsed woman suffrage.

If females voted, the veteran politician predicted, they would also participate in conventions, caucuses, and campaigns. "To any who are conversant with the manner in which our system of politics is conducted," O'Meara reasoned,

> the idea of the presence and participation of women therein will be distasteful and abhorrent—out of pure respect for the sex. At such scenes the bold or the bad would attend, perhaps; but we imagine few of the good or the gentle and modest could be brought to engage in the "filthy pool." Consequently the condition of things would be made worse instead of better in this single respect.

O'Meara forewarned that if women "demand all the immunities which men enjoy they must submit to all the exactions to which men are subject, under the laws of the land," and assumed that women would shun such a danger and prefer that men continue to manage "public life" and business. In a reference to Anthony, the editor concluded:

> no unmarried man or woman is competent to fully discuss or to thoroughly understand the question in point in all of its essential features. And the fact that the vast majority of the married women are the firmest of the opponents of the Woman's Rights movement is in itself a powerful argument against that mischievous late day hobby.

Meanwhile, Taylor's newspaper, the *Herald*, in an article entitled "Woman's Rights Feeling in Portland," credited the campaigner's lectures for "arousing the weaker sex to a sense of the grand future which awaits it when it has gained the political rights at present usurped by man."[29] After recounting the role played by the *New Northwest* and the Pioneer Society in the growth of local support for woman suffrage, the newspaper expressed fear for the future. "On the principle that the weak must use strategy where strength is lacking the gentle sea is keeping quiet at present, but when the proper time comes many a husband will be surprised at the bold front which his better half will show when she demands a right not conceded to her under the present complexion of politics." The writer maintained that many Portland males shuddered to think "of a refined wife, mother, sister or daughter struggling and jostling with wantons, and the ruder and more ignorant class of females to reach the ballot-box." The newspaperman doubted that much good would be accomplished by women voters and then advanced a unique argument against this reform which he attributed to "philosophers." "If all writers of prominence, known to history, are taken as authority, women would not—judging from her [*sic*] character—vote twice on the same subject, let it be for good or evil, as it would weary her, and she would want a new idea evolved, as she would desire a new type of bonnet or mode of dressing the hair."

While Portland editors and townspeople wrangled over the implications of her proposed reform, Anthony, who appreciated this attention, plunged into a busy lecture schedule. On 12 September, a day on which residents of the lower Willamette Valley complained about heavy smoke from a nearby forest fire, she crossed the river to East Portland. In her diary she referred in discouragement to "a stupid audience," but in a private home she took amusement in an astrologist, who, she wrote, "gave horoscope of my life . . . and hit upon a good many points of past."[30]

Duniway praised Anthony for wakening "the dormant feeling of duty and true womanhood in many a woman's heart in Portland, and scores of ladies in our community who never before gave the question a moment's consideration are now eager for the ballot."[31] The reformers went by train to Oregon City, where residents showed them the falls, the large woolen mills, and a noted flour mill. Boosters emphasized that these resources made their community the "Lowell of the Pacific." In the evening she spoke before what she deemed a "good audience". All anticipated a negative reaction from Editor Anthony Noltner's Oregon City *Weekly Enterprise*. A contentious man, Noltner had frequently railed at suffragists, thus drawing the wrath of Duniway, who once called him a "libidinous apology of manhood."[32] Noltner underestimated the size of Anthony's audience and dismissed her: "We have neither space nor inclination to criticize her speech, suffice it to say that we were very much disappointed in the abilities of the lady, and so were most of her hearers."[33] Instead of analyzing her arguments, the editor resorted to ridicule.

> We could not help thinking what a fine looking and useful woman she would have been had she got married years ago and would now be sitting in her parlor surrounded by a family of children, grandchildren and perhaps great grandchildren. She would then consider herself the peer of any woman. We wish she had been more fortunate in her younger days.

Besides his brief, abusive story, Noltner simultaneously published an equally harsh account of Anthony's lectures from the *Enterprise*'s unnamed Portland correspondent, who described her as "most horribly ugly" and predicted that "one look into her countenance would frighten a young child into convulsions." The critic accused her of "papering" the house. "Her logic," he asserted, "is that of all women—'because.'" The writer ridiculed her answers to questions, charged that she believed that the Bible was dated, and cried: "When a Christian people can sit and listen with patience to such stuff as this, we are almost prepared for negro-equality, Chinese suffrage, and woman's rights. But Heaven forbid!"

Noltner, a relentless opponent of woman suffrage, devoted almost the entire front page of his 29 September issue to the publication of a special sermon, refuting Anthony's lecture, delivered by Rev. Elbridge Gerry in Oregon City's Congregational Church. The editor recommended the sermon because of its "sound and logical arguments" and published an extra supply of the paper, which was soon exhausted. Only a small part of Gerry's refutation was based on Scripture. His arguments were wide-ranging, as he insisted that voting was not a natural right, but a political privilege; that all the arguments supporting woman suffrage could be as easily used to support "Baby Suffrage"; and that, far from being oppressed by male domination, women actually enjoyed a lofty position because of male chivalry. He denounced as libelous the charge that men "are all savages, brutes, looking upon women as legitimate prey." The minister countered Anthony's views of the social evil: "no woman ever yet voluntarily entered upon a life of sin and shame without there being, at least, two guilty parties." He, like O'Meara, feared the consequences of societal change. "Give women the ballot, draw them out from their homes, make them a factor in politics, and they will have political ends to gain; and the chances are," Gerry cautioned, "that the temptations to lead a life of easy virtue will be at least two where there is one now."

Gerry also discussed the inequality of wages: "the rule of society which regulates this matter of wages is not so unjust after all. It seems to be based upon the principle, that a woman is required to meet present necessities. Her work is temporary. Her destination is marriage." To his way of thinking, females who graduated from colleges—established for the benefit of young men—took positions from males, thereby preventing them from finding such suitable jobs as would allow them to enter into matrimony. This result, the preacher insisted, was deplorable: "taking human nature as it is today, we feel safe in asserting that every man or woman growing up in society in an unmarried condition adds to the danger of moral corruption."

After citing other fallacies of suffragists and objections to woman suffrage, including the accusation that "if there are women who will sell their virtue for gold they will sell their votes for gold, for position, for worldly advantage," Gerry concluded: "Men and women have their separate and legitimate spheres of action equally honorable, founded in nature, in reason and the Word of God. Any change must ignore eternal principles, and result in confusion and moral decay."

Angry with the editors of the Portland *Herald* and the Oregon City *Enterprise* for their "uncouth remarks" about Anthony, Duniway denounced them publicly:

> The truly deplorable specimens of humanity, whom we lately chastised into decency, have "returned to their wallowing in the mire". . . . they are attacking a woman so far above them in intellectual ability, moral stamina, and public and private worth, that we know of no comparison sufficiently strong by which to illustrate the matter. Some men seem to have been born destitute of all gentlemanly instincts.[34]

Following the lecture in Oregon City, the reformers went by train to Salem, which Frances Fuller Victor described as "probably the pleasantest town in Oregon."[35] In the capital, the woman suffrage question had recently been discussed in public letters. Mrs. Jennett Blakesley Frost, a New Yorker who had lived a few years in California and came to Oregon promoting her Civil War book, wrote against woman suffrage, evoking a letter of sharp disagreement from a local young woman who employed the pen name of "Rose Greenleaf."[36] Frost, who would later confront Anthony and Duniway in Albany, wrote: "I am not, nor never was, in favor of the suffrage movement. In endorsing such a platform as laid down by the Women's Rights Party, I should prove recreant to my God, traitor to my country and false to my sex." To endorse the "Woman's Rights platform," she continued, "I must believe the Bible is a fable, that the Savior of the world was an imposter, ridicule the sacred rites of the church, ignore marriage and encourage prostitution." She charged that

Victoria Woodhull was the actual leader of the suffragists and predicted that while "educated and refined" women would not vote, "the unprincipled and uneducated women" would do so. "If the right of the ballot is given to women," Frost warned, "our Government would pass rapidly into the hands of miserable despots, and the star of our Republic will set forever in degradation and shame. With the first vote polled by woman's hand the death warrant of our Republican Government is signed."

Samuel Clarke, the slight and nervous editor of the Salem *Statesman*—an important Republican daily—explained that he had published the two letters because of the importance of the woman suffrage issue. He observed that the two correspondents refused to change their opinions and humorously proposed that "the *Herald* and the *New Northwest* be allowed to settle the question by force of arms."[37] Clarke, however, encouraged readers to hear Anthony's addresses.

During her two days in Salem, the New York feminist delivered three lectures—including another "women-only" afternoon lecture on the "Social Evil,"—to large audiences. At the first evening meeting, held at Reed's Opera House, Clara Duniway sang the campaign song, her mother gave the introduction, and Anthony spoke on the "Power of the Ballot." Her second evening lecture was based on questions and objections to woman suffrage, covering much the same ground as her earlier effort in Portland.

Anthony met some interesting sympathizers in Salem, including two aspiring Oregon poets, Mrs. Belle Cooke and Mrs. Minnie Myrtle Miller. The visitor wrote about Miller's desertion by her husband: "Joaquin Miller—the Poet—took all the earnings himself and left three children and wife destitute and went to England and now comes home with published poems and famous. A sad story that of Mrs. Miller if true and it seems so."[38]

Miller studied the New Yorker's impact on her audience; perhaps her account for the *New Northwest* aptly described most audiences. She explained that Anthony was the only woman she had ever heard speak in public, except at a meetinghouse "when Aunt Tribulation Fear-The-Lord arose and through her tears nose and handkerchief told her 'experience'"[39] The female listeners "were as serene and unruffled as a Quaker's night-gown. It was not their funeral." But the men's responses were divided. Some suffered through the experience. One was "a very reluctant-looking man. . . . He was continually shifting his position, meanwhile casting glances at his wife to see the effect of everything upon her." Another sat "with his chin resting upon his breast and his eyes closed. His play was to be oblivious when Miss Anthony made a point." Another stared at the speaker, realizing that she was "logical, forcible, and conclusive," but he would be unwilling, Miller predicted, to argue against those who would charge the campaigner with sophistry. But not all males were uneasy; some smiled in agreement with Anthony's forceful message.

Between lectures, members of the Oregon Supreme Court called upon Anthony at the Chemeketa Hotel, one of the most handsome buildings in town. Judge G.W. Lawson, a state leader of woman suffrage and thus a target of ridicule—antisuffragists said he wanted to be a woman—encouraged his colleagues to consider her argument that women were entitled to vote under the Fourteenth and Fifteenth Amendments. According to Abigail, Susan convinced most of the judges, who urged

> us to make a case and test the matter of our personal enfranchisement at an early day, and we shall certainly do so, provided our brother judges of election prove so perverse as to render such action necessary. This we believe they will not do, for so much of the foremost judicial talent of the State is already committed to the fact of woman's right to vote that no judge who has a political ax to grind—and what politician hasn't?—will hardly dare to run the adverse chances that will follow such refusal.[40]

Salem newspapers ignored this interview but responded to the lectures. A Democratic newspaper, the Salem *Mercury*, edited by Jonas H. Upton, gave them brief but favorable coverage. He called Anthony "earnest, honest, and forcible" and denied that she was "vindictive and unsparing." This response surprised readers, for Upton and Duniway had clashed before over woman suffrage. Upton had opposed it on the basis of his assumption that women, enjoying exemption from the risks of military service, would be more likely to vote for war than men and from his fear that Mrs. Woodhull had converted suffragists to the merits of "legalized lechery."[41] Another Democratic editor noted the change in Upton's attitude and guessed that Anthony had converted him.

Upton's competitor, Clarke of the influential *Statesman*, had a completely different response; he had not been openly critical of woman suffrage until after he heard Anthony. Unlike Upton, Clarke gave considerable space to her lectures.[42] His first report was favorable. He complimented Duniway's singing and Anthony's entertaining delivery and stated: "the audience . . . was large and as intelligent as has been our fortune ever to witness on such an occasion."

Clarke impartially quoted some of the reformer's basic points: that the ballot is "the emblem of liberty, respect and integrity;" that "as the divine right of Popes has been overthrown, the last is, to overthrow the divine right of man"; and that "when women vote they will have the power to rob men of some of their freedom and license; then drunken, libertine husbands will be at a discount; the golden hope of this movement is to exact of man the same purity and chastity that he demands of woman."

A few days after Anthony's visit Clarke praised her for scolding in "decorous and womanly tones," granted the significance of the suffrage movement, and urged men to improve the condition of women. Then, however, he launched his attack. "She assumes," he complained, "as a foundation of her argument that man is an unreasonable tyrant, that he is almost universally unfaithful to his marriage vow, and that he defrauds his wife of her just earnings and denies her any voice in government or any protection under the law." He denounced Anthony for wanting marriage to be looked upon as a business rather than a "sacred obligation" and called her illogical for thinking societal ills could be remedied by simply granting woman the vote. He believed that the reformer glossed over the potentially negative impact of political ambition upon women. Clarke deplored her private "social evil" lecture in which she told women that "men were as a class unfaithful" and related "improbable anecdotes that were borrowed from a condition of society a political stump orator could scarce invade with impunity." He took solace in the fact "that when the first effect of Anthony's appearance wears away, the women of Oregon will realize that while she told many truths and told them well, she treated their own husbands and fathers unfairly." Clarke added:

> We resent the charge, brought by a disappointed and sarcastic woman—neither a wife or mother—against the race of men who are today carrying civilization to its highest point, raising

> human nature above its former level, giving woman more privileges than she has ever had, and whose motto is freedom, equality, common education and the elevation of the laboring classes.

He ended with an emotional denunciation: "She is not entirely disinterested, either, in adopting the role of a reformer, for she seems to have received a very handsome sum, even here in Salem, for her attempt to prove that 'all men are liars.'"[43] The accusation that greed motivated Anthony would be repeated by other foes.

Belle Cooke rushed to the reformer's defense. She asked, "How many papers in Oregon have ever been sufficiently exercised over the vast expenditures . . . on traveling circuses, negro minstrels, low theaters, and the like?"[44] The Salem woman stated that Anthony's private talk contained more valuable information and theories than the public orations delivered by politicians; furthermore, she had not abused men as much as they abused each other in their political speeches.

While Clarke fumed over Anthony's doctrines, she moved northward and stayed in Milwaukie with a noted couple, Seth and Clarissa Lewelling. The guest wrote in her diary about the Lewellings's famous nursery and the spartan meals they served: "Strict vegetable diet and no tea, coffee, spices, or salt." The "desperately small" audience at the local schoolhouse was no more agreeable than the food.[45] The empty benches surprised the audience because Mrs. Gordon's successful suffrage lecture held a month earlier had attracted about two hundred.[46]

On 17 September Anthony, who must have been encouraged by good audiences in Oregon City and Salem and by her private conversations with sympathizers, completed the first leg of her tour with a return to Portland. The following morning, she hastily packed her bags for departure by steamer for speaking engagements at The Dalles, Walla Walla (the largest town in Washington), and Wallula. Duniway had scheduled appearances in The Dalles and Walla Walla to coincide with popular agricultural fairs, hoping to capture the attention of their large crowds.

# FOUR

# *Scattering the Reform Seed*

WITH PASSES FURNISHED by entrepreneur John C. Ainsworth of the Oregon Steam Navigation Company, Anthony, who left her hotel at 4:30 AM., and Mr. and Mrs. Duniway, boarded their steamboat. Fog delayed its departure; thus the boat docked at The Dalles at 8:00 P.M., the scheduled lecture time. Anthony wrote nothing in her diary about the confused rush to the Congregational Church, where one hundred people waited. The more excitable Abigail, however, provided an interesting account:

> Runners from the two hotels jostle and crowd us in the darkness, disturbing the equanimity of belated lecture-goers and making the evening hideous with their discordant yells. Getting into the nearest hack, we drive to the nearest hotel, to find that our baggage has been left behind, the people congregated and waiting for the coming lecture, and everything in commotion and confusion. Miss Anthony is capable of composing herself and making a good speech upon any occasion, no matter how adverse may be the circumstances, so the people of The Dalles, who were accommodated in Mr. [Thomas] Condon's well-appointed church were treated to a lecture of one hour and a half in length, with which they were . . . intensely gratified.[1]

In encouraging readers to attend the lecture, Editor William Hand of The Dalles *Mountaineer*, who had been praised by Duniway for employ-

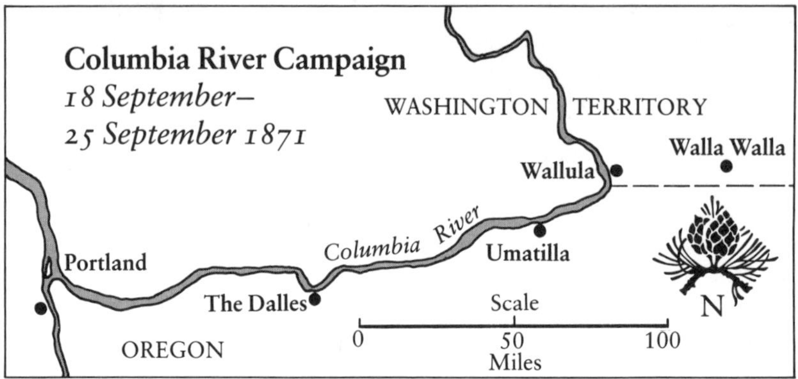


ing a girl typo at the same wages paid to boys, said he was "somewhat inclined" to accept Anthony's interpretation of the Constitution. Hand predicted "that when women enjoy the same rights and privileges with men, socially, politically and otherwise—then our Government will be conducted in a better and more economical manner." Hand, who had compared Duniway's editorial work favorably with her brother's, provided readers with frontier humor, including jokes about females: "Women are like horses—the gayer the harness they have on the better they feel." His reaction to Anthony disappointed Duniway, who had considered him to be an ally. He proved far more interested on the day of the lecture in the horses brought to the Columbia District Agricultural Fair than in the lecturer. Hand ignored Anthony for about three weeks and then expressed his preference for Jennett Frost, republishing much of her antisuffragist speech.[2]

At five on the morning following the lecture, the reformers took a fourteen-mile railroad trip around the rapids, boarded the steamer *Tenino*, and proceeded to Umatilla, where the boat laid up overnight. They walked up to the village, where Duniway recalled that what was once "known as a thriving commercial town is now a rocky succession of sand hills, and what once were streets and stores and dwellings look now to be abodes of owls and bats. Trade has taken another direction, and this dilapidated town bewails its wind-worn raggedness and weeps o'er days departed."[3] In Umatilla the New Yorker was surprised by an invitation to have a glass of wine with a man who Duniway identified as a bartender whose mother had known Anthony in Rochester.[4] Duniway explained that her companion only took a polite sip, but news of this incident traveled ahead of Anthony to Walla Walla; the minister and officials of its United Brethren Church, where the lectures were scheduled, quickly met and refused Anthony the use of their building. Other denominations followed suit in barring the reformer.

But if the turbulence awaiting them at their destination was not enough, the reformers first had to endure another rough road trip. The tour manager gave a picturesque account of the travel into Walla Walla:

> with the early dawn our steamer is off again, and for three or four hours we steam the rapid current, and at last we reach Wallula, which looks like a ragged fragment of poor, tattered Umatilla which the wailing winds had wafted to this barren rock and left in desolation. As this God-forsaken spot is now the head of navigation, we here met the stage, a huge, ungainly omnibus, with six fine horses and a manly driver, who handled the lines with that dexterity for which his class are so particularly famous. Miss A. mounted the outside of the lumbering vehicle. We tried the seat beside her for awhile, but soon yielded to the burning sunshine, exchanged with not an unwilling hombre and seated us beside a placid Chinaman, who seemed oblivious to all surroundings. Oh, that Walla Walla road! Pen cannot paint or picture portray it! Driving up a long and narrow grade upon the rugged hillside, where a careless move would upset our coach and land us in eternity, we suddenly met a loaded prairie sloop, drawn by four horses with a leader of the mule fraternity. Our driver stops suddenly to give the teamster opportunity to get out of the way of the coach.
>
> "Hold on, good friend; you'll smash my hub to smithereens!" yells the busy teamster.
>
> One of his horses, a piebald, rat-tailed caricature upon well-kept horse-flesh, rears and dodges as if he expects the great stage coach to devour him bodily.
>
> "Your horse is young and skittish," says one of our passengers. "Young d—m me; he's seventeen years old."
>
> "Ah, I see; he's quite a colt."

> Everybody laughs and we are by this time disentangled from the disagreeable proximity, and on we go, through the stifling dust and over rocks and ridges, down sidelong declivities and up steep ascents, feeling all the while an intense longing to plant our feet upon terra firma and trust horse-flesh nevermore. But the long ride of thirty miles is over now, and we drive up to the Walla Walla Inn, looking like pilgrims to some ancient Mecca, or the forlorn hope of a caravan of forty-niners.[5]

Instead of describing the billowing sand and rut-filled Walla Walla road as most travelers did, Anthony wrote about stage driver Amos Bradley, who assured her that they would be on schedule and then gave his life story. He was the son of a New York paper manufacturer, had run away from home at the age of fourteen, had never written his mother, and had not drunk whiskey in eight years. Anthony, who liked to interview riverboat captains and stagecoach drivers, called Bradley a "whole-souled fellow."[6]

Walla Wallans and visitors to the Washington Territory Agriculture, Manufacture and Arts Fostering Society Fair awaited Anthony's arrival. Men and women excitedly spread the story that the visitor was being denied the use of churches. Moreover, advertisements in the two rival newspapers—the *Statesman* edited by Democrat William H. Newell and the *Union* edited by Republican Edward C. Ross—and brief news stories publicized the visit. Editor Ross, who also practiced law, quickly indicated the condescension that would characterize his coverage:

> As most of our people are under the impression that a woman's rights are to sew on buttons, darn stockings, cook a square meal, tend baby, retail scandal and run up big store bills, there will most likely be a large audience to hear Miss Anthony announce and explain the other rights of woman. To our contracted intellect there appears to be a great objection to woman suffrage in the very constitution of the sex. Voting by ballot is the silent expression of the opinion of the citizens, and as no woman—save a deaf and dumb one—ever had a silent opinion upon any question she could not exercise the right of suffrage.[7]

With all of the Walla Walla churches unavailable, Ben Duniway sought an alternative place. The best location, the City Hall, was reserved by the Pixley Sisters, a dramatic troupe of six persons presenting "chaste entertainments" before and during fair week.[8] Arrangements were made to utilize a new schoolhouse, where Anthony gave two public presentations. During her busy schedule the visitor delivered an afternoon talk to ladies in City Hall; her third public address was moved from the crowded, distant schoolhouse to the Bank Exchange Hall, a large room often used for large social gatherings, located to the rear of the Bank Exchange Saloon.

Although the appearance of smallpox in the city reduced the number of fair-goers, such large crowds—attending partly out of curiosity to see the woman who had aroused church leaders—appeared for the first lecture that half could not gain entry. In her public lectures Anthony discussed familiar subjects and wrote in her diary that she "cleared up the Free Love" question to the satisfaction of at least one visiting minister.[9] She strolled the dusty fairgrounds with Duniway, who complained: "Many women were out in fine array, their trailing skirts reminding us of fallen Psyches, and so marring our ideas of the fitness of things that we were poorly prepared to appreciate much that would otherwise have appeared harmonious."[10] Though unimpressed with the fair, Anthony enjoyed the new home, orchard, and hospitality of a leading Walla Walla citizen, Mrs. Lucy Isaacs. Although tourists often visited the Whitman Mission, site of the valley's major historical event, the 1847 Whitman Massacre, apparently Anthony did not do so. But she must have been told about Narcissa Whitman's missionary work and murder at the hands of some Cayuse Indians.

Editor Ross's lengthy coverage in the *Union* was critical, accusing the New Yorker of making "scattering" remarks for an hour and forty minutes. "No man," he insisted, "with any pretensions as a public speaker would care to risk his cause upon such an effort as Miss Anthony made."[11] Ross carped:

> One of her strong points seemed to be that, as the women, the married ones in particular, are at present treated [as if] they did not have their full share of the financial income of the partnership, as she denominated the condition of wedlock. Did it ever occur to Miss Anthony that over half of the married

> women do not ever contribute by their earnings to the funds of the concern? That they simply manage the household, control the servants and entertain company, while the husband is slaving at his trade, profession or business to get money to pay the bills?

The complainer then portrayed women:

> We are free to admit that the brain of woman is composed of as fine material as that of man, and that intellectually she is his equal. But we are not willing to admit that when the Almighty created man with broad shoulders, deep chest, large waist and narrow hips, knotted muscles and prominent cords, indicative of physical strength, with an innate, irrepressible desire for out-door labors and pursuits, and at the same time created woman with narrow shoulders, broad hips, and rounded muscles, indicative of grace and beauty, with an unconquerable penchant for dolls and needle-work, that He ever intended them to be equal in all things. Therefore, we hold that it is simply a physical impossibility to greatly enlarge the pursuits of woman.

Women, Ross admitted, might be typesetters—for females had "delicacy of touch and dexterity of hand"—or clerks; furthermore, he conceded that women were generally not as well paid for the same work as men. He could not, however, agree that the ballot would remedy wage inequity.

As had happened in other towns, an editor—partly motivated by a desire to prevent the suffrage movement from spreading—denounced the campaigner only after her departure. The *Statesman*'s editor, Newell, whose fiery disposition was known all over the region, had been surprisingly calm during her visit.[12] After her first lecture, Newell admitted that she had submitted "an able argument in favor of extending the ballot" to women and that she was a better "orator than we had been led to expect from the criticisms of her lectures that appeared in the San Francisco papers." He appreciated Duniway's entertaining remarks at the conclusion of Anthony's first speech and summarized: "The advent of these ladies in Walla Walla has created quite a sensation, a female speaker in this part of the country being a novelty."[13] But Newell had no sympathy for novel and unorthodox ideas.[14] The week after Anthony's visit, the editor censured the campaigner and her manager for making a raid upon Walla Walla; moreover, "Miss Anthony, in the course of her travels through Oregon and Washington Territory, is reported to have bagged over $5,000. Men, when they go forth on electioneering expeditions, usually come out behind; the 'strong-minded' seem to manage these things better."[15] The Walla Wallan proclaimed that the woman's rights movement "is worse than the small-pox and chills and fever combined."

The editor of the Albany *Democrat*, Martin Van Buren Brown, was visiting Walla Walla, and he, too, disliked the New Yorker.[16] She is "a beautious young maiden of 55 tender summers," he wrote, and her private talk "is said to have abounded in richness and to have somewhat startled those of her fair auditors who didn't before know how lots of things in this world were done. This modest virgin was accompanied by Sister Duniway," who made a better impression "than did the Anthony."

While both Walla Walla newspapers criticized the reformer, they and other townsmen disagreed over the propriety of the actions of local church officials. The *Union* editor pointed out that contributions to the building of the churches had been made by a wide variety of citizens, and that refusing both the suffragist and Unitarian minister John C. Kimball the use of the building "is a species of bigotry . . . an infringement of good breeding and Christian charity that cannot fail to give our community a bad name." Another Walla Wallan summarized: "Among the best minds and greatest reformers of the age Miss Anthony stands recognized and honored. And yet . . . there was found for her no place in the Inn of the Walla Walla churches."[17] The *Statesman*, however, argued that "most persons will think that the church officials acted wisely" since the visitor did not talk about religion.[18] "As it was," Newell rationalized, "she was permitted to speak in buildings suitable for miscellaneous gatherings, and thus the desecration of church edifices was avoided."

Duniway published a more enthusiastic version of the visit.

> At Walla Walla (where the people are advanced so far ahead of the ministers as to be justly indignant over the insult to them and their speaker which locked the church doors in the face of

> the rightful owners of the only decent lecturing places in the beautiful little city) Miss Anthony held wonderful and enthusiastic meetings, first in the new and commodious district school house, which proving too small to hold the hundreds who flocked to hear her, was reluctantly given up for the only available hall in the place—a hall good enough in its way, but unfortunately, situated back of a saloon, where the tender-footed preacher who locked his church against us couldn't go in on a complimentary ticket because the hall was in such an unrighteous locality! Miss Anthony made scores of converts and frightened the few old fogies in the city almost out of their wits. The *New Northwest* gained a large number of new subscribers, and the women are unanimously resolved to use their right to vote.[19]

In Walla Walla as elsewhere men and women told the New Yorker about local conditions and prospects. In response to her inquiries, she learned that wheat growers planted in either the fall or spring and that some averaged a rewarding fifty-six bushels per acre. Perhaps in this town she discovered that there were those favoring a division of Oregon and Washington along the Cascade Mountains. According to an editor at The Dalles "the eastern and western sections are as irreconcilable as two cats tied by their tails and thrown over a pole."[20]

The New Yorker could see the different landscapes as she returned along the Columbia Valley to Portland. Duniway took advantage of delays in transportation, thus her companion spoke in tiny Wallula and again at The Dalles. At Wallula Anthony stayed with T.J. Peabody, the Wells Fargo Agent, and his wife and must have been pleasantly surprised to find that they subscribed to the New York *Revolution*. Duniway said that the second lecture at The Dalles was given to an appreciative audience; Anthony, fatigued by her busy campaign, called it "very small."[21]

The schedule permitted no rest. Soon after her arrival back in Portland on 26 September, Anthony visited a suffragist and grumbled: "found her ill—took tea and then back to St. Charles fully resolved never to accept private invitations in Oregon."[22] The following morning she and the Duniways boarded a train for Albany and the crowds attending the Linn County Fair. Her five days in Albany—the third largest town in

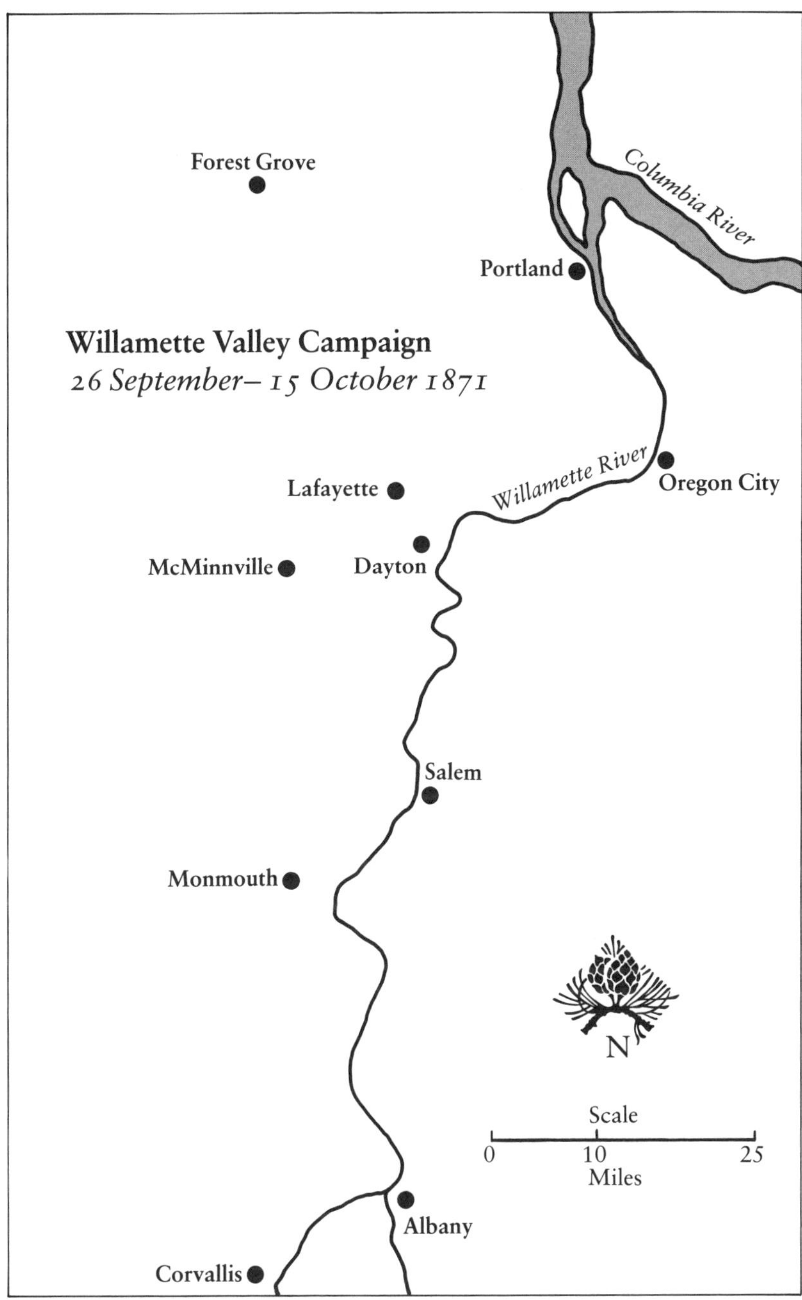
Forest Grove
Columbia River
Portland
Willamette Valley Campaign
26 September– 15 October 1871
Willamette River
Oregon City
Lafayette
Dayton
McMinnville
Salem
Monmouth
N
Scale
0
10
25
Miles
Albany
Corvallis

the state—were difficult. The first problem was finding accommodations; fairgoers packed the hotels. Anthony finally took a room in a private house and rushed to the courthouse and lectured on the "Power of the Ballot" to an audience without "deadheads."[23]

The next morning she breakfasted at a hotel and found her meal to be typical of her touring fare—"a total failure." This tasteless food was followed by a splendid private dinner—her "first square meal in Oregon"—in an Albany home, which prompted her to write to the *Revolution* about one of the state's deficiencies. Its editor paraphrased her opinions:

> Oregon . . . [a] new and beautiful State, needs a large emigration of sensible industrious women. She has not been in a town in which a good hotel, or even an excellent boarding-house of the New England species, might not make a fortune. Outside of Salem and Portland she has not been in a hotel deserving the name. A colony of good cooks would find plenty of hungry mouths with recollections of Eastern dinners sharpening their appetites.[24]

Later in the day she toured the fairgrounds, a mile and a half south of Albany, and expressed her displeasure: "in nothingness surpassed only by the Walla Walla Fair."[25] Her second lecture, on the Fourteenth and Fifteenth Amendments, attracted a smaller audience than the first. Anthony explained the reason: "Duniways so sure of their old home, but I find much dislike of them and my audiences suffer from it."[26] She failed to mention in her diary entry that when she asked for questions, the antisuffragist Frost—who had come to the fair to challenge Anthony—arose, posed questions, and sparked a controversy. According to the Albany *Democrat*:

> The sympathies of the audience seemed on the side of Mrs. Frost, though all three ladies manifested tact and ability in their intellectual sparring. The scene was decidedly interesting. We thought Mrs. Duniway exhibited a little too much temper, but man, the poor weak creature, often does the same thing, much to the injury of his cause.[27]

The following morning Anthony lectured free of charge in a circus tent, calling it "hard work." In the evening the activist attended a speech by Frost, who had announced that she would oppose the feminist's doctrines and "show that the greatest curse that could befall the good and virtuous women of this country would be woman suffrage."[28]

The antisuffragist's speech in Albany, which included many of the same ideas she had published in her public letter at Salem, was the first of a series she would deliver in the Pacific Northwest against Anthony and her allies. For a time Frost dogged her opponent, attempting to counter her influence. The most complete account of a Frost speech came from a sympathetic listener. The Californian began by apologizing for her lack of experience as a public lecturer and then stated that she had attended both of Anthony's addresses in Albany.[29] After pondering the reformer's message, the antisuffragist had concluded:

> I was more than ever convinced that the ballot in the hands of woman would prove destructive to our social, civil and religious liberties, and result in untold misery to woman herself, and, as a Christian, a woman, and a mother, I felt it my sacred duty to use my influence, and such ability as God has given me, in opposing this destructive doctrine.

She fought woman suffrage for three reasons: it "will destroy the Government of the United States as it now exists . . . it will cast aside the Bible, encourage infidelity, . . . and it will rob woman of everything which should be held sacred in the relations of life, and subject her to the buffetings of this tempestuous world only to be clothed with ignominy and disgrace." According to the reporter, Anthony interrupted the lecturer at this point and challenged the accuracy of her generalizations. Frost snapped that her opponent could speak later.

The antisuffragist then asserted "that woman, in her present position, governs the world—her influence pervades every circle, it commenced in the garden of Eden. . . . The pirate on the seas quails before the influence of woman; the word 'mother' sharpens the courage of the soldier upon the battlefield and mitigates the sufferings of his dying bed." She recalled how important the word "mother" had been to mortally wounded Civil War soldiers she had known and insisted that the influence "of women [*sic*] is everywhere felt, and will so continue while she remains in her present sphere; but the ballot in the hands of woman will utterly destroy this influence." Frost charged that most suffragists were infidels—this blow brought hisses from Duniway[30]—and the speaker continued, "They ignore the Bible, blaspheme the sacred name of Jesus, and are creating dissensions and discontent throughout the social circle." Referring to the New Yorker she sarcastically commented, "I never could see how it was that an old maid who had neglected to fill the office in society for which God in his providence had wisely created her, should essay to lecture married women upon child-bearing, maternity and other kindred topics, when, as a Miss, who was never married, she is supposed to be innocently ignorant of all such matters."

After arguing that many female suffrage leaders favored the free love ideas of Victoria Woodhull, she maintained "that every mother . . . is already represented, through her sons, who, if they be trained properly, will represent her aright." She boasted that her two sons "were never arraigned before a court of justice, as were the sons of a certain person [Mrs. Duniway] the other day, who, instead of being at home teaching the lessons of life, was absent from her family inculcating the pernicious doctrine of Woman Suffrage."[31]

Both of the suffrage leaders were visibly annoyed with Frost's personal attacks; one observer joked that "both were pretty badly Frost-bitten." Anthony's diary entry called her detractor "the weakest silliest acting and talking woman I ever saw—fairly dirty in her insinuations."[32]

The following night men and women, anticipating more excitement, squeezed into the courthouse to hear Anthony's response. She had studied part of the day so as to counter the objections raised by her California critic and other opponents. In her rejoinder the New Yorker probably mentioned that in the East antisuffragist lecturers sometimes trailed their opponents, thus she was accustomed to tactics such as Frost's. To Anthony's way of thinking, such itinerant foes, like negative editors, confused the public, but she believed that in Albany her reply had "brushed away the Cobwebs."[33] Frost, however, remained unconverted and would be heard from again as she continued to trail the reformers. On Sunday the suffragist prepared and delivered her first temperance lecture in Oregon. Again she expressed satisfaction with her performance, but the Albany *Good Templar*—no champion of woman suffrage—only reported that the speaker was interesting and that she stressed "the influence and power which the ballot would give to women in the temperance reform."[34] In the evening Anthony attended the sermon of an antisuffragist preacher.

Duniway applauded her companion's efforts in Albany: "The irrepressible advocate of human rights met with most gratifying success. . . . Her lectures were largely attended, and the deep and silent interest of her immense audiences was the most flattering tribute they could possibly pay to the sterling worth and genuine good sense of one of the noblest specimens of true womanhood."[35] She judged that "the brains and worth of Albany all favor Woman Suffrage, just as intelligence and moral stamina do everywhere." But the Oregon editor also wrote some harsh words: "The whisky rings are opposed to us, and so are a few ignorant old fogies and a soft-pated preacher or two, who (the preachers) live off of the exertions of a few honorable, church-going women." She maintained that "roughs" opposed reform and that the Albany *Democrat* was "irresponsible."

At the time Anthony visited, a temporary editor managed the Albany *Democrat*. He was as hostile to woman suffrage as the regular editor, Martin Van Buren Brown, and voiced displeasure with the campaigner even prior to her arrival, insisting that she was unqualified to speak about marriage. The editor chided women: "Somebody says that the giving of the ballot to women would not amount to much, for none of them would admit they were old enough to vote until they were too old to take any interest in politics."[36]

The *Democrat* practically ignored Anthony's presentation. The editor, who left during the course of her first lecture, merely noted: "Miss Anthony is a well appearing lady and she speaks with much earnestness and apparent candor, impressing her hearers with the conviction that she means all she says. Her age . . . is perhaps on the shady side of fifty."[37] Editor Brown returned to his desk and resumed this line of attack. He, like Frost, sought to discredit the distinguished visitor by calling her a follower of Victoria Woodhull. In an editorial entitled "The American Commune," Brown decried an unprecedented "licentious spirit" now threatening western civilization: "In France it is known as the Commune. . . . In this country it is rapidly developing and attempting to organize under the Woman's Rights standard." The writer did not accuse all advocates of woman's rights of sympathizing with the "immoral views and sentiments of the French Commune," but he boasted that he could "prove from their own lips that the leaders of the movement are Communists and enemies to Christian civilization." Brown believed that he had exposed a domestic menace: "We accord to Miss Anthony and Mrs. Woodhull the right to teach, and to all who wish to do so the right to echo their sentiments, but we claim the privilege of stripping the gauze of sophistry from their clamor for the ballot and exhibiting them in their true character." At the same time the Portland *Bulletin* joined Brown in an attempt to link woman suffrage with every dangerous "ism" by publishing a report that Europeans generally classed suffrage "with Mormonism, Oneida Communism, and Free-loveism."[38]

The next opportunity for Anthony to attract large audiences was at the Oregon State Fair, scheduled for 11 October. Duniway, taking advantage of the time prior to the fair's opening, scheduled a hectic interim canvass for her co-worker—a rapid tour of agricultural towns west of the Willamette to consist of two days in Corvallis and a single day each in Monmouth, Dayton, Lafayette, and McMinnville. This swing, part of which was made in a private wagon, would conclude with a brief rest and lecture at Forest Grove. The Duniways took a brief leave of Anthony but made arrangements for friends and relatives to transport the speaker to lecture sites.

On 2 October, as Anthony started her tour, she calculated that she had raised $735 in California and Oregon—a figure considerably smaller than that cited by editors opposed to her campaign—and she seemed puzzled that she had earned only eighteen dollars as her share from a large Corvallis crowd. Following her second lecture in that town she wrote in her diary: "felt most terribly blue—can it be some evil to the loved ones at home or in Kansas?"[39]

G.W. Quivey, editor of the Corvallis *Benton Democrat*, was another critic. He disliked Anthony's old-fashioned dress, dismissed her modern interpretation of the Fourteenth and Fifteenth Amendments, complained that she sometimes met objections "in the true Yankee style of answering one question by asking another," and preferred the antisuffragist lecture of Frost who "must command the thoughtful consideration of the moral and upright."[40] Editor Quivey renewed his attack after her departure through name-calling (she was a "Transcendant bilkess!") and with a joke: "A Boston paper says the best way to improve the lot of woman is to put a good house on it, and a good man in the house."[41]

Anthony traveled a few miles north to Monmouth College, where a large audience filled the chapel. In Dayton she drew a meager crowd but relished the luxury of staying in her hotel bed until noon. Her next stop was Lafayette's Methodist Church, which was crammed with town folk and farmers, some of whom had driven fifteen miles for the occasion. Many of these farmers were in a celebratory mood, having recently received $1.20 per bushel for their wheat—a price which meant that "nearly every farmer in the county will get out of debt this season." On Saturday evening, 7 October, she delivered the "Power of the Ballot" to a large audience at the long, narrow, and unfinished Mohawk Hall in McMinnville. The town's newspaper, the *West Side*, was one of the few in the mid-Willamette Valley to praise the campaigner. A few months earlier its editor, Thomas B. Handley, had been unable to understand "how any true lady on God's footstool can argue that dabbling in politics will in any way enhance her happiness," and he had predicted that within ten years after women received the ballot Americans would suffer from "a petticoat government more disgusting than the reign of Mary Queen of Scots and more tyrannical than that of Queen Elizabeth."[42] But Anthony dispelled such fears; Handley, who seemed converted, summarized:

> Owing to the coldness of the weather, the largeness of the hall and many other disadvantages, Miss Anthony did not display the vivacity and perfect freedom that she did the night previous at Lafayette. It must be said that she took Lafayette as by storm, and it was the leading topic of conversation on the streets of that town that she had converted nearly all to the belief that the women of the period were fearfully abused and 'Give us Suffrage' was the cry. She obtained a few converts here. Her lecture was well put together, and caused frequent bursts of laughter, for she has learned that an occasional humorous anecdote lends charm to her addresses. She . . . left McMinnville with the knowledge that a larger audience outside of Portland had not heard her speak.[43]

Voices in McMinnville raised a broad range of concerns. A male correspondent, using the pen name "Man's Rights," accused:

> An unchaste woman will infect with moral leprosy every virtuous woman with whom she comes in contact. Happily man, being so infinitely superior to woman, is not subject to moral contamination. He can wade through all manner of filth and wickedness, and come out pure and undefiled; but let a woman come in contact with evil, and straightway she becomes inoculated with its deadly poison.[44]

Anthony's hostess aired a more concrete grievance. Her husband had fled with most of their property, their five children, and had married a young California woman. Having heard other depressing accounts of desertion in the Pacific Coast, the New Yorker concluded that a marriage in the region was "practically any thing but an indestructible tie."[45]

On Sunday the campaigner climbed aboard the 6:00 A.M. stage for Forest Grove, where she rested at the home of John T. Scott, Abigail's father. Her appearance the following evening in the local Congregational Church was occasion for a youthful prank: "Some boys," she wrote, "threw Cayenne Pepper on the hot stove . . . and made terrific coughing and almost stopped me from speaking. Dr. [Sidney H.] Marsh [President of Pacific University] and all the College [were] dreadfully mortified."[46] The next day Anthony visited the college and then went on by stage to Portland, which included jostling over six miles of corduroy road. She made diary entries about the telegraphic report of the great Chicago Fire and her "first splendid view of Mt. Hood, St. Helens, and Jefferson."

Duniway preceded her companion to Salem and scheduled lectures in the Marion County Courthouse and on the fairgrounds. The effort started badly. On 11 October—much to her distress—Anthony missed the southbound train and had to cancel the courthouse meeting. When she arrived the following day excited families, enjoying gorgeous fall weather, crowded the streets. One visitor wrote: "Everybody had fair on the brain. The hotels and many private residences are crowded. . . . Gamesters, sharpers and blacklegs are having a sumptuous feast of filthy lucre, and many a poor fellow quits their company lighter in pocket." Another observer commented about the number and variety of fair-goers, including "a row of old ladies, standing near the railroad track, dressed in homemade blue frocks, long gingham aprons, ruffled caps, and large sun bonnets, smoking their pipes."[47] They were gaping at the first railroad train they had ever seen.

Anthony and Duniway must have been disappointed with the small audience that attended their meeting on the fairgrounds. While the sideshow—featuring the 417-pound Vancouver Fat Girl, contortionist Madam Forrestelle, a Mexican dwarf, and the ever-popular Pixley Sisters—attracted large paying crowds from the ten thousand people roaming the grounds, only one hundred sympathetic listeners paid the fifty cent admission to hear the agitator's talk held in a circus tent. Fortunately, fair managers asked Anthony to give an afternoon lecture on 13 October in a copse near the pavilion. This address, which called for voluntary donations rather than an admission charge, drew the largest audience she enjoyed during her western crusade—Anthony estimated it at one thousand while her tour manager boasted that it was three thousand. Pitching her voice above the clamor of the sideshows, the New Yorker delivered what she later called "a real Patrick Henry" speech.[48] She was pleased with her presentation and with the fact that only forty persons attended the Frost lecture delivered earlier that day. An antisuffragist analyzed the contest: "Mrs. Frost . . . has made several efforts to reply to Miss Anthony, but she is not very logical in her style, and Susan makes light work of her, poor thing, but she is too innocent and confident to ever find it out, so Susan's shafts fall harmless."[49]

Portrayed as the "old clown" by one newspaperman, Anthony was ignored by most other writers, who instead stressed the exhibits, horse races, and Colonel David Taggart's platitudinous featured fair address. Delighted with her co-worker, Duniway enthused that Anthony "held that every woman was, in common with all other creations of the good All-Father, brought into existence primarily for her own highest personal good, and secondarily for the good of others. Old men and women, young men and maidens listened to her words of wisdom, believed, and were converted."[50]

The editor of the *Oregon Statesman* continued the criticism he had directed at Anthony following her earlier Salem visit. In announcing her circus tent lecture Clarke sarcastically commented: "She will be pleased to see as many present . . . as have a half dollar to give her in return for the pleasure they will experience in beholding her beautiful form, and listening to her melodious voice."[51] In summarizing her outdoor speech, which was given to what he called "a curious multitude," the writer complained: "It seems that woman's first duty, according to Anthony, is to love herself, the next to love her God, and after that she can waste some attention on her husband, if he behaves himself so as to deserve it."[52] He wondered how an old maid knew so much about men and praised male listeners who "grinned and bore it bravely."

Anthony's presence at the fair affected Colonel Taggart, who delivered the fair's annual address. Partly because he had puffed the Pacific Northwest greatly to eastern newspapers, Taggart, a military paymaster, had been given the honor of making the featured speech. Among the colonel's many platitudes were a few aimed at women. The soldier remembered his youth when he "deemed that petticoats covered only angels," and he directed some disjointed remarks at those unsophisticated men presently holding such an idea:

> The cause on which woman smiles will always prosper—even female suffrage, whenever they shall be unanimous on the subject, if female unanimity were a possible attainment. While by the law of Nature she is denied the physical strength, and some rudely assert, the mental vigor of her *once* lord and master—I say "*once* lord and master" out of respect to Miss Susan B. Anthony—yet by the same law the impulses of her heart, if native and unperverted, are always right.[53]

The orator then admonished women to attend to their crucial, traditional role:

> It is in your power by industry, frugality and kindness to make the fires burn brightly in the hearth of the home . . . By your conduct a weak-minded husband may be dragged down to destruction. By your efforts an outlawed husband may be led back to decency, virtue and happiness. . . . Oh, ye! To whom much power is given exert it in mercy, let your influence go forth to unpeople the haunts of vice and the dens of infamy; let it go forth to incite striving man on his arduous way; let it go forth to win back *erring* man to wisdom, virtue and honor.

The reformer heard these words and perhaps challenged them in her major speech on the fairgrounds. Taggart's perception of woman's role was the traditional one that Anthony battled constantly. She did not summarize it in her diary and saved her refutations for later in the crusade. Instead she recorded his characterization of her; "I am slab-sided spinster—failed to get a whole man" and returning through "Salt Lake to try for a fraction of one."

The state fair gave Anthony evidence to support her generalization that frontier men did not protect women; but in fact sometimes preyed upon them. According to one writer, "Only two accidents happened that I heard of, and those were two runaways in the shape of two men running away with other men's wives."[54] One seduction case received considerable publicity; one newspaperman expressed his disgust with two hundred men and boys crowding the police court to hear details. "They had" he charged, "come from the beer cellars, the dens of filth and the courts of death in hopes of enjoying a repast of scandal, and came with foul bodies, fouler breaths and foulest minds."[55]

At the state fair and every other stop, Anthony solicited women's signatures on a petition demanding the right to vote and also asked them to donate a dollar to the cause. The signatures and the money went to the National Woman Suffrage Association, which compiled lists of names to be submitted to Congress in an attempt to prove that females favored enfranchisement. In Salem and elsewhere the New York feminist sold woman's rights documents, including Stanton's lecture on marriage and divorce and Woodhull's memorial to Congress, and assured her one hundred buyers that these publications would help them convert neighbors to the suffragist cause.

For two nights Anthony camped with all of the Duniway family on the grounds adjacent to the fair (the *New Northwest*'s office had closed so that the Duniway boys could leave their newspaper jobs and enjoy a vacation). Several hundred Oregonians pitched white tents and enjoyed their outing. Duniway explained that families arrived at the "Donnybrook" prepared "to make money, spend money, patronize sideshows, camp out, eat dirt, breathe smoke, sleep on the ground, race horses, and be gay."[56] Anthony, however, found camping to be disagreeable. It was the first time she had ever camped, and she wrote that the occupants of her tent were "packed side by side like herring," and that she preferred a "nice bedroom and hair mattress."[57] She never forgot the occasion and never slept outdoors again.

With no prospects for a good audience in Salem, the two reformers decided against scheduling a Saturday night lecture. Thus Anthony returned to Portland, where she wrote in her diary that an argument with "coarse men" prompted feelings of remorse. On Sunday she packed for the next leg of her tour, a series of appearances on Puget Sound. The famous visitor estimated that during her five weeks in the Willamette, Columbia, and Walla Walla valleys she had earned $500. She left no written evaluation of the campaign's impact. Her tour manager, however, wrote a glowing summary: "Miss Anthony has sojourned in the Northwest about thirty-five days, has made thirty speeches, traveled one thousand miles, and, we may safely add, has converted fifteen thousand people. Has any other preacher done as much?"[58]

# FIVE

# *North to Puget Sound and Victoria*

ON 16 OCTOBER Anthony and the Duniways disembarked from the steamer *Fannie Troup* at Monticello, a small Cowlitz River port, and boarded a battered stagecoach for what they knew would be an exhausting ride to Olympia. A trip to the small towns rimming Puget Sound seemed profitable. Abigail had explained to her companion that California suffragist Laura de Force Gordon had been well received by residents, including editors, and that suffragists from such places as Olympia and Seattle had written their enthusiastic support for a visit by a national leader.[1] These folk, like suffragists in Oregon, wanted an experienced reformer to give impetus to the movement: they needed publicity, organization, and converts. For several years some Washingtonians had insisted that women deserved the right to vote under the territorial election law of 1866, which had extended suffrage "to all white citizens."[2] Some members of the recently convened territorial legislature pledged themselves to fight for a bill that would enfranchise females. Thus local suffragists believed that Anthony might be of crucial help in persuading politicians to enact such reform.

The knowledge that influential citizens in various towns eagerly awaited their arrival helped sustain the three reformers as their stagecoach bounced along a winding road up the heavily forested Cowlitz Valley and Cowlitz Mountain to Pumphrey's Station, a stop on the eighty-five mile route to Olympia. The weary travelers dined on trout that caused Anthony to dream "most uncomfortably until awakened by her driver at 2:30 A.M." Guided by the feeble light of its lanterns, the stagecoach laboriously followed a crooked, root-infested mountain road. At times the passengers were forced to walk several miles while the driver repaired his vehicle. Perhaps a fellow foot-traveler told Anthony that when the railroad was completed it would take only ten hours to travel between Portland and Olympia—not the forty-eight hours presently required by coach. Reaching the territorial capitol with "fagged out bodies and wearied brains," the reformers moved in "double quick time" to private homes, where Anthony napped prior to her appearance in Olympic Hall. After her talk she boasted that "scarce a man could have done it after such a ride."[3]

In another rendition of "The Power of the Ballot," she reiterated the points she had voiced from previous platforms. The audience, which included some legislators, was a disappointment. Fewer than one hundred chose to pay the unusually high $1 admission fee; the ticket price had been doubled because it had been agreed that one-third of the gross receipts would be sent to Chicago fire victims. The meager proceeds prompted the speaker to turn over the evening's entire net receipts of $30 to the fund.

Editors of the four local newspapers were probably in attendance. These men, struggling to find subscribers and advertisers in the territorial capitol, had expressed no reservations about Anthony's visit. The *Tribune*, the only daily in Washington, had treated her forthcoming lecture more lightly than its competitors. In announcing it, Republican Editor Charles Prosch commented, "If she would come in company with a few hundred marriageable girls, her mission would be more welcome and successful. At present there are scarcely enough women on the Sound to set up a claim to any rights."[4] This shortage of females had prompted a joke that appeared in New York City on 5 August 1871 in *Woodhull and Claflin's Weekly*: "A voice from Washington Territory, 'Send us wives!' Thousands respond, 'Take ours!'"

The press response to the talk was brief, diverse, and favorable. H.J. Munson's *Echo*, a weekly temperance paper, summarized that her "style of argument is systematic and philosophical, her manner dignified and ladylike" and that despite her ninety-mile stage ride she "held her audience spellbound."[5] Prosch, of the *Tribune*, applauded the reformer for speaking "with her usual ability and logic, carrying conviction to many minds," but he denounced the $1.00 admission fee: "There are few

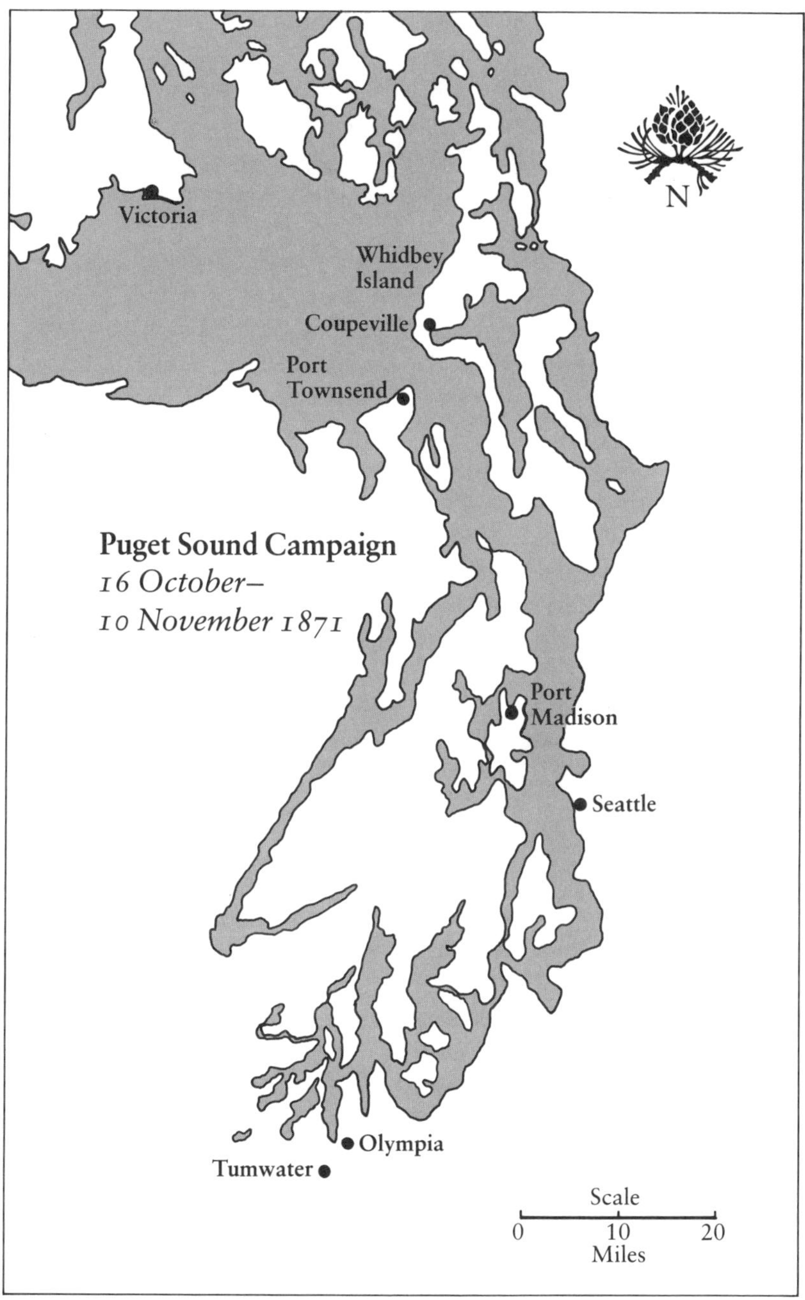
Victoria
Whidbey Island
Coupeville
Port Townsend
Puget Sound Campaign
16 October–
10 November 1871
Port Madison
Seattle
Olympia
Tumwater
N
Scale
0 10 20
Miles

in this community who can afford to pay a dollar for any kind of entertainment."[6]

Republican Elisha T. Gunn, editor of the *Transcript*, published only a brief notice. But veteran editor John Miller Murphy of the *Washington Standard* complimented Anthony at length: "She presents her arguments in graceful and elegant language, her illustrations are ample and well chosen, and the hearer is irresistibly drawn to the conclusions which she seeks to inculcate."[7] Murphy, a noted Democrat, listed the major points of the speech and, anticipating that he would be criticized for supporting equal suffrage, emphasized that his support was a personal decision, not that of the Democratic Party. The reform, he insisted, was "a question upon which Democrats as well as Republicans may honestly differ. We do not depart in the least from the principles we cherish and have so long advocated, nor do we intend [to] do so. It is simply a question of right, upon which we wish to be on the side of RIGHT."

On the day following Anthony's speech, Daniel R. Bigelow, a Republican member of the Territorial House of Representatives, invited Anthony and several legislators to his Olympia home.[8] At this dinner, men undoubtedly boasted to the famous guest about Puget Sound, calling it the "Mediterranean of the Pacific." Here and elsewhere there was talk about the fact that only a few American tourists were aware of the beauties of the Pacific Northwest. Many visited Yosemite Valley—as had Anthony and Stanton a few months earlier—but few journeyed to the Northwest corner of the nation where they could hunt bears and cougars, fish for salmon and trout, climb Rainier and St. Helens, marvel at towering forests, and enjoy sublime vistas. In summary, a local writer maintained that the region's scenery "is unique, and as diversified as it is peculiar."[9]

Many predicted that Puget Sound's safe anchorages would someday accommodate a busy commerce. Envisioning a great civilization where pristine forests now stood, boosters insisted that Washington Territory, like New England, would become prosperous, not through a reliance on agriculture, but through the development of its outstanding commercial and manufacturing capabilities, especially lumber and coal.

In conversation with Olympians and later with other residents of Puget Sound, Anthony learned that although Washington Territory was not "an earthly paradise," it was believed superior to life on the Atlantic

Coast. "A poor man," residents explained "can earn a living here easier than in the East, as labor is in demand, wages are good and provisions cheap. A man can subsist bountifully by his rifle and fishing rod alone, so that the procuring of food need give him no trouble."[10] To develop the territory, residents wanted an influx of hard workers and warned that "literary men . . . loiterers or followers of the fickle goddess, are not wanted and had better keep away."[11] In discussing the need for more women, the visitor learned of a need for female school teachers—the pay was too low to attract males—and for domestics. Boosters promised, "One hundred girls could find positions within one week after their arrival in the Territory."

Bigelow's liberal views of women—his wife was also a suffragist—must have pleased the New Yorker. He argued, for example, that "the fashionable female portion of our country do not want to vote because they do not want to make the exertion which the duties of citizenship would require. And here we find the origin of the idea, that it is feminine to do nothing." He complained that an Olympia female described another as "a perfect lady because she did not know how to do anything."[12] At the dinner party, the host most likely compared his wife, Elizabeth, a frontier wife who had endured every pioneer hardship, with ornamental women. Anthony was also greatly impressed with Mrs. Bigelow, calling her a "splendid" wife.[13]

At this and other social occasions around Puget Sound, residents may have told their famous guest that during the first session of the territorial legislature in 1853, Seattleite Arthur Denny had introduced a bill that would have given white women the right to vote. Anthony was also informed that the International Order of Good Templars in Olympia and other places championed equal suffrage. These prohibitionists wanted women to help them control the liquor traffic. Bigelow talked not only about the need for equal suffrage, he also rehashed a suffrage bill he had recently introduced in the legislature. (In studying the possibility of passing his bill, the politician probably mentioned that his Republicans barely outnumbered Democrats in both houses—by 5 to 4 in the Council and 16 to 14 in the House.) He lauded the assembled legislators for inviting the famous suffragist to address them in a forthcoming session, and he rejoiced over the fact that an attempt to secure the service of an antisuffragist lecturer to rebut Anthony had been tabled.

Olympians long remembered 19 October. With many fashionably dressed ladies among the crowd assembled in the house chamber, a special house committee escorted Anthony and Duniway to the forum. As the applause faded, the calm speaker, who was handsomely gowned in a gray silk dress that had been a present on her fiftieth birthday, stressed that "this was the first time in the history of our nation that a woman has been allowed the privilege of addressing the lawmakers in session."[14] In one of her most effective speeches delivered on the Pacific Coast, Anthony provided ample evidence to support her contention that women enjoyed the right of suffrage under the provisions of the Fourteenth and Fifteenth Amendments. During her straightforward address she stressed the importance of the ballot: "The idea of free government does not appertain to those not enfranchised. . . . By all men's definitions of the term, the withholding of the ballot and representation while taxes are imposed, is the most abject of servitude."

In her conclusion she disagreed with Bigelow's bill that would require the women of Washington Territory to vote on whether they wanted the right of suffrage. The speaker resisted it,

> because it submitted the matter to the women, who were in a condition of servitude and incapacitated from voting on the question. It was hard to break loose from the restraint imposed by popular sentiment, and only those who have used the ballot know its value. You might just as well leave the decision of school matters to the children, who would prefer to romp and play, the regulating of the sale of liquors to the saloonkeepers . . . or that of brothels to the prostitutes.

In lieu of Bigelow's bill, she proposed a declaratory act "requiring the proper officer to register the names of women and making it the duty of the judges of election to count their votes, the same as those of the men." If this were done she predicted "the most gratifying of results—the immigration of a large number of good women to the Territory." Anthony having heard in the East and in Wyoming the theory that woman suffrage would entice men and women to underpopulated territories, obviously counted on the assembled lawmakers to be moved by such an argument. Apparently this tactic failed; the territory's prosuffrage legislators rarely, if ever, used it themselves. It appears that the campaigner might have stopped advocating the correlation between equal suffrage and increased population, for none of the regional editors, including Duniway, reported it in their subsequent summaries of her talks. Washingtonians had a more conventional solution to the problem of underpopulation. They reasoned that the Northern Pacific Railroad, which had recently started its long-awaited construction northward from Kalama on the Columbia, would bring sufficient immigrants to their remote but promising location. To most residents the locomotive, not the ballot, was the obvious way to draw people.

Duniway was also asked to speak and recited a brief history of the suffrage "movement in ye land of Webfoot." One listener said that the Oregon newspaperwoman used "well-chosen but very emphatic language," warning "those having political aspirations that now was the accepted time of salvation; to take heed of the indications of the times, before it was too late."

Anthony's logical address won considerable support. Editor Gunn now praised her: "Miss Anthony is a woman of more than ordinary ability, and the able manner in which she handled her subject before the Legislature, was ample warning to the members of that body who oppose woman suffrage to be silent."[15] Duniway evaluated her companion's speech as "calm, courteous, convincing [and] dignified"; she enthused that it had "converted hundreds . . . to a knowledge of the truth as it is in the Constitution."[16]

But the majority of the lower house proved unmoved by Anthony's assertions. The day after her speech, a lawmaker introduced exactly the kind of declaratory act she had urged; it failed by a close vote of 13-11, with Bigelow, who preferred his own plan of action over that urged by the famous reformer, voting no.[17] Immediately after this vote an antisuffrage legislator moved that Bigelow's bill be indefinitely postponed; his motion passed 16-11. This reversal failed to discourage the visiting reformers, however. Editor Duniway assured her readers that "the names of the immortal eleven will be heralded throughout the great Northwest. We hope to get the bill through in proper shape before the close of the session, as we hear every day of some new convert in one house or the other."[18] Anthony wrote in her diary that the 16-11 count did not represent a test vote and could not be taken as a true barometer of opinion. But in actuality the vote to postpone Bigelow's bill did reflect the strength of antisuffrage sentiment and the lower house further showed its opposition by rejecting a proposal to print Anthony's address.

Following her appearance before the legislature, the Easterner continued her scheduled lecture tour. The excitement generated by her appearance before the legislature resulted in a brisk sale of lecture tickets. She talked to a small group in nearby Tumwater; the next evening she spoke again in Olympia. In this final performance she drew hearty applause as she refuted objections to her reform.

Building upon the enthusiasm they had generated for their cause, the two suffragists, eagerly aided by local allies, prepared for a suffrage convention to be held in the territorial capitol on 8 November, the day of their expected return from their swing around the Sound. It seemed appropriate to conclude the campaign with an enthusiastic convention; more than one hundred men and women agreed, attaching their names to the notification of the scheduled meeting, whose announced objective was "to arrange some plan by which to secure concert of action among the women voters of the Territory."[19]

Anthony and Duniway deemed the just concluded Olympia visit an auspicious beginning to the Puget Sound effort. The New Yorker had delivered effective speeches, had won enthusiastic support for the forthcoming convention, had enlisted promises from a number of politicians, and had not been criticized by a single local editor. The Portlander rejoiced over the fact that the Olympia press—unlike that of Walla Walla, Portland, or Salem—had been unanimously fair to Anthony and the cause.

Yet scarcely had the visitors steamed for Victoria, B.C. before Prosch launched an attack in his *Tribune*. The Republican editor rebuked his rival, Murphy of the *Washington Standard*, contending that Murphy had "thrown up his position as a Democratic standard bearer, and marches boldly into the front rank of the woman suffragists."[20] Murphy's name, Prosch joked, "will shine in the constellation of which Train, Woodhull, Stanton, Tilton, and Anthony have long been bright and shining lights." Other politicians, Prosch prophesied, would also rally around the "petticoat banner." Turning to Anthony, he quoted a Seattle news story which spoofingly claimed that Anthony was actually a wife and mother and jested: "If so, Susan is very wicked; for she is palming herself off for a spinster. Who'd a thought she could practice such deception?" In another column he mocked:

> We are mortified that many of the very susceptible people converted to the new faith by Miss Anthony and Mrs. Duniway are already wavering, and betray signs of backsliding. Just so did they of Walla Walla. . . . For the credit of Olympia, it is hoped the flock here will remain steadfast, and thus spare the feelings of their fair captors.

Murphy, who had engaged in many political battles with Prosch, anticipated this criticism and denied that his conversion to woman's suffrage was recent or opportunistic. Murphy elaborated:

> The *Tribune* elevates our frank avowal of what have been our profound convictions for many years into the dignity of leadership, and attributes to us the gushing enthusiasm of a new convert, anxious before many witnesses to proclaim our devotion to the "new departure," as it calls woman suffrage. The profound (we had almost put it elephantine) sage, who presides over the *Tribune*'s tripod, has grown frisky in his old age, and dances through a column of verbose pleasantries, with an agility which must have caused great beads of sweat to decorate his hoary brows.[21]

Duniway soon jumped into the fray, pointing out that Prosch was the only Olympian who had changed his mind. At the time of their visit, the newspaperwoman recalled, Prosch "was as devoted a Woman Suffragist as even Theodore Tilton; but—alas! for the frailty of human nature—no sooner had the good evangelist of the new gospel of freedom to woman departed than he hied himself quickly to the husks of man's rights political doctrine."[22]

In good weather the sixteen hour voyage from Olympia to Victoria presented unforgettable scenery—magnificent stands of timber that grew to the water's edge, shining water, and snowcapped mountains. One Olympian bragged, "Nowhere in the world can be found a grander tableaux of water, forest, and snowy mountains than is to be witnessed from the bosom of Puget Sound."[23] Foul weather ruined the view, and the churning straits nauseated Anthony and her traveling companions. They disembarked in Victoria during a rain that, Abigail wrote, poured "down in a heavy Oregon fashion." Apparently the three itinerants selected Victoria for an extended effort because it was on the steamboat route, because Anthony would have a chance to teach her doctrines before a foreign audience, and because there was a better opportunity to sell tickets there. Victoria's population of 5,000 made it the largest urban center north of Portland.

Anthony strolled Victoria's streets and welcomed visitors at her hotel. She learned that 1871 had proved a crucial year in British Columbia's history: Canada's Conservative Prime Minister, John A. Macdonald, had promised these remote residents a great railway to the Pacific Coast if British Columbia would join the Canadian Confederation. Thus remote British Columbia had recently joined a barely four-year old nation—one that lacked the strident nationalism so characteristic of the United States. Anthony, however, heard concerns similar to those expressed by Oregonians and Washingtonians; for example, that Victoria needed additional settlers. One promoter summarized: "We are assured that there are, in California and other states and territories on the Pacific slope, thousands of precisely the description of settlers of which this Province stands so greatly in need, and who would not hesitate to come here if informed of the nature of the country and its advantages."[24] She learned about the great natural resources of Vancouver Island and the need for money, railroads, and female domestics. Like western Americans, western Canadians expressed hostility to Chinese laborers, denouncing them as "long tailed, almond eyed gentlemen," and calling them derogatory names similar to those the traveler had heard ever since her arrival in San Francisco.

But Anthony noted a major difference between Victoria and Olympia. In her six day stay in Olympia, concern about woman suffrage had been intense; during her five days in Victoria she had to seek ways to arouse interest. In Olympia she had received meaningful support from local women; in the Canadian city only a few women came to visit her, and it proved almost impossible to get them into lecture seats. Duniway later explained that "the idea of the ballot for a woman was even more unpopular than in the United States, though all, by strange inconsistency, were intensely loyal to their queen."[25]

Anthony's first two evening performances in Alhambra Hall were similar in format and content to those delivered in Olympia, but the audiences, which averaged somewhat fewer than one hundred persons, were about 95 percent male. She began her first speech by admitting that she had not found time to study local laws regulating suffrage; therefore, she would speak as if she were in America. The Victoria *Standard* of 25 October, was as much interested in describing the visitor as in evaluating her ideas. It estimated her age at forty-five and explained that "although somewhat stern-looking . . . for her sex, she is not without a smile at times." During her initial talk the suffragist asked Victorians either to visit or write her with their objections to woman's suffrage; she especially wanted communication with "divines, lawyers, or editors." Few, if any, accepted the invitation. Thus, according to the *Standard*, at the second meeting "she brought forward the arguments usually advanced against the doctrine, if we may so term it, and dealt with them one by one, and we must say, handled them without gloves."[26] She urged listeners to bring women to the third lecture, but not more than a dozen would appear. Disappointed with her indifferent reception by local men, the veteran campaigner delivered a provocative speech designed to fill the hall for her last lecture.

Editor David Higgins of the Victoria *Colonist* had praised her as being "in every respect the best lecturer who has visited us since [Rev. William Morley] Punshon" and judged this third address her most effective effort. The visitor, he reported, made sweeping statements about the benefit of suffrage and the status of women:

> She claimed that by the admission of women to the franchise wars would cease. Every step of science had been obstructed by the prejudices of the world, which had to be met and overcome. It is true there is nothing about women voting in the Bible, nor is there anything about men voting. . . . Men of libertine depraved habits were afraid that, if women got the same privileges they have, they would be just as abandoned. But all that woman claimed was the right to separate themselves from a drunken, brutal, libertine husband, and refuse to bear him children and thus pass down his vices and degradation to future generations (cheers). The speaker claimed that when Laura Fair was tried she was not fairly tried because she was a woman. Mrs. Woodhull was vilified and abused because she is a dealer in stocks and a Spiritualist, and she (Miss Anthony) and Mrs. Stanton are abused by the Press of America because they have extended their hands to assist an erring sister.[27]

Following these provocative assertions, the speaker attempted to arouse her listeners further by addressing the local climate for reform. Anthony reported that a local minister and some ladies had visited her hotel, explaining that it was a mistake to charge admission. They complained that Victorians would only buy tickets for minstrels and circuses; furthermore, they maintained that local women did not want liberty. The reformer refuted such sentiment, charging: "It was said that there is no town in America in which wives got so many floggings as in Victoria." A concession was made, however, in a final effort to attract women to her forthcoming and final Victoria appearance: she announced that there would be no admission charged. The crowd laughed and applauded when she explained that she had decided upon a free lecture because "she wanted to see if the women of Victoria had so sunk their womanhood that they were happy even in their degradation." The amused audience voted its thanks. The veteran campaigner exploited the moment by requesting a vote on woman's suffrage. Every hand voted yes.

As Anthony had anticipated, her provocative comments and free admission decision packed the hall for her fourth effort. She regretted, however, that fewer than twenty women sat before her. According to Editor Higgins the speaker again voiced challenges and accusations:

> She began by examining the Common Law of England and said that by it a man may whip his wife with a stick no bigger than his thumb. . . . Missionaries ought to go about and enquire. (a laugh) If a wife rebelled against a whipping and tried to run away she might be restrained. She knew a man who tied his wife to a bedpost to keep her from running away. It had been done here, too (cries of NO!). Oh, I've had half a dozen wives to see me today, so you needn't talk. In England a man may sell his wife. The present condition of women is similar to that of slavery before the war. . . . Drunkards might apprentice their children to rumsellers and brothels and the wife could not prevent them. . . . The women of England and the United States are slaves, and the movement is designed to break the very last link in the chain of slavery.[28]

She continued with a familiar argument that everywhere men took jobs from women, who necessarily had to leave their domestic duties and labor outside their homes. "Go and look at your Victoria dry goods stores where great big six-foot men are measuring off tape. (Laughter). You ought to be ashamed of yourselves for crowding women out of work." The skilled campaigner aroused listeners by generalizing that "not a woman in Victoria is satisfied with her lot. If they say they are, don't believe them." The crowd laughed and cheered, Duniway wisely passed the hat, and the visitor bade farewell.

The lecturer considered this final effort "a tip top speech."[29] Duniway reported that rowdies in attendance apparently hoped "to end the meeting in a roaring, laughing riot."[30] The Oregonian applauded her companion's ability to control detractors; for example, when the crowd became too hilarious, the veteran would pitch "some bomb of truth . . . and quiet would be restored."

Duniway noted differences between the audiences in Victoria and those in America. "We were struck," she wrote, "with the regular Johnny Bull features of the really intelligent audience. There is an indescribable difference of nationality that is everywhere palpable to the understanding, but it is not possible to tell just why it is or what it consists in." But Duniway could easily pinpoint one difference: Canadian blacks, appreciative of the New Yorker's abolitionist work, reminisced about abolitionism at her hotel and attended lectures. The Oregon editor continued:

> The colored people came out in force to every lecture. We find them intelligent, industrious and law-abiding. While there seems to be no desire upon the part of the races to intermarry or mingle socially, there is not that prejudice of caste existing here which we see in Portland. A colored man is spoken of as Mr. and a colored woman is always addressed as a lady.

Editor Higgins attended the four lectures and gave them considerable coverage. Duniway appreciated his efforts but regretted that he, like American editors, must worry about pleasing readers; thus in his account of her last lecture he only dared to publish "a coarse outline of her premises, without attempting to elucidate, by explanation or metaphor, any of the really vital principles of which her logic is constructed."

Higgins opened his columns to those exasperated by Anthony's generalizations and accusations. Using the pseudonym "A Male Biped," one correspondent, making many of the same arguments as American opponents, contended that pregnant women could not be legislators, that a jury of both sexes could not be locked up together, that a mother could not leave sick children for jury duty, that women could not soldier in bad weather, and that "Nature's God" made women physically unfit for the work of men and had "made her gentle, confiding, loving and trusting."[31] He believed, contrary to the claims of woman rights advocates, that in the present state of society only a small percentage of women became prostitutes and that divorce had increased in the United States only because of the agitation created by suffragists. "Society may be wrongly organized," he judged, "but Female Suffrage will not reform it." One woman called the campaigner "a shrewish old mischief-maker who, having failed to secure a husband herself, is tramping the continent to make her more fortunate sisters miserable by creating a dissension in their households."[32] In another column a critic, using the pen name, "An Insulted Husband," accused:

> America, the home of many humbugs, which produced Brigham Young, Barnum . . . and many others, has, it appears, another human curiosity in Miss Anthony. This specimen from over the way, comes amongst us, and because our ladies fail to recognize or encourage her in her vagaries, she gets very rabid and snarls and snaps at "the women of Victoria who had so sunk their womanhood that they were happy even in their degradation." The degradation referred to is that of whipping, which this female firebrand appears to believe is the rule here. Surely, the complete immunity from castigation of such an obnoxious creature as Miss Anthony is sufficient answer to this libel. Men in British Columbia no more countenance bad husbands than do the women quack apostles in petticoats. They look upon such people as sexual mistakes.

Anthony, who clipped these negative letters for her scrapbook, anticipated and appreciated them. She knew that they reflected the fact that she had accomplished one of her purposes—some British Columbians had become aware of the issue of woman's rights.

While Victorians expressed their disgust or pleasure with the suffragist's assertions, the reformers resumed their tour. Following another rough crossing of the Strait of Juan de Fuca, they arrived at Port Townsend, the port of entry into Washington Territory. Their brief stay was interesting; the two travelers visited some nearby Indian huts, where the New Yorker reported seeing "boys perfectly naked . . . eating clams."[33] They heard citizens predict that the Northern Pacific Railroad would build its terminus in Port Townsend. Residents here, as well as in other ports, talked incessantly about high real estate prices and the great future that would follow the arrival of the locomotive. Port Townsend society, however, discussed a variety of topics besides the railroad. The issue of woman's suffrage had been thoroughly debated here, and Anthony and Duniway would have agreed with another recent visitor, historian Frances Fuller Victor, that despite their isolation the inhabitants were "wide-awake, intelligent, courteous, and modish."[34] Between two lectures here, Anthony nervously crossed by a small sailboat to tiny Coupeville on Whidbey's Island where she had been invited to visit the home of Thomas Coupe, a fellow suffragist and Republican member of the legislature who she had met in Olympia. The visitor enjoyed her stay, especially conversation with "two splendid wide awake women."

Both Port Townsend editors disapproved of woman's suffrage. A Swede by birth who had learned English in the territory, Julius Dickens had recently established the *Cyclop* and evidenced his hostility in his announcement of Anthony's call. He repeated a rumor that "the ancient virgin [had] never kissed a son of Adam more than two years old."[35] "She will tell us," he gloomily predicted, "how the avalanche of old maids about to be precipitated upon the latter half of the nineteenth century will serve a good purpose; how it will be their duty to prove that although a woman may have the misfortune to die unmarried, her life is not necessarily a failure." Dickens then sniped at the practices of local women:

> Port Townsend contains its full share of women who deserve to be called "fair," though, we are sorry to say it, one sees too many who buy their complexions at the drug store, and appear on the streets under false colors, as plainly seen as store signs. This most reprehensible practice does not deceive the gentlemen, whose eyes are keener than is supposed in detecting the cheat, and who regard a painted woman with mingled pity,

> fear and aversion. . . . A woman should be content with the beauty God designed she should have.[36]

Editor Al Pettygrove of the Port Townsend *Argus* responded to the reform message with the somewhat unique idea that only intelligent men and women should enjoy the right of suffrage. Such voters "would know what voting meant and have personal interest enough to make him vote right. . . . such a plan would effectually shut out corruption, and would be a reform."[37] He hoped that Anthony would support his idea; if so, he promised her his assistance. The New Yorker ignored Pettygrove, but her companion denounced his proposal. Pettygrove, in turn, became livid:

> Universal suffrage is a humbug, and if the idea is carried out, it will be the rock upon which our Republican Government will be totally wrecked. The ballot is a sacred thing, and should be guarded as such, and only entrusted to those who can properly use it; it is a matter of little moment whether the voters be male or female.[38]

On 31 October the weary travelers steamed from Port Townsend to Seattle, where the stumpers hoped to wage a vigorous campaign among its twelve hundred inhabitants. The older traveler, however, arrived in a depressed mood; she wrote, "the stench of something kills the life in me . . . Mrs. Stanton's letter pretty scolding about the San Francisco $320 check I failed to get off."[39] The dismal skies of Seattle and a "hard" room at the Occidental Hotel—it advertised itself as the only "first-class hotel on the Sound"—added to her discomfort. Anthony felt in no mood for her first lecture. Her condition improved, however, when she moved from the hotel to a private home; she called this a "splendid change." The fact that she and her co-reformer—now without Mr. Duniway who had returned to Portland—moved in with Mrs. Amanda D. Wiggin probably raised a few eyebrows, for their hostess had lectured in several towns on spiritualism and held seances. But this association did not prevent one noted Seattle lady, Mrs. Sarah B. Yesler, from inviting Anthony to dinner. A rainstorm limited Anthony's first Seattle audience to fifty people, but a second speech, held on 2 November, attracted a large crowd, half of whom were women. During three full days in this port, Anthony met many Seattleites, who insisted that despite the depressed condition of the lumber trade, their city was the leading commercial center on the Sound. They emphasized that their harbor held a vital place in the coasting trade and was continually busy with the movements of steamers, tugs, and three-masted lumber schooners; that shipbuilding and sawmilling meant jobs and profits; that coal mines on Lake Washington provided a vital industrial fuel; that farms on local rivers fed loggers and mill workers around the Sound; that there were plans to build a canal between Lake Washington and salt water; and that Snoqualmie Pass, the route followed by those driving cattle and sheep from such grazing lands as the Yakima Valley, must be utilized by the Northern Pacific Railroad. Because of the port's many advantages, residents felt, it must win the bitter competition for the railroad's terminus. The soaring increase in the price of land reflected this optimism.[40]

Considering their port far superior to that of Portland, Seattleites surely reminded the travelers about the low water level of the Columbia and Willamette Rivers, which resulted in ships being impeded by sandbars. The fact that Harvey Scott had recently urged Oregonians to solve their problem with a dredger seemed proof that many places around Puget Sound were indeed superior choices to Portland. Duniway refused to show regional partiality in the conflict; in fact she puffed Puget Sound. Perhaps the fact that the suffrage campaign went so well in its various towns was a major reason for her flattering paragraphs. (Clark Crandall, another Portland editor, traveled to Puget Sound at about the same time as Duniway; he argued, however, that his native city was superior to all of its northern rivals.)

But Anthony had come to the Puget Sound Basin to push her reform, not debate the bright prospects of the rival seaports. She was pleased that the Revs. Daniel Bagley and John F. Damon of the Methodist and Congregational churches championed woman suffrage. These ministers and other prominent citizens helped the visiting reformers organize a Seattle suffrage society in Bagley's church. The society elected women as officers, including Mrs. Yesler as president, and chose both men and women as delegates to the convention scheduled in Olympia. Anthony then took time from her work to straighten out her financial affairs: she sent checks, including one to Stanton.

The two Seattle newspapers gave varied responses to the distinguished visitor. Samuel L. Maxwell, independent editor of the *Intelligencer*, had shown little inclination to support woman's suffrage, and he, like many other editors, had published several humorous articles about women. He apparently enjoyed these stories; for example:

> Did you ever see a thin girl take a bath in the surf and come out with her bathing dress sticking tight to her, like a poor woman's plaster? Funny, wasn't it? Well, it's nothing to a fat girl in the same posish. I do think of all the comical sights in the world, the funniest is a fat girl when she comes out of the surf. . . . I don't think men look any better, but we don't expect grace and beauty in our sex, and can stand the sight. If you are very much in love with a girl and want to break the spell, take her to the beach and see her in her surf toggery. If that don't knock the spooney out of you, you had better marry her and call it square.[41]

Maxwell, who called the *New Northwest* a "valuable journal," also appreciated Anthony:

> In handling this subject of woman's equal right with the sterner sex to the ballot, she evidenced a familiarity with, and brought to bear, every salient argument in its favor, thus answering satisfactorily all of those frivolous objections so often urged, and at the same time showing in a conclusive manner that woman's condition in life would be really improved, and her sphere for usefulness much enlarged when accorded equal privileges with men.[42]

But Beriah Brown, editor of the Seattle *Territorial Dispatch*, violently disagreed with his competitor. Known on the Pacific Coast for his combative disposition, Brown had edited newspapers in San Francisco, Portland, and Olympia prior to his recent move to Seattle. (Many westerners recalled that his opposition to Lincoln had prompted a mob to destroy his San Francisco press.) Maxwell called his competitor a "blackguard" and "shallow old braggart."[43] Brown's editorial about Anthony's Seattle speeches became the talk of the town. The famous campaigner, he admitted, was talented, earnest, and persuasive. "Hence many honest people," he warned, "embrace her doctrines simply because they cannot immediately controvert her arguments; they are subjugated by superior mental force, not convinced by their own experience, observation, and comparison of facts."[44] Brown warned:

> It is a mistake to call Miss Anthony a Reformer, or the movement in which she is engaged as a reform; she is a Revolutionist, aiming at nothing less than the breaking up of the very foundations of society and the overthrow of every social institution organized for the protection of the sanctity of the altar, the family circle, and the legitimacy of our offspring, recognizing no religion but self-worship, no god but human reason, no motive to human action but lust. . . . The whole plan is coarse, sensual and agrarian, the worst phase of French infidelity and communism.

The editor charged the speaker with deception. "It is true that Miss Anthony did not openly advocate free love and disregard of the sanctity of the marriage relation, but she did worse—under the guise of defending women against manifest wrongs, she attempts to instill into their minds an utter disregard for all that is right and conservative in the present order of society." The outraged editor concluded by linking Anthony, Elizabeth Cady Stanton, and Victoria Woodhull and asked: "are our sisters, wives and daughters, prepared to accept the teaching of brazen harlots and open advocates of licentiousness? We trust not."

Brown—who was called many things by Duniway, including "a drinking, chewing and smoking leper"—renewed his denunciation a month later in an editorial entitled "Beastly Doctrines."[45] He singled out Stanton and Woodhull as being particularly dangerous. "Emancipation from political disabilities is but the initiatory step by which they propose to abolish all the social and moral restraints heretofore thrown around women to protect her from the unrestrained licentiousness of the baser sex." Anthony, the editor complained, had referred local "unsophisticated women" to "the more advanced and carefully prepared works" of Stanton and Woodhull.

At about the same time that Brown fumed over her first lecture, Anthony described her recent experiences in a letter, mentioning continuous rain and overcast skies: "It has been very tantalizing to be on this wonderful Puget Sound these ten days, and never see the clouds and fogs lift themselves long enough to give a vision of the majestic mountains on either side."[46] After a favorable description of the countryside, she summarized her work in the Pacific Northwest: "I have traveled 1,800 miles in fifty-six days, spoken forty-two nights and many days, and I am tired, tired. Lots of good missionary work, but not a great deal of money."

But there was no time for rest and little opportunity to sell lecture tickets. Duniway had scheduled appearances in two mill towns, Port Madison and Port Gamble, where saws, whistles, and steam puffs shattered the forest solitude. Meigs and Gawley owned the mill at Port Madison, where about two hundred workers daily manufactured 100,000 feet of lumber. Pope and Talbot Company's two hundred fifty employees produced about 150,000 feet of lumber at Port Gamble. Each company owned the town site, shops, shipbuilding facilities, a fleet of ships, a company store, and a hotel.

Arriving at Port Madison, the diarist wrote: "Went to forlorn hotel—babies and Irish mother in sitting room and no other—dreary prospect for Sunday."[47] Fortunately mill owner George A. Meigs invited Anthony to stay with his family; she called their comfortable home a "haven of rest." She visited a new ship and then climbed a hill for a spectacular view of the Cascades. The campaigner delivered two talks to sympathetic audiences and noted that Meigs attended.

At the Port Gamble wharf a local woman met the itinerant reformers and led them to her home. An often retold incident occurred here. Anthony gave the basic details: "just before starting for lecture her husband came in and said he didn't keep hotel—that his wife had no right to invite us in."[48] The visitors moved to a hotel "where," Duniway complained, "there were indifferent accommodations for ladies."[49] Mill workers, the angry Oregon editor asserted, expressed indignation over the incident but the "boorish" husband, "who owns and possesses that woman in fee simple," felt that he had "taught her a lesson of subjugation which she will not dare to forget." Duniway predicted: "When that lady gets the right to vote and hold property and office she'll turn a new pin in that fellow's nose."

Washington's Territorial delegate, Republican Selucius Garfielde, who surprised Anthony by admitting that he had not thought much about woman suffrage, introduced her to her Port Gamble audience.[50] The reformer summarized the disappointing occasion: "small audience—

very poor speech—cold house. A generally disagreeable time." Duniway made an interesting comment, however, about the women of Port Gamble:

> The wives of the mill men live in houses by themselves and the men take their meals at the company's cookhouse, leaving the women nothing to do but keep their homes. Yet these women are strong suffragists, who, with one accord agree with the slave Tom, that they "would like to have a little more that is their own and a little less that is master's."[51]

During the following day Anthony, who was unimpressed with this town of three hundred, kept recalling being ordered out of the house by the irate husband. In the evening she boarded a steamer and enjoyed conversation with Seattle delegates who were also journeying to the Olympia Woman Suffrage convention. Their vessel ran late, and the New Yorker had to hurry from the wharf to a cup of coffee at a private home, and then over to Olympic Hall.

As they had hoped, the convention was a successful conclusion to the Puget Sound canvass. Anthony beamed over the fact that between two and three hundred men and women from various towns braved venturing out in a rainstorm to participate in the two-day meeting. Far more skilled at conducting such a convention than the other participants, she deftly guided the proceedings. In private talks before the opening of the convention, she instructed delegates that they should choose women to be their presiding officers. Owing to her conviction that eastern male leaders had proved untrustworthy in the struggle for woman suffrage, Anthony wanted western women to have the places of leadership in their fight for advancement. She understood that these women needed to learn how to manage such a meeting and wanted both sexes to see that women could successfully conduct a convention.

Anthony and four others, including Daniel Bigelow, drafted a constitution for the Washington Territory Woman Suffrage Association. The document reflects her influence: the association's objective was to encourage Washington women "to claim and insist upon her right of suffrage as guaranteed by the Federal Constitution and the amendments thereto, and especially conferred in the suffrage law of this Territory."[52]

The veteran also influenced proceedings by submitting a number of resolutions, all of which were adopted. One of the most important endorsed the plan of action she had pressed upon the territory's legislators: the passage of "an act declaring it is the duty of judges of elections to receive and count the votes of all women citizens possessing the requisite qualifications, the same as they do those of men." Another resolution related to political tactics: Washington women had a responsibility "to give their influence and votes to no political party or nominee, unless fully pledged to practically recognize the right of the women citizens to vote or hold office." A final resolution urged women "to organize associations, hold frequent meetings for lectures and discussions, circulate tracts, speeches and newspapers, and enroll the names of women who will vote at the next election." Clearly the delegates had adopted the veteran's entire program, and she also congratulated them for electing females to every leadership position in the new association.

Emotional exchanges throughout the second evening session excited the crowd, many of whom probably never forgot this unusual event. Opponents of woman suffrage came by invitation to participate in a debate. One who accepted was Representative James H. Lasater of Walla Walla whose "character," a tactful biographer explained, "was too positive and aggressive to render all men his friends."[53] The contentious lawyer hotly disagreed with suffragists; some accused Lasater of being drunk.[54] According to one newspaper, Anthony, "referring to the loudness of his demonstration . . . very aptly compared him to the jackass, and thought that in a braying contest he would take the first premium."[55] The audience also relished the sharp disagreement among the ministers present. Editor Murphy summarized: "The Bible was dragged in as a cudgel and wielded with all the force which ignorance and bigotry could command, to stay the revolution which is slowly but surely taking place in popular sentiment."[56] Murphy emphasized that Rev. John C. Kimball—he served the New England Unitarian Missionary Association, toured the Pacific Northwest, and at Walla Walla had been influenced by Anthony's doctrines—easily refuted those ministers who used the Bible against woman suffrage. After lengthy debate, delegates accepted Kimball's interpretation of scriptural intent: "Resolved: That as members of this Association we believe that in advocating the equality of the rights of women with those of men, we are carrying out the spirit and principles of the Gospel of Jesus Christ."

One bitter critic considered her invitation to address the convention to be insulting and refused. Frost, following her clash with Anthony and Duniway in Albany, had continued to condemn their doctrines throughout the Northwest. Just prior to the start of the convention, the antisuffragist lectured in Olympia; she then proceeded to Seattle, where she censured suffragists for being infidels and free lovers. Her two Seattle audiences varied in size; the first attracted about ninety people; the second was much smaller. The *Intelligencer* reported that the speaker engaged in "anomalous orating" and that "in an avoirdupois point of view [she was] decidedly weighty."

The press focused on confrontation at the convention, not the commendable cooperation between Republicans and Democrats. Surely many delegates rejoiced to see political opponents—like Republican Bigelow and Democrat Murphy—working in harmony. While these talented Olympians battled over other various local political issues, they served in concert on the convention's committees.

Anthony was the busiest person on the convention floor, but she took time to help local ladies establish the Thurston County Suffrage Association, which selected a committee "to wait upon the Legislative Assembly and urge legislation in behalf of woman's rights to a voice in national and local politics." Drawing on her experience, Anthony warned about the inconsistency of politicians and emphasized that this local association was in a good position to watch and pressure legislators.

The convention delegates—whose female members were dubbed "crowing hens" by the Walla Walla *Statesman*—rewarded their leader.[57] They chose her to be the association's delegate to the forthcoming National Woman Suffrage Convention, awarded her $100 for expenses, and thanked her for her efforts to win suffrage for women, especially those residing in Washington Territory.

The Olympia press responded with interest to the convention. Gunn of the *Transcript* continued to be impressed with the organizer. "She is," he stated, "an able advocate of the cause she has espoused, and the women of the territory cannot help being proud of her as their champion. Her logical power has convinced many, and the cause of Woman Suffrage has been promoted by her efforts. The ladies of the territory cannot help but feel grateful to her, for her services and assistance in securing a permanent organization."[58] Still a bit apologetic for his support of woman's suffrage, Murphy published the official proceedings of the convention in his *Washington Standard*, explaining that he did so because woman's suffrage was an "absorbing interest" and because women had no press of their own.[59] The Democratic editor, however, did more than apologize; he commended women for their able management of the meeting and for seeking and listening to opponents. "Each and every objection," he enthused, "was fairly met and answered, and the cause came forth from the ordeal unscathed, triumphant." Opposed to temperance reform, Murphy ignored the fact that the Good Templars presented supportive resolutions at the convention.

Prosch's *Tribune* continued the criticisms initiated two weeks earlier. The Republican editor sarcastically referred to the convention as "the grand event of the period."[60] He complained that the two travelers had dominated "the novices" and judged that enthusiasm was wanting on the second day. "Many having seen how it works, manifest no further interest in the movement." Prosch, who thought the title "Mrs. Chairman" amusing, predicted that the woman's suffrage movement in the territory had peaked and would be "absorbed by questions of more vital importance."

While editors evaluated the exciting and unusual convention, Anthony reflected on an incident that occurred after its adjournment. She wrote in her diary: "band serenaded me at 10:20 Capt. [C.H.] Hale a rich widower at bottom of it—alas, alas, poor soul—[I went] to bed at 11 to be called by policeman at 1:30 A.M."[61] She and her companion had to be awakened early so as to catch the south-bound stage. The return to the river port was even more exhausting than her first experience had been. Anthony, who refused supper after the fatiguing ride, grumbled that the "log road beats all hard jolting yet" and that she had traveled the "roughest road ever known."[62] She never forgot this bruising ordeal.

The three and one-half week long campaign to Puget Sound communities had worn out the middle-aged suffragist, forcing her to cancel meetings in order to rest. Soon, however, Anthony was ready to plunge back into her missionary work, looking ahead to future efforts on behalf of her sex rather than reflecting back to assess her northern tour.

Duniway, however, recorded her summary of the campaign: "it succeeded financially, pleasantly and, for our cause, profitably."[63] This brief Washington effort—it was the most impressive campaign waged by a reformer in the territory since its creation in 1853—accomplished as much as longer ones in Oregon and California. From Olympia to Victoria she had alerted men and women to the unfortunate status of women and the promise of remedy through equal suffrage; she had delivered a memorable address to the legislature; she had inspired leading citizens everywhere to continue the fight for enfranchisements after her departure; she had sold prosuffrage publications; and she had played a major part in organizing a territorial association to be affiliated with the National Woman Suffrage Association and two additional local associations. Before she stumped Washington Territory, local supporters of equal suffrage lacked inspiration and organization. Anthony provided both. Her enthusiasm aroused local leaders and goaded residents into meaningful discussions about her reform.

One civic leader in Olympia, Albert A. Manning, wrote that "No question ever so agitated our community as has this question of woman's demanding the ballot. One hears of it everywhere."[64] Manning quoted an emotional deacon who cried that he "had rather see his wife or daughter in their grave than voting." Another antisuffragist wailed that "The seed sown by Miss Anthony is already bearing fruit. We hear of several cases of disagreement between man and wife on political questions."[65] The reform also prompted Democratic editors Murphy and Brown, who had been friends while publishing the Olympia *Washington Standard*, to exchange insults. Barney O'Ragan, a former editor, wrote a public letter in which he promised to "die an old bachelor" rather than marry a suffragist.[66] He cried:

> Who but a political demagogue or a soulless man would think of putting a ticket into the hand of his wife or sister and trotting her up to the polls on election day to be made a target and laughing stock of by drunken and foul mouthed men . . .? Who wants to see his wife or sister go into a jury room . . . and . . . listen to testimony that often brings the blush of shame on the cheek of the greatest loafer in the land? Who wants to have his wife or sister live with a man a few days or months, then discard him to pick up with another who may suit her fancy? I for one do not. They are none but such as Susan B. Anthony, Mrs. Duniway, Mrs. Stanton—a host of old maids and fast women,

> who to gain notoriety, accumulate money, or to gratify passions I dare not mention—none by such can believe in woman's rights, woman's suffrage, or free love.

Anthony's influence was obvious not only in the press but also in territorial politics. Olympia women "waited on the legislature," talking to its members and attending sessions. These lobbyists requested a married property act, a prohibition law, and the franchise. Near the end of the session legislators took up a variety of bills, including those being urged by local activists. Politicians enacted a married property law; its proponents hailed it as the most liberal one in the nation. One suffragist generalized that the law passed because "the genial rays of eternal truth and justice are beginning to dawn upon and warm the granite hearts and stolid brains of the prerogative sex." More immediate reasons for this law could be attributed to the teachings of the New Yorker and the efforts of local men and women.[67] But the victory was temporary; the next legislature repealed it. At the same time that the married property bill was enacted, a prohibition bill narrowly failed in the house.[68]

But woman suffrage was the crucial issue. On 23 November its proponents rejoiced when Representative Lasater, a Democrat and notorious suffrage opponent, moved that Bigelow's bill be reconsidered. He explained that he had reintroduced the issue because some of his colleagues had neglected to take it seriously. "The question was," he ruled, "an important one and they should meet it like men, and not like schoolboys." Immediately two representatives reiterated arguments for the enfranchisement of women, including Anthony's basic assertion that the political participation of her sex would improve society. To the dismay of reformers the suffrage bill failed 17-12, with Lasater voting no. A suffragist interpreted the defeat: "Bargain and Sale, Truck and Dicker are the order of the day. The demoralization, even of good men, is fearful."[69]

Disappointed local women continued to pressure representatives for a measure that would enfranchise them. The *Tribune* belittled these efforts: "A delegation of ladies was on hand to encourage and stimulate its advocates by their presence. We are informed that they went fully prepared to starve out the refractory opponents of the bill; being provided with an ample stock of cookies, doughnuts, confectionery and apples, to supply the wants of the inner man of their friends while battling for their rights." Editor Prosch pointed out that Representative C.J. Noyes led the successful fight against the bill and predicted: "Mr. Noyes is a marked man from this time forward. He won't get any doughnuts nor cookies when next the female woman suffragists prepare a feast for their friends."[70]

Realizing that a suffrage bill could not be passed and worrying that the territorial election law of 1866 might be repealed, suffragists faithfully attended every legislative session. According to one chronicler, some legislators during the session's waning moments tricked the anxious observers by promising that the existing law would not be altered. After the women departed the hall antisuffragist members introduced a unique measure that made the old law ineffective and in both houses passed it by nearly 2-1 majorities. Simply entitled "In Relation to Female Suffrage," this law stated "That hereafter no female shall have the right of ballot or vote at any poll or election precinct in the Territory, until the Congress of the United States . . . shall, by direct legislation upon the same, declare the same to be the supreme law of the land."[71] This unusual measure, receiving Governor Edward S. Salomon's signature on 29 November, definitely blocked territorial women from voting in forthcoming elections.

Some writers have sought reasons for the passage of this unique law—for Washington was probably the only territory at that time to turn the controversial woman suffrage issue over to the federal government. Several years after its passage editor Murphy simply explained that "it was probably intended to be merely an expression of the assembled lawmakers." Historian T.A. Larson judged that the bill was "designed to squelch, once and for all, the persistent appeals to the election code of 1866."[72] Both interpretations have merit but are incomplete. One factor in the decision to pass a new law was that the question of the enfranchisement of Washington women had become so important in the fall of 1871—Anthony's crusade was the major explanation for this unusual agitation—that it consumed a considerable amount of time, especially with the lengthy debate in the lower house. At least one editor, who must have spoken for other commentators, protested that such discussions over suffrage wasted time.[73] Another possible factor was that the legislature concluded that their new law defused all the constitutional arguments for suffrage. They were sparing election judges from women who, as Larson notes, confronted them with the 1866 territorial law, but they were also rejecting those women who currently insisted—as Anthony had instructed them—that they had the right to vote under the amended Federal Constitution. Furthermore, some must have assumed that the new 1871 law would squelch the novel and well-organized suffragist agitation, including the tactic of "waiting on the legislature." Opponents assumed that these local reformers must now turn to the distant Congress for the realization of their demands. In summary, antisuffragists had various reasons or excuses for what they considered to be a clever shift of the suffrage problem from the territorial to the national capital. If they thought, however, that their hasty measure had permanently disposed of the controversy, they were to be disappointed. Washington suffragists—one of whom stated that they were not discouraged because "all great reformatory movements necessarily sustain many defeats before they fully triumph"—soon sought ways to repeal this despised law at the territorial legislature's next session.[74]

# SIX

# *Final Oregon Efforts*

WHILE ANTHONY STUMPED PUGET SOUND, the Portland editors she had left behind continued to condemn her. The *Bulletin*'s O'Meara and the *Herald's* Taylor (who worried that Portlanders' enthusiasm for woman suffrage had grown considerably since Anthony's September lectures) both insulted her while she made Puget Sound stops. Persistent fears of her teachings prompted O'Meara to impeach her integrity; such an offensive was a significant change for him. After hearing her in Portland, he had disliked her doctrines but judged that the reformer was "a lady possessed of much ability and earnestly zealous from the best of motives in behalf of the sex." In October, however, the Irish editor attacked her character, stating that she had acted selfishly in giving only a part of the proceeds of an Olympia lecture to victims of the Chicago fire. "She cares in cash," he cried, "just one-third as much for the sufferers as she does for Miss Susan B. Anthony."[1] The angry editor warned, "If . . . converts to her faith are thus to demonstrate their benevolence, it will hereafter be rough on any who are prostrated by misfortune, if they depend on the Anthony crowd." Duniway, who had long opposed O'Meara, replied that he desired "to willfully misrepresent Miss Anthony and poison the minds of the people against her."[2]

O'Meara found another basis for censure in an old clipping. He quoted Anthony as once having maintained that because it was unhealthy, "no two persons, no matter who they are, should habitually sleep together."[3] The Irishman duly noted that the reformer presently slept alone but sneered: "But how comes it, we are curious to know, that Miss Anthony fails to advocate the Sleeping Alone' crochet now-a-days? Did she try it until she found it unpopular and inoperative? Sleeping alone," he reassured, "will not do—Miss Anthony to the contrary, either theoretically or practically."

The *Herald* was also sarcastic. Taylor often cast barbs at suffragists; for example, a fortune could be made, he asserted, by "starting out some of the long, lean, bloodless, scraggy woman-women, with directions to threaten to hug any man who refused" their entreaties to buy suffragist newspapers. On another occasion Taylor reported that the New Yorker had recently chided Colonel Taggart for his state fair speech and mocked: "We don't think Anthony ought to take any exceptions to what the Colonel said, for according to our recollections the allusion was to ladies only."[4]

Such caustic comments seemed to be one way editors could see to counter the reform leader; another was to support Frost's antisuffragist talks. The California visitor followed Anthony's trail to Portland, advertising her own lecture as "celebrated" [for] "showing that the ballot in the hands of women will destroy all our civil, political, social and religious institutions."[5] Among those endorsing Frost was Editor H.L. Herman of the Portland *Catholic Sentinel*:

> The evils attendant upon the teaching of Women's Rights, as proclaimed by Susan B. Anthony, Mrs. Woodhull, and others, are so apparent to all right thinking people, that any effort made to counteract or destroy their pernicious doctrines, should be encouraged. Mrs. Frost, a lady of highly intellectual attainment, has, by her lecture at Albany, Salem and other places . . . done much good toward reclaiming many who were inclined to look favorably upon the views expressed by Miss Anthony.[6]

Although Duniway was the only Portland editor to support Anthony, none of the others joined Herman in sanctioning Frost's emotionalism. The *Herald* said that Frost's illogical points matched the "fallacies" of suffragists; for example, she predicted that equal suffrage would lead to free love and asked her listeners "how they would like to see a daughter, only eighteen or twenty years old, present them with three or four

Columbia River
Portland
Pacific Ocean
Salem
N
Willamette River
Eugene City
Oakland
Roseburg
Portland to California Campaign
11 November–26 November 1871
Jacksonville
OREGON
CALIFORNIA
Yreka
Scale
0
50
100
Miles

children, yet could claim no father for them."[7] The best assessment of the antisuffragist appeared in Scott's *Oregonian*: "From all we hear, we are inclined to think her decidedly a talkative woman but not remarkably argumentative; rather smart but scattering, and upon the whole not calculated to do a great deal of harm to her own or her opponent's cause."[8]

Upon Anthony's return to the St. Charles hotel, all of the male editors awaited a chance to rebut her. Physically exhausted from her demanding trip to Puget Sound, the campaigner—who quickly learned of the hostile mood of the press—twice slept long hours and cancelled visits to Vancouver and Kalama. Her disappointed tour manager Duniway had long pushed these visits, particularly to Kalama, home of Mrs. M.L. Money—the only other female editor in the region and who was lukewarm about equal suffrage. She and her husband had launched the Kalama *Beacon* at about the same time that Duniway started her newspaper. The *Beacon* spoke for the Northern Pacific Railroad and for the superiority of its terminus, Kalama, over Portland, Vancouver, and Seattle. The Moneys hoped that Kalama would become the region's great commercial center; thus much of their writings championed the new hamlet against the older communities. Mrs. Money had heard Anthony's first Portland lecture but remained unconverted. Duniway called Money so "blind to her own best interests as to raise her puny pen against the suffrage movement." Money responded by stating that she had no great interest in the cause and could not see how an increase in the number of voters could end "the present corruption or abuse of the ballot." She asserted, "We have the best interests of our sex at heart, but a good acquaintance with the world has taught us not to expect too much from the fair sex." Money praised Anthony's integrity but complained that Duniway was guilty of "unladylike tirades."[9]

Although Anthony's last week in Portland was less hectic than her first one, she busily advanced her reform in a variety of ways. She planned Oregon stops during her overland journey back to California (emphatically refusing to risk seasickness), visited local sympathizers, worked to organize a county woman suffrage association, granted a newspaper interview, and delivered a final address. At the St. Charles, as well as at other stops, Anthony carried on correspondence with her family, especially with her concerned mother. The traveler also wrote to Stanton and to California suffragists as she continued to try to advance national reform efforts from her temporary base in the Pacific Northwest. During spare moments she studied eastern newspapers and clipped relevant columns from the regional press.

In these final days her most important public activity in Portland was her assistance in establishing the Multnomah County Woman Suffrage Association. She and Dr. Mary A. Thompson, a controversial eclectic physician advertising batteries and "instructions on the use of electricity as a remedial agent," served as organizers, and visited suffragists, requesting them to sign a call for a convention. Twelve women—Duniway boasted that they were influential and respectable—believing in the practical application of the principle of "no taxation without representation" and desiring a "concert of action among the women," endorsed the call.[10] About two dozen responded and hurried through the afternoon rain for the meeting at Oro Fino Hall. Huddled around a large but inefficient stove, the ladies conducted an efficient meeting. The New Yorker relied upon Dr. Thompson, who in the 1850s had labored for woman suffrage in Illinois, and upon Mrs. Harriet Williams, who had soldiered with Anthony in the New York temperance ranks. Probably Anthony and such experienced allies had prepared a short constitution in advance; the Portland women—a reporter dubbed them as "man's aggressiveness-defying women"—studied and signed the document. One of its articles explained that "the object of this Association shall be to encourage such cooperation among women as shall cause them to assume their responsibilities as citizens."[11] Anthony boasted that the participants were "of the very best positions." They elected a slate of female officers, most of whom were housewives, but a domestic, a physician, and an artist were interesting exceptions. To prepare this group for the difficult suffrage battle, the veteran campaigner penned a comprehensive resolution:

> We urge the friends of Woman Suffrage throughout the State to organize Associations in their respective towns and voting precincts; hold stated meetings for lectures and discussions; circulate tracts, speeches and newspapers, enroll the names of all women who will present their votes at the next election, and of all men who will give their influence to induce women to exercise their right to vote, and use every other moral means to encourage women to assume their rightful position as voters;

> and we respectfully solicit the judges of election to fulfill their duties in receiving and counting the votes of women citizens precisely the same as they do those of men.

The women unanimously approved this statement and then chose its author to serve as an assistant delegate for their association at the National Woman Suffrage Convention.

None of the Portland's dailies took the convention seriously; the Olympia editors had been more supportive of such a meeting. Some Portland newspapers published the official proceedings, but accounts in the *Oregonian* and the *Herald* were attempts at humor, not analysis. The *Oregonian*'s reporter wrote a flippant account that reflected the fact that his newspaper had changed its approach: it would generally ridicule or criticize rather than describe or evaluate Anthony's campaign. The reporter related how he bashfully had tried to get a story about the convention but had gallantly retreated because some participants "felt a little timid about exercising their Constitutional prerogative in the presence of gentlemen."

The *Herald* provided a briefer account of the meeting; it stated that the assembled women had prepared to vote in local elections and joked that any man who stood in the way would be routed by their "lingual sword."[12] This breezy tone characterized the newspaper's coverage of later meetings of Portland suffragists. Its reporter ignored ideas and concentrated upon appearances: "Instead of meeting skeletons wearing green goggles and a nazarine blue dress," the writer expressed surprise to see "some of the most robust, lively-looking pieces of femininity to be found in this market, and they were sociable, laughing creatures, and apparently live on something besides vinegar and squashes."[13]

The campaigner's final speech scheduled for 15 November, the day following the convention at Oro Fino Hall, attracted scant newspaper coverage. The *Oregonian* entitled her scheduled talk "The Final Scold" and summarized:

> We felt satisfied, when she began, that she would have a last say, if the world would only hold out, and tonight we are to get the final scold . . . unless the great suffragist shall, like the theater people, conclude to add a "positively the last," and then a "most positively the last." After all, we don't know but we are

> glad that Miss Anthony came here, and that she has had her scold, if for no other reason than it has shown how very harmless her mission has been.[14]

Probably newspaper criticism and exhaustion contributed to the visitor's apprehension, as she wrote in her diary: "terrible depression of spirit with feeling of impossibility to make this last speech in Portland."[15] According to her summary the evening went just as badly as she feared: "small audience and not one second's lighting up of brain—the barest, boldest points and no thought beyond. Altogether it was and is the most terrible experience of my life . . . of being compelled to speak when the spirit said nothing but no, no." In a letter to her mother, she described her anguished feelings: "the hurt of it stings yet. I never was dragged before an audience so utterly without thought or word as last night and, had there been any way of escape, I would have taken wings or, what I felt more like, have sunk through the floor."[16]

Some of her audience sensed that their leader seemed more anxious than she had been during her first Portland address. Only the *Oregonian* dispatched a reporter; he wrote that the lecturer reviewed the history of the woman suffrage movement, restated familiar arguments for the enfranchisement of her gender, and faulted Colonel Taggart, especially for instructing women "to make home pleasant and to lead men to lives of sobriety and virtue." She spoke, the writer judged, "with much less force than her reputation led many to believe she might . . . and contradicted herself."[17] In her synopsis Duniway sensibly emphasized the distinguished visitor's long campaign in the Pacific Northwest, rather than her concluding lecture. The newspaperwoman boasted that her friend's "sojourn among us has won the hearts of the people as no statesman has ever been able to do since the gallant Edward Baker took the public heart by storm [in 1860]."[18] But even her coadjutor deemed it necessary to explain Anthony's uninspired delivery. "Evidently the speaker was very much jaded from the effect of her recent herculean labors as the Woman Suffrage 'wheel horse,' but she did not swerve one hair's breath from the line of her argument, and the audience appeared unwilling to leave the hall at its close." The *Oregonian*'s "feeble" reporter, Duniway accused, had been inattentive and inaccurate.

Between visits with Portlanders on 16 November, Anthony granted an interview to the local editor of the *Herald*. Seeking a good story, Murphy goaded the reformer into making extreme statements. According to his interpretation, she was shy but became combative under provocation:

REPORTER. When women get the ballot, what use will they make of it, what good do they propose to accomplish?

SUSAN. They propose to do away with vice and immorality, to prevent the social evil by giving women remunerative employment; to forbid the sale of spirituous liquors and tobacco, and to teach men a higher and nobler life than the one they now follow.

REPORTER. Then I suppose you will do away with the grammatical distinctions which express the genders of the sexes also, and we shall not know whether it is a masculine or feminine who is in office unless the name is specified?

SUSAN. To be sure we shall; we shall do away with such words as editress, poetess, doctress and other such expressions which are absurdities. We do not call Rosa Bonheur a paintress, though no man can equal her in painting cattle; we call her an artist.

REPORTER. How will you distinguish between the Christian names of married men and women; will the wife call herself after the Christian name of the husband?

SUSAN. No; a woman is as much entitled to her first name as a man, and she should retain it; and for that, her surname also. Hereafter, instead of calling a married woman Mrs. John Smith . . . she will be known as Mrs. Abigail Smith.

REPORTER. I understand one of the follies which the women clamoring for rights intend to do away with, is the power vested in man to make the proposition of marriage; you intend, I believe, to stimulate the courage of the girls to make propositions also.

SUSAN. I believe a girl has more right to make a proposition of marriage than a man, and when she becomes independent of him she will do it. Now she is a pauper, dependent on man, but when she earns a good salary, and maybe a better one than her lover, she can approach him without shame and ask him to unite with her for life. At present she cannot do it, as she is a pauper on his bounty; and said she, emphatically, no person can be independent unless he or she has pecuniary means. . . . I would have a woman marry for love alone; I would place her in a position to be able to earn a competent livelihood, and live independent of man until she finds someone who she thinks would increase her happiness. When woman gets the ballot she can receive positions under Government the same as men now do, then they can become arbiters of their own destiny.

REPORTER. . . . Perhaps [women] can become Congresswomen and Senatoresses.

SUSAN. Exactly; women should go to Congress, and they would have a higher ambition than to be the wife of some Congressman or Senator. They would be the ideal women, and fulfill their mission to do away with immorality, which would give us a more moral and intellectual race of people. Then asylums, penitentiaries, jails and policemen would be done away with, and we should reach the highest happiness. As it is at present, a race of imbeciles, tainted with disease, are peopling the world, for, said she, don't you know that the sins of the father curse the children for generations.

REPORTER. So it is said, but is the father entirely to blame—is woman in no way responsible for the curse?

SUSAN. Man is the grosser animal, and it is his money that causes the downfall of poor innocent girls.

REPORTER. Then the girls are aiming for pecuniary independence in order to be free, for according to your theory, unless they have money they are slaves, so they sell themselves for money.

SUSAN. You have three hundred prostitutes in Portland and you think these creatures do not curse unborn generations. Now when women get the ballot they will do away with this class, as they will furnish them employment. Hereafter if men are found using their wiles upon innocent girls, women will vote to place them in asylums, and with them, the whisky-drinkers and tobacco-chewers and smokers.

REPORTER. Then you will have to place nine-tenths of the people of this country in asylums, for I suppose that number either drink or use tobacco.

SUSAN. Emphatically, then we'll do it; we'll build large asylums and confine them there until they are cured, for they are morally insane.[19]

At this point, the reporter maintained, the reformer became quite angry, indicating that he should leave so that she might greet visitors, and she warned: "Now, if you make me look ridiculous in tomorrow's paper, you shall be the last reporter that ever enters my room." He promised not to ridicule her but would only publish her ideas, "which the public will be most anxious to see, as they are at least unique."

Probably Murphy's report was fairly accurate; his attitude as well as her continuing fatigue and frustration over her last appearance explain the fact that she lost her temper and made a few extreme statements before terminating the interview. At no other time in her tour had she argued that there were three hundred prostitutes in Portland—the 1870 census listed about a dozen women with "doubtful" occupations—or advocated the construction of large asylums for the "morally insane." If Murphy's story had been embellished, Duniway would no doubt have rushed to her co-worker's defense and reprimanded him; her attacks on erring newspapermen were already famous. Interestingly enough, Duniway complimented Murphy for his candor and fairness and granted that he made "a pardonable effort . . . to get the better of the argument."[20] Instead of rebuking him, she republished a large portion of the interview but wisely deleted this last and most controversial section.

Immediately following Duniway's evaluation of the interview, the *Herald* reporter, denying that he had tried to best Anthony, responded with additional information obtained from "the goddess of woman suffrage."[21] The reformer, Murphy remembered, would not state that a woman who disliked her husband should divorce him for "a more pleasing affinity," but she did advise separation if the husband became abusive or "if the union became disagreeable to both." The newspaperman complained that his subject "had an ideal love which ordinary mortals seldom reach, and that happiness in a married state was to have the husband and wife act like two ninnies, both besmearing each other with trifling little kindnesses and honeyed words, which would pale after a short time."

During the last hours in her hotel, the noted guest received callers who thanked her for her extensive campaign and wished her success. Anthony also jotted in her diary the receipt of a startling correspondence from A.T. Stevens, a thirty-two year old teacher. He asked for an opportunity to propose marriage. In a letter to her family, Anthony seemed to have taken his proposal seriously. Anthony advised her family: "If any of the girls want a rich widower or an equally rich bachelor, here is decidedly the place to get an offer of one. But tell brother Aaron I expect to survive them all and reach home . . . as single-handed and penniless as usual."[22]

The reformer noted testimonials from three prominent local merchants and from lawyer John H. Mitchell, who would soon begin a long and notorious career in the United States Senate. No journalist sent flattering words; however, a few composed facetious farewell thoughts. The *Oregonian* predicted that the distinguished visitor, who, it jested, had frequently promised that she would "never, never, never" cease her agitation, would travel to Washington "and lead the charge of the strong-minded upon the honorable, franchise-monopolizing members of Congress."[23] Another reporter joked: "We did intend to go and kiss the good old girl for her mother. . . . As we could not be present to shake her wrinkled hand, we will whisper in her ear we earnestly hope she will yet get a husband, reform, and settle down and become a model woman and worthy to be imitated."[24]

While newspapermen laughed over their parting shots, Anthony went by train to Oregon City, the first of many stops on her journey to a suffrage meeting in Sacramento. Despite the fact that there was little advance notice—publicity would be a problem all the way to her destination—men and women elbowed into the courthouse where she would be speaking. They anticipated a spirited reaction to the extensive criticism leveled at her in Anthony Noltner's Oregon City *Enterprise*, particularly that of Rev. Elbridge Gerry. Her listeners were not disappointed. Recovering her enthusiasm for the rostrum, she vigorously countered Gerry's arguments. He probably failed to attend—at least he did not respond when Anthony called for him—and none of his friends defended him from her slashing attack, which brought laughs and applause. "Hope," an unidentified female correspondent, wrote a favorable assessment for the *New Northwest*, praising the lecturer for systematically refuting all the "common objections to woman suffrage, at least to those who are not so blinded by prejudice that logic fails to convince them of anything."[25]

Two weeks earlier, Noltner had explained: "We have tried in our advocacy of principles to be courteous to our opponents, always aiming to be fair and just."[26] He could not, however, uphold such high standards in his response to this second visit. The editor reacted exactly as he had to Anthony's September call: he insulted her and gave ample space to an unnamed antisuffragist. Noltner acknowledged that he had been subjected to the reformer's "gentle abuse" but maintained that "it did not hurt us, and we are happy to say that our love for dear Susan and her dogma is not at all diminished. We might say something mean if it was not for the respect we had for old age, and also for the uniform she wears."[27] Exasperated by Noltner's mean spirit, Duniway charged that his newspaper was "so dirty that we always feel impelled to open it with a pair of tongs."

The paper's unidentified special correspondent (who Duniway believed was Gerry) disliked Anthony's looks—she possessed "not the most distant approach to beauty"—her "harsh" voice, and her "nervous" gestures. Unable to guess the speaker's age, he judged that "from the care-worn and far away expression she carries in her face, we should say that a long and dreary existence has been hers; unblest by a joy in the past, or a hope for the future." He singled out as dangerous her ideas about the Bible, a book he appreciated because it "so clearly defines the differences of men and women, in nature and in duties." The unidentified critic then provided his own definition of woman's role: "to watch over and beautify the sacred precincts of home; to train up her sons to be strong towers of Christian virtue and manliness, and her daughters to be as the 'polished corners of the temple.'" To his way of thinking the home made the nation great. "The moral power of our nation over the nations of the Old World, can only be maintained by preserving the sacredness of home-life in the domestic virtues of American women." He admonished: "Oh, Christian mothers see to it that your duty is not neglected. See that the feet of your loved ones are tending towards the paths of purity and goodness."

Pleased with her sizable audience and her spirited refutation of Oregon City critics, Anthony stopped briefly at Salem. The veteran campaigner realized from her October visit the impossibility of drawing a paying audience in the capital, thus she had arranged a meeting in tiny nearby Buena Vista where a number of its villagers apparently supported reform. In June they had hosted the Oregon and Washington Health Reform Association where male and female speakers proclaimed "the hygienic mode of preserving health and curing disease." However, because no one met her at the station, Anthony reboarded and journeyed to Albany, where she conversed with sympathizers. The traveler proceeded to Eugene and stayed in another hotel serving "poor enough fare."[28] The town had recently received rail service and citizens rejoiced that the locomotive's whistle had replaced the stagecoach's horn. Some Eugeneans and farmers insisted that entrepreneur Ben Holladay's threat to bypass Eugene unless they paid $60,000 and gave land demonstrated his unacceptable tyranny over Lane County; the majority, however, argued that his Oregon and California Railroad had sharply increased property values and wheat prices.

The campaigner's arrival a day early meant that she somehow had to publicize on Sunday morning that evening's lecture. She overcame this difficulty by resourcefully employing the sheriff to carry notices to the town's six churches. This tactic worked. A large, enthusiastic crowd squeezed into the courthouse, where lamps were lit and the bell rung. The following evening she drew another good audience but wrote: "foolishly put admission down to 25 cts."[29] Eugeneans turned out in large numbers because of her reduced admission, because the press had publicized her, because this would be her only visit, and perhaps because they wanted to hear her denunciation of a recently opened "hurdy-gurdy" show. Its performers (called "sisters of soiled virtue" by one disgusted resident) had attracted large male audiences.[30] Anthony most likely sided with Duniway in promising that when Eugene women won the ballot they and male allies would "abolish such pit-falls."

Upon the advice of Duniway, the campaigner visited with Rev. J.H.D. Henderson, a prominent Eugenean. Since his supportive letter to the *New Northwest* in May, he had not shown much public enthusiasm for woman suffrage. Henderson had been busily promoting railroad service to Eugene and selling lots in his addition to the town. Sensing that he still had hopes for a return to political office and that he worried because many of his parishioners disliked his suffragist ideas, Anthony shrewdly discerned that he was a "good (careful) friend."

The city's two newspapers—the Republican *Oregon State Journal* and the Democratic *Guard*—had occasionally commented upon Anthony's Pacific Northwest campaign, but they had been giving much more space to Victoria Woodhull's opinions. While both newspapers denounced this radical feminist, they held different views of Anthony. Though the *Oregon State Journal* had not forthrightly condemned her, it was one of the few newspapers to use her name as a lead into an advertisement:

> Mark Stevens thinks the reason Susan B. is so hostile towards the wicked men is because none of them have ever proposed to her. If this opinion is correct, Susan will be railing away till the day of judgment. For this reason Mark has laid in a new supply of everything in his line, and more particularly a full stock of ammunition and pistols.

On 19 August, the *Oregon State Journal* had attempted to put the suffrage movement into historical context: "Woman for the last thousands of years has been moving on the ramparts of man. But it is only within the last fifteen or twenty years that they have made any decided progress." The newspaper also explained that women editors "demanded the enfranchisement of woman as necessary for the purity of our politics."

An acting editor of the *Oregon State Journal* took the middle ground in reporting Anthony's Eugene visit. Refusing to attend to her specific arguments, he merely pronounced that some were true and that others were "illogical and in no wise calculated to advance the interests or welfare of society in any respect."[31] Anthony was, he reasoned, critical of men, especially newspapermen, because they "are never willing to do the women justice." The writer thought he was being fair in advocating that women alone should decide whether or not they wanted to vote. To avoid being labeled a supporter, he ended on a hostile note:

> Miss Anthony did one thing, we learn, in this community which she will be held responsible for, and that is that she caused hard feelings in several families, where such a thing had not existed for years. Arguments were engaged in between husband and wife until they were not tempered with courtesy which should govern such things. If it has come to such a pitch already, what will it be when the women vote?

The *Oregon State Journal* joked that Anthony's extensive campaign to the region "will doubtless result beneficially . . . as it is said that a woman is pretty apt to tell about everything that she sees and hears."[32] Duniway, ever optimistic, chose to interpret positively the newspaper's assessment of Anthony. The *Oregon State Journal* responded. "We think Mrs. Duniway is a little inclined to attribute bad motives to all who oppose Woman Suffrage, and to flatter those who do not take an open stand against it. It would not be becoming in any man to speak disrespectfully of any cause in which so many respectable people were honestly enlisted."[33]

But George G. Buys, a twenty-eight-year-old Democrat from New York, made absolutely no attempt to be fair in his Eugene *Guard*. Intolerant of minorities and fearful of social change—for example, he accused three "strong-minded" Oregon girls of teaching "Heathen Chinee" because they wanted them as husbands—he had heard Anthony at the state fair and had expressed his disgust. "This mad hen," he grumbled, gave an address that "was a mixture of ridiculously false statements, and invective against all human beings of the masculine gender."[34] He continued his savage denunciation by stating that the

> venomous old shrew . . . remarked that she thought more attention ought to be paid to improving the human race; that instead (of) offering premiums for fine calves the Agricultural Society ought to offer rewards for the best babies. Susan ought to keep a baby on hand all the time, as a sample of what she could do in the way of stock raising, and as an incentive to her followers to take measures to produce better ones. Susan . . . go home and raise fine babies, if you are not too far advanced in years.

A few weeks later Buys quoted radical feminist Victoria Woodhull's doctrine that wives should choose suitable men, not necessarily their husbands, to sire babies. In a rambling column, the outraged editor applied this radical notion to the campaigner:

> Imagine Miss Anthony, or some other lump of loveliness, entering your room and after holding you in conversation upon all subjects till she has tested the strength of your mind, but before declaring that you are an "affinity," or that you are a suitable "sire," she wishes to be better informed as to your physical proportions, she would politely, if not affectionately, invite you to stand up and submit to her manipulations, and if found without blemish be told that you are her "affinity," and that "in the pursuit of her aim of giving to the race better specimens of womanhood and manhood," she had selected you to become the "sire" of one of her children, and desired to "breed herself" for that purpose! Our gallantry and politeness would forbid a refusal.[35]

In an effort to diminish Anthony's appeal, Buys' emotional report of her first Eugene address played upon fears by linking her with two unpopular individuals: black leader Hiram Revels—Buys knew that many readers detested blacks—and editor Woodhull. He added:

> Susan says she used to be as good as a nigger, but since the war only two classes of human beings are on an equality with women. Idiots, insane persons and women are the most

> degraded of the human race. No woman, says Susan, should marry until she has a home—one which she has earned. If this were the custom there would not be a marriage once in ten years. But then it would be nuts for the boys that did marry . . . Susan says there are thousands of women who are not fit for wives and mothers. These women, she thinks, should be allowed to hold office. We venture the assertion that in nine hundred and ninety-nine cases out of one thousand women who are not fit to become wives and mothers are fit for nothing but subjects for the undertaker . . . Susan knocks the wind out of the sails of the Bible, when it opposes woman's rights, by saying that the Bible was made for the times in which it was made, and has no reference to the present. The statement, from a Christian standpoint, is blasphemous.[36]

Buys concluded on the subject of marriage. Anthony, he noted, recommended that women should be married by Methodist ministers because they deleted the word "obey" from vows. The editor countered with a humorous clause to be added to the wedding ceremony: if a wife found that her marriage did not "quite come up to her expectations, she may leave her husband and go home to ma."

At 5:00 A.M. on 21 November, the day following her last lecture in Eugene, Anthony climbed aboard a stagecoach for the long trip across the mountains separating the Willamette and Umpqua valleys to a point near Red Bluff, California where she could once again enjoy rail travel. The traveler, as was her habit, rode beside the driver, taking pleasure in his conversation and that of his "thoroughly bright" wife, and their girls.[37] However, the sixty mile ride to tiny Oakland, Oregon was fatiguing, especially the twenty miles on corduroy road. She described the experience:

> Sixty miles of my 350 miles of staging, and it, if possible, more than matches Monticello and Olympia . . . This route has one point of superiority—we stop but once to afflict our stomachs with the horrid cooking of Chinamen or any other men. I am really making up my mind that cooking is out of man's sphere, for he does set before us such villainous compounds.[38]

Like others, the middle-aged passenger commented favorably upon the meals prepared by the woman operating the Oakland station: the only "cleanly tasting hotel food . . . outside of Portland and Salem." Naturally her thoughts turned to reform:

> When good women cooks are honored as are teachers and ministers, then we shall have first-class brained women entering the profession. And surely the person who ministers wholesome, palatable food to the stomachs of mortals does quite as much—nay, more—for spirit and intellect than any and all other ministers.

Anthony's accommodations, however, were terrible: "a little speck of room, in corner of dining room at foot of stairs and bar room—thin cloth partition and perfectly noisy."[39] The campaigner was gratified, though, to note a good audience at the Oakland Academy, and praised the postmaster for making lecture arrangements.

The next day she continued stagecoaching in the Umpqua Valley to Roseburg and depicted a section of this infamous road:

> twenty miles of 'Joe Lane black mud' as they call it, because old Joseph Lane settled right here in the midst of it. It is heavy clay without a particle of loam and rolls up on the wheels until rim, spokes and hub are one solid circle. The wheels cease to turn and actually slide over the ground, and then driver and men passengers jump out with chisels and shingles to cut the clay off the wheels.[40]

The Roseburg stop was challenging. Bethenia Owens met her stage and quickly assured Anthony that she had received her telegram requesting lecture arrangements. She then reported that she had engaged the best lecture site (though the Methodist minister had winced at the use of his church), and that she had hired a boy to place posters around town. News of the lecture had aroused Roseburg "as though the coming of circus had been announced," but she warned that many opposed the suffragist. A saloon keeper had warned Bethenia Owens that "we will checkmate you, for we are getting up a free supper and a free dance at the hotel, and I'll bet you don't have a baker's dozen at the church."[41]

The Roseburg woman told her guest about her own unusual personal history. She had come to Oregon with her family in 1843, had married at the age of fourteen, had a son two years later, and had defied convention by obtaining a divorce when she was nineteen. She also related that she had struggled for an education and boasted that by hard efforts her millinery shop in this trading village had prospered. Impressed with her accomplishments, Anthony called her a "splendid woman." The milliner was similarly inspired by the reformer; she told her guest that the New York *Revolution* had made her into a suffragist.[42] Bethenia Owens-Adair (she hyphenated her name after her marriage to John Adair in 1884), who was secretly studying medicine, would go on to become a controversial physician and a local fighter for temperance and suffrage. She always credited Anthony as being a force in her life, referring to her as a "foster mother."

In the evening the two ladies passed the noisy hotel where the "anti-Anthony dance" attracted a lively crowd. Fortunately, many other men and women—some showed surprise that the meeting was to be held in a church—chose to hear the campaigner. The following morning five local women evaluated the condition of frontier women with the New Yorker and enthused that they had taken inspiration from her address.

While the Roseburg group conferred with the reformer, William Thompson, editor of the Roseburg *Plaindealer*, composed his report of the evening's lecture. He declared that he was "grieviously disappointed" with her talk, finding it difficult to take notes.[43] "She has," Thompson grumbled, "the gift that all married men are compelled to admit has been given to woman, a fluent tongue, but of politics, law or logic she is as ignorant as a child." The editor thought it was peculiar that the speaker covered many topics for two hours in a church without making "the slightest reference to the Almighty, or any allusion to the influence of religion upon the morals or happiness of the sex."

At noon Anthony's stagecoach began its day and night run, with only brief rests at Canyonville and Grants Pass, to Jacksonville. In good weather travelers commented upon the dense forests, mountain ridges, and deep canyons. But in Anthony's account of the mountainous journey to the Rogue Valley, she took more interest in learning the biographies of the stage drivers than in the scenery. She rode beside these men, one of whom claimed to be a reformed gambler from Michigan. A moonlit drive turned to clouds and rain and the passenger commented: "had on driver's waterproof coat over my own waterproof—still blankets got wet." She retreated inside.[44] She reached her destination mid-afternoon on 26 November, tried to nap, and arose at 6 P.M. for her lecture.

The editors of Jacksonville's two weeklies sat in the Methodist Church, scribbling notes as the famous lecturer covered familiar themes. According to their summaries, they heard different things. Harrison Kelly, of the *Oregon Sentinel*, reported that she drew a good audience despite the fact that lecture notices had failed to arrive. In a very brief summary—the kindest she had received since those penned in the *New Northwest*—Kelly wrote that she "gave an able and interesting discourse . . . Miss Anthony has studied her subject well, and manifests great ability in presenting her views to the public. Her lecture was reformatory throughout, and can't be otherwise than productive of great good."[45]

Charles Nickell's *Democratic Times*, which had once humorously advocated extending the ballot to a woman who had proved her worth by hauling firewood, faulted the feminist's appearance.[46] She possessed "not the most distant approach to beauty." Nickell stressed Anthony's economic argument: "she thought that young women should be taught the different trades—blacksmithing, shoemaking, carpentering, etc. etc.—in order to support themselves, and not be reared, as they now are, in comparative idleness, waiting for someone to marry them. The arguments advanced in support of her theory were as novel as the theory itself." The *Times* disagreed with the *Sentinel*, arguing that her message "accomplished but little for the advancement of the cause."

After her two-hour performance, the speaker retired to her "cold and forlorn" hotel and slept until called at 3 A.M. A few hours later her stagecoach—at times whitened with snow—labored up the mountains into California, completing her Pacific Northwest campaign. Bundled against the storm the famous passenger probably spent less time reflecting on this strenuous tour than thinking about future appearances: Had notices been distributed for her two talks in Yreka? How would the San Francisco press respond to an address? And, most importantly, what action could she and allies take at the National Woman's Suffrage Convention in Washington that would convince men—in or out of politics—that women deserved the right to vote under the provisions of the Fourteenth Amendment? It was not Anthony's way to dwell upon a completed campaign when another lecture hall demanded her attention.

# SEVEN

# *Ramifications and Assessments*

In California Anthony found time to reflect upon her completed crusade. She knew that very few Pacific Northwest residents had traveled their new area so extensively, and that few outsiders witnessed so much pioneering. She boasted that her adventure "had effectually settled . . . the fact that woman was capable of much more physical endurance than was required to cast a ballot."[1] More specifically, she assured San Franciscans that her tour had been successful; in a letter to Duniway she said that she believed she had sown "some good seed" and anticipated "good fruit." The traveler sent a similar message to the *Revolution*: "Washington Territory and Oregon are pretty well aroused to thought, and, I think, action too."[2] Such positive assessments rested upon solid evidence: her campaign was characterized by appreciative audiences, individual promises of action, public letters, the sale of suffrage publications, the collection of signatures, and the establishment of four new organizations dedicated to the advancement of women. In audiences composed of townspeople and farmers, the reformer was able to win the respect of both. Surely the reaction of a Portlander to one of her lectures was by no means unique: "At first I thought her almost homely. But as the subject warmed her and the fire of intellect at length kindled in her eyes lighting up the strong features of her face and the rough channels of thought, she seemed like another woman . . . she made a deep impression upon the great mass of her hearers."[3]

Perhaps the campaigner had not made as much money as she had anticipated, but such missionary work rarely generated much income. In 1871 the 171 lectures she delivered from coast-to-coast earned $2,771 towards the retirement of her debt.[4] While Anthony's purse remained thin, her major objective—the promotion of the woman's rights movement, especially equal suffrage—had been attained in the Pacific Northwest and in Victoria. A Canadian scholar judged that the Anthony visit to Victoria began a suffrage campaign in British Columbia that lasted until 1917, the year woman suffrage won. Journalist Michael H. Cramer asserted that British Columbia women owed much to the campaigner for planting "the seeds that eventually led them into the polling booths and legislative halls."[5]

Even critics acknowledged that her meetings in schools, churches, halls, and courthouses had alerted pioneers to the condition of women and their needs. From his editorial desk in Salem, Samuel Clarke continually expressed great alarm about the crusade's impact. Early in 1872 he recalled that Anthony "sowed seed, which has at least afforded a plentiful crop of discussion." The antisuffragist conceded that her message attracted the attention of the state's "best women" but growled that it ignited "a raging fire of divorces."

Newspapers served to publicize her efforts. Some editors not only reported her campaign but also lent a degree of support: the Salem *Mercury*, the McMinnville *West Side*, the Olympia *Transcript*, and the Seattle *Intelligencer* applauded Anthony's message, logic, integrity, and speaking skills. However, these editors refused to ally themselves to her cause because they lacked commitment or feared the taunts of anti-suffragists. The only editors who consistently championed Anthony were Duniway's *New Northwest* and John Miller Murphy's *Washington Standard*. Realizing that he was out of step with fellow Democrats, Murphy did not attempt an elaborate defense of woman suffrage; he simply ruled that it was right. Perhaps Anthony and her co-worker were surprised that the region's two temperance newspapers, published in Albany and Olympia, furnished very limited assistance despite the New Yorker's assurance that her sex would cast ballots for temperance.

Editors were not the only ones influenced by the campaign. From such diverse meetings as those held in private parlors to the huge outdoor gathering at the Oregon State Fair, listeners carried her teachings back to homes, halls, churches, and street corners. It is impossible to determine the number of converts or the number of suffragists inspired to renewed efforts, yet Anthony through her integrity, intelligence, devotion, and energy obviously attracted new allies and rejuvenated old ones. From Coupeville to Jacksonville, men and women promised to battle for woman suffrage; Anthony jotted down many of their names in her diary. An unknown number of sympathizers in this far distant corner of the country, like many easterners, enlisted for a long fight. Undoubtedly some became discouraged—Walla Walla and Olympia editors gleefully stressed early signs of backsliding—but other 1871 critics, especially in Portland, saw little such evidence.

Two regional women immediately followed up on the visitor's work for the advancement of their sex. Minnie Myrtle Miller, an admirer of Anthony, soon gave her first public lecture. The fledgling nervously assured that she "did not come to stir women up to rise in mutiny," but instead entreated males to recognize the rights and individualism of females.[6] A more experienced and famous fighter, Duniway, also took advantage of the public's heightened interest in equal suffrage. Anthony's visit had been crucial to the Portland reformer. By touring the region with the veteran, she had learned at first hand the rhetoric and tactics of reform, acquired additional subscriptions and many columns of stories for the *New Northwest*, and, of equal importance, she soon became acquainted with suffragists, including Stanton, Lucy Stone, and Henry Blackwell. Duniway often stressed her indebtedness to Anthony: "I became quite thoroughly initiated into the movement and made my first efforts at public speaking."[7] In late 1871 the Oregon reformer immediately put into practice what she had learned: she directed the establishment of a suffrage study group in Forest Grove and gave lectures there and in Portland. With an admission fee of fifty cents her first Portland address, "Women's Duty as Citizens," received attention in her brother's *Oregonian*: "What Miss Anthony left undone in this vineyard to make naughty and aggressive man behave . . . Mrs. Duniway proposes now to do."[8] Antisuffragist Samuel Clarke wrote Californians that Duniway was "a mature female as regards age, self-reliance and absence of any timidity, who drank in all the wisdom Susan Anthony could inculcate" and won women to equal suffrage through her lectures and her *New Northwest*, "which is reckless and somewhat vixenish."

During the early 1870s lectures Duniway expounded on themes voiced by her mentor, including the promise that enfranchised women

William H. Newell was the Democratic editor and proprietor of the Walla Walla *Statesmen*. The week of Anthony's visit, Newell said that Anthony had submitted "an able argument in favor of extending the ballot to women." The week after her lecture, Newell proclaimed that the woman's rights movement "is worse than the small-pox, chills and fever combined." (Penrose Memorial Library, Whitman College.)

Anthony Nolter, editor of the Oregon City *Enterprise*. "We have neither space nor inclination to criticize her speech, suffice it to say that we were very much disappointed in the abilities of the lady, and so were most of her hearers." He went on to comment on Susan B. Anthony's "usefulness." "We could not help thinking what a fine looking and useful woman she would have been had she gotten married years ago. . ." (OHS neg. OrHi 4046)

Harvey Scott, Republican editor-in-chief of *The Oregonian* and Abigail Scott Duniway's younger brother. About Susan B. Anthony he wrote, "She is an elderly maiden lady, quite different in appearance from the vinegar-faced virago whom we had been led to look for from the representations of the San Francisco papers." About her campaign he said, "much more is expected from the suffrage of woman that can possibly be gained by it." (OHS reg. OrHi 83803)

Martin Van Buren Brown, editor of the Albany *Democrat.* Brown claimed that he could "prove from their own lips that the leaders of the movement are communists and enemies to Christian civilization." (OrHi 83806)

John Miller Murphy, Democratic editor of the Olympia *Standard.* "She presents her arguments in graceful and elegant language, her illustrations are ample and well-chosen, and the hearer is irresistibly drawn to the conclusions which she seeks to inculcate." Murphy emphasized that his support was a personal decision, not that of the Democratic party. (OHS neg. OrHi 83804)

Jonas H. Upton, editor of the Democratic Salem *Mercury*. He called Anthony "earnest, honest and forcible" and denied that she was "vindictive and unsparing." Upton opposed woman suffrage on the basis of his assumption that women would be more likely to vote for war since they were exempt from military service. (OHS neg. OrHi 83802)

Charles Prosch, Republican editor of Olympia *Tribune*. Prosch was initially supportive of Anthony and Duniway, but after they left for Victoria, B.C., he launched his attack in the *Tribune*. He rebuked rival editor Murphy for his support of Anthony and claimed that other politicians would soon rally around "the petticoat banner." (OHS reg. OrHi 83804)

Daniel R. Bigelow, a supporter of woman suffrage, put forth a bill that would require the women of Washington Territory to vote on whether they wanted the right of suffrage. Anthony disagreed with his bill "because it submitted the matter to the women, who were in a condition of servitude and incapacitated from voting on the question" and because "only those who have used the ballot know its value." (OHS neg. OrHi 72696)

David William Higgins, editor of the Victoria *Colonist* during Susan B. Anthony's 1871 visit. He commented that Anthony was "in every respect the best lecturer who has visited us. . . ." He attended all four lectures and gave them considerable coverage. He opened up his columns to readers exasperated by Anthony's generalizations and accusations. (Provincial Archives of British Columbia)

would uproot evil (for example, female voters would "banish from our cities the painted and gaudily bedecked creatures whom sensual man keep from occupying respectable positions in society"),[9] the conviction that the amended federal Constitution granted female suffrage, and the plea to the state legislators that they should enact laws beneficial to her gender. In 1872 Duniway acquired a national reputation as she expanded her efforts: she actively participated in eastern suffrage meetings and lectured about women, national politics, and other topics in Illinois, Iowa, Wyoming, Utah, and California.[10] Following another admonition of her mentor, late in 1872 she attempted to pressure Oregon legislators into passing favorable laws. Duniway voiced ideas in Salem that she had heard the suffrage leader advance from numerous Pacific Northwest platforms.

Not only were the Oregon reformer's themes similar to the New Yorker's, but so were her platform techniques: she was factual (the veteran instructed the novice not to deliver public lectures without careful preparation), frank, humorous, and questioning. She differed from the older woman, in that her first lectures lacked polish; moreover, she tended to be wittier and more sarcastic.[11] No matter how much Duniway subsequently changed her message and her tactics—for example, she stopped organizing small suffrage societies because they proved unrewarding—in her long and arduous battle on behalf of her sex, those she employed in the early 1870s clearly reflected that she was Anthony's disciple.[12]

While Duniway was the most famous of the New Yorker's local followers, others also received instruction in the tactics of reform. Although some pioneers had learned these lessons from involvement in the abolitionist, temperance, or woman suffrage movements in the East, most lacked personal experience in such reform organizations. Anthony taught the basic techniques: to organize associations at various levels; to adopt short constitutions, resolutions, and petitions at these associational meetings; to elect women to leadership positions in these organizations (Anthony emphasized her keen disappointment with men in suffrage organizations since the Civil War); to "wait upon the legislature"; to subscribe to suffrage publications; to counter isolation by sending delegates to national conventions; to fill the ranks with recruits; to lecture; and to converse with opinion makers, including ministers and editors. But Anthony did much more than simply inform about tactics.

She put her teaching into practice by helping establish local suffrage organizations in Portland, Seattle, and Olympia and by working to create a Washington Territory Woman Suffrage Association.

The veteran reformer had won eastern acclaim since the 1850s for her organizational ability. William Lloyd Garrison in 1857 said she was "a noble woman" who "worked indefatigably in . . . conventions."[13] In 1871 those on the other edge of the continent also acknowledged this skill, for she was the guiding hand in the meetings that founded all four regional suffrage organizations, and their conventions, constitutions, resolutions, and female leadership reflected her influence. Although these organizations would in time be superseded, they were significant models; for example, the 1873 convention establishing the Oregon State Woman Suffrage Association followed Anthony's teaching, with the exception that men received more leadership positions than she would have deemed appropriate.

Although Anthony won considerable support for and played a crucial role in launching a regional woman's rights movement, she also encountered considerable opposition from editors, ministers, Frost, and the majority of the population. Her campaign recruited many into the suffrage ranks, but it also intensified the opposition. Because Anthony stressed equal suffrage as the fundamental aspect of the woman's rights movement, her critics also concentrated on that subject. However, on the frontier as well as in more settled regions she met with apathy as often as hostility. Perhaps the general situation in the region was best exemplified by her last Willamette Valley schedule. Her concluding Portland address drew only the faithful, not the diversified throngs she had enjoyed in September, and indifference and opposition are the explanations. For these reasons Anthony traveled through Salem and Albany without arranging public meetings. In Oregon City a large and lively crowd greeted her because they anticipated verbal fireworks. There were good audiences in Eugene and points to the south in large part because she was a novelty there. But in general, the reformer had worn out her welcome. Many who came to her meetings out of curiosity would not return, while others who had heard or read her ideas saw no reason to pay fifty cents for a repetition.

An examination of her critics provides insight into the minds of many citizens. Antisuffragist Frost was a much less important or representative opponent than editors and ministers. Frost's writings and addresses were emotional, rambling, and sarcastic; although some cheered her negativism, there is no evidence that she changed the minds of those converted by the New Yorker. Frost actually added something to the campaign, for her efforts publicized the issue—this was one of Anthony's and Duniway's central objectives—and made settlers personally aware of the fact that itinerant critics contested suffragists. According to the *Oregonian*, Frost had some notoriety because of her "cheek and eccentricities" but faded quickly from public memory. In early 1872 any lasting admirers must have been chagrined by a story that she had slipped out of Victoria for San Francisco without paying for expensive clothing.[14]

Pacific Northwest ministers, Anthony understood, tended to be negative and shaped attitudes more than Frost. In 1870 Duniway had acknowledged their view: "the woman question is decidedly frowned upon by the clergy."[15] The New Yorker attempted to modify this situation through lectures and conversations. Undoubtedly she hoped that her "expediency" arguments would be persuasive: the guardians of public morality heard that woman suffrage would improve society, not undermine it. She met, however, with limited success. Her pupil encountered the same resistance from Oregon ministers early in 1872 and judged: "Of all men who oppose the movement, saloon keepers and ministers die the hardest."[16] But the New Yorker's accounts of the 1871 tour did not stress the liquor interest's opposition. Anthony's message prompted a reaction from churchmen, not saloonkeepers. In the region (as in the nation) this group divided over the suffrage issue. There is no evidence that she found adherents among the leaders of the region's Roman Catholic, Episcopal, or fundamental churches. On the other hand, she received endorsement from Unitarian, Congregational, and Methodist leaders. But Congregational and Methodist ministers did not as a body agree on reform issues; for example, Reverend Geary, a Congregationalist in Oregon City, published his antisuffrage sermon. Conversely Reverend Damon of Seattle, a member of the same denomination, enthusiastically promoted Anthony's work. While Walla Walla's ministers opposed her, an unknown number of Puget Sound preachers championed her reform at the Olympia convention called by suffragists. Unfortunately, no one detailed the opinions of the clergymen who hotly debated suffrage at this meeting, but surely both sides reiterated familiar arguments over the Bible, woman's role in society, morality, marriage, and divorce.

Perhaps Anthony influenced a few ministers by her denunciation of free love and by her promise that enfranchised women would align with them in a battle to close saloons, "hurdy-gurdy" halls, and brothels. But while her positive impact upon clergymen is mostly speculative, there is no doubt that she failed to enlist the editors of Portland's two religious newspapers—the *Catholic Sentinel* and the Methodist *Pacific Christian Advocate*—who disagreed about many religious matters, but both censured Anthony's liberal religious views. Secular editors also raised religious arguments against her. Perhaps the best example was the Portland *Herald*'s editorial entitled, "Philosophy Instead of Christianity," in which the writer accused that Anthony's private lectures were "a devilish contrivance to poison the morals of the wives, mothers and daughters;" moreover, "the whole system of woman's rights . . . is based upon an Epicurean philosophy, which is to substitute Christianity and virtually abolish its restraining influence and its ameliorating effects."[17]

While records of the response of clergymen are fragmented, there is a considerable body of information about editors' reaction. It is hazardous to assume that this group mirrored the majority opinion of readers on such a subject as woman suffrage. It seems reasonable, however, to conclude that editors at least spoke for many, if not necessarily the majority. Obviously Anthony—who clipped newspapers for her scrapbook and her lectures—and Duniway—who gathered them for her editorials—studied the regional press, assuming that its columns were a significant barometer of public opinion. The two politicians, like citizens everywhere, considered newspapers an important means by which to influence thought; thus both had launched weeklies—one on either side of the continent—to promulgate their ideas, and, to a lesser extent, to deflect shafts from antisuffragist writers.

During the 1871 campaign Duniway erroneously boasted that her coworker had "conquered the press and brought the whole fraternity to terms." Anthony's biographers, Ida H. Harper and Alma Lutz, were as badly mistaken; the latter summarized that "the press with a few exceptions was complimentary."[18] In actuality, most editors opposed Anthony. Of the thirty-three surviving Pacific Northwest newspapers responding to lectures, twenty were vehemently or mildly critical, and only eight extended compliments or enthusiastic endorsement, and five seemed neutral. What is even more striking about this editorial reaction is that the most widely read newspapers were hostile, including the Portland dailies—the *Herald*, (which complained of her "pernicious doctrines"), the *Bulletin*, and the *Oregonian*. Other significant newspapers that rejected the reformer were the Salem *Statesman*, the Oregon City *Enterprise*, the Albany *Democrat*, the Eugene *Guard*, both Walla Walla newspapers, and the Olympia *Tribune*.

It is easier to count the opposition newspapers than to account for their sentiments. There is no simple profile of the negative editors: their places of origin, ages, and political affiliations do not explain their sentiments. Men who arrived from all parts of the nation as well as those reared in the region took either side of the woman suffrage issue. Most critics were not transplanted Southerners—the region most hostile to this reform—but came from New York, New England, or the Midwest. Age had nothing to do with the division of editors into suffragist or antisuffragist positions—it was simply not a case of fogies battling the change championed by young editors. Journalists in their twenties were as antagonistic as those in their fifties. In 1871 woman suffrage was no more a party matter than was temperance. Republican newspapers, including the *Oregonian*, Salem *Statesman*, and Walla Walla *Union*, refuted the campaigner and such Democratic rivals as the Portland *Herald*, Walla Walla *Statesman*, and Eugene *Guard* expressed similar sentiments. It was true, however, that the Democrats wielded more savage pens and tended to engage in more personal denunciation. Such negative reaction was not the result of Anthony's party affiliations, for the New Yorker voiced no political preference and repeatedly explained that she would support any party that would enfranchise her sex.

Collectively the Pacific Northwest editors refused to consider woman suffrage a primary issue: traditional politics and the factors of economic development, especially railroads, were seen as more vital. Anthony's ability to arouse interest in the status of women, however, prompted columns about her and about females living near and far. Some male writers, such as O'Meara and Newell, apparently gave her more space than they had originally intended because the press, especially in Portland, thought it necessary to combat her campaign, even while realizing that in doing so, they gave the reformer the publicity she so craved.

Obviously the anti-Anthony writers recognized no compelling social, economic, constitutional, or political reason to enfranchise women. Chauvinism, a desire to maintain traditional male primacy, personal insecurities, and insensitivity were factors in their negativism. Historian Lee Nash provided an interesting reason why frontier newspapermen could not champion change in traditional sex roles: they recognized a "macho norm" that meant that those men "were expected publicly and visibly to be tough, combative, elemental, insensitive, uncompromising."[18]

Although it has been assumed in folklore, if not in the classroom, that frontiersmen favored woman suffrage because of their egalitarianism or because they realized that their female helpmates had earned the ballot on the basis of their arduous pioneering, only two male editors in 1871, Scott and Murphy, expressed such sentiments.[20] Not until 1896, in response to the pleas of Duniway, did the Oregon Pioneer Association take action recognizing the fact that frontier women had earned the ballot: "Whereas Oregon Pioneers of both sexes have equally shared the dangers and difficulties of subduing the Oregon wilderness, therefore, be it Resolved, That we use all honorable means to secure to both sexes equality of rights before the law."[21]

Instead of portraying Anthony as a politician who promised unattainable results in her expediency arguments, most opposition editors preferred to denounce her in general, rather than on such particularized grounds. A sweeping condemnation was safer, as well as easier, than an analytical rejection; furthermore, some editors might have rationalized that the reformer's own generalizations merited no attention or only counter-generalizations. A few editors, especially Scott and Murphy of the *Herald*, insisted that Anthony promised too much and was inconsistent. Scott reasoned that her "capital error . . . consists in the attempt to accomplish purely social results by political means." Clarke in the *Oregon Statesman*, said she illogically promised that woman suffrage would cure all evils and then faulted her: "she smoothes over the difficulties . . . as if woman was . . . an angel whose nature would survive the pollution of politics and sustain no blemish by becoming ambitious for office."[22]

The antisuffrage editors often dismissed Anthony with emotional, rather than rational arguments. These frontier newspapermen did what they could to scuttle her cause. They ridiculed her appearance ("That she likes money . . . can be seen . . . by the ghostly smile that flickers across her face, like a rat saturated with kerosene running off a bed of cold ashes"), questioned her character (she "loves a stiff cocktail, and imbibes her gin and bitters regularly before she makes a telling speech"), exaggerated her age (her name was not Anthony but Antony and she was the sister of Marc),[23] distorted her points, linked her with every current and dangerous "ism", and forewarned that if her liberal ideas about marriage, divorce, and woman's role won favor they would undermine society. To the disgust of suffragists, detractors sometimes delayed their attacks until the campaigner left town. The majority of editors probably had confidence in the power of their rhetoric; moreover, they believed that it was up to them as guardians of the community to protect it from dangerous notions. In rejecting the New Yorker, editors sometimes fell to making sarcastic or simplistic comments about frontier women in general. Scott and Murphy of Olympia were among the minority who comprehended many of the actual problems confronting the region's rural and urban women.

Thus in 1871 Anthony pondered the same kind of newspaper reports in the Pacific Northwest and Victoria as she had prompted elsewhere. Editors, ministers, and the public reacted to her ideas similarly from one coast to the other. Her scrapbook was filled with the negative newspaper clippings that she had courageously saved. Cognizant of the basic uniformity of the opposition (though perhaps in 1871 she was lampooned more often on the various frontiers—Oregon and Iowa were similar[24]—than in the older sections of the nation) the campaigner preached the same basic message and taught the same tactics at every stop.

Although mentioned earlier, one tactic of the frontier antisuffragists deserves elaboration. During Anthony's campaign and for many months afterwards, her opponents—Frost, ministers, and editors—maintained that the New Yorker and other suffragists soldiered under the command of Victoria Woodhull. In the early 1870s newspapermen made her the nation's most famous unconventional woman. She was editor of a racy newspaper, a presidential candidate, an advocate of free love and legalized prostitution, a proponent of economic and political radicalism, a peddler of gossip, and a recipient of much scandal as she shared living accommodations with both her former and current husbands. Although her newspaper, *Woodhull and Claflin's Weekly*, had a limited circulation, its spicy columns were quoted far and wide. By claiming that Anthony actually or secretly approved of Woodhull's dangerous doctrines, especially free love, critics hoped to frighten men and women away from suffrage. Opponents of a variety of reform movements have consistently publicized the most radical and menacing elements of groups battling for societal change: thus in the nation's history William Lloyd Garrison was heralded over Theodore Weld; Woodhull over Anthony or Stanton; Eugene Debs over Samuel Gompers; the Black Panthers over the NAACP; and militant advocates of ERA over the moderate majority. Apparently a useful way to discredit a reform movement is to concentrate upon its most notorious leader or extremist organization.

An Oregon editor, in employing this familiar scheme, even argued that any minister who favored woman suffrage thereby endorsed "notorious" Woodhull.[25] In detaching herself and the national organization in 1872 from the grasping Woodhull, Anthony was likely acting from awareness of the polarizing "free love storm" raging on the frontier as well as in the urban East. The radical woman's life, ideas, and political ambition were hindering, not helping the woman's rights movement. This continued to be true in the Pacific Northwest for months after Anthony departed, for regional editors hurled the words and deeds of Woodhull at Duniway as well.

The embattled Oregon newspaperwoman's attempts to counter the attacks on the radical feminist led to verbal duels with antagonistic editors. Some of them now lampooned her as they had Anthony: "Woman has no more use for the ballot than the editress of the *New Northwest* has for her prodigious ears."[26] Duniway shot back that her critics advocated the "man's rights party." One of her most interesting editorial battles was with her brother, Harvey Scott, whose *Oregonian* shifted the target of its batteries from a departed suffragist to a local one. In December 1871 the siblings clashed in their newspapers for the first time over two issues: the legal relationship between citizenship and suffrage and the notorious Victoria Woodhull.

Harvey's reaction to Abigail's journalism had been meaningful to her. In announcing early in 1871 that she was to be the editorial correspondent of the suffragist San Francisco *Pioneer*, he wrote "while we hardly see how Mrs. Duniway is to add to its interest, already brought to so high a standard, yet we hope she may be a benefit to its many readers and the world generally."[27] The brother was much more supportive a few months later when he wrote an editorial notice evaluating the first issue of the *New Northwest*. Scott concluded: "The sheet before us is full of vigorous writing with a strong flavor of practical good sense. We apprehend that Mrs. Duniway in the course of a few issues . . . will succeed in stating the woman question in a clear, full and spirited manner, so that if all are not convinced many will be disposed to listen."[28] Abigail thought that Harvey was neutral on woman suffrage and he, like some other editors, watched "the waves of public popularity," and would support the reform as soon as he knew that it was the "winning side."[29] To Duniway's great pleasure, Scott had endorsed Anthony's legal arguments, but after her departure he annoyed his sister by rejecting a fundamental point: he judged that "citizenship is one thing; suffrage is another."[30]

The siblings engaged in a livelier dispute over Woodhull. Duniway explained that this individual was not the leader of her choice and repeated an argument of her teacher: "But she is the only woman who can get the ear of the men who have usurped our rights, and women must speak through her until they get into power. Politicians always work to win."[31] Such politically expedient reasoning angered Scott. Although he had not denounced suffragist leaders in March 1871 when publishing a letter in which Anthony expressed love for and faith in Woodhull, calling her a "bright, glorious, young, and strong spirit," in December, the editor publicly cautioned his sister about the radical agitator.[32] Woodhull, he warned, was doing enormous harm to suffrage reform. Duniway and other moral suffragists should categorically reject the infamous woman's leadership because her "doctrines . . . are too abominable to be thought on without indignation."[33] Involved in what she called "a spirited controversy" with her brother, she resented his editorials and hurled shafts at him: he suffered from "a serious attack of the rabies," she needed "leather spectacles to see his logic," he used a "filthy style" by calling Woodhull a "bawd," and he required "a hauling over our editorial coals every week or two." In an editorial aimed at her brother, she insisted that she had never defended the "vagaries" of either Woodhull or Brigham Young. She obviously believed that in her reference to the Mormon leader she had equated two infamous violators of monogamy. To the delight of readers enjoying the family quarrel, Abigail lectured Harvey: "we do emphatically declare that men who seek to beslime the Woman's Movement by insinuations about the Woodhull had better turn their attention to man movement and the Young who heads it."[34] This provocative assertion was at some odds with the interpretation of Stanton and Anthony. According to historian Lois Banner, they "often argued that polygamy was in fact no worse than the man-made marriages of the regular society."[35] But the Oregon woman would have won nods of approval from both the famous suffragists when she lambasted her brother and other males: "There is not a more egregious folly under the sun than this man-made outcry that women are in danger of being contaminated by free love." She charged that men, who realized that free love was a bogus issue, employed the emotional term so as "to frighten weak-minded women into the belief that they need the domination of men to keep them virtuous."[36]

Despite her outrage, Duniway had already concluded in her first Portland speech that "The true women must rescue the leadership of the suffrage movement from such women as Mrs. Woodhull."[37] This is exactly the conclusion that Anthony would reach several months later. The Oregon editor explained that the "monstrous" writings of Woodhull led to her decision. It is probable, however, that her brother's editorial also influenced her thinking. Despite her dispute with him, she appreciated his shrewd political judgment, including his recent cautionary interpretation of Woodhull's impact which was sounder than Anthony's earlier declaration that the radical woman was politically useful and was unfairly assailed by male editors. In any event, Duniway realized, as did her brother, that radicalism in far away urban New York influenced the reform effort in rural Oregon and Washington.

Probably Duniway's newspaper as well as a few letters from sympathizers kept Anthony aware of the controversy over Woodhull and other aspects of the regional suffrage fight. The visitor left the coast convinced that her cause had a better chance of success in Washington than in either Oregon or California, but long experience had taught her not to anticipate an early victory. Through her campaign around Puget Sound, she had prepared local men and women for an extended battle for the ballot. It was, however, up to these concerned citizens to find the leadership, energy, and time required to win it. Victory came in 1883 when the territorial legislature granted women the right to vote. Anthony's campaign of 1871 was less responsible for this success—a temporary one as women lost the right to vote about five years later—than was the long agitation of Duniway and her allies in Washington Territory. According to historian T.A. Larson, the association established by Anthony in 1871 collapsed and Duniway's "work during the years 1871-1883 justified calling her the mother of woman suffrage in Washington."[38] There is evidence, however, that opinion makers of the 1880s had not forgotten Anthony's tour. Such Washingtonians as Editor Murphy in Olympia, Mary O. Brown and Sarah Yesler of Seattle, and the Isaacs women in Walla Walla all received inspiration from the New Yorker and for years these suffragists labored for the cause.[39] Because of her lasting influence—Duniway acknowledged it in the 1880s—the tireless Anthony might appropriately be called the grandmother of woman suffrage in both Oregon and Washington.

There is considerable evidence that Anthony's prediction that Washington women would be conscientious voters and jurors came true in the 1880s. Editor Murphy ruled that "Women make excellent jurors, honest and industrious officers, and intelligent voters."[40] Pioneer Phoebe Judson did not feel "any more out of my sphere with [the ballot] than when assisting [her] husband to develop the resources of our country," and also insisted that "At the polls, men were respectful; voting places were kept clean and free from loafers. The women, as a rule, allowed character, rather than party to influence their votes. It was not because of failure that we were deprived of equal rights, for it was a grand success."[41] In 1887 the antisuffragist Seattle *Post-Intelligencer*, in applauding the rescindment of the franchise, did not claim that women had been incompetent voters. It stressed, however, the traditional argument that women should not engage in politics because "the ideal American woman . . . is the woman whose first interest is her home, and who, after that, devotes her time to the church and to the amelioration of the condition of her brother men and sister women."[42]

Female voters, as Anthony had predicted fifteen years earlier, often supported prohibition. But her assurance that men would learn to appreciate the moral vote of females proved incorrect.

An examination of Anthony's prodigious efforts in the fall of 1871 reveals much about her. Biographers such as Ida Harper, Alma Lutz, and Katherine Anthony, in their coverage of the period from the launching of the *Revolution* in 1868 through her casting of an illegal vote in the presidential election of 1872, unfailingly praised their subject as she engaged in controversial journalism, politics, organizations, and lecture tours. The primary materials from both national and local sources indicate that beneath her earlier biographers' praise, she was a more complex character. Editor Horace Greeley, who both admired and opposed her, sometimes called her "Captain Anthony" or "the noblest Roman of them all" as he related and evaluated her reform work. In his 1871 estimation he wrote that no suffragist agitator was "more indiscreet, more reckless or more honest." The influential editor continued:

> We have no sort of sympathy with the object to which the fair Captain is now devoting her life; but we know no person before the country more simple-minded, sincere, and unselfish, and for these reasons, more honestly entitled to the regard of a public which will always appreciate upright intentions and disinterested devotion.[43]

Operated by an editor who was more conservative than Anthony, the *Revolution*'s assessment was similar to Greeley's:

> She is impulsive and sometimes impractical, saying and doing what her best friends regret; but she has an enthusiasm that mean and small natures are incapable of and cannot appreciate. . . . There is no nobler and more heroic person connected with the woman movement than Susan B. Anthony.[44]

The major weakness of her Pacific Northwest appeal was her sweeping promise that woman suffrage would greatly improve society. As indicated, those few newspapermen who were willing to examine her message—especially Scott and Clarke—objected when she assured that an outpouring of economic and social improvements would naturally follow the enfranchisement of females. Apparently Scott never changed his mind for in 1900 he ruled that it was "utter folly to assert that only through the ballot can Woman's wrongs be righted."

Her regional critics granted that she sincerely believed in her doctrines. Although accused of about every other possible personal shortcoming, apparently nobody denounced her for seeking political power for personal reasons. Her study of society led her to conclude that woman suffrage was the best, if not the only, way to improve society. She held that men wielded far too much power—politically, socially, economically, and sexually—and that the results were the societal flaws that she underscored in numerous speeches. Anthony preached the basic motto she had used in the *Revolution*: "The True Republic—Men, Their Rights and Nothing More, Women, Their Rights and Nothing Less." Corrupt politics, pay inequity and restricted professional opportunities for females, male-dominated marriages, drunkenness, and prostitution were difficulties that she believed would be resolved if woman voted. Another important factor in shaping her mind was her acquaintance with hundreds of talented and moral women—famous as well as obscure—whose collective voting power would, she foresaw, mitigate the excessive power of selfish or insensitive men. Her assessment that men had too much power and women had too few rights was obviously correct. Anthony and her allies genuinely, if naively, maintained that if this imbalance were resolved through equal suffrage then America would enter into a golden age. Time has demonstrated that the emancipation of women—and the redemption of society—has required more than the ballot.

The famous suffragist could be faulted in 1871 not only for her expediency arguments. Her interpretation of black suffrage and her neglect of Chinese workers also reflect limitations. While Anthony had evidence to support her contention that politicians, who needed to win black votes, no longer made scurrilous remarks about the physical appearance of blacks, she greatly exaggerated the improved position of blacks in American society. The *Oregonian*, summarizing one of her references to blacks, stated that "she ran a parallel between negro servitude before the emancipation, and women servitude as made by the laws. She showed that, so far as civil and political disabilities are concerned, neither the negro or the woman had much to boast of—the one over the other."[45] Many eastern reformers had disagreed with this equation of female and black status and had argued that vulnerable freedmen were in greater need of the protection of federal amendments; they denounced Anthony and Stanton in the late 1860s and in 1870 for criticizing the Fifteenth Amendment. She was aware of the condition of freedmen and the fact that Congress had to enact Force Acts in the early 1870s to enforce recognition of the civil and political rights of blacks as guaranteed by the two Reconstruction Amendments. This knowledge and her distrust of male character must have led her to realize that female suffrage would serve to alleviate male domination, rather than instantaneously terminating it. It would have weakened her argument to publicly acknowledge the limitations of suffrage; she instead exaggerated the benefits of the ballot, arguing, among other things, that newly enfranchised blacks were no longer "abused by men in power."[46] But such an interpretation about blacks was too simplistic. As historian Ellen Carol DuBois has recently concluded, Anthony and Stanton sometimes expressed racism and elitism.[47] It is also interesting that in the Pacific Northwest where there was widespread and vocal hostility to black suffrage, no editor denounced Anthony's simplistic interpretation of blacks. She would have won the wrath of outspoken regional opinion makers had she been more explicit about the local black situation; Portland, for example, operated a segregated public school for black children.

It is a bit surprising that as a labor reformer she did not complain about the treatment of the region's Chinese workers. From her days of association with the workers in her father's cotton mills, she had been interested in labor difficulties and sought their resolution. In 1871 she attended a labor convention held to consider the status of workers and had been elected a vice president of a new Labor Reform League. Despite her commitment to labor reform and despite the fact that she had seen and heard much about Chinese laborers on the Pacific Slope, she ignored this disadvantaged race and stressed only her disadvantaged sex. Lois Banner provides an explanation for this decision. Anthony's experiences convinced her that "the woman's movement must not scatter its strength but rather focus on one reform at a time." This practical decision was not shared by her friend: "The dream of a political union of the dispossessed—women, blacks, the working classes—continued to haunt Cady Stanton."[48] It is very probable that Anthony's fixation with suffrage restricted her appeal to her audiences. Stanton complained that her colleague unduly emphasized the ballot to the detriment of other women's rights issues. In her own lectures Stanton also addressed marriage, divorce, education, jobs for women, and prostitution. Anthony, it is true, sometimes handled these topics as they related to woman suffrage, but she could have emphasized them in talks. The Portland *Herald* and the Portland *Bulletin*, for example, discussed prostitution, the children of prostitutes, juvenile delinquents (then called "bad boys"), obscene periodicals (including the *Police Gazette*), and temperance. Anthony might have partially pacified her critics by stressing a broader range of societal wrongs. (She would do this in her 1896 visit to the Pacific Northwest.) Talks on these current topics as well as a discussion of national politicians—Duniway quickly learned that lectures on politics attracted audiences—would have earned money for the New Yorker and given her greater opportunity to spread her suffrage message.

It was unrealistic to expect that frontier women, lacking experience and money, could maintain suffrage organizations without sharing leadership, at least temporarily, with men. While the National Woman Suffrage Association could retain power in the hands of such unusually talented women as Anthony and Stanton, it is doubtful that frontier women—then a weak minority—could do the same. The suffragists in Oregon soon adopted the practice of the National's rival organization, the American Woman Suffrage Association, and awarded offices to men.

The New Yorker might be faulted on other grounds. As Larson has judged, her legal arguments were too complicated for most listeners;[49] furthermore, at times she scolded men or made sarcastic remarks that probably did little for her cause. Other reformers, including Laura de Force Gordon and Stanton, had the ability to instruct in pleasing or humorous tones. The Californian impressed Pacific Northwest listeners with her sunny disposition as well as with her oratory; Stanton was famous for her jolly manner.

Anthony's overall character and talents, however, overshadowed her faults. She was a woman of enormous energy and endurance: she had the capacity to master the physical and mental difficulties of an extended campaign in the frontier Pacific Northwest. She seemed able to look beyond the problems she encountered, writing in 1872 glowingly of her experience on Puget Sound: "How like a dream it all seems, and what a beautiful one, too, to live over and over."[50] She had the capacity to avoid boredom in the endless repetition of her message, but lifeless audiences could distract her. The reformer possessed the courage to continue her fight without becoming embittered. She was not only tolerant, but she was unusually dedicated, as all observers emphasized, to the woman's movement. Anthony was an effective speaker, in part, because she had the intelligence to master a large body of factual knowledge. (One modern biographer offered an original and erroneous explanation for Anthony's appeal as a lecturer. Her gray silk dress and pink accessories stirred males: "The effect upon the starved males of the Northwest was all that could have been desired by a more designing woman."[51]) She was a skilled politician, a fact that most biographers fail to develop, but Professor DuBois has recently emphasized this talent: "Stanton and Anthony were the leaders in establishing woman suffrage as an independent feminist movement. . . . Their politics led them to establish the National Woman Suffrage Association, from which they could proceed to build an independent movement of women for their own enfranchisement."[52] In the Pacific Northwest, the New Yorker demonstrated considerable political ability. She understood the tactics of reform (her long experience in the temperance, education, abolition, and suffrage movements—especially after 1868—was of tremendous value),[53] possessed the ability to judge character, had the capacity to understand local attitudes, and had the personal resources necessary to wage a long battle for her principles.

Besides her political talents, Anthony was an effective teacher long after she left the classroom. Although her biographers fail to stress it, the fifteen years she spent as a schoolteacher were very useful; in fact, she approached her audiences as if they were pupils—some of whom were unruly—who badly needed her instruction. In 1871 her lectures, discussion techniques, mastery of facts, enthusiasm, sense of humor, and ability to listen reflected on her mastery of the teaching profession. Like other successful instructors she was optimistic, operating on the premise that her listeners had the capacity to learn.

Stanton, who had observed her friend during the long western tour concluded: "Miss Anthony's style of speaking is rapid vehement. In debate she is ready and keen, and she is always equal to an emergency." In her old age Stanton still retold Anthony's great efforts during her first Pacific Northwest campaign. She praised her for "sailing up the Columbia River and, in hot haste to meet some appointment, jolting over the rough mountains of Oregon and Washington . . . lighting the fires of liberty. . .and scattering our breezy leaflets to the four winds of heaven."[54]

In summary, in 1871 she was an impressive figure. Few American reformers—male or female—so consistently fought to bring the better nature out of the citizenry. Long before and long after her Pacific Northwest tour, she remained steadfast. Her vision won converts.

EIGHT

# A New World of Organized Women

FROM THE TIME that Anthony left their region by stagecoach in 1871 to her return by rail in 1896, Pacific Northwest residents gained only a general understanding of her eastern suffrage work from newspapers. Readers of Duniway's *New Northwest* learned more, including details about the leader who personified the woman's rights movement. Many residents must have been pleased by reports of Anthony's praising them and the Pacific Northwest to eastern audiences.

On returning home in late 1871 Anthony once again faced obstacles to her campaign, though this time of nature's making: a snowstorm in Virginia City and a snowbound train in Wyoming. In 1872 the leader wisely disassociated the National Woman Suffrage Association (NWSA) from Victoria Woodhull, whose startling pronouncements and efforts to use the NWSA for radical political ends—she was now running for the presidency of the United States—brought enormous national criticism upon suffragists. In that same year Anthony, making good on her assertion that the Reconstruction amendments to the Constitution enfranchised women, voted for Grant. She was arrested by a federal official for illegally casting a ballot and tried. A judge found her guilty and fined her $100. The defendant refused to pay, hoping that her case, like that of Dred Scott, might be taken to the Supreme Court for a clarifying decision. It did not. Disappointed with the case's disposition, Anthony often recounted its history—now a cause célèbre—during her speaking tours. Even as late as 1896 she informed westerners that the judge in her case was "small-brained" and that a law review had once urged her to emigrate if she was "not pleased with our laws." For years Anthony also castigated the Supreme Court for its 1875 *Minor* vs. *Happersett* decision, a ruling that states could deny women the vote—an interpretation of the Fourteenth and Fifteenth Amendments in direct opposition to the New Departure argument that she had voiced in her 1871 campaign.

Pacific Northwest inhabitants interested in Anthony's career understood her frustration with the courts; they also knew that she and her allies faced other difficulties in the 1870s and 1880s, including conflicts within the movement over political party affiliations. In 1872 the Republican party, seeking the support of reformers, stated that it would respectfully consider "additional rights" for women. Anthony, though not Elizabeth Cady Stanton, rejoiced over this proclamation. At a May meeting, Anthony, Duniway, and others formed a campaign committee to work on behalf of the Republican party. The group supported Anthony's prematurely triumphant pronouncement that "woman is now fairly inside the political ring and can never again be snubbed out."[1] These activists soon learned, however, that Republican interest in woman's suffrage was shallow and short-lived; their platforms after 1872 offered no redress.

While most politicians chose to ignore the suffragist demands for reform, the NWSA, led by Stanton and Anthony, competed with the conservative American Woman Suffrage Association (AWSA) for membership. These factionalizing efforts diluted the power of the movement; neither group enlisted the numbers required to win state suffrage elections. Suffragists expended a tremendous amount of energy and as much money as they could raise in these futile referenda. Suffrage defeats attracted the Pacific Northwest's attention, particularly the one in Colorado in 1877. Anthony's hard campaigning there was of no avail—a failure she attributed to the impossibility of conveying her arguments to the large Spanish-speaking portion of the state's electorate. Such out-of-state politics, however, were less important to Oregonians, than their role in the controversial 1876 presidential election.

In 1883 Anthony, making her first ocean voyage since her nasty one to Portland a dozen years earlier, toured Europe, meeting with women and planning an international suffragist organization. Probably western admirers took a greater interest in their leader's efforts in South Dakota than in London. In 1890, at the age of seventy, Susan campaigned there for six months. A companion reported that "Like a true soldier, she could snatch a moment of sleep or a mouthful of food where she found it, and if either was not forthcoming she did not miss it." The suffragist slept in one-room cabins, drank brackish water, and traveled by wagon in bitter cold and blistering heat. For a combination of reasons the male electorate again denied women the privilege of voting. Perhaps newspaper exchanges made Pacific Northwest readers not only aware of this election result but also of the split that significantly contributed to it. Open disagreements between national and South Dakota suffrage leaders prompted newspapermen to poke fun of them and belittle their cause. The Aberdeen *Saturday Review*, for example, denounced Anthony. "We were well organized and working harmoniously, but she upset our organizations. . . . Everyone who does not fall down and worship her aged countenance, everyone who does not hang rapturously on the halting and inconsequent words consistently falling from her ever-open mouth are her enemies."[2] There can be no doubt that the sobering South Dakota experience had an impact upon both Anthony and Duniway.

Rebuffed in all but one state referendum campaign—Colorado granted equal suffrage in 1893—Anthony and her allies also aroused little federal support. In 1878 Senator Aaron Sargeant of California, responding to Anthony and others, introduced a constitutional woman suffrage amendment. This proposed Sixteenth Amendment was introduced in succeeding Congresses but never passed. Anthony unsuccessfully championed it for many years, but she switched the thrust of her effort from the fight for this amendment to the Federal Constitution back to state referenda campaigns. A reason for this change in tactics was the fact that in 1887 a Senate vote on the amendment failed by a vote of 34 no, 16 yes, and 26 absent. This devastating result clearly demonstrated that it was impossible to get the required two-thirds vote; suffragists must seek redress through state victories.

A shortage of money as well as a lack of political support hampered the movement. Duniway publicized this fact in 1877 by publishing a letter from Anthony. "If women had money," the New Yorker explained, "they might move the world. But they are making this fight with hands tied, financially, as well as politically."

There was another irritating problem that Anthony often presented to her follower. In 1894 she summarized this difficulty: "It is the dishearteening part of all my life work—that so very few women will work for the emancipation of their own half of the race!!"[3]

In the mid-1890s, after years of resounding defeats, perhaps all but the stoutest hearts questioned Anthony's continuing optimism. These men and women, however, pointed to signs of progress. The NWSA and AWSA merged in 1890 to form the National American Woman Suffrage Association (NAWSA). More important, public opinion had changed in twenty years. By the 1890s the idea of woman suffrage was no longer perceived as radical but was considered a liberal or even moderate issue. The persistence of the suffrage movement—its proponents unrelentingly kept their goal before the public—and the burgeoning political radicalism of the 1890s convinced many citizens that a ballot in the hands of women was much safer than one grasped by a radical Coxeyite or Populist. During the 1890s in the Pacific Northwest, as in other sections of the nation, conservatives worried about the emergence in 1892 of the Populist Party. It decried the new industrial society, proposed that the federal government play a larger role in the economy, and ran a colorful presidential candidate. Many also disapproved of the Coxeyites—the supporters of Ohioan Jacob S. Coxey—who in 1894 had led an "army" of unemployed men on a march to Washington in an attempt to convince the government to assist the jobless. In the depression years of 1894-95, many Oregon, Washington, and Idaho residents championed both the Populist party and Coxey.

Anthony and her allies did not threaten, as the Populists or Coxeyites did, the established political and economic order. Suffragists assured that they only wanted to participate in and improve the existing system; the Populists, on the other hand, sought major economic changes, including government ownership of the railroads. The NAWSA played solid moderate politics; for example, it now downplayed prohibition, and Anthony's message in 1896 was less threatening than it had been in the 1870s. The association's moderate political approach compared favorably with the radical programs voiced by politicians who sought to combat the economic depression of the 1890s—a contrast which won the suffrage cause some measure of respectability.

Suffragists could be pleased with the Portland *Oregonian*'s differentiation of these elements arguing for societal change. In the spring of 1896 it denounced only radical—not moderate or liberal—politicians canvassing Oregon. Editor Harvey Scott complained that radical speakers sought to influence the upcoming election by spreading "political and economic error" among the state's puzzled voters.[4] The Republican leader lashed out at "a swarm of wild eyed guerrillas and free lances of politics" of the type of Jacob S. Coxey and James B. Weaver (the presidential nominee of the Populist party in 1892) and Mrs. Mary Lease (a popular Populist orator). Although Scott lacked sympathy for Anthony's crusade, he understood that she was not to be linked with Coxey, Weaver or others who came to Oregon "like dramatic stars in the spring, to fill a vacant date." The editor did not list Anthony among the "mischief-makers." He, and many others, thought of her as misguided but sincere. Perhaps his sister, Abigail, had confided to him that she believed that the great suffragist leader preferred, as she did, the Republican to the Populist Party.

Anthony insisted that the NAWSA must concentrate on the suffrage issue; Stanton, however, pushed a broader reform and accordingly denounced the tyranny of husbands and ministers. She acknowledged that her co-reformer defended "co-education and prohibition" but emphasized that Anthony "solves every difficulty with the refrain, 'woman suffrage' as persistent as the 'never more' of Poe's raven."[5] The younger women in the NAWSA leadership felt much more comfortable with Anthony's liberalism than with Stanton's radicalism. Thus political radicals in and out of the suffragist movement made Anthony appear to be a moderate.

The 1890s brought other reasons for optimism besides the creation of the NAWSA and a more favorable political climate. Many states had by then granted women a limited suffrage—they could vote in school board elections and sometimes in municipal ones. Anthony considered this half-suffrage better than no suffrage. It was an opening wedge.

The movement also gained momentum as a new group of intelligent women had taken up the cause. Anthony delighted in the talents of Ida Husted Harper, Carrie Chapman Catt, Rev. Anna Howard Shaw, Sarah B. Cooper, and others. Another positive development in the 1890s was the fact that many more American women were attending high school and college. Such graduates often felt that their education made them more qualified to vote than many in the existing electorate, such as unschooled males and new immigrants. At the same time, the suffragist movement had been strengthened by support from such female organizations as the Women's Christian Temperance Union (WCTU) and the Young Women's Christian Association (YWCA).

In the 1890s opinion makers on the Pacific Coast wrote about the "new," "emancipated," or "awakened" woman who was defined as one becoming absorbed in social, economic, and political affairs. A growing number of such individuals rejected their traditional role and sought professional careers, especially in business, or positions as wage workers. Antisuffragists pondered and warned about the immediate and long range implication of the evolving status of females, cautioning prosuffragists that "If a woman becomes a man she must resign her privileges as a woman."

Anthony expressed pleasure with all this attention given to the status of her sex. Furthermore, she taught that much progress had been accomplished. "Fifty years ago," she assured the 1894 NAWSA convention, "there were three occupations for women—housework, sewing, and teaching." She noted that women found admission into formerly closed universities and industries. She concluded that the "single exception" to change was the fact women still did not enjoy the franchise.

Like other experienced politicians, Anthony recognized these currents of social change and developed tactics to make them work to the movement's advantage. In the 1870s and 1880s women began to form all female organizations whose purposes ranged from fostering intellectual development and friendship to social reform and charity. As one scholar stated, "By the 1890s . . . a new world of organized women had sprung into existence, reflecting a shared desire to participate in public life beyond the home and family."[6] To Anthony's way of thinking these women's clubs could provide recruits to bolster the thin suffragist ranks. In California in the mid-1890s Anthony and her coadjutators sought to attract women's groups to the suffrage banner by conducting an annual woman's congress. Pacific Northwest suffragists read about these meetings; in fact, the Woman's Congress Association of the Pacific Coast asked Northwesterners to join the organization and attend these annual gatherings. The regional association, meeting in San Francisco, urged women to think and act on "issues affecting humanity."[7] In 1895, Anthony was the Pacific Coast Congress's featured lecturer; the following year she returned and was one of several notable speakers, lecturing on the association's theme, "Women and Government." In both congresses the New Yorker received an enthusiastic welcome and provided momentum for those engaged in the 1896 California referendum campaign.

The congress was not the only means employed by Anthony and California allies in this fight. In the 1870s Anthony had stated that her sex would rally to that party that promised "freedom to women." Disillusioned by the Republican party's abortive action in 1872 and subsequent disinterest, Anthony and other national leaders still refused to be allied with any single party. She argued that "my position . . . is that of knowing no party save for its allegiance to freedom and franchise to women" and that women should not "divide on party lines until after they receive the ballot."[8] She asked each party to write platform planks favoring the enfranchisement of women; by late May 1896 California's Republican, Populist, and Prohibition parties had done just that.

Because she still appreciated the power of newspapers to shape public opinion, Anthony pursued editors for endorsements of her reform. In 1896 the California press was much more sympathetic than it had been twenty-five years earlier. Many editors championed equal suffrage; only a few ridiculed its chief advocate by reporting stories of her intoxication and by reminding of her inability to find a husband. One negative journal, the Sacramento *Record-Union*, congratualted suffragists for waging a "gallant struggle" and promised not to resist it by "sophistries, sneers slurs, or unfairness." Although the influential San Francisco *Examiner* refused to march with her, it allowed Anthony to publish a column every Sunday.

During this well publicized and crucial California campaign, Anthony received calls from Pacific Northwest suffragists to lead a rally in Seattle and to appear in Portland for the first Oregon Congress of Women. Scheduled for June 1896, this meeting was modeled after those held in California since 1894. To ensure success, its organizers sought Anthony, whose reputation and political skills were widely acknowledged. Like the National Women's Political Caucus that met in Portland in August 1987, the one held ninety-one years earlier also emphasized "consciousness-raising" and wide-ranging political discussions, including those on how to battle what is now called "campaign stress." Anthony recognized why Pacific Northwest sympathizers wanted her participation, but she indicated that California politics consumed her busy schedule. She would spend eight hectic months in that state. She agreed, however, to come north for nine days.

In Anthony's scheme, a smashing victory in California would lead to success in Oregon and Washington, but her political experience told her that victories could be attained in these states only after extensive organization and publicity. Anthony's nearly forty-five years as a leader had consistently demonstrated that recognition of equality would have to be earned in the political arena; men in the 1890s seemed no more willing to surrender power to women than they had been in the 1870s.

In the 1880s and 1890s the experiences of Pacific Northwest suffragists, paralleled that of their national counterparts: they rejoiced over some local political victories but more often suffered bitter defeats. In both Oregon and Washington legislators enacted measures beneficial to women, but Duniway and her allies, employing tactics taught by Anthony in 1871, by her correspondence, and by her advice given at national meetings could not win state or territorial suffrage. From the time the national leader concluded her first visit into the late 1880s, Duniway battled extensively for the cause, becoming the most influential suffragist in Oregon, Washington, and Idaho. Besides her deep involvement in their suffage campaigns, she published the *New Northwest* (it continued to be an influential source of fact and opinion for those seeking to improve the condition of Northwest women), attended national conventions, lobbied politicians, stumped her cause in towns throughout the Pacific Northwest, struggled to maintain some suffrage organizations, and appealed to various individuals for assistance. Despite the fact that Duniway and her volunteers labored for more than fifteen years for their cause, in the late 1880s into the mid-1890s it was at its nadir.

In the early 1880s it had seemed that Duniway and other suffragists had reason to be optimistic. In 1880 the Oregon legislature provided for a referendum vote in 1884. In June 1884 Duniway again met with frustration and anger when voters soundly rejected equal suffrage by a vote of 28,176 to 11,223. In analyzing this painful defeat the Oregon leader, who had tried to make her state the first to enfranchise its females, groused that eastern organizers had not supplied the money required for such a crucial statewide campaign and lashed out at political opponents for manipulating "the ignorant, blear-eyed, red-nosed, beer-guzzling pauper hordes who flood our land from foreign climes" into voting against women. Duniway ridiculed opponents, particularly such foreign-born voters: "if t'e vimmen gets as much rights as t'e mens, t'ey gets so schmart t'ey ton't vant to mind,' sagely remarked a valuable citizen who earns a living by dealing in second-hand trash."[9]

Anthony had closely followed this 1884 referendum campaign, writing on election day; "I wait with bated breath the news from Oregon, where today the men are voting on this question of woman's enfranchisement. My heart almost stands still. I hope against hope, but still I hope."[10] She faulted herself for not having participated in this suffrage fight, mailed Duniway $100 to cover part of her campaign expenditures, and urged eastern women to be financially generous with their Oregon sisters. Anthony's analysis of the 1884 defeat was much the same as Duniway's: "the women should stop asking legislatures to submit this question to the electors, to have it killed by the majority, made up of ignorance and whiskey, native and foreign."[11] Despite misgivings about conducting another referendum vote, Duniway, who preferred legislature balloting on the suffrage issue, told her disappointed supporters that they should immediately prepare for another public contest. Predicting a favorable vote within five years, the activist actually had to wait sixteen for the question to be put to popular vote again.

In 1883 Washington Territory suffragists had experienced a spectacular but temporary success when they received the right to vote. At a premature state constitutional convention in Walla Walla in 1878, Duniway and others had pleaded for equal suffrage, but delegates by a narrow vote of 8-7 rejected it. Although a similar measure failed in the 1881 territorial legislature, the next session enacted it. This exciting political victory prompted Duniway to provide a history of the "Grand Triumph" in the *New Northwest* of 22 November 1883. The editor acknowledged Anthony's tour of Puget Sound, emphasizing that her powerful message had prompted fearful opponents to engage in dogmatic negation"; in fact, from 1871 to 1883 they had resorted to "ridicule and misrepresentation."

Delighted with the action of the territorial government, Anthony in 1884 informed her Portland ally that if Oregon would join Washington in granting equal rights then " the land of the sundown seas" would be the "New England of the new century." Three years later reformers experienced a sunset as Washington's territorial supreme court voided the suffrage law. In 1889 they were again bitterly disappointed when

Washington males soundly rejected woman suffrage by a referendum vote of 35,527 to 16,613.[12] Many agreed with the Oregon leader that the producers and consumers of alcoholic drink, fearing that women voters would support prohibition measures, worked to thwart equal suffrage. Two prominent eastern suffragists evaluated the election returns, reaching conclusions like Duniway's. Henry B. Blackwell lobbied in Olympia and confessed: "I am forever cured of the dream of a prohibition alliance." Carrie Chapman Catt judged that "there was no doubt in any mind that 1889 was the saloon's hour in Washington."[13]

During her long fight for suffrage, Duniway occasionally wrote to Anthony or conferred with her at conventions. There were many signs of a close friendship; for example, in 1876 Anthony had asked her Oregon protege to join her in Philadelphia "and help us until taxation without representation shall be Done-away." The New Yorker also praised the Portlander's fiction: "My mother enjoys your story; thinks that Mrs. Duniway after all, understands human nature about the best." The national leader occasionally requested the regional leader to solicit petitions for the proposed Sixteenth Amendment. She candidly explained to Duniway why she preferred this strategy rather than the state referenda campaigns: "I have had enough begging my rights at the feet of the great unwashed rabble, native and foreign, white and black, with Mexican greasers added."[14]

Still convinced that Duniway was the Pacific Northwest's most important suffragist, Anthony freely furnished advice about reform tactics, reassured the remote Oregonian that she did not soldier alone, and soothed her when she related insults and lies voiced by mean-spirited detractors. In an 1884 public letter she encouraged her pupil to ignore the envious and jealous and "to work right along—as the moon did when it was barked at."

An obvious sign of the continued confidence was the fact that in March 1884 Anthony included Duniway in a small group that appeared before a United States Senate Select Committee. The delegation presented arguments for the proposed Sixteenth Amendment. In introducing Duniway, Anthony praised her for collecting petitions and for pushing the reform in the Pacific Northwest; furthermore, she hailed the Portlander as the person most responsible for the enfranchisement of women in Washington Territory. Duniway spoke optimistically about a suffrage victory in Oregon's June election but urged that Congress pass the amendment so that informed state legislators—not the disinterested and even illiterate state voters—would decide the issue.

Soon after Anthony presented a summary argument to the committee. She favored the method Duniway advocated. Anthony, aware of the hard work that her friend put into the Washington and Oregon campaigns, insisted that such undertakings required too much time and money: "I do not wish to see the women of the thirty-eight states . . . compelled to leave their homes and canvass each State, school district by school district. It is asking too much of a moneyless class."[15]

For some quarter century Duniway and Anthony apparently were in essential agreement on the goals and tactics of their reform movement. Both considered that it was wiser to wage a campaign for the votes of a few men in the state legislature than for those of the many thousands of ill-informed voters in a statewide referendum. Each advised that women must not push too many reforms at one time; Duniway taught co-workers that they must "be careful lest, in their zeal to accomplish too many reforms all at once, they make their fire too hot and by so doing jeopardize their own enfranchisement."[16] Anthony and Duniway agreed that the primary goal of the woman's movement was equal suffrage, but in the 1890s each employed her own tactics to attain it.

Their disagreements did not amount to much prior to 1896. An Anthony biographer contends that Duniway was one of the state leaders who became "alienated and hostile."[17] This generalization is too sweeping. After a twenty-five year association the noted women became somewhat critical of each other, but the Portlander was never hostile towards her old teacher. Since 1871 Anthony probably had cautioned Duniway on occasion to be less combative and caustic and to be more cooperative. At a meeting in 1889 they had argued over the advisability of linking suffrage and prohibition. Duniway concluded from her experience in the Pacific Northwest that men would vote against woman's suffrage because they feared that if women voted they would support laws prohibiting alcoholic beverages. She warned against teaming the two reforms, but suffragists with a background in the Woman's Christian Temperance Union (WCTU) strongly disagreed. Ever since temperance leader Frances E. Willard came to the Pacific Northwest in 1883 to inspire existing groups (called unions) and to establish new ones, the WCTU had been an active social and political force. Some of Willard's supporters proclaimed that her suffragist arguments convinced the Washington legislature to grant the vote to women. It is a debatable generalization, but there is no doubt about the fact that after 1883 hundreds of WCTU members in western Washington championed their enfranchisement.

Duniway, however, railed at those who combined suffrage and prohibition. She became livid when reading some political pronouncements of regional WCTU officers. For example, in 1891 a Washington State president had predicted that when "the right of suffrage (is) restored to women, she will be admitted into the Prohibition Party as an active member, and thus men and women will form a power strong enough to answer the prayers of an oppressed people and accomplish the annihilation of the liquor traffic."[18] Duniway must have quoted such writings to Anthony and others, insisting that such sentiments frightened men into voting against equal suffrage.

Anthony, who believed that the WCTU could be a useful ally, chided Duniway for her certitude. Undoubtedly Anthony reminded Duniway that in the frustrating South Dakota campaign of 1889-1890 she had struggled to separate the suffrage and the temperance issues. The New Yorker comprehended the basic political fact that an open alliance with the WCTU frightened voters. But Anthony assured that WCTU members might support a suffrage amendment without simultaneously advancing their controversial principles.

Duniway accepted her mentor's view of the WCTU but understood that Anthony and other national officers still disapproved of her for personal and political reasons. Catt stated privately, and probably to Anthony, that "I now believe that Mrs. Duniway is a jealous minded and dangerous woman."[19] In the later 1890s Anthony would never again express the confidence in her colleague that she had demonstrated since the 1870s; in 1896, for example, the national leader instructed the state leader to concentrate on the upcoming Oregon referendum and to stay out of the Idaho suffrage fight, which would be managed by an eastern organizer.[20] It must have been extremely difficult for Duniway to stay clear of a battle where she had long been a leading contender. They would talk at length about Idaho and the WCTU when Anthony visited Portland in 1896.

It should be kept in mind that suffragists, frustrated by continual failures and disagreements over goals, also fervently clashed over tactics, personalities, and power. A famous suffrage leader, Mary A.

Livermore, for example, confided that she nearly left the cause owing to "the rows and wrangles and splits and divisions." Historian Robert Booth Fowler noted rivalry with the NAWSA, including the fact that in 1900 Shaw unsuccessfully competed with Catt for its presidency and explained that "Catt and other NAWSA leaders liked to keep controversy far from the public eye . . . [because] there was a strong norm that harmony was both expected and essential."[21]

In some ways the disagreements between Anthony and Duniway were similar to those between Anthony and Stanton. The national leaders surrounding Anthony often complained to her about Stanton's excesses; they made similar complaints to her about the Oregon leader. Stanton and Duniway were too opinionated and independent for the NAWSA leadership. Controversy among politicians in the same organization is ever present, and it led the New Yorker to lose confidence in the Oregonian. Anthony and Duniway expressed mutual respect and friendship until Anthony's death; during the national leader's 1896 visit the two women cooperated closely and publicly endorsed each other. According to Duniway, by that year Anthony had come to agree with her about the danger of uniting prohibition and suffrage. During the California struggle, Duniway quoted her leader as saying: "I have done all I could to keep the two questions separate. . . . The two movements cannot successfully unite to win for either cause."[22]

Difficulties between these two reformers certainly did not contribute to the fact that the Pacific Northwest's suffrage movement was in the doldrums between 1887 and 1895. Duniway complained that the equal suffrage cause was almost "quiescent," but she did not fault her mentor or other outsiders. The discouraging situation resulted from regional conditions—suffrage defeats in both Oregon and Washington, the inability to organize or mobilize large numbers of sympathizers, the perennial shortage of money for political purposes, and the sale in early 1887 of the *New Northwest*. After surrendering her editorship, Duniway began spending long periods of time in Idaho. In her autobiography, she explained this change: "Seeing that progress in my work for Equal Rights had encountered a blockade in Oregon and Washington, I ceased open activities therein and turned my entire attention to Idaho, where my husband and sons had gone in quest of health and change of climate . . . and were engaged in the stock business."[23] Without a forceful leader, a solid organization, or an inspirational newspaper, the cause suffered in Oregon, Washington, and Idaho, too.

In 1894 and 1895 conditions changed. The Duniway family returned to Portland and Abigail became editor of the *Pacific Empire*, a Portland weekly published by another reformer. Although this publication was smaller and much less forceful and influential than the *New Northwest*, it helped to revive the Pacific Northwest's suffragist movement, which the editor lamented, had seemed to be "a forlorn hope for nearly a decade."[24] Anthony wrote Duniway a warm letter wishing for the newspaper's success and concluding: "I believe you love scribbling with your pen better than [any] other person I know."[25] Duniway, upon her return, aided other women in establishing the Oregon State Equal Suffrage Association (OSESA); this group organized reformers, especially members of Willamette Valley women's clubs and societies. In Oregon, Washington, and Idaho both educated and organized women expressed a new willingness to soldier for suffrage. In 1895 the Oregon legislature responded to increased suffragist pressure and approved a measure that would allow men—once again—to ballot on woman's suffrage. The referendum, originally scheduled for 1897, was delayed until 1900. Demonstrating her old energy and combative spirit, Duniway prepared for the fight, urging members of a local suffrage organization to join Portland's new woman's club, "where they could meet the women who had not yet become suffragist, but who would gradually become such without proselytizing by mere fact of association."[26]

Optimistic about their chances, Oregon women in 1896 urged Anthony and other eastern leaders to take time from their California struggle and help them launch their northern one. Washington women, too, began preparing for a referendum contest. They brought Duniway to Seattle and Olympia to mobilize members and told her that they desired Anthony to campaign in Washington as well as in Oregon. Inspired by her California accomplishments, especially the endorsements won from diverse politicians and editors, Oregon and Washington activists predicted that Anthony could do much to rejuvenate their reform movement. She had been called from San Francisco in 1871 to launch a campaign; in 1896 she was summoned to help revive it. Conditions differed in 1896 in that Anthony was not needed to introduce the rudiments of the suffrage movement as she had in 1871. Citizens had become more knowledgeable, especially from the energetic efforts of Duniway. While small suffrage groups (most met in western Oregon and Washington) needed the publicity that would inevitably follow from Anthony's appearance, she was primarily required—Duniway especially advocated this—to mobilize club women and other supporters for the forthcoming state suffrage contests and to teach the political tactics being employed in California. Nobody concluded that Anthony alone could win Pacific Northwest political battles, but reformers agreed that she could recruit thoughtful and often prominent women. She was required as much in 1896 as in 1871 because, after twenty-five years of intermittent effort, regional suffragists were little closer to success. With the Colorado victory only three years past and promising campaigns currently being waged in California and Idaho, Oregon and Washington reformers assured themselves that with outside assistance from Anthony and the NAWSA coupled with a renewed state effort their hour was not so distant.

NINE

# *Revival of the Regional Suffrage Movement*

DURING THIS SECOND REGIONAL VISIT, Anthony saw much less of the Pacific Northwest than she had observed twenty-five years earlier. The comforts of rail travel between Ashland and Seattle must have reminded her of the hardships of the 1871 campaign, and she commented on both rural and urban growth. She was aware of the region's great population increase that began around 1883 when the Northern Pacific provided the first transcontinental rail service.[1] For the next ten years Oregon and Washington experienced spectacular growth; the boosters' predictions to Anthony and everyone else in 1871 had been realized. The census figures recorded a major population increase:

| | OREGON | WASHINGTON | PORTLAND | SEATTLE |
|---|---|---|---|---|
| 1880 | 174,768 | 75,116 | 17,577 | 3,553 |
| 1890 | 313,767 | 349,390 | 46,385 | 42,837 |

The 1893 depression ended the boom; the Pacific Northwest, like the rest of the nation, suffered from the economic reversal.

In 1896, as in 1871, Anthony was curious about the region's politics, economics, and society. Urban dwellers informed her that the immigrants who had contributed to the region's boom were hard workers from the Midwest and from Northwestern Europe. Unlike some other regions, Pacific Northwest residents were not damning immigrants from

Southeastern Europe because these groups were not entering the region in large enough numbers to be of concern. Regional newspapers, still carried negative accounts about Chinese and Indians. In the 1880s there had been a bitter debate over the Chinese, who had been the victims of unemployed workers. *Oregonian* editor Harvey Scott's remarks about the Chinese were perhaps typical. "They are not a particularly desirable people and are subject to the usual criticism and strictures that apply to man in his natural state."[2] Scott emphasized that they were valuable because they performed laundering, housework, land-clearing, and other unpleasant tasks.

Anthony was also reminded that the region's cities still competed with each other to attract immigrants, trade, and investments as they had in 1871. She could have read the Seattle *Post-Intelligencer*'s comparison of Oregon and Washington: "the makeup of the two states is totally different. We are progressive, they are backward; we move ahead, they lag behind; we speak out, they dodge behind meaningless sentences . . . we say what we mean, they say what nobody means. . . . they are for Populists, we are for Republicanism."[3] *Oregonian* editor Harvey Scott saw it differently, insisting that Portland builders "were men and women of a morality, religious conviction and sturdy force of character not exceeded by any class of people in America."[4]

All visible evidence of regional growth and all talk about the great boom of the 1880s and early 1890s was tempered by the fact that in 1896 the Pacific Northwest was still recovering from an economic depression. Conditions had improved and residents rejoiced over signs of an improved economy, but the region had not returned to the flush days of the late 1880s and early 1890s. A Seattleite recalled the booming year of 1891 "when money may be said to have flowed like water and the whole Puget Sound region was undergoing a reign of prosperity."[5] The city directories, traditional voices of boosterism, had become subdued in the mid-1890s. A Portland edition admitted that for several years it had been "ominously silent as to future prospects" and acknowledged little progress during the business depression.[6] Seattle's directory admitted that the city had not escaped "the depression in business" and that in the 1890s "people were wont to go about looking down along their noses" because the "trade and commerce were discouraging."[7] Both Portland and Seattle publications took solace, however, in the fact that their population losses were less than feared. (In early 1896 Duniway had visited Seattle and observed that the city had "suffered severely from the financial panic that left her with a formidable array of empty, mortgage laden buildings as a luckless inheritance." She reported that residents were learning "economy and thrift" and that "the recuperative power of the vigorous young West is as noticeable here as elsewhere in our borders.")[8]

Some leaders explained that the Pacific Northwest did not want another boom but instead favored steady and substantial growth. Portland and Seattle, as well as smaller places, hoped to attract factories and foreign trade. Despite the spectacular population increase of the 1880s, the Pacific Northwest still believed it needed residents and continued to encourage settlement by additional families. In making their appeals, some boosters gave the current economic hardships scant attention; in fact, in 1896 a regional immigration board published a pamphlet that sounded as positive as the message that Anthony had heard twenty-five years earlier.

> There is no section of the United States which should . . . attract such universal attention as the Pacific Northwest, not alone that it has vast areas of fertile and cheap agriculture lands, offering comfortable homes to millions of home-seekers, that its rich mines, vast forests and many other resources offer safe investment for capital, nor yet that it adds to these the advantage of an exceptionally fine climate, but also that it is the last and only remaining great section of the United States, which is a new country, and offers those opportunities which are alone offered by a new country in process of settlement and development, and that the building of the Nicaragua canal, now assured for the near future, will double the value of its every resource.[9]

Anthony brought her political message to Oregonians just as they argued over the results of a recent state election. From her experience in California, Anthony understood that politics were far more important in 1896 than they had been in 1871. Elections continued to be exciting occasions for leaders and followers in the 1890s as they had been in the 1870s, but 1896 was a particularly significant year. Because of growth in Portland and Seattle, city politics had acquired some of the unsavory aspects characteristic of politics in older cities to the east. But politicians stressed state over urban politics. The continuing depression and the great battle over the free silver issue created intense political excitement. For years there had been a bitter debate in the nation over the coinage of silver. Those who mined it (joined by inflationists) advocated the use of both gold and silver as the monetary standard of currency. Advocates of the gold standard, on the other hand, feared that the unlimited silver coinage would destroy the value of the dollar. In 1893 Democratic President Grover Cleveland got Congress to repeal the Sherman Silver Purchase Act, a decision that alienated western Democrats. The traditional struggle between Democrats and Republicans, the controversy between Republicans who favored silver coinage against those who did not, and the Populist Party's efforts to become a major political force all intensified Pacific Northwest politics in 1896. In Portland and Seattle, Anthony heard or read such political terms as "political rings," "demagoguery," "bossism," "silverloons," "silver barons," "gold bugs," and "gold barons." All of this was part of a great controversy over bimetallism, which, many politicians explained, boiled down to the old struggle between debtors and creditors.

The Oregon election of June 1896 had attracted unusual national attention. Not since the great controversy of the state's role in the presidential election of 1876 had so many evaluated and commented upon the state's election returns. Oregon's political contest was looked upon as an early round in a great national fight between Republicans, Democrats, and Populists. Here, as in other states, Republicans—the majority party—had split over the gold standard, as a sizable faction of Silver Republicans bolted the party. The conservative *Oregonian* blamed this harmful division on "greed, treachery and betrayal."[10]

Besides the rift in the state's major party, many spoke about the vigorous campaign waged by Oregon Populists whose candidates angrily blamed the wealthy for the depression and insisted that only their party would protect the peoples' interests and resolve the nation's economic problems. Populists, in opposition to the Republicans, championed the silver standard as the way to increase the money supply. In Oregon, as would happen nationally, some Democrats and Populists fused behind county or city candidates. In these yeasty Oregon politics, national Populist champions, including James Weaver, Jacob Coxey, James A. Sovereign and others brought the Populist doctrine to Pacific

Northwest audiences. Sovereign, a leader of the Knights of Labor and an officer of the Populist Party, delivered hardhitting talks for free silver, decried the "money power," and recruited Pacific Northwest laborers to his party's standard.

Visiting and local politicians also debated important issues besides bimetallism, including the protective tariff and immigration restriction. Continuing his role as political teacher, Scott warned the electorate: "The confusion of parties and politics in Oregon is greater than ever before in the history of the state."[11] He worried that voters confused by complicated economic issues would be victims of demagogues. Bitter disagreement intensified all the customary political rituals: hard-hitting newspaper editorials, torchlight parades, political oratory, band music, and excited sidewalk arguments. One colorful Portland parade featured two hundred fifty twenty-one-year-old marchers carrying banners declaring they would cast their first ballot for the Republican candidates. This event attracted parents and friends; a male's first ballot, all suffragists knew, was important to him, family, and friends as a political rite of passage.

On 1 June the campaigning ended and the voting took place. It was a surprisingly quiet election day as voters chose from a lengthy ballot, headlined by candidates for two congressional spots, the state legislature, and the Portland mayoralty.

With upcoming California politics in her mind, Anthony read and heard in Portland that every political party denounced the election returns. Angered by the fact that they had narrowly lost the two congressional elections, Populists conducted fiery protest meetings, where leaders shouted that political schemers had cheated them out of victories. Republican regulars groused about the party split that had allowed an apostate, William R. Ellis, to be elected as a silver congressman; the silver wing worried about its future because the regulars retained control of the state legislature and would choose a gold senator in the next election. Democrats had not fared well and feared the rising Populist Party. Many political observers growled that the ignorant electorate had nearly chosen Populist Martin Quinn to Congress. Quinn, a self-educated Portland laundry driver, they moaned, would have embarrassed himself and his state if elected. Some acknowledged that "the fact that a man can leave the driver's seat of a laundry wagon and drop into an upholstered chair in the halls of Congress shows the possibilities of

American citizenship."[12] The Portland *Telegram* had reported that Quinn jumped "from the obscurity of an $11 a week job, handling soiled linen, to the proud eminence of representing the state."[13] Perhaps when Anthony and Duniway huddled they grumbled that Oregon women, who had a much better education than Quinn, could not even vote much less run for Congress.

Observers at the national and regional level pondered the Oregon election returns seeking evidence that its citizens supported the free coinage of silver. The Seattle *Post-Intelligencer* maintained Republican factionalism was disastrous for the region, as it forfeited its leadership position and allowed Populism "to raise its head with the prospect of making Oregon once more the laughing stock of the whole country."[14]

All Oregon politicians considered the implications of the recently concluded state election and planned strategy for the fall's presidential election. Many, arguing that men had voted illegally, concluded that the election demonstrated the need for a registration law. Republicans emphasized another unfortunate consequence of the June election: an old foe, ex-Governor Sylvester Pennoyer, was elected as Portland's mayor by Democrats and Populists. This prompted a fear that the Populist would succeed from this office to the United States Senate. One critic insisted that Pennoyer's victory meant that the city proclaimed "to the world its possession of a spirit of asininity at a time when . . . wisdom is so badly needed by it."[15]

Thus the recent election results consumed enormous attention and undoubtedly detracted from Anthony's efforts. In California, as well as the Pacific Northwest, there was, Anthony complained, a "frantic free silver whirl" that kept men from attending suffrage meetings. To give her campaigners an opportunity to reach voters she proposed that they appear at political meetings and make a short appeal "usually after all of the party orators have exhausted themselves, and the audiences, too."[16]

The national questions of silver, immigration, protectionism, depression, disagreements with Spain over Cuba, and local problems—such as labor difficulties and transportation needs—were all more significant to Pacific Northwest opinion makers than the reform that the New Yorker advanced. It seemed inappropriate to squander attention on the merits of the enfranchisement of women; in other words, the region's men were repeating what the nation had said to suffragists in the Reconstruction period—this was not the time to push their reform. In the late 1860s as well as the late 1890s politicians often informed suffragists that the resolution of complicated and pressing political problems was not to be found in the addition of thousands of more uneducated voters.

When Anthony made her initial visit to the Pacific Northwest she confronted problems of frontier development; during her second one the region faced industrial difficulties. An example of the latter attracted attention in both states: Columbia River fishermen had struck canneries and violence ensued. The Washington National Guard had been summoned to keep the peace on the river's north bank. On the Oregon side fishermen, who had struck canneries at or near Astoria, complained that it was grossly unfair to cut the prices of salmon from five to four cents a pound. Packers hotly disagreed, insisting that competition with Alaska producers meant that they could not pay what the union demanded. Fishermen rejected this argument, insisting that cannery owners made substantial enough profits to maintain the five cent price. The murder of a nonstriking fisherman, the destruction of nets and boats, the appearance of armed nonunion fishermen at fishing sites, and rumors of arson received considerable newspaper coverage prior to and during Anthony's visit. There was a running argument among Oregonians over whether the governor should send national guardsmen to the lower river. The *Oregonian* urged such action, complaining that "irresponsible wandering Greeks and Russian Finns" belonging to the union terrorized honest nonunion fishermen. The newspaper advised: "Cannerymen should protect such men, and not give out gear to tramps who are here today and gone tomorrow, and who are not American citizens."[17] Because it concluded that "the river fisheries are in something like a state of siege," that "armed ruffians" had murdered fishermen, and that there was a danger of more violence, the *Oregonian* urged militia deployment.[18] Other opinion makers disagreed, accusing the newspaper of inflaming the situation. The Portland *Telegram* said that the assignment of guardsmen would waste taxpayers' money and would only serve to provide young men with a summer outing. The editor acknowledged that "Life and property have been destroyed," but concluded that "The Oregon National Guard was organized and is maintained to contend with bodies of lawbreakers, not to perform detective duty or to pursue individual criminals."[19]

There was another political side to the dispute. Some Republicans charged that the fishermen had struck at the behest of local Populists; leaders of the fisherman's union conceded that most of its members supported the Populists but denied party boss control. Anthony was aware of these bitter labor disputes, but she knew that it would not advance her cause to voice an opinion. Supporters of Portland's Woman's Congress understood that the labor agitation on the lower Columbia detracted attention from feminist agitation on the lower Willamette.

Politics in the spring of 1896 absorbed unusual attention, but it did not consume life. From all over the Pacific Northwest there were vigorous complaints about the wettest May in memory. Anthony learned that farmers and gardeners speculated about the rain's impact on wheat, roses, and other plants.

Another group, bicyclists, also grumbled about the miserable weather. When Anthony visited in 1871 the Pacific Northwest was enjoying an ice-skating craze; in 1896 there was a so-called "bicycle mania." Just prior to her Portland arrival, Anthony, in a widely publicized interview, gave her opinion of the sport: "I think it has done more to emancipate woman than any one thing in the world. I rejoice every time I see a woman ride by on a wheel. It gives her a feeling of self-reliance and independence the moment she takes her seat; and away she goes, the picture of untrammelled womanhood."[20] She would see these emancipated females enjoying the sport everywhere in the Pacific Northwest, where writers emphasized the significance of bicycling. A Portlander asserted that it was "the greatest pastime of the century."[21] Everywhere cities drew up ordinances that restricted sidewalk riding, required lights and bells on bicycles, and set speed limits; for example, in Seattle no cyclist might travel faster than ten miles per hour. Bicyclists formed clubs to promote better roads, excursions, races, instruction on riding and maintenance, and road courtesy. Careless cyclists injured themselves and pedestrians both; women and men called reckless riders "idiots," "scorchers," or "mashers." One writer summarized that "the devotee to the wheel is, like any other devotee to pleasure, selfish in the prosecution of his desire."[22] Fearing injury, some expressed the hope that the so-called "spidery wheel" would only be a fad; farmers worried that the bicycle, like the electric streetcar, was replacing the horse and the inability to sell horses and horse feed reduced their income. An

Oregon farm publication editorialized on "The Passing of the Horse," noting these changing market conditions and asserting that bicycle races were taking money that had previously gone "to support horse-racing events."[23] Others also speculated about the future: a Seattle editor believed that the "bicycle masher" needed to be punished; if not, then "respectable girls" would not bicycle for exercise.[24] Some female bicyclists complained not only about scorchers but also about dogs that chased them. Some wags recommended that women carry a pistol in their bloomers, a costume that Anthony thought appropriate for women cyclists. An *Oregonian* reporter said that those who did not want to fire a pistol should have a large bloomer pocket "big enough to carry a real bulldog in, which will, in short order, chew up the curs which run after them."[25]

Perhaps the bicycle craze as well as political and economic conditions were topics of conversation on 5 June when Anthony visited Abigail Scott Duniway's home in Portland. The national and regional leaders evaluated indicators of the status of local women, including suffragism, the new women's clubs, the WCTU, marriage, divorce,and the condition of working women. Females continued to be underpaid and restricted to such traditional professions as school teaching.[26] In the 1890s female teachers suffered from a competitive market and feared losing reappointments. Only a few females had entered traditionally male professions, but Drs. Mary A. Thompson and Bethenia Owens-Adair—two suffragists who had supported Anthony during her first visit—practiced medicine and pushed various reforms. Classified advertisements must have discouraged Seattle and Portland female job seekers; most positions were for cooks and housekeepers. The status of the region's urban women in the 1890s depression was worse than it had been in frontier days. Duniway must have emphasized that though regional newspapers gave much more attention to her sex in the 1890s than in the past, the Sunday society pages described fashion, cooking, and home furnishings rather than the secondary status of women.

Abigail told Susan about the career and death of her daughter Clara ten years earlier, the marriages and careers of her five sons (Anthony praised Clyde for doctoral work in history at Harvard), her exile on an Idaho ranch, her financial problems, and her present concern about her husband's deteriorating health. Ben would be dead a few weeks after Anthony left the Duniway home.

Anthony, in turn, stressed the great struggle that she, NAWSA leaders, and local suffragists waged in the well-publicized California fight. She probably confided to her friend that she disliked being away from her Rochester home and in California for most of a year and that she engaged in "the cruelest thing in the world—that the men of each state make their women go down on their knees to each individual man and beg him to vote to let them vote!" Despite the fact that suffragists had difficulty raising money, the veteran politician anticipated victory, in part because three major political parties endorsed her cause and because eastern and western suffragists labored harmoniously in converting male opinion. Impressed with all that had been accomplished in California, Duniway had written her leader after the Republican Party endorsement: "Your triumphs in California are marvelous. Hurrah, and again hurrah! I believe now the women of the Golden State will win. All honor to you and your noble confrers!"[27]

While the two reformers agreed upon the California referendum campaign, they very much disagreed upon the one being waged in Idaho. In 1895 the NAWSA planned the Idaho fight, sending one of its most capable political leaders, Carrie Chapman Catt, to investigate the political situation and to take charge of field work. The association also wanted Idahoans to see Catt and thereby learn that a national suffrage organizer was not a "short-haired woman with bloomers."[28]

Anthony, who was greatly impressed with Catt's administrative ability and energy, was glad to give a younger woman control of arranging state campaigns. The two political planners must have spent considerable time conversing over the Idaho situation, especially over Duniway's suitability as their Idaho lieutenant. They understood that the Oregonian, who knew many Idahoans, wanted to lead them. Catt reported that she had heard that Duniway "was very unpopular and without influence" in Idaho and Portland.[29] The WCTU and Mormons had both expressed criticism of her, but even more damaging, as Catt wrote, the national group was "down on her [because] she talks all the time, and is always making out that she is neglected." Catt acknowledged that Anthony liked Duniway but would deny her the position of "chairman of the committee on campaign" because the NAWSA officers wanted to conduct a well organized fight in Idaho. This campaign also revealed operational differences between the association and Duniway. Catt, probably speaking for the national leadership wrote: "One great cause of our failure has been that nearly every association has a quarrel on and they are divided as to what they want to do. . . . We are split up into a dozen factions, each thinking it knows best what ought to be done."[30] Catt summed up the problem; "We say we need money, but we need something far more, and it's how to bury the individual in the organization. Until that art is learned we are doomed to disappointment."

Duniway was the last person capable of being buried in an organization. She was too independent; furthermore, she expressed hostility to eastern efforts to organize western states. It was her opinion that outside organization had led to a Kansas defeat and that non-organization had meant success in Colorado. She predicted defeat if Emma Smith DeVoe, a field representative of the NAWSA, tried to organize Idaho's women the way the association proposed. Such views rankled the NAWSA leaders, including Anthony. The national group concluded that Duniway wanted "to be at the head of things herself" and that Idaho women willingly cooperated with them. After unsuccessfully attempting to resolve political differences with Duniway, Catt bluntly concluded: "I shall . . . never again trust" her.[31] Understanding that Idaho needed "tactful management," the NAWSA in 1895 assigned another skilled worker, DeVoe. The following year the national group sent Mrs. Laura M. Johns to help organize suffrage clubs, to lecture, and to work with political leaders. DeVoe and Johns won considerable support from opinion makers and the public. Historian T.A. Larson judged that Catt sent DeVoe instead of Duniway to Idaho because she feared that Duniway would rile the WCTU and because the Oregon leader "had cast her lot with the Republican party, whereas the national leadership thought it wise to avoid identification with any one party."[32]

Duniway had definite ideas about how to win the Idaho suffrage fight and wanted to participate. At the NAWSA's 1895 convention she had delivered her opinions on political tactics and on her return from the convention had stopped in Boise to help organize suffragists. In Portland Duniway reminded Anthony of her reform activities in Idaho and her basic convictions: western women were more willing to work with a western leadership rather than with the eastern dominated NAWSA; furthermore, Duniway's long involvement in Idaho meant that she should play a significant part in the campaign's final months. The Portlander reminded her mentor that for nearly twenty years she had labored for the enfranchisement of Idaho women, pleading with politicians, distributing thousands of copies of the *New Northwest*, and traveling 12,000 miles by "river, rail, stage, and buckboard."[33]

Anthony remained unconvinced. She firmly advised her friend not to participate in the Idaho fight. Hurt by this admonition, Duniway bluntly told her old teacher that Idaho sympathizers did not want the national organization to send workers. Although she acknowledged that there was truth to this charge, Anthony reminded that Idaho suffragists had frequently asked her to campaign. She explained her refusal by emphasizing that the California fight was more important, for if it joined the ranks of suffragist states then less populated ones would soon fall into line. The NAWSA president added that she had preferred to return to Oregon and Washington to help launch a renewed suffrage campaign than to take time to speak in Idaho where the suffragists were so "cranky."

During their discussion of Idaho politics, Duniway remembered: "I said to Miss Anthony, 'What would you think of the irony of Fate, if Idaho wins and California loses?' She answered, 'Impossible! California is managed by our trained workers from the East.'"[34] The New Yorker also made it clear that it was difficult to leave her crucial California campaign and that Oregon must not be in the habit of calling her to battle for equal rights. "Wendell Phillips," she recalled, "used to say that the people used to treat him as they did the town pump. All they had to do to the pump was to lift the handle and the water came. So you seem to think of me in Oregon."[35]

Anthony's and Duniway's disagreements over control of the Idaho campaign and later over the reasons for the 1896 California defeat would eventually influence the management of the Oregon suffrage movement. In August, Anthony dispatched her trusted lieutenant, Catt, to Boise, where she played a critical role as speaker and organizer. Angered by the fact that an eastern officer had been picked over her to work with Idaho suffragists, Duniway found some solace in an invitation to lecture in the 1896 California fight. The fact that the reform indeed prevailed in Idaho and failed in California led the Portlander to tell her mentor and others that California suffragists complained that they might have won the election if they had not been dominated by eastern leaders. Duniway also incorrectly assumed that these outsiders would not invade her "bailiwick . . . except by invitation."[36] Anthony, who had conducted an exhausting campaign, disliked Duniway's criticism of her tactics. But whatever their disagreements in June 1896 the two women cooperated so as to assure that her second regional visit, especially her work in the Oregon Congress, advanced their reform. The public was unaware of their differences. Anthony and Duniway had agreed—as Anthony and Stanton had years earlier—that public squabbling would hurt their cause.

After a day's stimulating and wide-ranging conversation with Abigail, Susan went by rail to Seattle. In the absence of any suffragist organization there, the Woman's Century Club sponsored the two-day campaign. In accepting her invitation, Anthony wrote, "I shall be very glad to go to Seattle, Tacoma, and Olympia, for I would love to see that beautiful Puget Sound once more."[37] Time restraints made sightseeing impossible: the Century Club worked out a busy schedule—she lectured and conversed at length with sympathizers and potential political workers. Organized in 1891, the club explained that it "had its inception in the minds of a half dozen women who felt its need in the sordid atmosphere of a rapidly developing western city."[38] Its stated purpose in 1896 was "to promote the intellectual growth of its members, to stimulate investigation in social and political ethics and to lend its influence toward the solution of the altruistic problems of the day." Members presented diverse papers on relevant topics including suffrage, municipal reform, temperance, domestic and foreign politics, woman's progress, political economy, music, art, and literature.

On the day of Anthony's arrival, the Seattle *Post-Intelligencer* publicized her visit. Taking material from other newspapers, it compiled biographical information, emphasizing her suffrage efforts. The account stated that public opinion had changed since the early 1850s when the New Yorker began her struggle on behalf of her sex and proceeded to evaluate her dress and lecture style: "Latterly Miss Anthony has changed her austere ideas about dress. She delights in rich, becoming raiment, and is a picture in her silks and laces. She likes to have all her fellow workers equally fastidious and criticizes radical attempts at 'reform' dressing in their public meetings."[39] The campaigner also told the reporter that "I can't write a speech out. I must have an audience to inspire me. When I am before a house filled with people I can speak, but to save my life I couldn't write a speech."

Arriving early in the morning, Anthony was hosted in the home of Mrs. Kate Turner Holmes, the wife of a prominent druggist, and a well-educated proponent of kindergartens—she called them "the very foundation stones of good citizenship." Seattleites came to call; Anthony particularly enjoyed reminiscing with John F. Damon, a Congregational minister who had in 1871 introduced her to a Seattle audience. In the evening the Century Club held a reception in the guest's honor attended by members and invited guests, including Mrs. Mark W. Harrington, wife of the president of the University of Washington, and at least one female university student.

Following the reception, a *Post-Intelligencer* reporter interviewed Anthony. He described her appearance:

> She is not by any means handsome, but is certainly a remarkable looking woman. Her face is long, thin and very pale. Her eyes, while apparently expressionless, have an elusive something in their depths that compels attention. Straight locks of snow-white hair, parted in the middle and falling down over her ears gives her a resemblance to an old family portrait. . . . This impression was heightened by the rich though slightly old-fashioned black gown she wore.[40]

Although she appeared fatigued at the interview's start, the reporter noted that Anthony perked up while retelling events of the woman's suffrage movement. The reformer chided Washington for being "a back number" or "dead" state ever since its women lost the franchise. She talked about how she, Anna Shaw, and others were fighting to convert California to equal suffrage. In discussing the political tactics employed to attain this great objective, she underscored the importance of having the state's political parties endorse woman's suffrage. Anthony explained, "with such a plank in the platform, speakers can address meetings in favor of woman suffrage in the coming campaign, and as they will be advocating the acknowledged principles of the party they cannot be stopped."

In 1896 as in her first visit Anthony did more than talk about herself and her cause. In personal conversations or in group discussions she asked Seattle women about their views of economic, political, and social conditions. There was probably a general discussion about the status of working women, including teachers, domestics, prostitutes, and others. There must have been discussions about specific groups or individuals.

Undoubtedly she learned of the recent death of Angeline, the daughter of Chief Seattle, as editors, ministers, educators, and other opinion makers made frequent reference to this strong-willed Indian woman. The Seattle *Times*, explained that "She was by common consent regarded as representative of the era which has forever passed away, and her life was a protest and not always a silent one against the new order of things."[41] The writer predicted that "It will take time to regenerate the Siwash, but time and new ideas will do it." Anthony and her visitors must have exchanged ideas about the controversial subject of divorce and expressed disgust with the details of a current case in which a woman separated from a husband who "repeatedly urged upon her to enter upon a life of shame, and thus support him in idleness."[42] Anthony's callers acknowledged the long-standing prostitution problem and probably made reference to an editor who argued that because it could not be eliminated from Seattle, officials should restrict "disreputable women" to a designated district.[43] In discussions about the double standard of morality, Seattle ladies could refer to a recent adultery case that had prompted a thoughtful *Post-Intelligencer* editorial. "There is ruin," the editor judged, "for the woman; the man gets off scott free, and that is the end of it. The woman should not escape the consequences of folly, but the man should suffer no less for the sin."[44] Undoubtedly Anthony sympathized with the wife and repeated in Seattle what she had said twenty-five years earlier—the double standard resulted from the excessive power of men. A unique problem was probably brought to Anthony's attention: a federal official had ordered the deportation of several Japanese girls, who were, he ruled, brought into the country in violation of the contract labor laws. Claiming to be domestics, not prostitutes, the girls protested the decision by hours of "hysterical wailing" that unnerved inmates in the King County jail.[45]

Surely in Seattle and elsewhere, residents complained to Anthony about medical quacks who advertised extensively in major newspapers. Females often fell prey to these charlatans. At about the time of Anthony's visit Professor W. Fletcher Hall, who spoke on the "physical life of woman from the cradle to the grave . . . and all the conditions necessary to that highest early good-home and domestic joy," would appear on the stage with Hermann the Healer, who claimed to have the ability "to cure the deaf, lame, palsied, paralytic, and rheumatic by the laying on of hands."[46] The popular Dr. Sanden, too, would be in town, proclaiming that women could be restored to good health, not by medicines, but by wearing his electric belt.

Interviews and conversations gave Anthony a chance to teach and learn, but her lecture was the featured part of her Puget Sound visit. She appeared at the Seattle Theater, a site for many lectures and entertainers, which was currently advertising a performance by actor Eddie Foy in "The Strange Adventures of Miss Brown." Anthony's lecture tickets sold for fifty cents, the same fee she had charged twenty-five years earlier. The Century Club decorated the theater tastefully; the club's president, Annie M. Brown, gave the introduction. According to the *Post-Intelligencer*, the speaker chose to stand during her entire ninety minute talk. The newspaper introduced its coverage by reminding that Anthony's "unselfish efforts in behalf of her sex were heartily derided for a couple of generations but whose lifework now commands respect and admiration" even from those who were unwilling to endorse "the lessons of her mission."[47] To the reporter's surprise the famous speaker did not draw as large an audience as anticipated and very few men attended. The extemporaneous speech "was so thoroughly interesting that the silence which it commanded was rarely broken, even by applause."

In her lecture she probably made about the same points that she published in the San Francisco *Examiner*. To win the support of the educated women in the audience she reminded them that the powerful trusts and corporations, unlike women, influenced "the ballot box" and that city and state governments had both failed "in the management of the dependent, defective and delinquent" classes.[48] Thus drunkards, criminals, and paupers had become a public responsibility. Anthony stressed that "in a great measure it falls to the lot of women to care for the unfortunate victims, the deserted wives, the betrayed girls, the abandoned children. Men have the sole power over the condition which produce these wrecks, and then the women are called in to repair the damages." She predicted that if women influenced a state legislature it would result in better schools, safer streets, and improved prisons.

Her talk, like many of her interviews, consisted largely of reminiscences, and Anthony boldly stated that she did not enjoy any more rights in 1896 than she did when she joined the movement nearly a half century earlier. "I am working," she continued, "for my unfortunate sisters who have taken to themselves the luxury of husbands." Anthony explained how useful the vote had been to various groups—a theme that had been emphasized in 1871. The suffragist acknowledged the meaningful benefits for women obtained from the New York legislature but insisted that her sex would have enjoyed even greater gains had it been enfranchised. She complained about the conservatism of New York, Pennsylvania, and Massachusetts; this attitude led suffragist leaders to turn to the West. They hoped to achieve two goals in the region: to help enfranchise women and to enlist their Congressmen in support of the proposed Sixteenth Amendment. She expressed disappointment that Washington males had rejected equal suffrage and urged another state vote on the issue. In summary, she wanted referenda elections in each Pacific Coast state.

A male listener stated that he had heard Anthony's 1871 Seattle address and commented, "Wonderful woman; hasn't changed in any way since she was here last." Following her talk Anthony stayed in a hotel, not a private home, because she feared missing her 4 A.M. train to Portland.

While the campaigner wearily journeyed south, her Seattle supporters awaited the editorial response to the speech. The *Post-Intelligencer* generally interpreted controversial speakers, and the New Yorker was no exception. Thus far this newspaper, the most influential one in the state, had been fair in its reportorial coverage, but an editorial exasperated her allies. The writer failed to meet Anthony's major points and provided only a rambling rebuttal to the argument for woman's suffrage. The editorial praised local women for their business acumen and "power for good"[49] then repeated a traditional argument:

> The reluctance most men have to seeing women enter the political arena is that they still idealize her, and prefer to see her queen of the home, the wife, sister, mother and daughter, bringing to each capacity a potentiality which man even as a voter falls far short of, and expanding in a delightful world of her own, into whose sanctity men gladly enters [*sic*] with relief from those turgid experiences from which domestic woman is now happily free.

The editor's historical interpretation explained that "While men hunted and fought and fished and gambled with pebbles, she became the architect of the home, the decorator of the walls, the designer of fancy ornaments in shells and berries, and the originator of the potter's art." The editor reasoned that women without the vote could still attain their ends through "her domination of man, and if she is of the temperament or caliber which does not dominate him, her vote would only be another weapon in his hands."

Although the *Post-Intelligencer*, a Republican voice, editorially repeated views similar to those it had enunciated ten years earlier, suffragists preferred its response over that of the Seattle *Times*, a newspaper that claimed to be politically independent. The *Post-Intelligencer* had acknowledged the speaker through news stories and an editorial. The *Times*, on the other hand, had only announced her visit and encouraged readers to attend her lecture because, as it correctly predicted, she would not give another in Seattle. But it, like other regional newspapers, did not report her talk. The Tacoma *Ledger*, for example, had joined the Olympia *Standard* in publishing favorable suffrage editorials. However, these friendly journals ignored Anthony's Seattle lecture. The *Ledger* surprisingly did not mention the speaker's attempt to revive the cause—one that the editor endorsed. After encouraging women by reminding them that their struggle had led to partial suffrage in several states, he advanced the increasingly popular argument that women voters would help contribute to "the safety of the nation" because "government would be better and purer with woman suffrage than without it."[50] The editor sought to strengthen his opinion by reminding that in 1890 Washington had 443 male and only 4 female prisoners, "And yet," he complained, "we have disfranchised the women."

Anthony left Puget Sound with the belief that there was little chance for immediate success in Washington because her backers lacked leadership and organization. Furthermore, the public was indifferent. To her way of thinking it made more sense to concentrate her forces in California and Oregon, but Washington, which seemed so unpromising in 1896, would surprise the nation in 1910.

On Sunday morning, 7 June Anthony returned to Portland, granted a newspaper interview, and became the house guest of Abigail and Ben Duniway, who invited their sons and daughters-in-law for dinner and an evening's conversation about her 1871 and 1896 visits. No doubt everyone rejoiced over the current issue of the *Oregonian*, which publicized the Woman's Congress and published biographical sketches of Anthony and her Portland allies. The newspaper correctly explained that "The congress is not, nor is it intended to be, a woman-suffrage organization, but an independent federation of all societies in which women alone, or men and women together, are organized on planes of perfect equality and genuine good fellowship."[51] The account maintained that the visitor had a worldwide "reputation as a leader of women's hosts" and that she and Duniway agreed that the cause of women was necessarily the cause of men. To further publicize the event, the newspaper provided illustrations of the Portland ladies who would serve as officers of the Oregon Congress, and it also furnished the entire program for the three-day, nine-session event.

Acknowledged everywhere as the most influential newspaper in the Pacific Northwest, the *Oregonian* carried even more information on the day the congress convened. Its coverage included a thoughtful interview with the principal speaker. A reporter praised Anthony's political acumen: "She is thoroughly well informed on all political topics, and is as familiar with the workings of national, state, and county political machinery as is the author [James Bryce] of the *American Commonwealth*."[52] It seemed to the writer that Anthony headed the suffrage movement because of the "force of her arguments."

In recalling her role in the struggle for the ballot, Anthony explained that while she and other female teachers had earned only $8 a month pay, less qualified male teachers received $30. She had then concluded that only the ballot could remedy this inequity. In Portland she reiterated the point made in a Seattle interview: her reform was "further advanced in the West because the West contains the more liberal and progressive element from the East, and that any good cause or measure for reform is more readily accepted here." She had not followed this line of reasoning in 1871. Although there is no record of a Pacific Northwest journalist's disagreement with such a liberal interpretation of western attitudes, it might have been discounted by an opponent as nothing more than a political ploy—one used by strident Populist orators as well. Anthony also expressed the wish that western congressmen from equal suffrage states would take the lead in passing a Constitutional amendment because "in the old states . . . we could not possibly obtain a footing through the legislatures." The visitor recounted the progress of women in business and perceived:

> It is very remarkable when one thinks of the difficulties encountered, what a wonderful work has been accomplished. It was easy enough during the slavery agitation for Northern men to denounce men hundreds of miles away in the South for their evil practices, but it is not so easy for him to waken to an evil when the people who are robbed of their political rights are right in his own family—his wife and daughter.

When asked if she favored educating the sexes in separate colleges, she responded with a decisive no: young men and women should become acquainted because they would deal with each other long after graduation. Man, she insisted, needed to have contact with woman as his intellectual peer; if he did not, then he had "an altogether wrong opinion." Anthony added, "When educated in separate institutions the only knowledge a man has of women is what he sees of girls who are fixed up in a parlor to receive him and the women who do menial work about the college."

Meanwhile, Duniway published a letter about the availability of free tickets while defending the need for an admission fee to the congress. She asserted: "there isn't a man or woman who cannot raise a quarter . . . to help along with an uprising of the feminine forces of the commonwealth as is to be represented at this congress."[53]

The first annual meeting of the Oregon Congress was held at the Taylor Street Methodist Church. Its opening session started late because of logistical problems; meanwhile, well-dressed women and men grumbled about the wettest May on record and the current clouds and showers. The crowd also chatted about the impressive program schedule and the church's floral decorations, especially the word "Progress" in letters two feet high made from roses. Many of those attending belonged to church groups, WCTU clubs, fraternal organizations, and unions. Most delegates lived in Portland. A few men paid the admission fee and congregated in the rear pews or stood. In welcoming Anthony, Duniway recounted the suffrage movement's history, which she called "a story of hardship, ridicule, and abuse of intolerant pioneer feeling in this state, when women were considered equal only to the tasks of the kitchen and farmyard in the counties and towns."[54] According to a newspaper reporter, such negative attitudes surprised those in the audience who had never before encountered them. Duniway boasted that the Oregon

Congress resulted from a movement she had started twenty-five years earlier when she, an "unknown, inexperienced" wife had initiated a "great battle" for equal suffrage. The Oregonian referred to her 1871 campaign with the New Yorker: "Together we traveled up and down, sometimes on steamers, sometimes on horseback when we often fell off, but always got on again—sometimes on foot, but continually progressing."

Following prolonged applause, Anthony responded, "I am egotistical enough to feel that in a degree I am worthy of some little consideration, for I have devoted my life to not only a cause which I feel sacred, and which I know will eventually triumph, but in my best way I have tried to make the world better; better through the uplifting of women." No doubt she hoped that these words would appeal to the intelligent ladies sitting before her who voiced concern about the condition of their sex but were not yet suffragists. The speaker, like Duniway, recalled the 1871 tour. Unfortunately, no one published a detailed account, but merely reported that she said they went "a-gypsying . . . all over Oregon and Washington, overcoming such obstacles as few women would care to encounter in their efforts to advance the cause of their sex, which they have always claimed to be the cause of man also."[55] Anthony then lectured on the history of the national movement, reminding again that it was nearly fifty years old and that Stanton, Frederick Douglass, and others had played important parts. At the conclusion of this opening address, Duniway remarked that the present tributes to the heroine were "far different than the uneatable eggs and brickbats offered during the early 70s when Miss Anthony was first here." There is no evidence that anybody protested Duniway's exaggeration.

To attract and teach an audience, the famous guest spoke at every session of the Congress. That afternoon she urged that women unite for voting reform; in the evening she emphasized some themes from her 1871 "Power of the Ballot" address. To those who still believed that women could influence society without the vote, Anthony patiently explained that politicians only counted votes and ignored petitions submitted by church people. She asserted: "so long as woman had no vote, her influence would be nil in state or national affairs."[56] The lecturer argued that "Man had given over to woman the work of repairing all the damage done by man in society, reclaiming the drunkard, caring for homeless children, and other such charitable work."

While the clubwomen pondered this sweeping assertion made at them, the reformer added that she did not object to this work but thought it unfair that the men who produced "all this misery and suffering" should vote while women "who did the repairing" lacked the privilege. Anthony then reminded that Oregon prevented idiots, the insane, and women from voting. The teacher bluntly predicted: "Give us the political fulcrum, and we will plant our lever and move the world to a higher and nobler civilization."

Fatigued by the heavy demands placed on her during the long first day, the aging veteran delayed her appearance on the following morning. Anthony's topic went unreported, but she offered to meet at the conclusion of her speech those who had questions about woman's suffrage. Late in the afternoon she delivered a twenty minute discourse that was, a reporter judged, "a powerful appeal to women to make a united effort to secure the ballot by appealing to political leaders of all parties, and not only asking but demanding that they be given the consideration to which they are justly entitled."[57]

At this or some other session Anthony summarized the political tactics being employed or that would be employed in the California referendum contest. She instructed that the first step had been "to awaken public sentiment and to create an active and efficient corps of workers." Then these men and women "must talk suffrage in season and out of season, whenever and wherever they can obtain a hearing." These workers also must place information in newspapers and distribute literature. The last phase of the campaign would be "conducted in direct line with that of the political parties": distinguished speakers, including Catt and Shaw, would lecture around the state.

At the evening session she used her old teaching device of fielding questions. Anthony maintained again that women should sit on juries, emphasized the importance of the forthcoming votes on suffrage in California and Idaho, reminded that in two years Oregon and Nevada voters would decide the issue, and implored her listeners to participate in the Oregon campaign.

Anthony told her audience that she also wanted the best of the church seats reserved for men. Duniway interjected that they had been seated in the rear or stood and quipped, "now that we want to get the men to vote for woman's suffrage, we not only want to give them the front seats, but the softest cushions."[58]

On the last day the featured speaker's exhaustion again made managers rearrange the schedule. In her addresses Anthony repeated her plea for a united Oregon suffrage movement; perhaps she returned to this basic theme because she saw many new faces. According to Duniway, she also introduced a new topic by maintaining that "Woman's province is always to be the housekeeper, and she would certainly be qualified to keep the house of municipal and state affairs of administration." The reformer wanted both sexes together "to cleanse the political pool."[59] Duniway introduced Anthony for her final address, calling her "the noblest Roman of them all." The veteran campaigner praised the Congress of Women for demonstrating "that women are at least as capable of participating at the ballot-box as men."[60] Anthony appealed to the nonsuffragist ladies:

> The large number of women graduates from our different universities and colleges, the Chautauqua circles, economic clubs, literary societies, in all of which, like in the churches, most of the membership is made up of women, proves conclusively that women are as capable in promoting the political welfare of our country as men, and I wonder what in the world are men thinking when they allow women to be deprived of expressing their opinion at the ballot box.

She concluded by using American foreign policy to support her reform. She assured that if American women voted, then the "Cuban patriots would soon be free." Thus, the reformer joined many other national leaders in urging Cuban independence, but she added an original idea: following their liberation Cuban men, improving on the record of the Founding Fathers, should frame a constitution that provided liberty and equality for women. The audience applauded, but Northwest editors dismissed her admonition.

The aging leader consistently sought opportunities to train a younger group of feminist leaders. One tactic was to give them important assignments at various meetings. Mrs. Sarah Cooper, a Californian who Anthony wanted at this Portland meeting, arrived on the second day and immediately made an impact. Nationally prominent as a proponent of kindergarten education, she zealously worked for humanitarian reform and enjoyed Anthony's trust and respect.[61] A Congregationalist, a skilled administrator, a solid writer, and a memorable speaker, Cooper had presided over the 1896 Woman's Congress in San Francisco. One of that city's noted women, she had once opposed equal suffrage before becoming a zealous convert. At the Oregon Congress the feminist praised Anthony's ability to be more effective than ministers in winning businessmen to her reform and exclaimed that "we do love her." Cooper proclaimed that equal suffrage would improve society in numerous ways, including adoption of sensible child rearing practices and the necessary reformation of municipal politics. The female element, she explained, "is as much needed in municipal housekeeping as it is in the household." She recounted her career in California's kindergartens and complained, "After all this work, after helping to establish 46 kindergartens and following 9,000 children for 18 years I am not allowed even an educational ballot."[62] She aroused her listeners by asserting an old argument: "If it was safe and right to bring a million of colored people in the voting population . . . it surely is as safe and right to bring in the mothers."[63] At one point someone proposed three cheers for Cooper. There was "a fluttering of handkerchiefs" and then some feeble cheers. The *Oregonian* reporter facetiously urged women to improve their cheering because men rendered more rousing party yells.

There were many other effective speakers. Duniway's son, Willis, served as secretary to the Governor of Oregon and spoke in his place. Assuring the audience that the governor was an enthusiastic supporter of equal suffrage, Willis then gave his own opinions. The speaker insisted that he knew something about the "struggles of the great women in this movement." The secretary then added, "Their purposes were high, noble and unselfish, and they sought the betterment of women. . . . The fallacy that woman's right destroyed mother's love or woman's influence of home is one that I can readily deny from practical experience."[64] His brother, Hubert, delivered a history of the woman's suffrage movement, including his involvement as a boy working on the *New Northwest*. After he finished his mother crowed, "People have said that Mrs. Duniway is traveling around the country and leaving her children to grow up in drunkenness, viciousness, idleness, and no one knows what, and here you see the result."[65] Long a champion for suffrage, Dr. Bethenia Owens-Adair gave an address which recalled Anthony's 1871 Roseburg visit. To the delight of the Duniway family, Anthony, Cooper, and their coadjutators, several other speakers also spoke enthusiastically about their reform. These lecturers covered diverse and timely topics, including women as journalists, women as physicians, women as potential legislators, women and philanthropy, and women in the union movement. Some reported on such organizations as the Union for Unemployed Women, the Boys and Girls Aid Society, and Lady Maccabees. Duniway later published many of these papers and reports in her *Pacific Empire* and hoped they would be brought out as a history book.

Prayers, readings, and many musical performances were interspersed between lectures. The delegates showed their approval of the nine sessions through regular attendance, warm applause, and compliments.

On the afternoon after the conclusion of the congress, Anthony and Duniway crossed the Columbia River to Vancouver's Methodist Church for a meeting sponsored by the WCTU. This effort seemed fruitless: newspapers were late in getting the right meeting date, the audience was smaller than anticipated, and the talks of the two ladies prompted little interest beyond the church. Though fatigued by the demanding three-day congress, Anthony lectured on Washington's suffrage history and requested listeners to unite so as "to restore the rights from which they had been deprived."[66] Two Vancouver weekly newspapers paid scant attention to this meeting, where women called for moderate political action. Both editors preferred to evaluate two visiting controversial male politicians demanding radical change. Populist spokesman Jacob Coxey decried the depression and provided strong remedies; Granger Mortimer Whitehead castigated the gold standard. A Vancouver editor, who gave only a perfunctory report of Anthony's discourse, enthused that Whitehead delivered "the most powerful and convincing political address ever heard in this state."[67]

While the visit to Vancouver did little more than tire Anthony, she spent three more profitable days back in Portland, attending formal and informal suffrage meetings and two receptions. The experienced politician insisted that Oregon suffragists needed a stronger organization and hundreds of volunteers for local work. Although the referendum vote was two years in the future, she impressed upon sympathizers that her California experience taught that they must start work immediately. Anthony instructed Portland women, as she was telling California suffragists, how to conduct a campaign. She again emphasized the need for political party endorsements, for getting as much information in newspapers as editors would allow, and for money. Anthony also advised: "Since women desire to enter politics, they should be shrewd enough themselves to study political methods and learn the fine art of expediency." Women must not speak out on a vast array of political issues but should "talk and urge only their own emancipation." The teacher added that a referendum campaign required considerable effort:

> Every woman, every man must feel an individual responsibility. They must talk suffrage in season and out of season, wherever two or three are gathered together. They must introduce the subject and secure a discussion at every picnic, farmers' meeting, debating society, social gathering, whenever and wherever they can obtain a hearing. . . . These advocates must be willing to sink all other interests, put them aside until after this great issue is settled.[68]

On 8 June, the first day of the Congress, Anthony wrote in her diary that "It seemed the best [citizens] of the city at different sessions." To achieve victory the politician argued that these prominent women must be brought into the upcoming suffrage struggle. Surely she applied the lessons of the 1893 Colorado victory when suffrage societies, women's state clubs, the WCTU, and others collaborated. Catt, a national leader who put tremendous effort into that successful state campaign, brought details of its strategy to Anthony. She, in turn, stressed to Duniway the need to organize and cooperate. The Oregon leader must have bluntly responded that association with the WCTU would mean another devastating political defeat. As a scholar of Colorado's 1893 victory concludes, "The successful referendum campaign . . . proved virtually impossible to repeat in other states until much later."[69] This was not obvious to Anthony in 1896; she simply tried to apply the political tactics of one western state to another.

The national leader discovered, however, how difficult it would be to enlist Portlanders in a suffrage coalition. Many told her that they would not serve under Duniway's leadership, emphasizing her domineering character and sarcastic tongue. The New Yorker, who recalled that in 1871 some Albany residents expressed dislike of Abigail, understood that the Oregonian continued to inspire some women and exasperate others. A resourceful politician, Anthony sought to resolve this leadership problem in a public talk delivered to Oregon suffrage leaders. She recommended that they form "a city organization, separate and apart from the state suffrage association . . . to be officered by wholly new recruits of your able, fashionable society women, who will lead public sentiment for the amendment campaign in this city, leaving Mrs. Duniway free to direct the work for the state."[70] The speaker also advised, "Don't push Mrs. Duniway into the presidency of your city campaign. She doesn't want it, ought not to have it, and it is not just nor wise to ask her to accept it. Find your most available society woman and put her at the head." Anthony assured that Duniway would be a willing co-worker with this new leader. The veteran politician asserted that the impetus provided by the congress would make it easy to hold suffrage meetings throughout Oregon; moreover, Duniway, who had friends everywhere, should coordinate these gatherings.

Anthony, who had played similar politics in selecting leaders and dividing power in the NAWSA and in some state organizations, had tactfully provided sound advice. Ever since 1871 she had been training Duniway as a suffragist leader; in 1896 the teacher concluded that her pupil must share power with another respected society woman, who need not have been an active suffragist. The politician did not urge Oregonians to rally under Duniway's banner, fearing such action would mean defeat in the next referendum battle. The only workable strategy, the New Yorker concluded, was such a division of Oregon's leadership.

Duniway did not publicly object to these tactics in either her newspaper or autobiography; in fact, she published Anthony's political advice in the *Pacific Empire*. While Anthony told the Portlander about the need to divide power, she also softened this recommendation by emphasizing her friend's recent contributions to the local suffrage movement. In 1895 Duniway had led a small group in reviving the movement, had edited the *Pacific Empire*, and had competently managed the recently concluded congress. Her impromptu talks and her famous humor won applause. On one occasion she quipped: "Woman . . . was not an angel and it was well she was not, for if she were she would hardly be a congenial companion to her mate, the average man of today."[71]

Duniway boasted to her mentor that she now enjoyed a closer relationship with Portland's elite, many of whom attended the congress. A shrewd and experienced judge of people, Anthony well understood that the link between the reformer and the rich was tenuous. A long and frustrating referendum campaign in Oregon would undoubtedly mean that some club women would become disenchanted with the strong-willed Duniway and leave the ranks. And so some did. Anthony had often instructed suffragists not to endorse a presidential candidate in 1896, for it would mean that other parties would be hostile to the cause when the referendum vote was taken. Duniway, however, could not remain on the sidelines during the exciting race and endorsed William McKinley over William Jennings Bryan.

Anthony's political maneuver was a thoughtful attempt to compromise a difficult leadership problem. She took further political action at the end of the Oregon Congress by trying to recruit Portland women into the suffrage ranks. At dinners and receptions she sought to accomplish this by both personal and group solicitations. One day she managed to attend two receptions and a luncheon; each social occasion was sponsored by a Portland club and attracted both the city's leading women and newspaper publicity. The well-dressed and well-mannered Portland elite that enjoyed the table decorations and stimulating conversations with their distinguished guest were just the type of influential women that Anthony wanted committed to the suffragist campaign.

The luncheon was hosted by the Home for Unemployed Women. The guest of honor charmed the ladies. In fact, "her lively conversation" demonstrated "deep interest . . . in everything pertaining to woman's work in Portland."[72] Surely the fact that Anthony had been interested in the condition of working women for as long as she had been interested in suffrage impressed her listeners. She explained to those supporting a home for unemployed and poor Portland women and girls that the 1890s depression had brought even greater suffering in the eastern urban centers. Undoubtedly she repeated an old argument: if working women had the vote then their social and economic condition would improve. One woman attending the luncheon commented upon Anthony's energy. After a demanding three-day congress, receptions, and dinners the visitor seemed "to have imbibed deeply of youth's renewing waters of the elixir of life."

In the afternoon the visitor attended a reception sponsored by the prestigious Portland Woman's Club. Her wide-ranging address included the statement that from her own experience in Rochester she endorsed "all clubs where women met for literary and social purposes."[73] Anthony was demonstrating to these influential ladies that she was not limited to only the suffrage reform; she had time and interest for intellectual pursuits. This must have been an effective technique. After a brief rest Anthony went to an evening reception sponsored by the Portland Women's Union, an organization that maintained a boarding house for working women. She probably repeated much of what she had said at the earlier luncheon, commended its members for helping those struggling to support themselves, acknowledged this and other enthusiastic audiences, and answered questions. Duniway appreciated the fact the Portland's elite—she called them "our local 400"—honored "our chieftain."[74] She appreciated Anthony's attempt to win support among the wealthy. In fact, right up to the time she journeyed to the train station the national leader repeatedly explained to small local groups the tactics required to win a state referendum.

As the New Yorker traveled back to Sacramento, she reflected on her short but successful Pacific Northwest campaign. She appreciated the fact that the newspaper coverage of her and her cause had changed. Journalists no longer mocked her; indeed, they respected her ideas and appearance. The whole atmosphere had improved. In fact, in 1887 Oregon Senator Joseph N. Dolph had instructed fellow lawmakers that "the movement for woman suffrage has passed the stage of ridicule."[75]

Thus, late in the century in California, Oregon, and Washington, as in the nation at large, Anthony now received respect. Stanton emphasized the change, "from being the most ridiculed and mercilessly persecuted woman, Miss Anthony has become the most honored and respected in the nation."[76] She believed that the change in attitude was obvious in 1883 when Anthony sailed to Europe and "never were expressions of regret for an absence, nor more sincere prayers for a speedy return, accorded to any American on leaving his native shores."

Anthony acknowledged the friendlier response she received during this second visit to the Pacific Northwest; in fact, she was probably about as satisfied with her nine days' work in 1896 as with her nearly ninety days in 1871. During the last campaign she had convincingly argued that women should vote because they were citizens and because the ballot in their hands could improve Oregon society. In stressing the equality argument up and down the Pacific Coast, she instructed, "Every rational man, every just man, ought to see that the time has come when the women of the nation must be recognized, must be admitted to the rights and privileges of citizenship, for which they have waited so long and to which they are as much entitled as any male citizen."[77]

In both tours she had done much to advance woman's suffrage; in Portland, as elsewhere, her intelligence and demeanor won allies. A charming, grandmother-like figure, she had, one supporter enthused, "endeared herself to all."[78] Optimistic as ever, Anthony had reason to believe in mid-1896 that suffragists would organize a solid campaign prior to the Oregon suffrage vote. Although her political tactics now emphasized political party endorsements, her political message in 1896, especially of the need for organization and dedication, had changed little. Meetings in Portland and Seattle had added to her conviction that club women would be won over to suffrage and could make a great political contribution. It is interesting to note that the militant English suffragette, Emmeline Pankhurst, came to America in 1909 and, like the moderate Anthony, thought clubwomen to be "a perfect basis for a suffrage movement."[79]

Many Pacific Northwest supporters solicited Anthony to extend her stay and help organize the ranks for the suffrage battles. She insisted, however, that she must return to Sacramento in order to try to win the endorsement from the state's Democratic Party.

The three-day Congress was as great a success as its planners had hoped. Portland's two daily newspapers dispatched reporters who gave ample and favorable coverage. Impressed with the first day's sessions, the *Telegram*'s reporter lauded the women—both speakers and audience—for their "brain power, aptness, and eloquence of speech, and pure patriotism, and clean Americanism."[80] He asserted that these women should vote because they demonstrated that they had had "instilled into them from the cradle up, the principles of true citizenship." Repeating a point voiced by Anthony, Duniway, and others he favorably compared these informed women to "ignorant foreigners" who voted. The writer praised the distinguished visitor: "one glance at the open countenance, one look at the wrinkles, which, not time, but the fighting of the battles of the cause she had espoused for so long has wrought, and the listener feels that every word uttered by Susan B. Anthony is with her a religious conviction and comes from the heart." The *Oregonian*'s reporter also applauded Anthony for "her eloquent and logical way of presenting her ideas" and for "the fact that in all her many addresses she never goes over the same ground, and always has new ideas and thoughts."[81]

The *Telegram*'s writer believed many had been converted to equal suffrage, that collectively the speakers were excellent, especially the San Franciscan. "If ever pure womanhood, honesty of purpose and ability was combined in one person, that person is Sarah B. Cooper."[82]

The *Oregonian*'s reporter was less expansive than his competitor, but he, too, applauded the speakers, musicians, audience, and those responsible for the congress. He judged that the large attendance meant that the congress was a financial as well as an educational success. At least one woman journalist covered the convention. Sarah I. Lyman of the *Rural Northwest*, stressed that despite her age Anthony still addressed every session and enlivened each "by her wit as well as by her delightful reminiscences."[83] Lyman appreciated Cooper, describing this featured speaker as being "very attractive . . . showing by her face that elevation of expression which comes from a lifetime spent in self-denying labors for others."

Although reporters refrained from the snide and condescending comments characteristic of their response to Anthony in 1871, the two major Portland newspapers did not go so far as to embrace her cause. Reporters seemed very impressed with the activists, but their editors probably did not attend a single session. Scott of the *Oregonian* conceded that the congress "illustrates the activity of women in affairs that mark the intellectual growth of the era, and the direction of these activities."[84] Some of Scott's views were similar to those he enunciated against the reform in 1871, including his criticism of suffragists who argued that the ballot was "a panacea for all the evils of society." According to Scott, "Women's clubs, and unions and congresses have not revolutionized society, but they have developed individual women by the thousand, and these are working in quiet, womanly ways for purer society, better government, juster laws." He judged that Oregonians could be proud of the congress and the way it presented issues "without involving the state in suffrage experiments which have already been too widely extended."

The *Telegram* did not give an editorial response; instead its columns sometimes chided the congress for not taking action against the enormous, fashionable hats that women wore to the theater. "If the woman's congress desires to embalm itself in the gratitude of Portland's male tyrants it should formally condemn the wearing of big hats at public assemblies by the downtrodden sex."[85]

Duniway ignored the editorial pages of the Portland dailies and republished much of the reporters' accounts of the nine sessions. She had no time to write her own summaries for the *Pacific Empire* because she was so involved with the congress, hailing it as "an unqualified success." These three days were some of the most enjoyable in her life as a reformer. She enthused in her autobiography: "Never has a more successful public function transpired in Oregon than our Congress of Women."[86] She recalled that Anthony "was delighted to note the clever manner in which almost all the speakers sandwiched their speeches and papers with the suffrage sentiment and also the heightened applause which followed every allusion to our proposed equal Suffrage Amendment." Duniway judged that the congress helped bring men back into the Oregon suffrage movement. It was her conviction that they had left ten years earlier because of the mistaken strategy of mixing equal suffrage and prohibition.

But she knew that Anthony disagreed. Susan stressed that both the national and the state WCTU were cooperating with her in the California campaign; in fact, she had convinced Frances Willard not to hold the WCTU convention of 1896 in that state (Anthony privately called it an "invasion") because she did not want to "divert public thought from the enfranchisement of women to prohibition."[87] Suffragists, Anthony taught, had avoided the temperance question so as to keep the liquor business from becoming a foe.

The visitor also reminded the Portlander that the WCTU was much better organized in Washington and Oregon than the suffragists. (In 1899 Catt would observe this same condition in her Seattle visit.) In Seattle and Portland, WCTU leaders reminded that they had long championed equal suffrage, desired another referendum campaign for this reform, and promised to give the NAWSA assistance in a fight in either Oregon or Washington. Thus Anthony assumed that in the Pacific Northwest she could count on the same type of help she was getting from the WCTU in California.[88] An advocate of organization and cooperation, Anthony taught that an adroit suffrage leader could combine with Pacific Northwest temperance women. It seemed obvious to her that Oregon and Washington suffragists were too weak to reject WCTU assistance; furthermore, there was no way to keep the temperance women out of a referendum battle. Duniway remained unconvinced. She feared cooperation with the WCTU in such a contest because that organization would alarm the liquor interests, who would once again employ whatever political tactics that were necessary to block the reform. But apparently Anthony had convinced Duniway to seek political accommodation with the organized prohibitionists, for Abigail wrote that suffragists would unite with local WCTU members "under the single banner for an amendment campaign."[89] In time Duniway rejected the accommodation recommended by her mentor and again denounced the WCTU. Anthony was undoubtedly displeased with this additional sign of Duniway's independence, which led the teacher to take further action against the student.

# TEN
# *Oregon Becomes Crucial*

BETWEEN 1896 AND HER LAST VISIT to the Pacific Northwest in 1905, Anthony overcame difficulties resulting from advanced age and illness and continued her active life. Her old friend, Elizabeth Cady Stanton, compared her with Theodore Roosevelt: "the nearest example of perpetual motion."[1] In 1900 one of Anthony's closest friends judged that at the age of eighty she was at the zenith of her powers, but a stroke that year and old age sapped her energy. Between her visits to Portland, Anthony followed a demanding schedule: attending conventions, traveling twice to Europe on behalf of her reform, preparing part of a major history of woman's suffrage, maintaining a large correspondence, and continuing to provide leadership for the NAWSA even after she surrendered its presidency in 1900. Her message had changed little during these years. Her primary emphasis was still on the great need for woman suffrage, but she also argued that divorce was an important option for wives, that suffragists should become clubwomen so as to win such groups to the equal suffrage cause, that females should be admitted to universities, and that political parties should endorse equal suffrage. Anthony's energy, dedication, and persistence made her the subject of considerable writing. Her biographer claimed that more was written about the aging leader than any other contemporary woman. Her eightieth and eighty-fifth birthdays received national attention; while Seattle and Portland newspapers made little of these celebrations, her regional admirers honored them. In 1900, for example, about seventy-five women from Salem and nearby communities attended a banquet "as a manifestation of the high esteem in which Anthony is held as an advocate of progress in all lines of reform."[2]

While Anthony enjoyed an outpouring of friendship and admiration, she also had to cope with the death of loved ones, including two brothers and Elizabeth Cady Stanton. To an ever increasing degree she depended upon the love and assistance of her sister Mary, with whom she shared a home in Rochester, and upon her co-leaders, including Shaw and Catt.

Anthony's relationship with her old friend and ally, Stanton, had often been difficult. A recent biographer concluded that from the mid-1890s until Stanton's death in 1902 it "alternated between affection, annoyance, and animosity."[3] They disagreed over the new generation of female leaders (including Catt) that Anthony had brought into the movement; over Anthony's emphasis on equal suffrage rather than other issues; and over the relationship between the NAWSA and the WCTU. Although the notable reformers disagreed in old age as they had in middle age, they did not break their important bond. Each pursued her own interests, but Anthony still called upon Stanton to make key speeches. In 1902 Anthony noted that the two were not as close as they had been, but she deeply mourned her old friend's death

In several ways the relationship between Anthony and Duniway was like that between Anthony and Stanton. The independent Oregonian and the New Yorker were friends who drifted apart because of disagreements over political tactics, the WCTU, and such NAWSA leaders as Catt and Shaw. In 1898 Anthony told an ally that Duniway charged her with being an "autocrat," who employed improper political tactics. She wished that her Oregon critic would seek "to convert men to vote for suffrage" so that she would not have "time to be bruiting around . . . falsehoods."[4]

Anthony realized that her independent ally continued to be the most important figure in Oregon's suffrage movement, that her bluntness and sarcasm both attracted and repelled followers, that, as her son, Ralph Duniway, correctly summarized: "life would have no meaning for her whatever if she could not live it according to her own notions," that she disagreed with the national suffrage leadership, and that she had been instrumental in 1899 in persuading the Oregon legislature to provide a vote on suffrage in 1900. Anthony also knew that Duniway's co-workers praised her for receiving an invitation to speak before state lawmakers. This was the first time that a female in Oregon had addressed both houses; Anthony might have recalled that in 1871 she had been the first of her sex to appear before the Washington Territorial Legislature.

Pleased that there was an Oregon vote scheduled on equal suffrage in 1900, Duniway attended the NAWSA annual conventions at Grand Rapids in 1899 and in Washington the following year. At both meetings the Oregonian was a featured and controversial speaker, insisting that she had a more effective way to run a state suffrage campaign than did NAWSA leaders. Duniway contended that local, not national, individuals should organize and direct these campaigns. To her way of thinking recent defeats in Kansas and California resulted from outside agitation; Oregonians, she asserted, "do not like professional agitators, but they love liberty."[5] She bluntly predicted that a suffrage victory in Oregon could be won by waging a quiet campaign and by refusing to use public endorsements by the state's leading men. In her speech at the Washington convention, reprinted in the *Oregonian*, Duniway observed: "A delightful calm has settled over our political arena, but it is the calmness that precedes the success that is in sight."[6]

Convention delegates must also have been rankled by the Portlander's assertion that "Every good woman in the world likes men a great deal better than she likes women, and there isn't a wise woman in all this goodly land who isn't proud to say so."[7] Duniway irked those suffragists that she called "man-haters" by praising marriage and by warning that women who predicted that with the ballot they could change men only succeeded "in driving nails into the closed coffin lid of their own and other women's liberties."[8] The Oregonian always tried to separate the suffrage reform from the prohibition movement and maintained that a letter from Anthony saying she did not link equal suffrage with "sumptuary legislation" had impressed the Oregon legislature—a statement that irked prohibitionists in the suffrage ranks.

In 1900 the Portlander waged what she called "a still hunt campaign;" her biographer explained it as "an emphasis on persuasion of influential voters through personal contacts and educational publicity rather than a mass appeal through a public campaign which would stir up opposition."[9] Opposed to what she called "hurrah work" [demonstrations], she privately corresponded with Oregon politicians, editors, and liquor industry leaders assuring them that most women opposed prohibition. In summary, Duniway's tactics were fundamentally unlike those that the NAWSA leaders had employed in California and Idaho. The Oregon leader insisted on a quiet campaign; the national leaders, drawing upon a long reform tradition and current practices of political parties, wanted to alert the public through a vigorous one. For many years in the Pacific Northwest Duniway's political tactic stirred up both vigorous endorsements and denunciations. In 1899, for example, an editor criticized those advocating "a stillhunt canvass" because they "are not giving the voters an opportunity to read up on the subject, but will trust to hornswoggling him into their way of thinking by means of a little judicious chin-music."[10]

In 1897 Duniway wrote a letter to a Rochester, New York newspaper disagreeing with Anthony in her own home town. Anthony had been quoted in the newspaper as saying that the NAWSA had played a critical role in the 1896 Idaho victory; Duniway disagreed:

> We all concede the devotion to the cause of our beloved and honored Miss Anthony. We gladly accord to her and her cabinet of co-workers due credit for their earnestness, brilliancy and eloquence. We love them every one, and hope to have them visit us often, as invited guests; but we are thoroughly convinced by our many Western defeats, under their management, that every locality is its own best interpreter of its own plans of work.[11]

Annoyed with Duniway's interpretation of the Idaho and California struggles, Anthony privately criticized the Oregonian, reminding that leaders should follow the political plans established by the NAWSA board. She advised that those in disagreement should bring change by electing new board members. The veteran absolutely rejected the Oregon leader's insistence that eastern suffragists should stay out of western referenda battles. Anthony expanded on her views to a Duniway critic:

> There are no methods that are good for the East that are not equally good for the West. . . . I have been in nearly every state . . . and I have never seen that one place required any different tactics from every other. All we have to do is to educate a majority of the men of any state to want to have the women of their households and of everybody else's households enfranchised."[12]

She reasoned that if men could be convinced to endorse equal suffrage then the powerful liquor interests could no longer win enough votes to prevent the reform's passage; this had been the case in Colorado and Idaho and would be the case in Washington.

Anthony ridiculed Duniway's still hunt tactic, saying privately that the Portlander was "all off" on the issue. In 1895, if not earlier, Anthony had expressed her displeasure with Duniway's political tactics. She expressed her concern to their mutual friend, Rev. Thomas Lamb Eliot: "I have written Mrs. Dunway [*sic*] I hope this time there'll be no trusting to a 'Still Hunt' as she termed the campaign of 1884. There is no way but by personal education out of prejudice and selfishness—to carry a measure that means even-handed justice to the other half of the human family."[13] Undoubtedly the national and regional leaders had argued over this fundamental issue in 1896 when Anthony campaigned in Portland. The visitor insisted that the still hunt had been tried and failed because "our opponents always can make a stiller hunt."[14] Anthony lamented that "it is such a pity that she cannot see that her still hunt scheme provided quite as disastrous a failure as any of our open and above-board campaigns!"[15] The national leader fervently argued that the only way to win a state referendum campaign was through an open discussion in newspapers and from the political rostrum. Despite her deep hostility to her friend's favorite tactic and independent attitude, Anthony advised national workers not to enter Oregon during the 1900 suffrage fight "unless duly and formally invited by Mrs. Duniway, and pledged to speak on precisely such lines as she directed."[16] Although she deferred to Duniway's wishes, Anthony predicted that "there is hardly the ghost of a chance of Oregon's carrying the amendment, even under the best possible management, with the National and State societies harmoniously united and working together with one spirit and purpose, which is an impossibility with Mrs. Duniway." Anthony roundly denounced her co-worker: "Duniway's . . . head is so full of crotchets that it is impossible for her to *cooperate* with anybody; she must simply *control*." To avoid being blamed for the predicted suffrage defeat in Oregon, the national leader kept the NAWSA out of the fight, but she also stated that in case of victory she wanted Duniway to receive "the entire credit." Duniway attracted considerable attention from her allies by conducting her own style of campaign. The local commander called upon the NAWSA for two veterans and praised them, in part, because they followed her orders.[17]

Oregon and national leaders closely studied the 1900 referendum returns. Under the Portlander's management the suffragists went down by a close margin—28,402 to 26,265. This was a much better showing than the first contest in 1884. The negative Portland plurality of about 3,500 made the difference; Duniway blamed her brother, Harvey Scott, for this negative vote. He had promised not to use his influential *Oregonian* against his sister's reform. Late in the campaign, however, Scott delivered what she called "disreputable attacks" and rallied all the antis "and their co-workers, the gamblers and fallen women."[18]

The *Oregonian* had argued that suffrage would bring few societal benefits and "would probably do women a good deal of harm."[19] It reminded that a large majority of Oregon males in 1884 had rejected woman's suffrage and that even in 1900 only a minority of females wanted the ballot. Duniway fumed over the newspaper's conclusion that "woman is as little fitted for political as man is for domestic life;" and that furthermore, "womanly women" rejected suffrage through their intuition and "manly men" denounced it "through their judgment and reason."[20] After announcing the suffrage defeat the newspaper joked that some women would not be happy until they voted and that "they won't be happy when they do."[21]

The *Oregonian* had raised a frequent, and apparently effective, argument by ruling that only a minority of women wanted the ballot. The newspaper had stated that "until women in any appreciable numbers of force ask for it, the suffrage seems to the average man of intelligence a purely speculative rather than a practical question."[22] Some NAWSA leaders also faulted Duniway for failing to demonstrate that a large number of women wanted to vote. Since the 1850s reformers, both in and out of the suffrage movement, had organized local groups and encouraged them to compile signatures on petitions, memorials, and other documents. Lists of women would prove, reformers argued, that a large number sought enfranchisement. It was Duniway's experience that local organizations and the lists they compiled made little impact upon either politicians or voters. Thus she rejected what Anthony had taught in 1871 and 1896. The Portlander attracted sympathizers, including some regional and a few national figures who supported her tactics. One veteran reformer, Henry Blackwell, endorsed her "quieter plan" because it did not "create antagonism."[23] The *Woman's Journal*, the most prominent suffragist publication, applauded Duniway for avoiding "sensational methods" in 1900 and recommended that those planning referenda campaigns should study the one that narrowly failed in Oregon. This newspaper denounced the Oregon Association Opposed to the Extension of Suffrage to Women, accusing it of allying with "gamblers, saloon-keepers, and proprietors of houses of ill fame." It did not attribute the defeat to these organized opponents but reasoned that it was owing to "the solid position of the ignorant and vicious elements, and the stubborn, age-long conservatism that yields to modern progress only reluctantly and by slow degrees. Secretary of the Navy John D. Long had called it 'a slowly melting glacier of Bourbonism and prejudice.'"

Anthony, however, dissented. According to her interpretation Oregon suffragists failed largely because of Duniway's inappropriate still hunt, a disregard for organization, and an inability to control her emotions. Duniway's denunciation of her brother after the election, Anthony feared, damaged the cause. She must have disapproved of the Oregon suffragist's counterattacks in the *Woman's Journal*: "The big editor out-Heroded Herod in his persecution of our cause." Furthermore, she hoped that Harvey would recover "his mental equilibrium."[24] Anthony worried about antagonizing the powerful newspaper. If the *Oregonian* ended its opposition—and Susan considered Harvey to be a convertible friend—then the reformers might win the next state suffrage battle. Anthony's reading of the Oregon election returns led her to predict that improved tactics would achieve the political goal. Early in the twentieth century some Oregon women, especially newcomer Clara Colby and Portland journalist Sarah Evans, supported the national leader's interpretation; these two feminists and an unknown number of others agreed that Duniway's sharp tongue and inept political management hurt the movement. Thus, disaffected local women joined NAWSA leaders in turning against Duniway's domination. They wanted, instead, to adopt Anthony's political tactics in Oregon's next suffrage campaign.

While her local and national opponents planned to replace her, Duniway, who did not yet understand this threat, continued to push for another state campaign. She wrote that for about a month after the crushing 1900 suffrage defeat that "she was prostrated" (she could not even celebrate the Fourth of July) both by the *Oregonian*'s unanticipated opposition and by the negative vote.[25] Abigail soon became reconciled with Harvey and stumped for voting reform in southern Oregon. The Oregon State Equal Suffrage Association (OSESA) also overcame its bitter frustration with the election defeat. Some of its members faulted Duniway's leadership but all agreed with her that another amendment should soon be put before the voters.

The 1900 Oregon suffrage defeat worsened Duniway's relationship with Anthony and her lieutenants. During her 1896 visit Anthony had sought to disperse leadership between Portland clubwomen and Duniway, but the stratagem failed to weaken the Oregonian's influence. Anthony and others on the NAWSA board understood that the Portland leader enjoyed significant popularity; in fact, some admirers, hailing her accomplishments, called her the "Susan B. Anthony of the Northwest." Early in the new century the national officials sought to replace her. A major figure in the scheme to circumvent the state's aging veteran was Clara Colby. She had moved from Washington, D.C. to Portland in 1904 with her *Woman's Tribune*, a suffragist newspaper that she had edited since 1883.[26] Duniway bitterly resented Colby's challenge to her regional authority, suspecting that the NAWSA wanted the newspaperwoman to replace her. Apparently the embattled suffragist and the challenger, who wanted to play a major part in a state referendum battle, sought to keep their political and personal disagreements private, for Colby's newspaper did not publicize their differences. Duniway heatedly and repeatedly told friends that the newcomer was a silly carpetbagger whose newspaper was a weaker voice than the *Woman's Journal*.

Somewhat embarrassed by the fact that her optimistic predictions for the 1900 election had been erroneous and that national leaders treated her with a "we told you so" attitude, Duniway understood that she had lost influence in the NAWSA. She stopped attending national conventions, curtailed her writing in the *Woman's Journal*, and did not invite eastern leaders to Portland. In part to appease the national board she organized some local suffrage groups along their guidelines. In 1904 she did not yet fully realize that outsiders and dissident insiders threatened her authority. If Duniway had understood that there would be a direct challenge, she would not have reduced her influence. In 1904 the OSESA failed to get a referendum vote and Duniway, who complained about old age and poor health, resigned as the organization's president and became its honorary president. A woman she trusted, Viola Coe, replaced her. Duniway often assured her family that she enjoyed her new office, for it provided her with time to carry on domestic duties, to regain her health, and to write.

Although Duniway was not upset by the inability of the OSESA to conduct a referendum contest in 1904 and was predicting a victory when the reform was next sent to the voters, the NAWSA leadership undoubtedly faulted her for delaying the vote. The national leaders, joined by some local ones, concluded that Duniway and her followers—they dominated the OSESA—could not win an election and that her tactics would not gain supporters. To Anthony, Shaw, Catt, Colby, and others Duniway's failures to win in 1884 and 1900 and her inability to get a vote in 1904 were reasons for pessimism. Her blunt language continued to make these and other refined reformers wince; for example, the Portlander in 1905 informed a San Francisco audience that "A woman who doesn't like men is always a vinegary, cross-grained creature, who owes an apology to the men for living. She ought to steal away and die."[27] It was time to make a political change in Oregon. In her autobiography Duniway understated the lively political situation of 1905 when she wrote that the NAWSA's Portland convention "disarranged our plans" for the 1906 suffrage campaign."[28]

The state suffrage organization was responsible for the national convention coming to Portland in 1905. Oregon suffrage leaders instructed Dr. Annice F. Jeffreys Myers—one of Duniway's trusted coworkers and her personal physician—and her husband, Jefferson Myers, a noted attorney, suffragist, and president of the Lewis and Clark Centennial Exposition Commission, to attend the 1904 NAWSA convention and issue an invitation to hold its next annual convention in Portland. The national officers accepted because they were eager to hold their first convention in the Far West, because they wanted to participate in a national celebration of the lives of Lewis and Clark, because a Portland meeting would allow them to recruit Oregon allies as part of a move to wrest control from Duniway, and because they wanted to teach the proper political tactics that would result in a 1906 suffrage victory. It is also possible that the NAWSA chose a Pacific Northwest site in part because the WCTU in 1899 held its first Pacific Coast convention in Seattle. This widely publicized meeting aroused significant regional interest in the WCTU agenda.

In the early Progressive period of the 1900s the NAWSA leadership had concluded again that their emphasis should be upon state referenda, not national politics. It seemed to them there was now an even better chance of winning suffrage fights because of the Progressive spirit manifested in state legislatures and governors. It would be more difficult to get a Constitutional amendment through Congress, where conservatives still had considerable power, than to win equal suffrage through the more enlightened states. Once this decision had been reaffirmed NAWSA cast its gaze upon Oregon, which clearly was a progressive leader among states. It would make a favorable battlefield.

Suffrage leaders rejoiced over a measure recently enacted in Oregon which allowed for public proposal of laws by initiative. They interpreted this new law to mean that reformers could accumulate the required number of names, submit their petition to the proper authority, and then wage a campaign for the initiative's enactment by popular vote. It would not be necessary to seek the legislature's approval, a problem that hampered suffragists in many states. Anthony was particularly enthusiastic about the initiative because of her successful experience since the 1850s with collecting names. She had insisted that victory would only come when the public was sufficiently aroused; the solicitation of names and the publicity that would ensue from this activity would attract support. The old politician also thought that local organizations, which were dear to her heart, could play a vital role in the collection of signatures. But all of this enthusiasm was tempered by the fact that Duniway rejected this approach. She preferred to work through the legislature and avoid a noisy public battle. The Portlander wanted to use the 1900 tactics; Anthony and her allies called them hopeless.

The NAWSA leaders thought beyond the battle in Oregon and anticipated that a victory south of the Columbia would arouse women across the river border. Anthony's longstanding assertion that one success would lead to another seemed logical in 1905 because of the Progressive spirit. Anthony also studied conditions in Washington state. In 1898 she complained that incompetent leadership there had resulted in "inaction & inertia" and judged that Seattleite Dr. Sarah Kendall could revive the cause.[29] After its 1898 defeat the state's suffrage movement had nearly collapsed; only a few attended its 1904 convention. A national meeting in Portland, Anthony predicted, would attract Washington delegates. Furthermore, some eastern suffragists would travel to Puget Sound, preaching the need for new leadership and organization. In summary a Portland convention would fan the reform fires in both Oregon and Washington.

The national organization anticipated that California would also be influenced by a favorable Oregon vote. An eastern publisher in 1905 explained NAWSA's thinking: "Evidently . . . public sentiment in these three States is ripe upon the question, and only needs to be organized in order to achieve success. It is to be hoped that the Portland Convention will supply the needed stimulus."[30]

To bring about a string of political victories on the Pacific Coast—this region in 1905 looked more promising than any other—the NAWSA knew that it was absolutely necessary to establish a new and cooperative Oregon leader. Anthony fully supported the plans to depose her former protégé but her advanced age meant that others worked out and implemented the details. Even before the NAWSA convened in Portland, its board sent two field workers to Oregon. Mary N. Chase arrived in January 1905 and Gail Laughlin came a few months later. These respected, experienced New England daughters, assisted by some state suffrage officers, organized suffrage clubs across Oregon, including Ashland, Medford, Drain, Cottage Grove, Portland, Scappoose, Astoria, Seaside, Hood River, The Dalles, Pendleton, Moro, and Freewater. These local clubs elected officers, received encouragement to send members to the NAWSA convention to be held in Portland, and learned how to persuade neighbors. Knowing that Duniway saw little value in such organizations, Chase and Laughlin ignored her. The challenge to the veteran state leader occurred even before the convention.

Duniway supported the 1905 national convention coming to her home town for her own reasons: she sought to impress visiting suffragists with her talented co-leaders and to use the convention to publicize the forthcoming state suffrage campaign. The 1896 congress had helped mobilize support for the 1900 fight; another major meeting should help suffragists win in 1906. The Portlander wanted Anthony to make a third trip to the Northwest, but this time she was not being asked to provide lessons on political tactics and leadership. Anthony's major contribution, Duniway assumed, would this time be symbolic. This was a political miscalculation. After the 1905 convention several national workers remained in Oregon, enlisting local allies and controlling the 1906 campaign against Duniway's wishes. In her autobiography Duniway admitted making "a serious mistake" by inviting the NAWSA to Portland.[31] She had brought her political opponents into what she called her own "bailiwick." In 1904 Duniway had resigned as president of the state suffrage association and was its honorary-president. Her close friend, President Viola Coe, encouraged the OSESA to cooperate with the NAWSA. But at the same time she listened to Duniway's heated complaints about political trickery and betrayal. Coe probably approved of the scheme to deprive the aging veteran of power, but Duniway blamed others for political treachery. Although her influence had been reduced, Duniway would still complement the NAWSA convention as being a "brilliant success from start to finish."

In their public invitation to the Portland convention, Honorary President Anthony, President Rev. Anna Howard Shaw, Vice President Carrie Chapman Catt, Recording Secretary Alice Stone Blackwell, and other officers of the NAWSA insisted that the aim of their organization was to establish "a government of men and women—not by women alone, not by men alone, but a government of men and women, by men and women, for men and women."[32] The signers explained that they did "not claim that women's voice in the government would at once sound the death-knell to all social and political evils," but they believed that if the government represented "the interests and the beliefs of women and men" it would be improved. The invitation also described the host state: "One hundred years ago Oregon was an untrodden wilderness. The transformation of that primeval territory into prosperous communities, enjoying the highest degree of civilization, could not have been accomplished without the work of women."

An editor of the *Woman's Journal* encouraged attendance at the convention by emphasizing that the "four embryo cities" on the Pacific Coast "are destined to become centers of commerce between America and eastern Asia. San Francisco, Portland, Tacoma, and Seattle will equal or surpass New York, Philadelphia, Boston, and New Orleans. As the populations of the Orient far outnumber those of Europe, so the commerce of the Pacific will in time exceed that of the Atlantic."[33]

As suffragists prepared for the Portland convention, many also sought to obtain twenty thousand names on petitions to Congress in support of a bill that would allow women to vote for members of the House of Representatives. It had been years since the Congress had expressed any degree of interest in woman's suffrage; it was hoped that Roosevelt's

Square Deal—a domestic program aimed at aiding various groups—would include support for equal suffrage.

Some preparing for the 1905 convention predicted that the eighty-five year old Anthony was too feeble to make the fatiguing railroad journey to the Pacific coast. Friends and physicians advised her to stay home. The suffragist leader told a Portland journalist: "Oh, these doctors. They said I couldn't make the trip and live, but I passed over the highest grade as nicely as could be, and I sat and watched myself all the time expecting to die every minute; but I didn't."[34] In fact, Susan and her sister, Mary, enjoyed their travel. Arriving in Chicago on 21 June, they rested, attended a reception, and boarded a special car that carried delegates, who were described by Mary as "a right wide-awake jolly company." Another passenger stated that there were sixty-five delegates, including four males, on "the woman suffrage train" that was "heavily laden with talent and wisdom."[35] Journalists wrote extensively about the travel of eastern reformers to the far coast; along the route groups honored Susan and other noted leaders. As they traveled Anthony, Shaw, and other leaders handled NAWSA business matters.

Mary, who suffragists humorously called "Miss Anthony's young sister," was a vigorous seventy-eight-year-old retired teacher who kept a diary of the journey.[36] Like other delegates she expressed pleasure at stopping in Wyoming: "It . . . seemed like treading upon sacred soil and strongly tempts all women to come here to live under this banner of freedom." Impressed with the fact that Wyoming women had long been enfranchised, delegates picked bunches of Wyoming wildflowers to take home as souvenirs. In Idaho the reformers again felt uplifted by the fact that this state's women voted, but some, like Mary Anthony, thought the state lacked population and cultivation. She explained, "Strangers do not get a favorable impression of the country, but some lady delegates whom I afterward saw at the convention, were . . . enthusiastic in its praises."[37]

The travelers delighted in the Columbia River Valley's scenery; Anthony must have recalled the 1871 steamboat rides through this beautiful region and remarked about changes, including the growth of The Dalles and the appearance of numerous fish wheels that scooped out spawning salmon. At The Dalles, Duniway and other Oregonians climbed aboard the special car bound for the convention. Arriving at their destination on 27 June, the Anthony sisters immediately expressed pleasure with Portland; both compared it favorably to a famous German river port. Mary wrote, "the general appearance of the city surrounded by a background of green tree covered mountains, reminded one of the old, historic German city of Heidelberg."[38] The Anthonys stayed at the Portland Hotel, the convention headquarters. Mary said it was well furnished, offered excellent service, and could "be classed with the best on the Atlantic slope." Susan enjoyed her picture window. According to her biographer, "Her room commanded a full view of Mt. Hood and she never tired of gazing at that shining summit, emblem of purity, stability, eternity. Her mind seemed constantly to follow its grand upward reach into the glory of the infinite."[39]

# ELEVEN
# *Symbols and Politics*

SUSAN AND MARY ANTHONY STAYED in Portland for fifteen days, participating in the NAWSA Convention, meeting with regional suffrage leaders and the public, touring parts of the city, and attending the Lewis and Clark Exposition. They launched into their busy schedule on the very afternoon they arrived. Although wearied by her long journey, Anthony met with journalists and then joined her sister on a drive into the city's west hills. As their horse team labored along the road, the Anthonys praised the homes and flowers that they passed, as well as, "the view of the city and surrounding country . . . that could hardly be equaled by many of the eastern or foreign cities."[1] The women saw the "lovely park" where the Sacajawea monument would be placed. Seeking to make Sacajawea into an important member of the Lewis and Clark expedition and to create a regional heroine, Portland women had asked Anthony to speak about her and provided her biographical details—both fact and myth—for such an address.

Prior to the opening of the convention on 29 June, Mary and many of the seventy delegates who arrived on her train attended the fair. Susan, however, rested and participated in several committee meetings to conduct NAWSA business.

Portland's three dailies—the *Oregon Journal*, the *Telegram*, and the *Oregonian*—sought to interview these NAWSA committee members. Each newspaper had already provided useful coverage of the convention plans. On 25 June the *Oregonian* published an extensive feature story evaluating candidates for the honor of the six most famous living women. The author listed Anthony in this distinguished group because she was brave, dedicated, modest, and largely responsible for the fact that "today none is scandalized by a woman speaking in almost any public place." An *Oregonian* editorial further acknowledged the various talents of Anthony and other suffrage leaders. Harvey Scott, a major proponent of the Lewis and Clark Exposition, urged his readers to pay close attention to the proponents of woman suffrage and reminded that "Public ridicule, social ostracism, petty persecutions, no longer prevail against it."[2] This time around, his newspaper would not respond the way that it had to both Anthony's 1871 visit and the suffrage cause in the 1900 state campaign, but one of its writers could not resist a tinge of sarcasm. He joked that the NAWSA convention would last longer than those conducted by men because women enjoyed talking too much, and like some 1871 critics, he referred to Anthony as a "dear old soul."[3]

After interviews with the distinguished convention visitors, the Portland press carried details about the status and goals of the suffrage movement. Pacific Northwest newspapers, like those in other regions, had clearly changed their approach to Anthony's reform. Although they did not necessarily fall in with her teachings, they no longer made condescending remarks about them. In this third visit she was spared the personal abuse that had characterized the first one. The press was now willing to give Anthony a forum. In 1905 Oregon journalists sought Anthony's specific opinions, but she frequently offered only generalities. Her lieutenants, who attended these interviews, provided details. The aging leader sometimes interjected to clarify her own views; thus it is safe to assume that she generally agreed with the other spokeswomen. The eastern feminists instructed reporters that advanced age meant Anthony could only play a limited role in committee meetings and on the convention floor and that her friends sought to make "her duties . . . as light as possible."[4] A Portland newspaperman explained that Anthony's friends prevented reporters from visiting with her but that he had "begged his way past a cordon of guards into the presence of this distinguished woman." The eighty-five year-old politician told him about her 1871 campaign when she and Duniway "toured the state, sleeping in tents and addressing large audiences."[5] She recalled becoming friends with Portlanders Rev. Thomas Lamb Eliot and Harvey Scott and remarked on the great physical changes that Oregon had since

Abigail Scott Duniway with her newspaper *Pacific Empire*. (OHS neg. OrHi 78930)

Mary Anthony and her sister Susan in a 1905 portrait done by Grace A. Woodworth. (Seneca Falls Historical Society)

Reverend Anna Howard Shaw became president of NAWSA in 1904 after Carrie Chapman Catt resigned to attend to her husband's illness. (OHS neg. OrHi 83659)

Carrie Chapman Catt. In 1900 she was chosen to succeed Susan B. Anthony in the presidency of the NAWSA. She declined the offer of running the Oregon campaign due to her husband's failing health. (University of Rochester Collections)

Gail Laughlin, lecturer for the NAWSA. (OHS neg. 83658)

Dr. Annice Jeffreys Myers, president of the Oregon State Equal Suffrage Association. (OHS neg. OrHi 83657)

Emma Smith DeVoe, Lecturer and Organizer for the NAWSA. (OHS neg. OrHi 83650)

Clara Colby, Lecturer and Organizer for the NAWSA. (OHS neg. OrHi 83651)

Laura Gregg, organizer for the NAWSA. (OHS neg. OrHi 83656)

National American Woman Suffrage Association Convention in front of the Oregon Building at the Lewis and Clark Exposition, July 1905. Susan B. Anthony is in the front line, 6th from the right. Abigail Scott Duniway is to her right. (OHS neg. OrHi 59438)

Kate M. Gordon
Gail Laughlin
Cora Smith Eaton
Carrie Chapman Catt

undergone. Duniway also provided details about that 1871 tour, recounting that she had anticipated from newspaper accounts that Anthony would be a "cranky old maid" but that she had been surprised to find instead "a softly spoken and motherly-looking woman."

Portland writers emphasized that despite her age Anthony—she must have been the oldest politician to ever work the region—was still the "central and most interesting figure among the great women who are here. She has done more for the cause than any other, and in her declining years is the best loved among all her sister workers."[6] Delegates referred to their leader as "Miss Anthony" or as "Aunt Susan" and praised her leadership and domesticity: with all of her work for the cause, she still cooked, darned, marketed, and entertained. Close friends revealed that their unpretentious leader was actually happiest when at home. One explained that Anthony "has two personalities, and one day she will walk down the street with head up and the next day she will be like a dear, peaceful old grandmother as she goes to market."[7] Thus to win public support reformers sought to portray their champion as reasonable and willing to fulfill woman's traditional role.

Portlanders quickly understood that the eighty-five year-old Anthony was unable to give major talks and interviews, or to conduct business meetings, and that she expected President Anna Shaw to do the speaking and handle leadership responsibilities. Elected president of the NAWSA in 1904, the strong-willed and intelligent Shaw enjoyed Anthony's support. The president frequently consulted with her mentor, who served as honorary president of the NAWSA. In interviews with journalists, Shaw analyzed the suffrage movement and evaluated chances for equal suffrage victories in the West, especially in the next Oregon election. The president insisted that suffragists were "no longer laughed at, and there is a wave of kindly feeling even among the conservative. Great men with large minds are taking up our cause."[8] Shaw boasted that many women had either joined the suffragist ranks or lent it support. Anna Gordon, NAWSA secretary, interjected that she wanted the press to inform the public that "we look like other people, dress like other people and talk and walk like them. We are not a bit different. We are only working for what most of them believe, but haven't the courage to ask."[9]

Shaw explained that eastern leaders looked for success to come first in the West. She began by comparing the two regions. "It is to the West we look for greatest results in this movement because Eastern States have too great a foreign element and a foreign element is something which cannot be overcome in one generation. Foreigners and negroes are the greatest menace against equal suffrage for women which we have to combat. . . . Because enslaved classes once emancipated become the greatest tyrants on earth."[10] Shaw generalized that western women were more progressive than their eastern sisters; even young, idealistic, and energetic New England married couples were moving west.

Oregon was crucial to these female politicians. The NAWSA executive committee announced that its membership was currently designing tactics to assure a victory there in 1906. The *Oregonian* pointed out that they were "mapping out a plan of campaign by which they will fight for their rights in this land of the free and home of the brave."[11] President Shaw recounted that "Oregon workers have always been enthusiastic but their numbers have been very small." She boasted that the reform ranks, however, had been increased during the first months of 1905 by the establishment of fifty new local suffrage groups and that eastern delegates currently recruited workers during visits or stays in Portland homes. Shaw and the NAWSA field workers, of course, did not reveal that limiting Duniway's power was part of their political strategy. The president rarely mentioned the Oregon politician, though another easterner hailed her as "one of the great minds" in the movement.[12]

These interviews also provided details about national leaders. Some learned that Shaw was probably the first American woman to earn theological and medical degrees. Vice president Catt, Secretary Gordon, Co-editor Alice S. Blackwell of the *Woman's Journal*, and Biographer Ida Husted Harper were portrayed by journalists as being intelligent, energetic, and gifted leaders. Surprisingly the Portland newspapers failed to point out that there had never before been such a gathering of female talent in the Pacific Northwest.

At 2:00 P.M. on 27 June President Shaw called the convention to order; a writer said that this meant that "the Rose City" was now "the battle arena" for important American women.[13] Wielding a gavel made of historic wood presented by Oregon Historical Society Curator George H. Himes, Shaw acknowledged yellow-ribboned delegates and guests. Delegates came from every state in the Union—New England was particularly well represented—and most guests were Portlanders. The church's attractive decorations prompted comment; a participant described the sanctuary as "a bower of flowers. There are roses and all the blooms which grace Portland's yards, and they are arranged with taste and artistic effect to make the big auditorium the more pleasant."[14] Alice Blackwell summarized: "The great graystone Congregational Church has its auditorium hung with American flags and bunting of the suffrage color [yellow]; portraits of Lucy Stone and Susan B. Anthony stand back of the pulpit, and along its front runs the word 'Progress' in large letters made of Oregon flowers."

The national president quickly demonstrated her ability to chair a convention; she had the prerequisite oratory and organizational skills to handle diverse speakers and complex business. Viola Coe, president of the Oregon State Equal Suffrage Association (OSESA), spoke first, welcoming the delegates and acknowledging her friend Duniway's long service. Other Oregon women talked briefly; then it was Anthony's turn. Those who had heard that she had become feeble expressed surprise at her strong voice and fluent delivery. As on many past occasions, she rendered a sketchy history of the suffrage movement, emphasizing that she and Stanton had met considerable hostility from prejudiced men. "The day of universal scorn for equal suffrage," she emphasized, "has passed, and today we have gallant and courageous champions among the sex, the members of which 50 years ago regarded our proposals as a part of that system of iconoclasm which threatened the very foundation of the social fabric."[15] Anthony maintained that when she came to the region in 1871 only a few women supported suffrage. The speaker added that she had raised $1,000 in Oregon for her $10,000 *Revolution* debt. "It was," she recalled, "almost the first money I ever earned, and I shall always be grateful to Oregon."[16] Anthony had received a standing ovation when she appeared on the platform, and at the end of the session listeners rushed forward, grasping for her hands.

Anthony presided over the evening session of the convention. A writer described her as a rare picture "in the high-backed oaken chair, her snowy hair puffed over the ears in old-time fashion, and the collar of rose point lace which seems to belong to dignified old age, forming a frame for her gentle but determined face."[17] Well-wishers heaped flowers upon her arms; she responded that fifty years earlier she had been pelted by eggs and had been the target of various epithets. She smilingly acknowledged that she now received showers of roses. Portland newspapermen appreciated this occasion and acknowledged Anthony's surprising energy. One wrote: "Although well advanced in years, she still retains her vigor and speaks with the same directness and force, which years ago won for her such an enviable position among platform orators." Another correspondent summarized: "Her voice was resonant and her direction of affairs forcible. 'Aunt Susan' will not see the fruition of her hopes, but it must be a great satisfaction to her to retain in her old age an active interest and a firm hand in the movement."[18]

During the session the suffragist introduced three men who sat among the many women on the platform. One observer laughed that Governor George Chamberlain, Jefferson Myers (the man who had extended the Lewis and Clark Exhibition's invitation to the NAWSA), and Tom Devlin, city auditor and the mayor's representative, wore "uncomfortable-looking black clothes with their hair pasted down slick."[19] Chamberlain and Myers enthusiastically supported equal suffrage; Devlin, however, "dealt in glittering generalities with snow on the mountains and bloom on the bush." Subsequent female speakers all acknowledged Chamberlain's valuable endorsement: Catt hailed him as "one of our soldiers," and Duniway enthused that his words "electrified" her.[20] Duniway's Centennial Ode had been read in the morning; Anthony then presented her old ally, reminding the audience that they "went gypsying 34 years ago."[21] One listener called the Oregon leader's talk both humorous and historical; another concluded: "Duniway, revered by all the women of the convention as the veteran of the Pacific Coast in the campaign for woman's emancipation, gave an address that teemed with brilliant sallies." Duniway went on to play an extremely important role at the convention, which she had eagerly anticipated referring to it as one of the important events in her career as a reformer. After the convention's conclusion she wrote her son, Clyde, that everyone expressed satisfaction with it and that "Susan B. Anthony and your mother were recognized as its stars."[22]

President Anna Shaw then read her annual address. She immediately indicated that she would let others praise Lewis and Clark but that she would honor Sacajawea, "the modest, unselfish, enduring little Shoshone squaw who uncomplainingly trailed, canoed, climbed, slaved and starved with the men of the party, enduring all that they endured, with the addition of a helpless baby strapped upon her back."[23] While such sentiments prompted little comment, Shaw was more controversial when she read:

> Sacajawea . . . Your tribe is fast disappearing from the land of your fathers. May we, the daughters of an alien race who slew your people and usurped your country, learn the lessons of calm endurance, of patient persistence and unfaltering courage exemplified in your life, in our efforts to lead men through the pass of justice, which leads over the mountains of prejudice and conservatism, to the broad land of the perfect freedom of a true republic, in which men and women together shall in perfect equality solve the problems of a nation which knows no caste, no race, no sex in opportunity, in responsibility, or in justice!

The leader proceeded to discuss the history and present status of the suffrage movement, the persistent challenge of prostitution, the difficulties of marriage and divorce, and the importance of child rearing. The crowd appreciated her thoughts, including the assertion that "motherhood is a direct service to the state, without which no state can exist, mothers should have the ballot to protect themselves and their children." Like other politicians, Shaw interpreted old election returns, emphasizing that woman suffrage had attracted many more votes in 1900 than it had in 1884. Taking aim at Duniway and other like-minded suffragists, the speaker insisted: "There is hope for the future success of our work only in organization adequate to its needs, active, persevering, aggressive, determined." Duniway chose to ignore this assertion and enthused that Shaw's speech "was never excelled by any paper of President or Senator, and never equalled by them in soul." A journalist concluded that the president's analytical and philosophical address "was one of the most comprehensive heard in Portland."[24]

Delegates followed a different schedule during the convention's second day. After a morning session in the Congregational church they journeyed to the Lewis and Clark Exposition fairgrounds, where they participated in a special women's day and attended a reception. Returning to the church, delegates heard another round of speeches, including two by Pacific Northwest characters. Idahoan May Arkwright Hutton, who had become a millionaire from a lucky mining investment, entertained listeners. She recalled that when she was a girl the young William McKinley patted her head, stating, "I believe when this lassie grows up that hers will be an enfranchised womanhood."[25] Colonel C.E.S. Wood, an unconventional Portland lawyer who consistently supported the underdog, assured women in a speech entitled "The Injustice of Majority Rule" that they would receive the vote. According to a listener he then applied "a liberal portion of cold water by wondering what they wanted with it" and that the vote would not "do as much good as its advocates hoped for." He gloomily predicted that women would take their "places on the chessboard to be moved in the game by the governing machine which many of you do not see."[26] Wood judged that "our voters were as much governed and exploited as were the peasants in Russia" and generalized that the majority of American voters "were little stuffed men going to a little stuffed ballot box." This was too much for President Shaw, who countered that "she would rather be a little stuffed woman having her own say about it than be ruled by a little stuffed man without her consent." The suffragist predicted that men would no longer be "little stuffed men" if they had "free mothers."

In the *Pacific Monthly*, Wood elaborated on his views of woman suffrage. After his convention speech, he related, a woman called him a socialist. The lawyer replied,

> "No, madam, . . . I am at the other extreme of political philosophy. I am an anarchist."
> "Ah, yes," she said, "substantially the same." And I would doubt if she ought to vote, if it were not that the intelligent voters of this land, and the intelligent press are in the same state of ignorance. Possibly she thinks I am engaged in the secret manufacture of bombs.

Ida Husted Harper, who, like Wood, was an intelligent and skilled writer, delivered a thoughtful suffrage speech. This close associate of Anthony concluded that in Oregon "There is not an intelligent man or woman . . . who does not admit that the enfranchisement of women is only a question of time." Many listeners were flattered when this easterner, like some other experienced speakers, predicted that the Progressive West would lead the East into reform: "It is not westward but eastward the star of woman's empire takes its way, for it was in the West that it arose. . . . It is to the strong, courageous and progressive men of the western states that the women of this whole country look for deliverance from the bondage of disfranchisement."[27]

The session held at the auditorium on the Lewis and Clark Exposition grounds was perhaps the least productive one. The crowd aroused itself, however, when Anthony was introduced "in order that the children might see her." Following hearty applause, the veteran suffragist responded: "I don't expect to be here when you get the vote, but I shall be somewhere in the kingdom, in the universe, and I shall rejoice with you."

The day's highlight was Anthony's reception. The *Oregonian* maintained that she received the greatest ovation ever given a woman in the state and the *Telegram* boasted that no queen ever received a greater honor. As she entered the Oregon building, a band played "Auld Lang Syne," and she acknowledged Elizabeth Cady Stanton's portrait hanging in the reception room. Joined by eastern and western suffrage leaders, the honored guest greeted a long line of well-wishers. Asked by friends if she was weary, Anthony stated that the hours spent shaking hands "did not make her nearly so tired as it did 50 years ago when no one came."[28] Many who attended sought to describe the emotional occasion, but the *Telegram* seemed to capture it best. "The great leader was as sweet and winsome as a mountain flower, and throngs of admirers of the grand old champion crowded around her to do her honor."

Saturday, 1 July, was a gorgeous summer day; delegates used it to discuss tactics appropriate for suffrage fights and to hear stimulating speakers. Two Oregon men appeared on the rostrum; the least effective was Judge Stephen A. Lowell of Pendleton. Like other Progressives he denounced the rich who seemed to be above the law. The Oregon judge complained that "the curse of the age is the lawlessness of law enforcement," and he won applause by asserting that equal suffrage could change this deplorable condition.[29] He pleased delegates by reminding them that most nineteenth century reformers were women and explained that this resulted from the fact that men were too busy pursuing dollars. Lowell concluded, "Not color or creed or sex but patriotic honesty must be the test of citizenship if the republic lives."

William S. U'Ren gave a more practical speech. Delegates appreciated that he had played a major role in getting the initiative and referendum added to the state's constitution. The Progressive spoke on the need and purpose of these political reforms and answered several questions, especially about the initiative. U'Ren advised listeners to push reform in open campaigns, in opposition to Duniway's still hunt tactic. Vice

President Catt, who was particularly enthusiastic about the Oregon reform, asserted that the only persons opposed to the initiative and referendum were those who failed to understand it or those who opposed democracy itself. She proposed a resolution that the NAWSA "affirm our belief in the initiative and referendum as a needed reform." This resolution temporarily failed.

The press explained that the inaction resulted from the fear that the resolution would hurt the suffragist cause in conservative states opposed to such popular vote reforms. Clara Colby presented a more specific interpretation: "Duniway counseled indefinitely postponing the resolution, in the fear that its adoption would advise the opponents of equal suffrage that a campaign was to take place next year."[30] Anthony, who missed the discussion because she had been resting and arrived late, immediately and successfully argued that initiative petitions should be circulated in Oregon prior to the 1906 vote. Later in the convention Anthony, Duniway (who had changed her mind) and others spoke for a resolution favoring the Oregon initiative and referendum reforms. It won enthusiastic approval. Long after delegates left Portland they continued to advocate the state's reforms. In an editorial entitled, "Progressive Oregon," Henry Blackwell assumed that every state would adopt the initiative and referendum. In his mind this direct legislation was "the refuge of reformers from the tyranny of organized self-interest, like Paul, they can appeal to Caesar."[31]

Another political tactic also attracted the aging leader's interest. Harper returned to the platform and led a dozen editors in a lively symposium entitled, "How can we best utilize the press?" Journalist Alice S. Blackwell, the daughter of pioneer suffragist Lucy Stone and reformer Henry B. Blackwell, was a skilled writer and lucid debater. She held the audience's attention. Drawing from her long experience the editor contemplated ways to get newspaper publicity. Blackwell conceded that, when appropriate, female editors should criticize individual males but warned that they should not "roast men as a sex."[32] Duniway reminisced about her *New Northwest*, digressed on the topic of her husband's commitment to equal suffrage, and praised the *Woman's Journal*. She insisted, however, that "secular papers could best bring the movement before the public." Anthony interjected, "That's all right, Abigail." Obviously Anthony considered the press as important in 1905 as she had in 1871. At one point the leader admitted that "it had been so long since she published the *Revolution* that she had almost forgotten the tactics at that time." The politician then reiterated her basic point, "Women's papers are all right, but it is through the great dailies we must convert the world."

A wide-ranging discussion of another tactic aroused Oregon delegates. A Michigan visitor asked if it helped the cause for suffragists to join women's clubs. Portlander Sarah Evans from the Oregon State Federation of Women's Clubs encouraged such action: "the woman's club is the cradle in which to develop suffragists." She pointed out that her organization began "with hardly any suffragists in its ranks, and now most of its members are converted." Duniway assented, insisting that the club movement had helped fill the suffragist ranks throughout the Pacific Northwest. Participants sided with these Oregonians; one concluded, "We must not let the women's clubs be satisfied with doll politics, but make them feel that we need the real thing."[33] Another tactic won hearty approval: it was resolved to double the membership of the NAWSA by recruiting men. Delegates acknowledged that males often had conflicting interests but thought that their inclusion could assist the cause. A few, however, still wanted women to realize their goal without reliance on male assistance.

Many remembered that the third evening's speakers were the most stimulating. Among the four able women who addressed the convention were Rev. Antoinette Brown Blackwell, an eighty-one year-old reformer, who defied tradition and became the first ordained woman minister. An honored figure among young reformers, she emphatically ruled that there was "no sane reason" why a woman should not be elected as mayor, governor, or president.[34] Another, Gail Laughlin, a dynamic New York lawyer who had been organizing Oregon women into suffrage clubs in 1905, took up Theodore Roosevelt's Square Deal. The reformer insisted that the president implement it "against the greatest trust in the world—the political trust, the trust which is the most absolute monopoly because entrenched in the law itself." Laughlin received hearty applause when she judged that "the exclusion of women from participation in governmental affairs means the going to waste of a great force, which, if utilized, would be a great power in the advance of civilization."

Though the convention adjourned for the Sabbath, NAWSA officers continued to push their reform on Sunday; several of them had been invited to preach in Portland's pulpits. The *Oregonian* declared that "the event of the day, which drew out the greatest church gathering seen in Portland for a long time, was the appearance of Miss Anthony at the White Temple" Church.[35] This Baptist congregation and its visitors heard Anthony speak "with her old time force" on the topic, "The influence which educational, charitable, and religious associations would have if women possessed the ballot." The reporter stated that when the veteran suffragist appeared in Portland's largest church the audience, some of whom had to stand, loudly applauded "as though it had not been Sunday, nor the place a church. Aunt Susan, as Portlanders are beginning to affectionately call her, was feeling fine . . . and got in a few of the best words for the suffrage question which have been put to the Oregon public." The *Journal*'s chronicle of this unusual Sunday noted that suffragists told various congregations that the Bible supported equal opportunity and that "the welcome that was accorded the women by the Portland pastors was sharply in contrast with the hostility that once was shown by virtually all the clergy when the equal suffrage campaign began in the middle of the last century."[36] Perhaps Anthony, who so often reminisced, thought about the Walla Walla churches that had been closed to her in 1871 and the hostile ministers of that first Pacific Northwest campaign.

The Monday morning session was extremely important to Anthony, who saw the national and state suffrage organizations unite in planning for the 1906 suffrage campaign. The leader delivered a memorable political speech. "Clad in soft blacks appropriate to her advanced age," a journalist wrote, the venerable leader eagerly anticipated the coming fight "with the ardor of a cadet, and yet she revealed the mild-mannered, sweet, womanly character she had, in which also are found the qualities of true generalship."[37] She encouraged carrying the warfare into the state's remotest parts and reminded that suffragists had lost the 1896 California struggle because they had not canvassed the state's rural counties. In prescribing tactics, Anthony declared, "I stand for the fight in the open . . . and am not in sympathy with those who argue for the still hunt." Once again she opposed aligning the campaign with any political party. Anthony predicted victory would come because Oregonians no longer looked upon suffragists "as social iconoclasts," because the reform had attracted so many more voters in 1900 than it did in 1884, and because Oregon was a Progressive state enjoying the initiative and referendum. Impressed with these new amendments, the veteran politician believed they were "perhaps the most salient movement of modern times for the emancipation of the masses from the power of the bosses." It seemed to her and her allies—they often told Oregonians about this difficulty—that political bosses inevitably opposed woman suffrage. In 1905 as in 1871 Anthony told Oregon women that men could provide valuable assistance but that they must wage their own campaign "in order to prove their capability." Suffragists must voice, she instructed, a positive message: voters should simply be told that the reform would improve Oregon. "It will inject into the electorate of the state an element that in the main will stand for the better things in government, and it will raise the women themselves to a higher position and give them a complete realization of the duties and responsibilities that rest upon all who owe allegiance to our common flag."

Dr. Annice Jeffreys Myers—not Duniway—told the excited crowd that Oregon women had carefully prepared for the fight and eagerly awaited it. She praised easterners Mary Chase and Gail Laughlin for organizing additional suffrage clubs so that Oregon currently had fifty-two clubs with a combined membership of seven hundred twenty. Jeffreys Myers thanked the NAWSA for meeting in Portland and for providing campaign funds. In conclusion she provided reasons for optimism about the election: the state Grange had provided rural audiences, Sarah Evans had written important suffrage columns in the metropolitan newspapers, and Portland's three dailies had published appealing photographs and favorable, extensive accounts of the NAWSA convention.

Aroused to political action, suffragists pledged money and cheered speakers, including Willis Duniway. Abigail's son delighted in the announcement that the NAWSA would help the Oregon suffragists. He, like his mother, maintained that hard working pioneer women deserved the ballot and that he wanted Abigail to vote. Willis won loud applause by concluding, "I claim no right or privilege for myself that I would not give to my mother, wife and sister, and to every law-abiding citizen." Proud of her son, Abigail informed the audience, "That, dear women from the north and south and east and west, is one of Mrs. Duniway's poor neglected babies."[38] It is not clear what she thought of his ringing endorsement of the NAWSA.

After Anthony's call for an Oregon political fight and its enthusiastic reception, most sessions in the last two convention days seemed anticlimactic. Neither Susan nor Abigail played as dominant a role in discussions. On 4 July Portlanders and thousands of their guests noisily celebrated the holiday with traditional fireworks, oratory, music, excursions, and picnics. National American Woman Suffrage Association delegates did not join the 50,000 celebrants at the Lewis and Clark Exposition. They quietly planned political strategy, pledged money for the Oregon campaign, enjoyed speakers, and conducted an election of officers. The only contested election was won by Florence Kelley, who as the new vice president urged that women should win state suffrage battles while Anthony "is still with us."[39] For Oregonians the most favorable election result was that of Portlander Annice Jeffreys Myers as an auditor. Energetic and intelligent, she had played major roles in inviting the convention to Portland, in hosting the Anthony reception and in donating money to the cause. Delegates praised her contributions. Some must have thought of Jeffreys Myers as Duniway's replacement. Friends hailed her election as an honor for both her and Portland. Duniway must have considered the physician's recognition partly as a reward for helping the national and local leaders combine against her.

At the evening session the NAWSA leadership acknowledged the Fourth of July. Mary Anthony, who had been silent during the sessions, now played a part. In her journal she had acknowledged that the holiday was properly only "man's independence day."[40] Organizers chose her to read the Declaration of Rights adopted at Seneca Falls, New York, in 1848 because she had been present at that historic meeting. Her famous sister then added her own commentary, emphasizing that whereas the Seneca Falls convention had been poorly publicized, the press now thoroughly reported equal rights meetings. The politician linked Seneca Falls with the Portland convention of 1906 and advised: "concentrate your best hopes and wishes, and your best dollars, on Oregon for the coming year."[41] Vice President Catt then gave a stirring extemporaneous address. In interpreting the Fourth she reminded listeners that in 1776 Americans denounced taxation without representation but that contemporary women still suffered from such detested discrimination. Looking to 1906 she predicted a suffrage victory which would prompt her and her husband to move to Oregon. Catt also believed that an orator in the year 2005 would live in a time when "One sex will not rule another; one race will not rule another; one class will not rule another; but there will be real liberty of equality and fraternity for all."[42]

During the concluding sessions, lecturers handled relevant subjects. Henry Blackwell denounced war and ruled that "a purely masculine government never did and never will keep the peace. A government of men and women is needed in order to establish international courts of arbitration, and to make war and bloodshed forever more unnecessary."[43] Blackwell emphasized the costs of armaments: "a battleship which lasts only 15 years costs more than all the land, buildings, and equipments of Harvard university, Hampton and Tuskegee colleges combined." Rabbi Emil G. Hirsch, who gave several addresses in the city and at the exposition, also delivered a thoughtful lecture. "It is," the visitor explained, "a strange anomaly in American public life that we have given our schools so largely into the hands of women. They are expected to teach the children history and patriotism, yet are not considered competent to vote."[44] The religious leader reasoned that women should be enfranchised because they paid taxes, performed public service, and were righteous. Newly-elected Vice President Kelley discussed industrial problems affecting women and children and judged that the current weakness of the suffrage movement resulted from the fact that it had not sought help from working people.

Two regional residents also voiced ideas. Sarah Evans reported that when girls studied civics they became suffragists. Mrs. Emma Edwards Green of Boise amused the audience by stating that although she was a Democrat and her husband was a local Republican official, they still enjoyed a peaceful home.

Shaw recalled that the last session was one of the most significant because several Oregon men representing various political parties endorsed the reform.[45] These politicians were introduced by state Senator Henry Waldo Coe, whose wife was president of the OSESA. Coe disagreed with those who argued that women should be at home rearing children and asserted that "the woman who takes an interest in the affairs of her country takes the best interest in her home."[46] The two most important political representatives were Portland Mayor Harry Lane—a Democrat who had been in office only a few days—and Republican Andrew Smith. Reformer Lane predicted that female voters would purify politics and described the ideal marriage as one "where the man helped the woman with the housework, and she helped him with public affairs." Smith favorably compared the convention's female speakers with Portland males and explained that he supported the suffrage cause because "he asked himself if his mother was not as well qualified to have a voice in government as any man." Mary Anthony thought that these Portlanders provided the convention with a memorable conclusion. She described them as leading businessmen who expressed a willingness to work for a 1906 victory and concluded: "never before have we been publicly endorsed by so many influential voters—one from each political party. It certainly should give us courage."[47]

Following hearty applause for these politicians, Oregon suffrage leaders presented flowers to national officers, Alice Blackwell gratified Duniway's request to relate some suffrage anecdotes, Shaw delivered final remarks, and Anthony closed the convention by again urging everyone to labor for an Oregon suffrage victory. That evening May Arkwright Hutton of Idaho hosted a dinner for Anthony, Duniway, and other prominent figures, who were, the *Oregonian* maintained, "the most distinguished body of women . . . ever gathered at one table in the history of Portland."[48]

The last public platform that Anthony and Duniway ever shared was at the unveiling of the Sacajawea statue at the exposition grounds. Both enjoyed the occasion, and, like the Portland press, they boasted about the Indian woman's achievements. The *Oregonian* announced that "The courageous Bird woman who died in obscurity and poverty after pointing out to Lewis and Clark the trail to a new empire, will be honored by a multitude this afternoon when the drapings of a huge American flag are swept aside from the beautiful bronze statue of Sacajawea and her papoose."[49] The *Journal*, too, commemorated her efforts: "Gallant men of the western states today honored the memory of a brave Indian woman—Sacajawea—guide of the explorers who a century ago accepted and nobly discharged the mission of President Jefferson and sought a route over which afterward moved the column of civilization's army to conquer this region."[50]

The celebration included a parade from downtown Portland to the dedication site. Officers and delegates from the recently concluded NAWSA convention boarded a tallyho and carriages that took positions in the long parade. Arranged by the Improved Order of Red Men, a national fraternity with several tribes (lodges) in Portland, the procession included hundreds of its own members; bands; floats showing Sacajawea, the Boston Tea Party, and Washington Crossing the Delaware (an observer said they were "of beautiful appearance and historical significance"); and cadets from Oregon's Chemawa Indian school.[51]

At the platform site the Sacajawea Association, which had long planned this historic event, directed the ceremonies. Thousands of celebrants sweated under the hot summer sun as they observed Indians in native costumes, listened to a band play patriotic music, commented on the statue of the famous Indian carrying her baby, and struggled to get near the speakers. Many commented about the huge crowd; one observer explained that Anthony's "presence . . . was sufficient to ensure that a large number would be there to see and hear her speak."[52]

Anthony, the featured speaker, delivered what one listener called a brilliant oration. Another believed it fitting that the New Yorker speak at the unveiling because she was "herself a guide to advancement among women." In her short address entitled, "Women in Discovery," Anthony called Sacajawea "one of the greatest of American heroines, second not even to Molly Pitcher," and she "pitied the woman who was unable on this occasion to worship at the shrine of the Indian squaw."[53] The reformer recounted the significance of American women in the nation's history and emphasized: "This is the first time in history that a statue has been erected in the memory of a woman who accomplished patriotic deeds." Statues had been placed in honor of philanthropists and others, Anthony noted, but this was the first to a woman who had "done a patriotic duty." She asserted, "If it were not for that brave little Indian mother, there would be no Oregon or Portland." The politician then turned from an unfamiliar historical figure and spoke of the future, encouraging the crowd to support the suffrage cause in 1906.

Duniway spoke on pioneer mothers, one of her favorite themes. She praised them: "for whether she was engaged in the domestic pursuits of peace or defending her rude domicile from wild beasts or wilder savages, she was equally with man a necessary factor" in the establishment of a twentieth century civilization. The Portlander's tone was different from her old mentor's: she bluntly asserted that the statue represented "the past subjection of womanhood . . . when woman carried man on her shoulders—a feminine atlas."[54]

Sacajawea had been popularized in a 1902 novel by Oregon City resident Eva Emery Dye, whose work as president of the Sacajawea

Statue Association earned her the right to give the presentation speech. She hailed the heroine and the role of pioneer women. According to her understanding of history: "with women and wagons, Oregon was taken. The Indians expected to see an army with banners when the white man came, but no, the mother and the child took Oregon."[55] Portland Mayor Harry Lane gave the speech of acceptance, praising Indian character: "When they have not been contaminated by the evils of the white race, they are the personification of tireless energy, patience and hospitality. All of the wars resulted from the white people ill-treating the Indians who had befriended them." Anna Shaw then gave the benediction and the well-dressed crowd rushed to escape from the stifling heat. Probably Susan agreed with her sister's assessment of the unveiling ceremony: "It was an interesting affair. This woman, with her papoose (*the future male citizen*) strapped to her back, was the subject of three excellent speakers from men and three from the women."[56] Sarah Evans described the unveiling:

> The picture will never fade from the memory of those who saw Miss Anthony and Dr. Shaw standing on the platform with the sun lighting up their silver hair like an aureole and their faces radiant with hope, as "The Star Spangled Banner" sung by an Indian boy raised a tumult of applause while the flag floated away revealing the idealized mother and babe.

These and other suffragist leaders had obviously celebrated parts of the Sacajawea story in an attempt to promote their cause. Knowing that Americans wanted heroes and heroines, they lauded her courage, dedication, and competence; furthermore, both pioneer and contemporary women had often demonstrated these same positive traits. Thus the Indian woman's remarkable life should prompt thought about the abilities and character of women in industrial America. Many could see little connection, but ten years after the dedication Shaw recalled that Sacajawea "was treated little worse than thousands of the white pioneer women who have followed her; and standing there to-day . . . she still seems sorrowfully reflective over the strange ways of the nation she so nobly served."[57] The connection between the Indian and the suffrage cause from 1905 to 1912 is obscure, but twenty years ago historian Ronald Taber argued that "Mrs. Dye formulated the Sacajawea myth which was to become closely identified with the woman suffrage movement, not only in Oregon, but throughout the nation."[58] The writer also maintained that Sacajawea was more "an image of perfect womanhood" than Susan B. Anthony. Dye, an Oregon suffragist, had contributed to and promoted the Sacajawea myth, but Taber fails to recognize that male opinion makers, including newspaper reporters, joined suffragists in contributing to it. Taber is incorrect in asserting that state and national leaders made more of Sacajawea than of Anthony. Furthermore, there is no evidence that suffragists emphasized the model of Sacajawea to Oregon voters in 1906. Experienced female politicians knew that a compelling Indian story would not suffice to win male political support.

On the evening after the dedication the Anthonys and other guests must have thought about the day's celebration, the talents of the statue's sculptor Alice Cooper, and Sacajawea's contributions. After a special dinner the reformers drove about the city in the tallyho "Jupiter," provided by the principal of the Hill Military Academy. Mary Anthony delighted in this "sunset trip to Portland Heights to look down upon the beautiful electric lighted city and fairgrounds, and the snow-covered mountains, St. Helens, Hood, and others."[59]

Anthony lingered in Portland for five days after the convention's conclusion, helping to prepare the Oregon suffrage fight. President Shaw, Vice President Catt, and other experienced individuals made political arrangements with local organizers. Anthony served primarily as an advisor. The visiting feminists enjoyed a reception given by the Portland Woman's Club and spoke about the recently concluded convention and the importance of suffrage in resolving social and economic problems important to clubwomen. Many, passing through the receiving line, complimented Aunt Susan's black silk dress—worn also when she had been presented to Queen Victoria and the Empress of Germany.[60]

This reception provided Anthony and her lieutenants a pleasant opportunity to publicize their cause. On 10 July they huddled with Oregon allies to plan their political campaign. At this meeting the NAWSA formally accepted the OSESA's request for its assistance. Shaw stressed that the national organization did not come into a state uninvited, that it had sent many workers into the 1896 California fight—which would have been won were it not for the opposition of the

Oakland and San Francisco liquor interests—and that it had not yet chosen a manager for the Oregon campaign. The national president predicted "perfect harmony" between state and national organizations. Anthony, emphasizing teamwork for Duniway's benefit, advised that an individual should not "work on her own hook. She must receive instructions from headquarters."[61] But Duniway ignored the admonition and remembered their parting as pleasant. Anthony stated: "My highest hopes are centered upon Oregon. You have a splendid set of voters here, and they have carried us to a point where failure is no longer possible." The leader told many Oregonians that she hoped to return in June and help celebrate the election victory.

After reaching agreements on the upcoming struggle, the national and local leaders thanked each other for their roles at the convention, predicted a successful campaign, and said farewell. During this last meeting—as throughout the convention—Portland suffered from a heat wave. Mary Anthony stated that on 8 July the thermometer read 115 degrees in the sun. After their final meeting the NAWSA delegates joined Portlanders in seeking relief at the river, the coast, or in the forests. Because of the heat Anthony rarely left her hotel. She heard or read of Shaw's message to the YMCA and laughed when the speaker admitted that "she liked to talk to men better than she did women, for when she was talking to men, she was talking to heads, instead of hats and feathers."[62] While Shaw busily pushed her reform to Portlanders, Anthony sometimes discussed it in her hotel. Among her guests was May Arkwright Hutton, who discussed a plan to assist aged and indigent miners. Susan and Mary toured some Portland businesses and heard about the city's growth and brilliant future. This boosterism may have reminded Anthony of what she had heard in 1871 and 1896.

One evening the Anthony women enjoyed a trolley car ride to Portland Heights and gazed down upon the well-lit exposition grounds. The aged sisters lacked the stamina to stroll about the hot fairgrounds, but they heard and read much about its activities. Anthony sought information about the condition of local women; probably the following newspaper items were brought to her attention. Eleven Portland female organizations worked together to create an association to protect unchaperoned women visiting the Lewis and Clark Exposition. The city's school board had recently passed a resolution—the *Oregonian* called it "ungallant"—that any teacher marrying after being given a position would be dismissed.[63] A Multnomah County official reported that there was a 100 percent increase in the number of divorces between 1904-1905 and the preceding year and that in that same time period there were twice as many divorces as marriages. Shaw also brought Anthony information about the local WCTU conference, especially its support of equal suffrage. Shaw, who practiced medicine, probably called to her friend's attention the provocative address of Dr. Ella K. Dearborn. At a homeopathic medical society meeting in Portland the physician had advocated euthanasia for criminals, degenerates, and those suffering from fatal maladies.

Anthony often reflected upon her successful Portland visit. She appreciated the warm hospitality; rejoiced over the courteous, complete, and thoughtful newspaper coverage; applauded the convention's sessions where speakers, discussions, and reports had advanced the cause; enjoyed the receptions and the unveiling of the Sacajawea statue; won regional allies to her reform; and delighted in the smooth management of the convention by easterners Shaw, Catt, and Harper and by Oregonians Coe, Jeffreys Myers, and Evans. This third visit to Portland was a greater success than her earlier ones. In each she had sought to organize women and to win the state vote for equal suffrage; the prospects for attaining both goals appeared brighter in 1905 than they had in 1871 or 1896, primarily because now talented and dedicated national and state leaders now cooperated in planning the Oregon campaign. Anthony could take satisfaction in comparing her last visit with her first; the movement had acquired significantly more support from educated women, politicians, (including Portland's mayor and Oregon's governor), ministers, and editors. Although the city's press did not wholly embrace suffrage, it was no longer critical or condescending. There was another generalization that could be made about the newspapers: reporters interviewing the NAWSA leadership and attending the sessions seemed more sympathetic with the suffrage cause than their editors.

Other eastern delegates considered the convention memorable as well. They often praised the Pacific Northwest for its cool evenings, rivers, mountains, flowers, and fruits. These visitors enjoyed the region's hospitality (many stayed in private homes), favorable press reports, and the resolve of local women. During the convention and for years after delegates talked glowingly about Portland, the Exposition, Astoria, Seattle, and the Columbia Gorge. Mary Anthony wrote that "Portland can well boast of as fine natural scenery and surroundings as any other town I have ever visited in our country." Catt went beyond this assessment and called it the "most beautiful city of the United States and of the world."[64]

Many Pacific Northwest women left the convention as enthused as their visitors. Joined by a few men, these activists resolved to soldier in the 1906 battle. Inspired by Anthony, Shaw, Catt, the Blackwells, Harper, and other guests, they immediately spread the reform message from Portland. These enthusiasts agreed with Evans who stated that the suffragist convention gave their cause "a new birth."[65] Even those not in the suffragist ranks applauded the well-managed convention. The *Oregon Journal*'s assessment began with a reminder to readers that most observers had believed that a woman's convention would include "disagreeable encounters, heartburnings, and such an utter lack of conventional business methods as furnish food for the sarcastic and joy for the ungodly."[66] The editor continued, "But there has never been a more businesslike convention held here than that of the national suffragists." He, like so many other opinion makers, complimented the delegates for being thorough, efficient, and fair.

Colonel C.E.S. Wood reacted differently. Although he agreed that woman suffrage was "a righteous cause" and called Shaw "a most eloquent and able woman," he insisted that the convention had not furthered the movement in Oregon. Wood ruled that while only women could bring the reform to a successful conclusion, they would not do so here because of widespread indifference. Portland, he said, had a population of more than 100,000, yet the convention's meetings at the church were never filled. "Women of national and worldwide reputation," he reminded, "were there; eloquent women were there; but apparently there were not five hundred women in Portland who took any interest in this interesting subject and this interesting convention."[67] Duniway and others responded that the various attractions at the Lewis and Clark Exhibition reduced attendance at the NAWSA Convention.

Wood's opinions about numbers and signs of indifference were not unfounded, but the regional suffrage movement was, as Evans insisted, transformed by the convention. Inspired by a long list of able speakers, new friendships, the pleas and symbolic presence of the aging Aunt Susan, and the reiteration of basic principles in discussions and reports, regional women and men voiced a new determination to fight on for eventual victory.

The NAWSA delegates underscored the Oregon suffrage fight, but the Washington suffragist movement also benefitted, as Anthony predicted, from the convention. Several Washingtonians attended, including ex-Chief Justice Roger S. Greene, who spoke at one session about his state's suffrage history. Puget Sound women caught the enthusiasm that infected those from the Willamette Valley. They returned home resolved to work harder for their enfranchisement. Several eastern delegates, including Harper and the Blackwells—editors of the *Woman's Journal*—toured on to Puget Sound, meeting with reformers. In Seattle they conversed with Dr. Fannie L. Cummings, president of the state's suffrage association, and other leaders. Henry Blackwell hailed the sixty members of the Seattle Suffrage Club, calling them "a noble band . . . resolute in their determination to reinstate equal suffrage at the earliest opportunity."[68] He spoke in the city's Unitarian Church and received extensive and fair newspaper coverage.

His daughter, Alice Blackwell, also wrote a glowing report about Seattle. She pleased its inhabitants by generalizing that no New England city could compare with it "in natural beauty" and praised its suffragists for their ability to utilize the press better than those in Boston. The editor insisted that the booming and beautiful city needed woman suffrage so as to provide more support of libraries, schools, and free hospital space. In fact, Blackwell in 1905 like Anthony in 1871 predicted a better future for the city if it adopted her reform. "Let Washington give the ballot to her wives and mothers, and the educational, artistic, and humanitarian side of Seattle will be built up and developed side by side with its great material expansion."

Late in 1905, suffragist organizations around Puget Sound reported increased publicity and membership; one reformer stated that the state's suffrage movement "got a great impetus from the Portland Convention."[69] The Oregon campaign of 1905-1906 would give Washington suffragists an opportunity to participate and learn; Tacoman Emma Smith DeVoe's experience in Oregon helped prepare her for the effective campaign in her own state. Thus, an increasingly important Washington suffrage movement can be dated from the NAWSA convention of 1905.

Aware that much had been accomplished in Portland, Susan and Mary Anthony began a tiring, month-long journey home. Accepting California invitations the sisters traveled as far south as Los Angeles. They wilted from the summer's sun but wisely punctuated their travel in hot railroad cars with evening rests in hotels. At Mt. Shasta both thoroughly enjoyed a cool mountain resort before proceeding through the scorching Sacramento Valley. Mary observed that Red Bluff was a typical town in that there was "a saloon to about every hundred inhabitants."[70] Annie Bidwell, a friend, greeted the travelers in Chico and took them to her impressive home, where they visited and rested for several days. Susan and Mary both expressed pleasure with the widow's vast property and her generous character. They also sympathized with local Indians suffering from prejudice. At a ceremony in which Bidwell donated land as a Chico park, Anthony asked men to show their appreciation to the donor by supporting political equality.

On 18 July the sisters arrived in San Francisco, receiving a warm welcome from the local Susan B. Anthony Club. Mary toured Chinatown and told her sister that its "miserable opium dens" were a disgrace "but no more than the saloons of the slums where men are so constantly stupefied with whiskey."[71] Susan stayed with long-time friend Ellen Sargent; they recalled Anthony's 1871 and 1896 California campaigns. In San Francisco, as in Portland, the Anthony women attended receptions and dinners, took carriage rides to scenic places, and enjoyed favorable newspaper accounts of Susan and her cause. Suffrage leaders as well as reporters solicited her opinions about reform politics. Anthony's public talks were brief, historical in subject matter, and concluded with pleas for a state suffrage amendment. At one occasion a male praised women's faces. Anthony retorted that "sensible women would be better pleased if men would praise their intellect instead of their physical charms," and if they sought "beauty in their minds instead of their faces."[72]

After about a week the travelers went through San Jose and Santa Barbara to Los Angeles. Here, as in San Francisco, the sisters applauded Shaw's speaking. Between social occasions, Anthony talked politics with suffragists and spoke generally to admirers. On 2 August Susan and Mary left for a visit with Kansas relatives. The trip was excruciating. The thermometer reached 110 degrees, and the old ladies sought relief by applying towels soaked in ice water. At Albuquerque they encountered Indians selling crafts. Mary bitterly commented, "This company, especially the men, show more signs of civilization, as they should, being politically the superiors of every woman in their country."[73] In Leavenworth, Kansas, they rested from their fatiguing journey across the Southwest, visited their sister-in-law, stood before their brother's grave, and took drives in a steamer automobile. On 10 August the Anthonys returned to their modest Rochester home and recalled their pleasant, profitable, and tiring West Coast trip. Susan would never return; Oregon suffrage politics, however, would prompt Mary to visit again in 1906.

Throughout the remaining months of her life Anthony avidly followed the unfolding Oregon battle, one she had helped plan and launch. Personal correspondence and reports in the *Woman's Journal* and the *Woman's Tribune* provided her with details. She was too infirm to command the fight, but she could still advise. Following the Portland convention, suffragists began their eleven month-long effort when Shaw hammered for equality in rousing speeches delivered at Oregon City and Ashland chautauquas. She reported the pleasing results to Anthony in California.

In October 1905 the NAWSA established Portland headquarters and took charge of the state election. An officer of the OSESA admitted that her organization had "put the actual work of the campaign in the hands of the National." The eastern leaders carried on several tasks simultaneously: they stepped up the effort to collect the eight thousand signatures required to place the suffrage amendment on the June ballot, solicited endorsements from organizations and individuals, and publicized their cause through conversations with editors, ministers, businessmen, club women, and ordinary citizens. The drive to get signatures on petitions united the reformers. Members of the OSESA gathered them on Portland streets and exposition walkways; Duniway collected them from the Grand Army of the Republic; Editor Clara Colby urged readers to get petitions signed and traveled herself to Willamette Valley towns, circulating them everywhere. In late December a state official announced that the required signatures had been collected. Reformers congratulated each other.

Meanwhile proponents of the referendum received organizational support from Grange chapters, churches, the Woman's Medical Club of Portland, the Sacajawea Statue Association, the Oregon State Federation of Women's Clubs led by Portland feminist Sarah Evans, and the Oregon WCTU. Governor Chamberlain, Portland Mayor Lane, William S. U'Ren, and other politicians espoused the cause. A veteran suffragist explained that in no previous state campaign had the reform counted "so many of the interests . . . back of it."[74]

Abigail Scott Duniway Day at the Exposition provided her and allies an opportunity to push the campaign. In November the OSESA convened in Portland and the national leaders dominated proceedings. Delegates listened to the three women who would play a critical role in the battle: Laura Gregg, an employee of the NAWSA who temporarily served as Oregon campaign manager; Laura Clay of Kentucky, who had stayed in the city after the convention's conclusion and had assisted state suffrage officers; and Gail Laughlin, an experienced politician and national organizer who had already met and organized many Oregonians. These veterans had directed the meeting and established its committees. Coe, president of the OSESA, chaired the state campaign committee, but it was the outsiders who actually commanded; in fact, their control was as complete as that of Anthony at the 1871 conventions in Olympia and Portland.

Gregg informed delegates that "In my interviews with ministers, editors, clubwomen, and businessmen, I find the prevailing belief is that we are going to win. In no previous campaign have I found such general sentiment in favor of equal suffrage as I have found in Oregon."[75] Laughlin and Clay delivered action-inspiring addresses; audiences learned that these speakers and other experienced field campaigners, including Julia L. Woodworth of Oklahoma, and Ida Porter Boyer of Pennsylvania, would engage in the Oregon fight. In February NAWSA President Shaw would move to Portland and direct the effort until the June election. These national figures assured Oregon women that they, under the OSESA leadership of Coe and Jeffreys Myers, would play a significant role in their own battle.

At times the visiting suffragists reminded local co-workers that they lived in a "state of magnificent distances. It will not be an easy task," they observed "to cover all the centres of population with meetings, to say nothing of reaching the voters on isolated farms. But this is the work which the women must do."[76] For the most part the Oregon campaign was like the one that Anthony had managed in California in 1896. It was much different than the one that Duniway had led in 1900, but the Oregonian still preferred her still hunt strategy to the open effort launched by outsiders in 1905.

From the East Coast came encouragement and financial assistance. Various state suffrage groups sent money; Anthony donated $100. The *Woman's Journal* of 9 December carried considerable news about the ongoing Oregon referendum campaign, reminding that "A victory in Oregon means a victory to every State." The newspaper bluntly asked its readership "What are you going to do for Oregon?" President Shaw, speaking in the state in 1906, emphasized this message: "the immediate battlefield is on the Pacific Coast and in . . . Oregon. Here rests the center of our hopes during the coming year; and we trust . . . another star will be added to the four already on the field of blue." Shaw praised the initiative that made the election possible, commended the state's suffrage workers, and appealed to voters.

> Let [Oregon] be the Star of Hope which will inspire us during the new year, strong in the conviction that the gigantic forests, the rugged mountains, and the mighty rivers of that great Northwest have developed in its men such a love of liberty that they will [share it with] Oregon's women."[77]

Campaigners in Portland took their message under stormy skies to churches, halls, theaters, businesses, and homes. A large theater crowd heard two public forums, where Laughlin was the featured lecturer. Suffragists working in the state's rural regions coped with more difficult conditions—rough stagecoach rides, winter storms, uncomfortable lodging and tasteless meals. Assigned to eastern Oregon, Mary Chase boasted that every man she met was a supporter. The field worker waged an effective effort in villages and towns; the Baker City *Herald*, for example, judged her convincing and challenged local men to hear her, "just to get the cobwebs off his brain so he can hitch up his moral suspenders a bit and get a better grip on the handle of the world."[78] DeVoe, who had skillfully campaigned for the cause in South Dakota and Idaho, left her comfortable Tacoma home and traveled across Southern Oregon in search of votes. If Anthony read about DeVoe's stumping Douglas County it might have reminded her of her own travel there in 1871. The Tacoman spoke in Drain, Yoncalla, Kellogg, Oakland, Stephens, Wilbur, and Roseburg. Travel conditions had hardly improved since 1871; she went by stagecoach through rain and mud and stayed in a less than comfortable assortment of lodgings. Like Anthony she struck up conversations with her stage drivers; one advised her to tell women "to jes go an' vote, and the Oregon fellers wouldn't say nothin to 'em." Another male supporter told DeVoe that he had twenty-five hounds and all would "yelp for woman suffrage until next June, and they are almost as intelligent as some voters."[79]

In the fall and winter of 1905-1906 Anthony watched intently as her followers labored in Oregon; meanwhile, she resumed her East Coast work. Frailty limited her travel; fortunately, the New York State Suffrage Association gathered in her hometown of Rochester, giving the ailing leader an opportunity to participate in proceedings. In mid-November she went to the White House and met with President Roosevelt. (At the Portland convention the NAWSA had decided to interview him about equal suffrage.) Anthony raised significant issues with the president, asking him, among other things, to speak for the woman suffrage cause in Oregon.[80] He replied that he did not interfere with state issues; as the months passed it became clear that Roosevelt was also not going to push a federal suffrage amendment. Disappointed suffragists denounced his Square Deal for its obvious exclusion of their reform.

Anthony waged her fight through correspondence to widely scattered allies and through her appearance at the NAWSA annual convention, held in Baltimore between 7 and 13 February. The old reformer arrived ill. Resting in a private home and under a nurse's care, she nevertheless insisted upon attending the second day's session. She surprised the convention by walking onto the platform and explained that she had come because money needed to be raised. Holding up her purse, she told the hushed audience, "I want to begin by giving you my purse. Just before I left Rochester they gave me a birthday party and made me a present of eighty-six dollars. I suppose they wanted me to do what I liked with the money and I wish to send it to Oregon."[81] Her emotional action prompted others to pledge a total of $4,000 for the distant battle. Anthony probably anticipated such generosity, as her lieutenants had informed her that "throughout the convention the work in Oregon . . . was the uppermost thought."[82] Delegates knew of the need to send money and lecturers, and, like Anthony, they paid particular attention to the optimistic account presented by OSESA President Viola Coe. She reported that the suffrage initiative petitions had 2,400 more names than required by law, that Gail Laughlin's prosuffrage argument had been filed with the Oregon secretary of state, who would distribute

100,000 copies of the document, and that various organizations had endorsed the cause. The Oregon leader, who was a close friend of Duniway, gave the pioneer suffragist credit for getting support from the State Federation of Women's Clubs. This organization, Coe recalled had previously been "noncommittal on the suffrage question." Coe answered many questions from concerned delegates about the political fight and predicted that Oregon would soon be represented by the fifth star on the suffrage flag along with Wyoming, Utah, Colorado, and Idaho.[83]

The state officer privately related to delegates some negative news that she had omitted in her optimistic public report. Duniway had provided a speech to be read at the convention; it lacked Coe's enthusiasm and mildly criticized Anthony's open effort campaign tactic. The Oregon delegate also reported that the strains of managing the campaign had weakened Laura Gregg's health; furthermore, there were too few workers and too little money to carry the reform message to the state's far corners. To wage an Anthony-type effort required lecturers to appear in remote hamlets, deliver many addresses in major cities, cultivate local leaders, organize clubs, and track community responses through newspaper clippings. In other words in 1905 and 1906 several experienced women were reliving the problems faced by Susan and Abigail in their arduous 1871 campaign.

Baltimore delegates also must have asked Coe about newspaper reports that in November eighteen Portland women who opposed suffrage had created the Oregon State Association Opposed to the Extension of Suffrage to Women (OSAOESW). Composed of wealthy women seemingly able to spend large sums in their effort, the group's members were called "antis." They circulated literature, raised money, and courted allies. A suffrage proponent explained that this new opposition "consists of a little handful of millionaires' wives, who are very comfortable themselves, and who think that all other women ought to be well satisfied with their condition."[84] Dr. Jeffreys Myers joined in the criticism, calling her female opponents a wealthy group that had never earned a dollar and were thus unable to understand the problems of workers. Duniway agreed and described the "antis" as a group of women who had inherited their wealth and sought something to do and that they were actually being "used as cats' paws to rake the liquor men's chestnuts out of the fire." The *Oregonian* also denounced these "antis" as being individuals "who can't or don't even button their own shoes."[85] The newspaper insisted that a solid case could be made against equal suffrage but not by "women who live in luxury and ease, and spend their time over rich gowns, bridge, whist, pink teas and beauty shows."

Coe reported that the local "antis" even boasted that they had defeated Oregon suffragists in the 1900 election and that they circulated literature furnished by Massachusetts antisuffragists. She ridiculed these female foes for refusing to debate suffragists and generalized that the public appearance of the Portland "antis" had also aroused statewide attention. A Corvallis newspaper, for example, called it the "prettiest political fight that ever took place," one that was between "excellent ladies who favor woman suffrage against those opposing it. The battle is straight slugging with no sparring for wind, and no lying down to escape punishment."[86]

Deeply concerned about Oregon, Anthony was among those who must have asked Coe about Duniway's role in the campaign. The relationship between Anthony and Duniway seemed strained, a fact that worried their friends. At the NAWSA Portland convention the two had publicly praised each other; when Anthony arrived a newspaper reporter heard her state that she and Duniway were warm friends and that Duniway was "a dear mother in Israel."[87] The Portlander in turn referred to her old teacher as "a beloved leader." Anthony also appreciated that Duniway—who still enjoyed great respect, influenced many Oregon opinion makers, and had a devoted personal following—had cooperated with the NAWSA during its Portland convention. At its conclusion Duniway told journalists that she anticipated a 1906 suffrage victory. But the notable politicians were more distant in 1905 than they had been during Anthony's second visit. Neither, however, saw any reason to break their old and meaningful relationship. In her autobiography Duniway stated, as mentioned earlier, that she had mistakenly supported the invitation to the NAWSA to meet in Portland. She later charged that the national leaders, wanting to manage the suffrage campaign, "held a supposedly secret conclave with a few of my ambitious eleventh-hour opponents and decided 'to take the Duniway bull by the horns.'"[88]

The date of this meeting is uncertain, but in November 1905 the OSESA convened. Some of Duniway's local opponents, including Clara Colby and Dr. Mary Thompson, aided by some NAWSA representatives took

Susan B. Anthony and Rev. Anna Howard Shaw at the unveiling of the Sacajawea statue at the Lewis and Clark Exposition. Mrs. Edna Shooks is unveiling the statue. (OHS neg. OrHi 37240)

*Sacajawea,* as sculpted by Alice Cooper. The statue now stands in Washington Park, looking up to the West Hills neighborhood of Portland. (Photo, John M. Tharp)

THE EVENING TELEGRAM, TUESDAY, NOVEMBER 7, 1905.

# MAJORITY OF CITY PASTORS SAY, LET THE WOMEN VOTE



PROMINENT FIGURES IN DISCUSSION OF WOMAN'S SUFFRAGE.

## Rev. Dr. Ford Believes That Two-Thirds of Portland's Preachers Favor Giving the Ballot to Mothers and Sisters.

Two-thirds of the ministers in Portland favor woman suffrage.

That is the opinion of Dr. Ford, of Sunnyside Methodist Episcopal Church, ... sion, with two ministers to be chosen later on each side.

The committee in charge of the discussion will consist of Rev. Edgar P. Hill, D. D., of the First Presbyterian ... purposes, and that a vote of the majority would not bind the minority. A vote would simply be an expression of individual opinion.

7 November 1905 article in the Portland *Evening Telegram*. (OHS neg. OrHi 83655)

*Oregonian* photograph of Gail Laughlin near the polls on the day of the vote. (OHS neg. OrHi 83964)

Suffrage cartoon that appeared in the 30 November 1905 *Oregonian*. (OHS neg. OrHi 83655)

THE SUNDAY OREGONIAN, PORTLAND, NOVEMBER 26, 1905.

Prominent Portland Women Who Oppose Woman Suffrage

Prominent Portland Women Who Oppose Woman Suffrage. President, Mrs. Ralph Wilbur; Vice President Mrs. J.B. Montgomery; Mrs. Gordon Voorhies; Treasurer, Mrs. Wallace McCammant, treasurer; Mrs. David Loring; Miss Eleanot E. Gile, secretary; Mrs. J. Thoburn Ross; Mrs. H.W. Corbett; Miss Failing; Mrs. Helen Ladd Corbett; Mrs. E. Wesley Ladd. (OHS neg. ORHi 83659)

# BALLOT BEATS COLD CREAM

## Dr. Brougher Says Women Will Grow More Beautiful If They Vote—Dr. Wilson Says Suffrage Will Give Them Hard Faces

Will equal suffrage aid in beautifying women? Or will it not; or will it have any effect whatever upon their personal appearance?

Deep is feminine interest in the problem. Womankind in Oregon is per-

his ideal of beauty in the home instead of at the polls.

"I should be sorry," he said, "to see our beautiful Oregon women developing into hard-featured ones. Will the ballot make the women beautiful? Look

Front page headline ran in 27 May 1906 *Oregon Journal*

Scandalous petticoat card that circulated around Portland only days prior to 1906 election. (OHS neg. OrHi 83661)

control of the state convention. Duniway had avoided this meeting, informing her son that she went to California because she knew that the "Eastern invasion would swamp us."[89] Although Duniway failed to mention it, after her loss of power some of her friends aided the new leaders. Duniway was angry with the NAWSA—in 1896 it had prevented her from entering Idaho and conducting the successful last phase of the suffrage contest—and in 1905 it had taken control from her in her own state. Despite her more than thirty years of struggle for equal suffrage the NAWSA and local foes had grasped power from her. But Duniway and her opponents wanted to avoid an open break. Recognizing her standing and fearing a division among suffragists, the Oregon campaign managers chose Duniway to help file suffrage petitions in Salem and to serve as a delegate to the NAWSA convention in Baltimore. The old fighter seemed pleased, for she acknowledged that the suffrage struggle was in "dead earnest" and voiced only mild reservation about the NAWSA's political tactics. Duniway informed her sons that "I am not able to carry the [campaign] load myself."[90]

But in January 1906 she expressed discontent about the NAWSA's management: "I begin to have grave fears less the imported old maids from the East, combined with a few Oregon fools, will defeat our Amendment by creating a reflex action."[91] Soon after she told editor Colby, who fully cooperated with the NAWSA against her, that "we are all being driven to our . . . defeat by the imported and cranky combination now in the bandwagon," and predicted that suffragists would get fewer votes in 1906 than they had received in 1900.[92] Colby undoubtedly relayed this negative assessment to NAWSA leaders.

State President Coe and perhaps another Oregon delegate summarized Duniway's criticisms to Anthony and others. They also related some good news about Duniway: in October she was honored by a special day at the Lewis and Clark Exposition and urged males to vote for suffrage and provided reasons why they should do so. One of her most original assertions was that distant Asian women watched the outcome of the Oregon suffrage battle. The state delegation also reported that Duniway had recently lectured with NAWSA representative Gail Laughlin.

Anthony and her allies anticipated Duniway's displeasure with the NAWSA's control of the Oregon fight; it was evident in her speech read before the Baltimore convention. But the Portlander, who had a reputation for blunt language, chose to be only mildly critical. In her rambling communique Duniway, who asserted that a suffrage victory might be won in her state, pointed out that the liquor interests and the idle class had joined against Oregon suffragists. She asserted that it was Anthony's open campaign that had aroused and united the reform's diverse enemies. Duniway referred to the 1900 effort, praising her own still hunt tactic, which had been "so adroitly managed that our opponents . . . were taken completely by surprise."[93] Thus Duniway only told the public that she disagreed with Anthony over tactics; she did not denounce her and others for grasping political power in Oregon.

Many who read or heard Duniway's opinions about tactics disagreed. One of her old colleagues, Jeffreys Myers, had stated that the 1900 failure resulted from a lack of organization.[94] Delegates at Baltimore must have reassured those from Oregon that an extensive, well-organized campaign being waged in their state's hamlets and cities was the best strategy, that Duniway would not bolt the fight, and that "anti" opposition organized by wealthy Portland ladies was to be anticipated.

Duniway's critique of the ongoing campaign and the fact that she published her Baltimore address in Oregon newspapers might have rankled some NAWSA leaders and their Oregonian allies. While Duniway's friend Coe and the national workers in Oregon predicted victory to state audiences and to Baltimore delegates, Duniway wavered. Her doubts must have discouraged some of her followers.

The NAWSA wanted to lead a team effort; Duniway would not subordinate herself. The fact that she published her views signaled her disagreement with her old mentor, and there was always the possibility of an open rupture among leaders. But throughout the campaign Duniway remained an important officer of what she called "our patriotic army of voters."[95] The Oregon politician remained loyal because she wanted to win, because of the death of her old teacher, because the NAWSA recognized her influence, and because of the foul blows of antisuffragists.

Following the conclusion of the Baltimore convention, Anthony journeyed to Washington for a Congressional committee hearing scheduled on her birthday. Illness prevented her attendance, but she was able to participate at an evening meeting of admirers celebrating her eighty-sixth birthday. Greetings were read to her from politicians, including some from the Pacific Northwest. Senator Weldon B. Heyburn of Idaho called her "one of America's noblest women"; Oregon Senator Charles Fulton judged that "by her noble life and work she has earned and will be accorded a permanent place in . . . history."[96] Washington Congressman Francis W. Cushman recalled that his parents had taught him "to admire and revere Anthony." Idaho Representative Burton L. French asserted that her service appealed to women and men all over the world, who thus were inspired to "higher thinking, nobler living, and a more earnest realization of man's responsibility to man." A short congratulatory message from President Roosevelt prompted Anthony to say that she would rather have his political support than his praise. Later in the evening she thanked her supporters and assured that "failure is impossible."[97] According to her biographer these are the last words she uttered in public; they became the "watchword of those who accepted as their trust the work she laid down."

Anthony returned from Washington to her home and soon suffered from pneumonia, but she still continued to push her cause. "Above all else her mind was concentrated," biographer Harper maintained, "on the approaching suffrage campaign in Oregon, where a victory seemed almost assured. She had not expected to go to that State herself but had intended to raise a great deal of money—had done so in fact—and to help in many ways." She asked her sister to return to Portland to care for Anna Shaw, who might bow under the strain as Gregg had, and to assist at headquarters. Shaw came to Anthony's death bed and conversed about the suffrage movement. The veteran complained that "It's too bad that our bodies wear out while our interests are just as strong as ever."[98] They reviewed the NAWSA strategy to concentrate on Oregon, where a victory, both agreed, would lead to others. Shaw recalled that "Each day we talked on the prospect of carrying Oregon and I would cull from the letters and newspaper clippings a fresh bit of hope to give her." In her weak voice Anthony responded, "Oh, if I were only able to be there! I long for it so." On 13 March 1906 her concern about Oregon ended when she died of pneumonia.

TWELVE

# *The Thinner the Population, the Deeper the Support*

ANTHONY'S INFLUENCE in the Oregon suffrage fight continued even after she had gone. Her death motivated some sympathizers to renewed efforts as memories of the leader lingered in their thoughts. The Oregon State Equal Suffrage Association like many other woman's rights organizations, sent a message to the national headquarters: "Renewed consecration to the principles of our departed leader and loyal efforts toward Oregon's victory for equal suffrage." And indeed Anthony's work in Oregon and Washington helped support reformer Henry Blackwell's admiring eulogy:

> Whether in the palace of the rich or the tenement of the poor, in the society of queen or seamstress, of the luxurious millionaire or the hardy frontiersmen, she, like Benjamin Franklin, remained simple, unembarrassed and sincere. It is said that most men and women cease to grow after they reach maturity, but Miss Anthony grew steadily in quality of mind and heart with advancing age, mellowing but not weakening as the years went by.[1]

Her death and Catt's well-publicized eulogy intensified the efforts of eastern sympathizers in their work for an Oregon victory. Catt expressed the sentiments of Pacific Northwest as well as eastern suffragists: "There were great women associated with her from time to time, women of wonderful intellect, of superb power, of grand character, yet she was clearly the greatest of them all. We shall never see her like again."[2] The NAWSA's journal, *Progress*, called the Oregon contest "a peaceful warfare for our own liberty" and was optimistic: "We are as sure of victory as were the men and women of the fifties who crossed the great prairies and desert, to the land of promise."[3] Some suffrage groups sent memorial contributions across the continent to the Portland campaign office. Mary Anthony donated $1,000. She, her niece Lucy E. Anthony, and President Shaw followed Susan's request and traveled to Portland soon after the funeral. A national news story explained that Mary at her sister's deathbed "heard her yearning prayers . . . for victory in Oregon and heard [her] . . . even in her delirium, beseech that the cause . . . might triumph on the Pacific Coast." Mary, who had long battled for suffrage and was more retiring than Susan, became "the bold, resolute champion of her sister's cause." At Umatilla, Oregon, Mary extended greetings:

> Miss Shaw and I are coming to place at the service of the people of Oregon our time and every possible effort to help bring to women the freedom which every true American man and woman should prize above life. It was the last prayer of my sister, and we come in faith that it will be answered by Oregon men with a splendid victory which shall make the State even more famous for its love of justice than it now is for its beauty and prosperity.[4]

Prior to traveling to the Rose City to take charge of the referendum campaign, President Shaw wrote to presidents of state suffrage organizations. She related that Anthony had asked that flowers should not be sent to her funeral but that the money should go instead to the crucial Oregon suffrage fight. The leader instructed her followers of the need to build for Anthony "an imperishable monument of freedom for women, and the enfranchisement of the women of Oregon must be the cornerstone."[5]

Shaw arrived exhausted and fainted in Portland's railroad station, but soon she and other easterners participated with Oregonians in a Sunday commemoration service for the dead leader. An old friend of Anthony's and a respected community leader, Reverend Thomas Lamb Eliot, recalled her 1871 visit, emphasizing that she had told him several times that while she would rather "be laid under the sod rather than have to go on with" reform work, she nevertheless could not shirk her duty.[6]

Duniway, who had already publicly underscored that Anthony's thoughts were centered on the Oregon campaign "during her last conscious moments," gave a reflective address. It was the only one that brought applause from the church pews. She, too, recalled that 1871 campaign, praising her mentor for having coped with frontier hardships and for having been always "the same genial, thoughtful, attentive, womanly woman, who could converse intelligently with the wisest statesman or could administer . . . a simple [medical] remedy" to a worried mother. Perhaps Duniway annoyed Shaw, Mary Anthony, and many others when she concluded: "The mantle of our risen leader now falls upon the shoulders of her only remaining sister, Mary S. Anthony, who, in this hour of Oregon's need, has stepped bravely from the niche, where for more than fifty years she stood as a living wall behind her gifted standard-bearer." Thus it might have seemed to national officers that the independent Oregon leader refused to accept the fact that Anna Shaw, not Mary, had been Susan's choice as her replacement.

Clara Colby recalled her long association with the "remarkable" Anthony, insisting that she had played a part in the "awakening of womanhood which was the distinguishing characteristic of the last half of the 19th century." The editor reminded that the reformer's last prayer was for an Oregon victory. "Surely this feeble death-bed appeal," Colby pleaded, "will be potent to touch the heart of every justice-loving man and woman in Oregon and so the prayer shall be answered."

Rabbi Stephen S. Wise of Portland admitted that Anthony had helped him understand how men had wronged women. He praised her dedication and ability to withstand ridicule. To the rabbi's way of thinking the great figures in history, including Moses, Jesus, Socrates, and Luther, had battled for liberty. "In so far as Susan Anthony was a sturdy and life-long battler for liberty," he added, "she belongs to this high and immortal succession." Wise reminded that the distinguished leader had wanted suffrage, better wages, higher education, and equal legal status for her sex. He emphasized that Oregon's real tribute to the departed leader's memory would be a favorable June vote. "A woman [Sacajawea] helped to give us Oregon," he concluded, "let Oregon help to give woman freedom."

It is very possible that a speaker read the *Oregonian*'s obituary of 14 March 1906. Although he did not change his mind about Anthony's demand for equal suffrage, Scott gave "her full credit for the sincerity of her effort, for the reforms in woman's position in the industrial world which her efforts brought about, and for woman's improved status before the law." He also acknowledged her sincerity and sense of justice.

Soon after this commemorative service the OSESA conducted a two-day conference in Portland's White Baptist Church. More than two hundred delegates from around the state joined a large number of city residents in restating the importance of their cause, reviewing the status of the campaign, and planning political activities for the remaining two months before the vote. Campaign manager Shaw, of course, dominated the sessions. The minister assured her co-workers that they were doing "God's work in seeking to establish justice." One session was a thorough discussion of the Oregon press; a participant boasted that only six newspapers in the state actively opposed the cause. Duniway and a few others reaffirmed the press's crucial role in the ongoing fight and she chided editors for failing to be supportive. If they had done their duty "in the beginning the grandchildren of women voters would be voting today."

Gail Laughlin proudly reported that there were 189 campaign committees in the state with some 4000 members. Speakers relished the news about the attitude of editors and the impressive organization of the state's suffragists. Those who had lectured in distant parts of the state, reported both difficulties and successes, but were optimistic about the election's outcome.

Some spoke more generally about relations between the sexes. Shaw insisted that "men as a class do not respect women as a class. . . . Women taking their cue from men . . . do not respect their own sex." She claimed that "nine out of ten will take the opinion of a man rather than that of a woman" and that many females wanted only the benefits of privileges, not the responsibilities of rights. Duniway argued that equal suffrage would benefit men as well as women. Mary Anthony read from some of her sister's speeches to the attentive and emotional crowd.

Women left the conference resolved to persevere in their fight, which they believed they would win this time. The Portland headquarters mailed pamphlets and a letter to male voters, soliciting their support. Duniway was among the distinguished local women signing the letter; it was similar to the one she had distributed in 1900. Lecturers again boarded trains bound for all parts of the state. Devoe, Gregg, Chase, Laughlin, Clay, Colby, and less well-known women from inside and outside Oregon followed a variety of ambitious speaking itineraries.

Leaders in the Portland headquarters assumed other tasks. Taking political parties as models, the NAWSA workers sought to organize committees in as many state precincts as possible. Laura Clay, traveling by stage coach, visited every precinct in large, remote Josephine County in southwestern Oregon. She also delivered more than fifty speeches in several counties and reported sympathy for her message.[7] On the other side of the state, Mary Chase stumped Haines, Cove, Bourne, Sumpter, and Vale. At tiny Cove she organized a campaign committee of fifty and she wrote from Sumpter: "Storming, big drifts on side streets. Organized a committee, and sure that good work will be done, for the people organized are influential."[8]

A new speaker, Mary C. Bradford, president of the Colorado Federation of Clubs, volunteered her services, heralding the importance of woman suffrage to the economic and social well-being of her own state. Shaw divided her time between lectures in the Willamette and Columbia Valleys and Portland. The president commented on her busy schedule: "This is intensely hard and interesting work." Although the minister rarely demonstrated a sense of humor, she did so when DeVoe informed her that a band would greet her arrival in Eugene. Shaw responded that the idea made her laugh, as she now knew how a circus performer in tights felt: "I shall not be in tights, however . . . but I am willing to be the circus rider for the sake of the cause. It is quite a step from a preacher to a circus rider, but I leave it up to you whether the step is up or down."[9] The president reported that her co-workers expressed enthusiasm for their work, as well, noting that Alice Stone Blackwell became "ten years younger" as the campaign progressed.

The NAWSA leaders drew from long experience in managing the Portland fight. They and local volunteers conducted parlor meetings, scheduled public rallies, arranged for debates, distributed literature, and carried out organizational duties. Mary Anthony worked in the headquarters and kept a watchful eye on Shaw's health; Lucy Anthony distributed literature to clerks in major department stores; Laughlin and Kate Gordon appeared before labor and fraternal groups. Alice Blackwell, co-editor of Boston's *Woman's Journal*, submitted prosuffrage material to the Oregon press and wrote extensive accounts for her own newspaper, boasting that nearly all the NAWSA leadership was in the state pushing the cause. In short the national and state organizations waged just the type of campaign that Anthony had long advocated.

Henry Blackwell, like his daughter Alice, wrote for the enfranchisement of Oregon females in the *Woman's Journal*. The aging veteran—he had traveled extensively for the reform—remained in the East but editorialized that if the cause triumphed it would "be worth millions of dollars to the state within the next five years in the increased number and quality of immigrants and increased value of real estate that will result."[10] This was actually another version of an argument sometimes advanced in Oregon and Washington since 1871: large numbers of desirable citizens would move to equal suffrage states. Alice wrote that many citizens predicted that the amendment would carry but that experienced advocates took nothing for granted: "We have the justice, the facts, the arguments, and the common sense of the question on our side. . . . The one point where the adversary has the advantage is in the power of the purse."[11] She exhorted sympathizers nationally to make financial contributions, reminding that "now is the time to help toward the realization of Miss Anthony's dying wish, that Oregon should become the fifth free state."

In recent years scholars have carefully analyzed the suffrage movement's arguments, especially for shifts in reasoning. Anthony and other proponents had long based their appeal both on natural rights—women were entitled to vote—and moral superiority—their votes would improve society. Late in her illustrious career, Elizabeth Cady Stanton had affirmed that women and men merited equal rights, but rejected the assertion that women were morally superior to men. In Progressive America many suffragists discredited Stanton's interpretation, insisting that women were more moral, honest, sober, and decent. Thus, they reasoned, this superior class should be enfranchised so as to realize an agenda of societal improvements, including the regulation of saloons and trusts, the elimination of prostitution, the establishment of schools and parks, and the reinstatement of a clean and responsible government.

The 1906 Oregon campaign demonstrates that suffrage speakers continued to advance both the natural rights and the moral superiority arguments. For example, early in 1906 a local leader, Eva Emery Dye of Oregon City, explained her support for the suffrage amendment. If women voted they would back political candidates of intelligence and virtue, and she predicted: "very few women will ever care for office, but very many women will take an active interest in politics. They will have parlor meetings for something else beside whist, and men will go to the polls with their wives and mothers, and the ballot will mean cleaner housekeeping for the nation."[12] In a letter to the Irrigon *Irrigator* Duniway emphasized that "our desire for the ballot is based on the Declaration of Independence and the Constitution of the United States"; she reassured readers that suffragists "are not asking for any right or power to govern men."

Oregon suffragists often made their appeal on the basis of the vital work of pioneer women. Clackamas County reformers, reminded that pioneer women "after braving perils of starvation, Indian wars and frontier hardships . . . after giving the best of our lives for the conquest of the wilderness, today ask for the ballot." A Portland woman bluntly stated, "If the pioneer mothers could face all the terrors of the wilderness, their daughters need not faint away before a ballot box."[13]

Like other Progressives, suffragists also denounced corporations and trusts and accused that the wealthy blocked democratic reform. While leading Oregon's political revolution early in the twentieth century, William S. U'Ren and allies consistently maintained that power must be taken from parties and bosses and given to the people. National and state suffragists employed this Progressive political language. The suffrage campaigners, in the typical political tradition, often used those arguments that they judged the audience wanted to hear. Feminists could be as pragmatic as either Republicans or Democrats, for they understood that they were in a contest for votes, not in a college debate advancing philosophical truths.

Charles Erskine Scott Wood evaluated the suffrage doctrines. He repeated points he had raised in 1905 at the NAWSA Convention: most women did not want to be enfranchised and their participation could not purify politics. Wood, however, favored the reform because presently "every male blackguard and ignoramus can vote if he wants to, and no woman, however cultured and intelligent, can vote if she wants to."[14] After concluding that justice was the best reason to support the cause, the social critic asserted that political involvement would improve contemporary females. "I have never conceived a half-baked intellect and an haremic docility and imbecility to be true womanhood."

On 30 April and on other occasions President Shaw, who did not publicly acknowledge Wood's support, advised state campaigners about both the message they should take to voters and effective political tactics. Reminding that men held power through the polling place, she requested in this first letter to campaign committee members that they and others personally distribute literature and ask men directly for their ballots. The leader especially wanted all teachers and ministers to receive suffrage material because these persons "ought to know that the votes of women who comprise eight-tenths of all teachers and three-fourths of all adult church members, would greatly increase the educated and moral vote of the State and thus make the church and the school of as much importance, at least in government, as is the saloon today." Shaw pressed committee members to remind men that women had done much to make Oregon "prosperous and progressive," and men could repay women by granting enfranchisement. The campaign manager wanted voters to learn that "vast corporate power and wealth" influenced men to vote against equal suffrage. If men actually believed in fair play they would empower women and they would no longer be content to have the opposite sex "classed politically with idiots, lunatics, and criminals." In summary: "The time is ripe for men and women of Oregon to arise in defense of home rule by placing in the hands of women, whose toil equally with that of men, has built up the State, the power to govern it, and not aliens and foreign corporations."

These instructions must have influenced many co-workers. The message they in turn voiced won the applause of many of Oregon's opinion makers—editors, ministers, teachers, and politicians.

Lucy Anthony wearied of taking various messages to men, complaining to an Oregon suffragist:

> Why in the world we can't decide for ourselves what we want to do, and what we as grown human beings supposed to have in common sense think we ought to do. Just seems so ridiculous when I come to think of it. We all try to think how patient, and lovely, and hopeful dear Aunt Susan was through it all and gird on our armor and go on. I feel a hundred times a day that I am not worthy to be her niece because I get so discouraged.[15]

Two Pacific Northwest activists received considerable attention. Tacoman Emma Smith DeVoe, who Shaw called her best field worker, was as effective in Oregon as she had been in Idaho ten years earlier. She delivered more than eighty evening talks to audiences scattered across Oregon. The fatigue, frustration, and fear of inadequacy which DeVoe expressed in 1906 was similar to that voiced by Anthony in 1871. But others were not nearly so critical of her. In a lucid, pleasing style, she repeated many of the arguments made by Anthony in her first Pacific Northwest visit. A Springfield, Oregon, writer provided what her coworkers considered to be an apt summary of DeVoe's lecture: "Under the spell of her clear logic and tender eloquence, the blind see, the deaf hear, and the most conservative recant." Impressed with her work in Oregon, the Washington Equal Suffrage Association arranged to make her a state organizer and lecturer. In October 1906 she became president of the Washington association. Her experiences in the Oregon fight, especially the awareness she gained of the tactics adapted by advocates and adversaries alike, helped her lead Washington women to a smashing suffrage victory.

Duniway also received publicity. She did not stump rural districts like DeVoe but remained in Portland, lecturing, chairing meetings, writing private and public letters, meeting with influential individuals, and carrying out other self-assigned tasks. Audiences anticipated and appreciated her witty, sarcastic, and provocative addresses. Duniway told listeners that attorney Ferdinand E. Reed, who had failed to be reelected to public office, agreed to lead the antisuffrage campaign. This reminded the old campaigner "of the boy who had fought another boy and been thrashed, and after retreating to a safe distance, exclaimed: 'Well, any way, if I can't whip you, I can make faces at your sister!'"[16] She told a teacher that "the low wages of disfranchised women injured both male and female teachers" and informed a club studying Shakespeare that he presented "many female characters, some were good and others bad, but not one was a fool."

Because so many experienced Oregon politicians predicted success and because talented women soldiered in the ranks, it seemed to state suffragists, including Oregon City campaigner Eva Emery Dye, that they must win. Long after the election a Portland feminist recalled that the national and local women composed the most impressive group to ever direct a suffrage campaign.[17]

But the campaign was in deep trouble. There was a degree of hostility among the reformers. It is difficult to unravel this story, but Duniway, of course, was deeply involved. Prior to the arrival of Shaw in 1906, she wrote to her son that she had bested her opponents, who she identified as "Dr. Mary A. Thompson and not more than two or three others—all Machiavellians—who juggled to get themselves on the Executive Board while I was in California."[18] Even a month before the election she seemed pleased: "Our campaign progresses satisfactorily. Dr. Shaw, Miss Blackwell, and Miss Gordon have appeared upon the scene."[19] But conditions were more complicated than Duniway reported to her son. Laura Clay, an energetic Kentuckian who donated a year of her life to the Oregon fight, complained that the national leaders failed to ask local women for their ideas. She observed "outrageous dissension" between eastern and state volunteers, a situation that weakened the effort. Clay's biographer interpreted the 1906 campaign: "Internal friction was a greater problem than the suffragists admitted publicly or recorded in their publications and official histories."[20] There was conflict between Shaw and Duniway over the national president's conduct of an open campaign and over her attitude towards the state leader. One participant recalled that Duniway greatly and rightfully resented Shaw's attempt "to dictate to her"; furthermore, each woman heard that the other was critical of her.[21]

Surely Duniway's negative attitude about Shaw, Colby, Thompson, and others meant that some Oregon admirers gave only limited support to the political campaign. Duniway did her part to present a harmonious front to the public, acknowledging in a letter to the *Oregonian* near the end of the fight that "I have, as the newspaper fraternity is aware, been keeping (for me) unusually quiet during our pending equal suffrage campaign."[22] The veteran explained that she restricted her effort mainly to letter writing because "so many thousands of good and loyal co-workers have volunteered their assistance." The record indicates that Duniway played a significant role through her speeches as well as through her numerous letters. In any event, biographer Ruth Moynihan incorrectly concluded that "Duniway resigned from the 1906 campaign in anger."[23] The Portlander's efforts won applause from her fellow workers. At a reception in Duniway's honor, for example, NAWSA representative Gregg praised Duniway for her long and substantial suffrage work. This event not only recognized Duniway's efforts, it was also an attempt to maintain and demonstrate unity.[24]

Dye's papers provide vital details about the campaign at the local level and her optimism about its outcome. She knew about the deep division among the suffrage leaders but remained silent. Duniway, however, chose to recall it, writing that she lovingly told the national officers that they would inevitably meet defeat in 1906 and that she planned to regain her control and push on until victory.[25] She predicted to an old suffrage ally that there was little chance for victory because the campaign's leadership included "imported old maids, and the 3 quack doctors and fake female politicians . . . who call themselves the 'state organization.'" She even accused some of the "old maids" working for the NAWSA of graft and of making a "loot" from suffrage campaign funds.[26] One campaigner recalled that Shaw also said disagreeable things about Duniway. Despite this personal rancor the two did not become involved in an open political and personal confrontation until after the June 1906 election. Everyone knew that an internal fight would be disastrous.

A greater difficulty for the reformers than their internal squabbling was their opponents' use of money and resourceful political schemes, especially those hatched during the battle's last month. As the campaign heated up, President Shaw alerted her co-workers that they were engaged in full warfare and that "for the first time in the history of any campaign, the anti-suffragists have organized against us." The campaign manager told DeVoe that capitalists and liquor dealers had combined forces to defeat them, and decreed a switch in tactics from Portland to rural areas: "we know that when corporate interests in thickly settled communities are organized against us, men, like sheep, follow the leaders of their own interests, and principle and justice flies to the wind." Based upon previous campaigns Shaw judged that "country people" remained loyal once converted to reform; city people, however, were fickle. "Therefore our whole effort will have to be made in the country and our majority will have to be from the rural districts."[27]

There were other difficulties. The terrible San Francisco earthquake of 18 April upset campaign plans and made it more difficult to raise dollars for the suffrage fund. Oregonians, Shaw lamented, donated only to this disaster's victims and brushed aside appeals from suffragists. The campaigner even maintained that after the catastrophe only Portland friends gave money.

While the suffragists struggled with organizational and financial problems, the "antis" made their political move. In early May attorney Ferdinand Reed opened a Portland antisuffrage headquarters, announcing that he headed a businessmen's effort against the amendment. Meanwhile the Oregon State Association Opposed to the Extension of Suffrage to Women (OSAOESW) wrote to enlist the support of Portland business executives, warning that woman suffrage added to the innovation of the initiative and referendum "would result in much fad legislation." Furthermore, if the controversial amendment passed it "would alarm the cautious investor, and would discourage the construction of new lines of railway and other enterprises which promise much for the prosperity of the state."[28]

After quick consultation with followers, business leaders, and politicians, Shaw responded to this letter. Convinced that the Southern Pacific Railroad was behind the larger attempt to unite business interests against the amendment, she complained that the railroad

> is opposed to equal suffrage for the same reason that it is opposed to the initiative and referendum, because it is easier for corporate wealth to control a Legislature than to control the votes of the men of Oregon, and easier for it to control the votes of half the people than it would be to control those of the whole people.

The suffrage president and her allies would often assert that corporations fought any reform that gave the people more power. By advocating this typical Progressive doctrine, Shaw assumed she would influence reform-minded Oregonians.

In mid-May the attack on the reformers broadened. Responding to the appeal of the OSAOESW, 190 Portland corporations and businessmen signed a critical statement and published it in the city's press. These well-known signers emphasized two points: woman suffrage would "be injurious to the general welfare and development of Oregon" and a majority of women did not want the ballot.[29] From now until election day these two generalizations prompted heated debate.

Writing in her *Woman's Journal* Alice Blackwell sought to discredit the idea that woman suffrage would hurt Oregon economically. Exasperated by the business class, she ridiculed their "preposterous prophecy" that linked female voting with economic stagnation, complained that large corporations opposed an expanded suffrage out of self-interest, and accused antisuffragist women of aiding big business against the good of the people. To win voter support, Blackwell revealed that Portland's wealthy Ladd family, especially Helen Ladd Corbett, had pressured many businessmen into signing. But she and co-workers assured that this action taken by these male foes would boomerang because workers and others would reject their dubious arguments.

To assist their beleaguered suffrage sisters, Idaho and Colorado sympathizers sent telegrams, letters, and editorials testifying to the fact that suffrage states did not suffer economically. A forthright Boise newspaper editor denied that the reform would injure Oregon's economy and wondered "how men of Portland could permit themselves to be led into signing such a statement."[30] National American Woman Suffrage Association leaders successfully urged Oregon editors to publish such material. The OSESA, employing census statistics to substantiate their claims, published a pamphlet which accused adversaries of attempting to frighten the voters "upon the ground that equal suffrage would hurt the business interests."[31] Again the suffragists cried that corporate interests and several very wealthy women joined against the proposed amendment. The pamphlet writers cited facts showing that in every suffrage state wages and population had increased and agricultural and manufacturing production had improved.

Reform women spent considerable energy in speeches as well as in writings responding to those businessmen opposed to them. Obviously it worried Shaw and others to be resisted by such an influential group, but it was difficult to evaluate the impact of its efforts upon Oregonians. Clearly the businessmen's statement to the press prompted the Federated Trades Council of Portland to denounce the signers and then to endorse equal suffrage. An unknown number of state newspapers also attacked these Portlanders; the Pendleton *East Oregonian*, for one, called the statement "hasty and unreasonable" and an insult to Oregon.[32] The editor, like others, pointed out that there were four hundred men and only two women in the state penitentiary and reminded readers of the prominent businessmen who had been implicated in the state's land frauds.

Another "anti" tactic frustrated suffragists and probably others as well. An opposition leader offered money to Oregon editors if they would run antisuffrage propaganda as news stories. These advertisements, appearing as news, asserted that the only women who voted were of the "lowest and most debased class," that professional agitators [Shaw and the other NAWSA leaders] kept trying to push the ballot upon disinterested women, and that women in suffrage states "are worse off than before they enjoyed the rights of franchise."[33]

Possessing money to cover large mailing costs, the "antis" sent a variety of publications, including *The Women's Protest* to most voters. Alice Blackwell publicly identified this pamphlet as a revision of one published in Massachusetts. The editor wrote that Oregonians had reassured her that distant politicians had little local influence and complained that Massachusetts "in suffrage matters is a hundred miles behind Oregon."[34]

Reformers held up one piece of antisuffragist literature as being particularly offensive, with Duniway, Shaw, Blackwell, and the others calling it "vulgar" or "obscene." This political card had a picture of a woman's undergarment and the words "No petticoat government in mine!"[35] An OSESA advertisement said the card insulted "every man's mother. Any cause must be hard up for legitimate argument when it resorts to this low appeal to prejudice." The Eugene *Guard* expressed a different opinion about the petticoat cards: "This is not a very dignified way of campaigning, but it is catchy and sometimes such methods win. The American is not always guided by reason or swayed by argument."[36]

Angered by the type of campaign being waged against the amendment, Duniway became more combative, delivering spirited addresses and writing provocative letters. She accused the Portland "antis" of hiring a Salvation Army-type band, complete with tambourines and the singing of religious songs, to attract a noon crowd. Instead of the customary street preacher, an orator appeared and denounced woman suffrage. The old veteran lashed out at the opposition's "fake religious exercises, slanderous advertisements, and vulgar pictures."[37]

On 26 May the *Oregonian* published a secret circular mailed by the Brewers' and the Wholesale Liquor Dealers' Association of Oregon to all two thousand of the state liquor dealers. The publication warned that it would take fifty thousand votes to defeat the suffrage amendment. Thus it was every liquor retailer's duty to find twenty-five "no" votes. The OSESA had the circular reprinted in newspapers, believing it to be a damaging exposition of their opponents. For years after the election national suffrage leaders rehashed the importance of this circular and republished it in newspapers and books.

Late in the campaign the amendment's proponents strongly pushed their theory that the liquor interests, the corporations, and society ladies conspired against them. One of their advertisements simply listed about thirty names of wealthy Oregon women alongside those of state breweries, including Weinhard's. Like the Pacific Northwest Populists of the 1890s, some suffragist campaigners attempted to simplify the battle as being one between the rich and the poor.

The political advertisements of the "antis" charged that debased moral conditions prevailed in the states that enfranchised females: "Wyoming is the most backward state in the West"; "Denver is the most corruptly governed city in the whole West. . . . It is an object lesson on Woman Suffrage. Ignorant women are easily handled by selfish and corrupt politicians"; and "Do you want Oregon classed with Utah? If so, vote for Woman Suffrage."[38] The OSESA met this attack with its own advertisements. These declared that the four suffrage states were enlightened, denounced the various "anti" tactics, and published endorsements from Oregon politicians and other notable citizens.

Suffragists challenged without success Portland's antisuffragist women to a public debate. But city ministers debated at a meeting that attracted considerable interest. Rev. Clarence True Wilson, a Methodist and president of the Anti-Saloon League, took up the side of the opposition in a debate with Baptist minister J. Whitcomb Brougher before a packed audience. Wilson, employing traditional arguments, expressed the fear that a woman's voting would lead to family discord, reminded that male family members already voted on behalf of females, doubted that women could improve politics, concluded that bad women would vote just as bad men were currently doing, and reasoned that because women could not fight they did not deserve to vote. The *Oregonian* quoted him as saying: "After the . . . toil of a day a man does not like to come home and discuss politics for the rest of the evening with his wife, who through the day has been hobnobbing with all the politicians of the day and learned to vote and talk with other men at cross purposes with her husband."[39] He also advanced an economic argument: "There is a man unemployed for every woman at work" because women worked for lower pay. He concluded that "this abnormal condition ought to stop, but woman suffrage gives an impetus still further in the wrong direction."

Clara Colby took notes for her *Woman's Tribune*, adding that the Methodist minister proclaimed that when men were unemployed they remained single, a fact that contributed to the "social evil."[40] Colby also reported one of Wilson's less conventional arguments. He dreaded "the influence of politics on the looks, the manners and the actions of Oregon women. I have seen the stern-faced suffragists from Colorado, and I pray that our beautiful and every way perfect women of Oregon may never look like them."

The *Oregon Journal*'s account reflected this jocular theme in its headline: "Ballot Beats Cold Cream." It reported Dr. Brougher's rebuttal which explained why suffrage would increase beauty: "Well just cause. But as this woman's reason was insufficient he went on. She must grow sweeter to look upon because she will have got her own way and she will be so happy over the chance to vote. Happy people are always good looking."[41]

Reverend Brougher and suffragists rejected or ridiculed Wilson. Many saw a delightful irony in the fact that the minister headed the antisaloon group yet allied with these very opponents in fighting against the enfranchisement of females.

Both sides appealed to Portland editors for support. Suffragists made much of the fact that only a few of them expressed open opposition, but they would have more reason for rejoicing had the *Oregonian*, *Journal*, or *Telegram* endorsed their cause. They took comfort, however, in the fact that all these Portland newspapers published material they submitted and reported their meetings fairly. The *Oregon Journal* devoted a special section to letters from readers on the suffrage question. Proponents of the amendment read these avidly, responding publicly to some of the negative ones. The NAWSA and OSESA leadership feared how the influential *Oregonian* would declare on the issue. Late in the 1900 campaign its disapproval had played, they believed, a critical role in defeating the reform. Three days before the vote Harvey Scott finally gave his opinion. He began by judging that while there were zealous advocates and opponents, the majority of voters were indifferent. He anticipated that no more than 35,000 voters would approve the amendment—not enough to pass the measure. On 2 June, Scott reported that his newspaper was wearied by the contention over the issue, assumed that men knew their own mind, and concluded that the *Oregonian* "does not favor the woman suffrage amendment." The following day he said that the campaign had been "waged with such bitterness, sarcasm, and vehemence in this city [that it] would be amusing were not the contestants so terribly in earnest."[42] It was too late for reformers to counter Scott. Probably they expressed relief that this powerful figure had not been as harsh as he had been in 1900.

The antisuffragists carefully orchestrated their last effort before the vote. They placed newspaper advertisements and public letters in the *Oregonian* very late in the campaign, assuming that their foes would thereby have little opportunity to answer them. The advertisements espoused traditional negative beliefs; one read: "Oregon electors don't want women to be their equals; they prefer to regard them as their superiors."[43] Another predicted that "The political arena will soon sicken any respectable woman, and she will leave it to her more hardened sisters to do the voting."[44]

Mrs. R.W. Wilbur, president of OSAOESW, insisted that, contrary to the accusations of the suffragists, only fifteen of the five hundred members of her organization were wealthy and that many teachers, stenographers, saleswomen, domestics, and mothers had joined. The members, the Portlander asserted, accepted the initiative law but opposed increasing "the number of voters, who are not only untrained, but whose life work makes it impossible, and, furthermore, undesirable, that they should be trained to the rigors of a political life."[45]

A leading antisuffragist, attorney Wallace McCamant, saw the political contest as between "those who honor women in the home and those who want to see her on the hustings—between those who would protect her in the performance of her duties as wife and mother and those who would impose upon her jury service and political responsibility."

Businessman Martin C. Banfield ruled that "Politics is a dirty mess, and woman suffrage will not improve it. . . . My own experience is that it is only an insistent few and not the contented many who want woman suffrage. There is nothing in the world . . . so beautiful as a mother doing her full duty by her family, her friends and her neighbors; there is nothing so distasteful or demoralizing as a mother up to her neck in politics while her children roam the streets."

Charles V. Cooper, a persistent antisuffragist, warned that "respectable women . . . whom we would naturally look to to purify the political atmosphere by her vote, her influence and her example, will not enter into the filthy political mess of modern politics; her whole nature shrinks from it, and she will not use her right to vote."[46] He argued that "her less fortunate sisters, the ignorant, the foreign women, and the women of the brothels" would vote and "give the unscrupulous politician greater strength." Cooper also turned to the Bible for evidence. St. Paul had said that women should keep silent in the churches; the antisuffragist explained that this admonition "means today that women should not vote."

At their last political gathering the suffrage activists evaluated the enlarged antisuffragist effort. Coloradan Mary Bradford spoke for all her allies when she concluded, "The methods being used against us are marvels of underhanded ingenuity."[47] Duniway denounced opponents as representing the forces "of vice, corporations, trusts, and tyranny."[48] Blackwell accused New York "antis," including Mrs. Lyman Abbott, and Mrs. George Phillips, of "making common cause with the liquor interests here."[49] The reformers laughed at adversaries for making absurd accusations that suffragists had tried to "bunco" Oregonians and had spent $10,000 in an attempt to buy the election. They shared campaign experiences and press clippings, including the Port Orford *Tribune*. It reasoned that there was more support for woman suffrage in coastal counties than in Portland because "people along the coast were greater readers and more intelligent than people of the interior, and that wherever intelligent, liberty-loving people got to studying equal rights they invariably favored equal suffrage."[50]

Oregon reformers well understood that the contest in their state had national ramifications; not since Idaho adopted equal suffrage in 1896 had a state granted the reform. They had a chance to make political history, and national and state workers, with good cause, congratulated themselves on what Blackwell called a magnificent campaign. They appreciated the *Telegram*'s assessment that they had waged one of the state's "most brilliant and consistently aggressive political campaigns." Duniway, however, remained ambivalent about the prospect of victory: at times she talked about a forthcoming celebration. At other times she would advise the "necessity of courage in the face of defeat." The national leaders also prepared volunteers for the possibility of failure. According to a newspaperman, they "shed tears as Dr. Shaw told of the manner in which Aunt Susan . . . took the defeat in California 10 years ago."[51]

Portlanders witnessed a most unusual election day; pairs of suffragist women and groups of young male opponents faced off near many of the city's sixty-six voting places. Such a unique confrontation, of course, attracted reporters and photographers. A local reformer, Dr. Esther Pohl, like some other Portlanders, had recalled the unfair election practices used to defeat equal suffrage in 1900; therefore, she enlisted and assigned some two hundred females to the voting precincts. On the eve of the election, President Shaw, who had earlier requested her Oregon supporters to pass out leaflets on election day, urged her workers to wake up "sweet-tempered," take positions at the polls, and be aware that they must meet provocation with dignity. Acting womanly, she instructed, would be a factor in winning a favorable vote. She complained that "a man could get drunk and fall in the gutter and do anything disgraceful and he would be only pitied . . . but a woman's slightest misconduct would reflect on all women of the state."[52]

Standing the required fifty feet from the polls and often timid, these neophytes—wearing American flags on their coats—frequently pleaded with men to support the amendment. They sometimes sold food so as to provide a chance to talk with voters and to pay for campaign literature, and they always handed out a prosuffrage card. The *Telegram* of 4 June said of these females: "the charge that only stern faced, mannish women, or the riff raff of the sex wanted equal suffrage was quickly refuted when the voters saw the class of women who were asking their support."

Many women from the national organization participated. Alice Blackwell and Ida Boyer solicited support at a difficult North End precinct. They reported that the day passed quietly and that "most rough people in this rough" precinct were courteous.[53] There were some exceptions; an unsavory character told Blackwell to "Go to Hell!" Male pedestrians quickly cautioned him not to swear in the presence of ladies. Police, operating under orders to protect suffragists from harassment, patrolled this and some of the other potentially rowdy voting places.

Drs. Pohl and Shaw went by automobile to the various polls, supplying food and encouragement, which was especially needed during

Handbill from the successful 1912 campaign. (OHS neg. OrHi 23881)

Abigail Scott Duniway at the polls to cast the first vote by an Oregon woman. (OHS neg. ORE 4599)

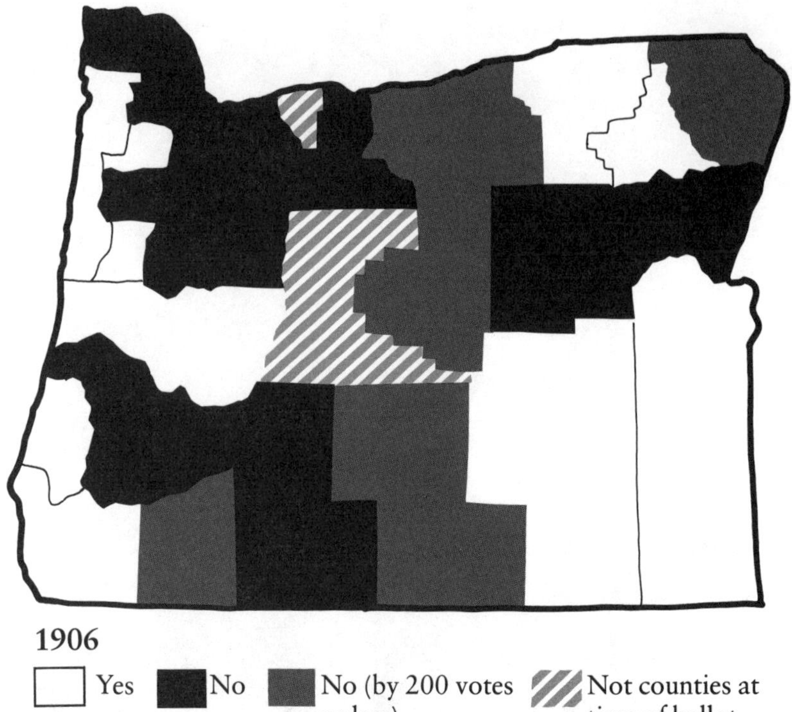


County by county voting patterns in the 1906 election. Counties in white voted yes and counties in black voted no. In gray counties the no vote won by less than two hundred votes. Areas with stripes have since been absorbed by other counties.

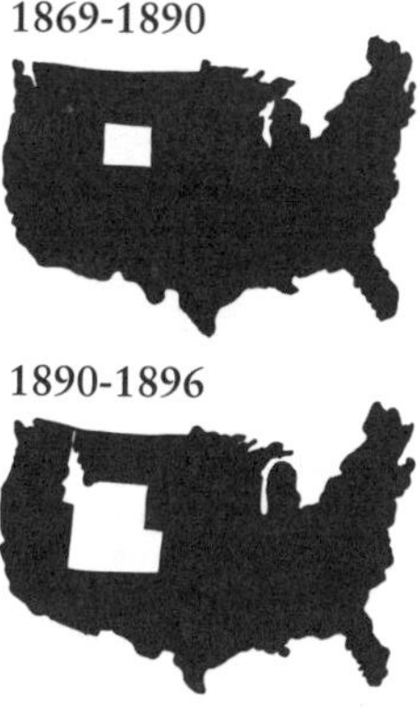


The maps at the right show the states and territories that had suffrage prior to 1910. The map below shows the suffrage map of the United States prior to the passage of the 19th or the Anthony Amendment. Limited suffrage meant that women could vote in city, county or school board elections but not in national elections.

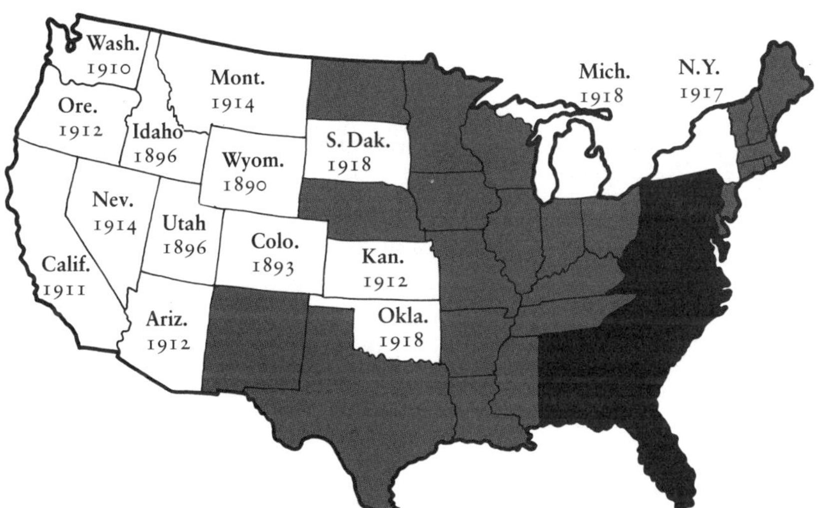


**Woman Suffrage, 1920** *(before the 19th Amendment)*

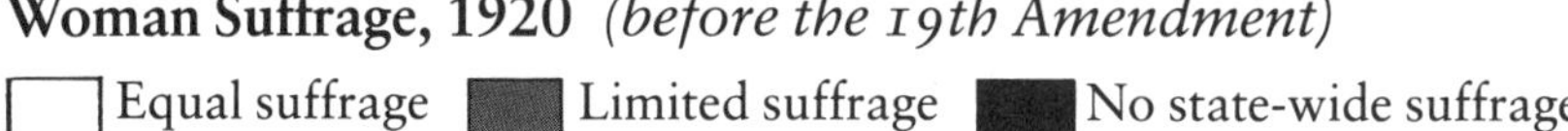

downpours. They encountered insults from "drunken, besotted wretches, who have no other means of support save what they get from their wives' washing or boarding houses."[54] One disgruntled voter growled: "Women should be at home scrubbing." The *Journal* called these vocal opponents "as tough a looking set of bums as can be gathered . . . in Portland."

In a few polling places members of the Portland Ministerial Association greeted voters. These churchmen acknowledged that it was very unusual for them to participate in a general election, but they explained that they were encouraging parishioners to support woman's suffrage and to oppose an amendment to local option. Obviously, ministers rendered much greater assistance to these reformers in the industrial period than they had in the pioneer one.

Prosuffrage women were not the only ones working at the polls. About three hundred young men and boys, aided by two women, also distributed political material and received instructions from "antis" checking precincts by automobiles. Their blue cards read, "Don't handicap Greater Oregon with woman suffrage." Shaw maintained that for the first time in a suffrage battle foes also distributed obscene cards, like the petticoat ones, which she charged came from "some vicious element among the men."[55] Liquor dealers paid those distributing the blue cards $3.00 a day with the promise of an additional $1.00 if the amendment failed. At polling places mature women and these young male opponents argued over equal suffrage and providing women greater economic and educational opportunities. Clara Colby snapped: "It ought not to be surprising that women will work at the polls for the freedom of their sex, but that a young man can be hired to work against it is astonishing; you must be hard up!"[56]

Suffragists maintained that their presence greatly reduced rowdyism at Portland's polling places and reported that ill-mannered men laughed that they had voted against the reform. It frustrated the reformers to see ignorant individuals—some of whom admitted that they could not read—cast ballots while they, who were better educated and better informed on local issues, could only plead or observe. Women working the polls provided impressions about voting patterns: middle-class workers carrying dinner pails endorsed the amendment; men of ease joined the lower class in voting no. Older neighborhoods of Portland's wealthy west side seemed particularly hostile. This reminded Shaw and other veterans of the 1896 California campaign; in San Francisco and Oakland the wealthiest and the poorest wards had rejected the amendment.

After handing out cards for more than ten hours, many of the two hundred suffrage workers (joined by some males) then watched the judges count the ballots—a process that lasted until the small hours of the morning. These Portland volunteers carried out this task in part because Shaw asked them and other workers to do so. She had warned the members of the state campaign committee that "it is rumored that immense sums of money are being spent [by liquor dealers] to buy up judges and clerks. We feel sure of victory if we secure a fair count."[57] A few judges had openly denounced the amendment, but observers—some of whom complained of nervous exhaustion—thought that ballots had been honestly counted. Reformers grumbled far less about the ballot-counting than about the fact that the liquor interests had paid men to vote no.

National American Woman's Suffrage Association leaders and other suffragists stayed up very late on election night and consoled each other as Portland returns indicated a terrible defeat. On 5 June the *Oregonian* quoted Shaw as saying that "Unless there is a covering of sod over me, I will be back in Oregon at the very next state election to fight for our cause." Duniway, too, predicted another election and eventual victory. Other reformers expressed disappointment but insisted that they were "not in the least disheartened." Shaw's initial explanation for the amendment's failure received applause from friends: "the liquor dealers" she wrote, "alone could not have defeated us. I attribute failure to corporations, which have expended a tremendous sum of money." The easterner continued, "One of the lessons of this struggle is that the majority of the voters are indifferent . . . whether we should be allowed to vote or not. . . . The progress and prosperity of the state have a good deal to do with our defeat. Men are satisfied . . . no one seems to be conscious of want."[58]

A few days after the election a large number of suffragists gathered in the Congregational Church where the NAWSA Convention had been held about a year earlier. The women had hoped this meeting would be a jubilation; it turned out to be a consolation. Ida Harper, who later interviewed national leaders, described the audience as "crushed" by their defeat but were happy that Anthony "did not have to add this disappointment to the many she had endured."[59] Although the final votes had not been tallied, it was obvious to these disappointed activists that all the Willamette Valley counties, except for Lane, had rejected the amendment. The prosuffrage counties were either on the coast or east of the Cascades; the voting returns demonstrated that the thinner the population the deeper the support. In the last half of the nineteenth century woman suffrage had been endorsed in underpopulated western states—Wyoming, Utah, Colorado and Idaho. In the early twentieth century the reform often won support in Oregon's thinly settled regions. Anthony and her lieutenants had correctly anticipated that an appeal to remote voting precincts would be successful but even Shaw had failed to realize that the Willamette and Columbia Valleys would be so negative. Undoubtedly those attending the meeting also evaluated the state's voting pattern and proposed ways of changing them.

The suffragist meeting featured speeches by campaigners, many of whom were returning east. Laura Gregg, the national organizer whose health collapsed during the struggle, requested listeners to be cheerful and to continue the fight. A Californian who had lectured on behalf of the reform stressed that Oregon's initiative law made it possible to arrange immediately for another election. Portlander Annice Jeffreys Myers assured her that steps had been taken to get another amendment before the voters in 1908. Many in the audience expressed an eagerness to work in another effort. The California speaker then noted regretfully that a victory would have inspired suffragists in her state. This was exactly what Anthony and allies had hoped—that one victory would lead to others on the Pacific Coast and at the same time put new life in the national movement. Such a happy result would not occur until the years from 1910 and 1912 when Washington, California, and Oregon approved equal suffrage.

President Shaw's afternoon address urged another contest and evaluated the one just completed. A splendid platform speaker, she aroused her audience when she angrily charged, "Never was a woman sold on the auction block more completely than have been the women of Oregon. I saw boys casting their first ballot, bribed to defeat their mother's freedom."[60] The minister was also upset by the fact that boys gave out the petticoat card, which taught "them to have a low regard for the mother that bore them." Shaw expressed surprise that there was as yet no reliable confirmation of the vote and stated that if she had the

$10,000 required there would be a recount. Like many of her colleagues, the president lambasted the political parties for their indifference in the referendum election and summarized: "From the day Susan B. Anthony put her dying hand on my head I have promised myself that I will never give one minute of my time, nor one cent of my money to any institution, nor any party, nor individual which works against the larger freedom of woman." The campaign organizer praised the political efforts of local volunteers, who labored long hours despite the demands of their own housework, reminding that "it means a great deal for a woman who has to get three meals a day to find courage and time to work for a principle." If Oregon mothers continued to work for their noble cause they would raise, Shaw predicted to them, "a generation of sons that will free you."

Duniway presided at the evening session. Veteran Alice Blackwell encouraged the depressed gathering. As an editor she emphasized the fact that of Oregon's 208 newspapers only seven had actively opposed them. Blackwell once again reminded suffragists of the influential power of newspapers: "Where editors stand today the majority of voters will stand tomorrow." She spoke glowingly of the long fight waged by those seated before her. "Even our opponents say," she boasted, "we have made the best campaign that has ever been made in the State on any subject."

Several speakers advocated another effort for the great cause. Gail Laughlin of the NAWSA aroused listeners with her positive perspective. She began: "When a monarch dies, the people cry 'The king is dead! Long live the king!' We say 'The campaign is ended. The campaign is begun.'" The activist reminded that liberty still lived in the state and that "we shall go forward to victory. Oregon, oh Oregon, we plead for thee!" Rabbi Wise also emphasized optimism and predicted, "I do not believe that defeat . . . ever will be repeated." The liberal religious leader solicited national help for Oregon's next fight, hoped that "in the future as in the past" the campaign would be conducted "without personalities," and exhorted women not to respond in kind if "high-bred gentlemen" threw political mud.

At some point in the proceedings Dye probably told suffrage workers about her recent letters to the editors of the *Oregon Journal* and the *Oregonian*, beseeching these opinion makers for help in teaching the public about the need for this reform. Dye advised Scott that her group had needed his editorial assistance in the past election and that she feared that Oregon would be the last West Coast state to adopt the inevitable reform. In her letter to Sam Jackson of the *Oregon Journal* she wrote: "The very fact that our clear-eyed, tall and handsome American girls have not stunted their growth with alcohol and cigarettes proves them fit to survive and triumph over the outworn traditions of medievalism. And every year but adds to their courage and stature."[61]

President Shaw gave the farewell speech. She began by indicating that the silk flag with four stars that draped across the pulpit had last been used on Anthony's casket. She continued, "Her last prayer was that another star might be added this year. Oregon was not true enough, not worthy enough. It may become so, and let that be our prayer. She, the apostle of freedom, longed more for your freedom than you longed for it yourselves." Shaw praised those men who had voted for the amendment and defended her own position: "They call us professional suffragists. I'd rather be a professional suffragist than a professional anything else on earth." She thanked Oregon women for their hospitality and encouraged them to continue their struggle.

Mary Anthony was ill and probably played no part in this final meeting. She still deeply grieved the loss of her sister but had assisted Shaw, as she had assisted Susan, in the Oregon fight. Many women thanked her for coming to the state and for her long hours of work in the suffrage headquarters. She returned to Rochester, continued to labor for the movement, pondered the bitter defeat, and became seriously ill. Many sent messages acknowledging her many contributions to the cause. Catt wrote, "Let me remind you that your life has been a blessing to womanhood, and the big suffrage army love you for all you are and all you have been." Mary died in February 1907.

While easterners packed to leave, Portlanders read OSESA president Coe's public statement. She praised the national leaders "who came to us without money and without price" and who, under Shaw, conducted a strenuous campaign.[62] Coe acknowledged the groups that had waged "a noble fight for the freedom of women: the state and local Granges, the trades unions, the WCTU, the pioneers, the socialists, and other organizations." She believed that by carrying out an "educative campaign" the citizens would overcome "the aggregation of corporate power and liquor interests" that had defeated the reform in the recently concluded election.

At the last Portland gathering and for years afterwards, suffragists sought to explain their bitter defeat; the final vote was 47,075-36,902. To inquiring newspaper reporters Shaw responded that the liquor dealers and the rich defeated the reformers: "The organized liquor traffic can lay its hand upon the State and play on it as a musician plays on the organ. In every hamlet it played on the avarice and the appetite of men. Then there was the greed of capital organized to defeat us."

To the campaign committees scattered across Oregon she provided a fuller explanation for the result. "It was an unequal fight. Liquor dealers, corporate interests, appetite and avarice were arrayed with the ballot against women—the home makers, the educators, the church supporters, the great moral force of society, helpless and ballotless."[63] Shaw expressed disgust with the opposition's "corrupt methods, which appeal to the low and baser natures of men and arouse the coarse impulse of man against woman." The president accused that some female allies did not work hard enough for the amendment's passage; some others became distracted by "side issues" and campaigned for candidates. "It is a useless task," she lectured, "to undertake to carry on two reforms at the same time."

Aware that readers everywhere were curious about the reasons for the Oregon defeat, Alice Blackwell evaluated the election in her *Woman's Journal.* The editor explained: "the liquor interest, the political machines [especially the Multnomah Republican machine], the trusts and corporations (including the Southern Pacific Railway, which is said almost to own Oregon) together with the natural forces of conservatism, and a quarter of a million dollars, made a combination too strong for the women to overcome."[64]

Blackwell also advanced a historical reason for the powerful opposition that overwhelmed suffragists. Women had done well in the battle for equal suffrage in 1900. Surprised by this close election, antisuffragists organized a stiff fight, spending an enormous amount of money to ensure success. Other observers sided with Blackwell. Some repeated the story that the head of the opposition revealed that $300,000 had been spent to defeat the amendment. The suffragists raised only a fraction of this amount, including an undetermined but small sum raised in Oregon and a generous donation of about $18,000 from the NAWSA. Most of the money covered printing, postage, and newspaper advertisements.

Blackwell also ruled that the "Trusts and large corporations, which would gladly deprive most men of a vote if they could, did not want to have any more voters to deal with, and were a powerful element in the forces arrayed against the amendment." She also denounced the character of her opponents: "We are informed that F.E. Reed, the manager of the anti campaign, had previously earned his living by acting as assistant and adviser for the women who keep houses of ill fame." On the positive side Blackwell calculated that 63 percent of Portlanders voted no; this was at least an improvement over 1900 when 65 percent opposed.

In the fall of 1906 Blackwell provided a more analytical explanation for the failure. Annoyed by eastern antisuffragist women who crowed that the referendum's rejection demonstrated that Oregon women were conservative, the editor asserted that Oregon was one of the most progressive states and emphasized that antisuffragists had waged the most "systematic and organized [state] campaign . . . ever made against an equal suffrage amendment."[65] Because Oregon was progressive and "liberty loving," the writer reasoned, antisuffrage groups were frightened into making such a major effort. Blackwell summarized that a combination of the "liquor interest," political machines of both parties, trusts, corporations, and "honest conservatives" worked against the reform. Reed, the antisuffrage campaign manager, acknowledged publicly the assistance of these groups and boasted that on election day he had poll workers in most of the state's counties and that in Portland 214 men served in this capacity. Blackwell taught that in Oregon, as in every other state, there is "a considerable unprincipled and vicious element which is naturally opposed to equal rights for women." She also reported that the Oregon "antis" received eastern encouragement and that most of the negative campaign literature came from Massachusetts.

After making the argument that a powerful political combination—not local conservatism—defeated the reformers, Blackwell then predicted a victory for equal suffrage because "you may deceive a majority of Oregon voters part of the time, but you cannot deceive them all the time." She reminded that "In the 22 years since the question was first submitted in Oregon, the antisuffrage vote has less than doubled, while the suffrage vote has more than trebled." Blackwell believed that the 1906 campaign itself proved reason for optimism. Few newspapers actively opposed the amendment; the "intelligent and leading" Oregon men, including political candidates were committed to the cause; the Oregon State Federation and other women's groups endorsed the reform; and the state's hard-working suffragist women vowed to campaign as long as necessary.

Laura Clay, who had spent considerable time stumping the state and working in Salem, agreed with Blackwell in asserting that "the corporations were opposed to the suffrage amendment, because they are interested in not having a larger electorate. The more extended the suffrage the harder it is for them to control the elections." The Kentuckian also identified "the liquor people" as our "most potent enemies. It was they who defeated us."[66] Like other participants in the fight, Clay insisted that the OSAOESW played only a minor role in the outcome. This antisuffragist organization recruited only five hundred members, a small figure when compared with the five thousand men and women who enrolled in the OSESA. Clay concluded by affirming: "I have learned to realize that this work is God's cause, and He is the leader of all our campaigns."[67]

During the campaign Mary Anthony lashed out at opponents. "Wholesale liquor dealers, saloon keepers, dive-proprietors, drunkards, gamblers and thugs generally, inside and outside of prison, are in full accord with the Oregon Society of Women Anti-Suffragists. Blessed companionship! How proud these women ought to be of the tie that binds!"[68] Mary's ally, Ida Porter Boyer, was less critical of the organized antisuffragist women. She wrote that they played no important role and actually served "as a cloak for the real antagonists, the corporations and the liquor interests."[69] Boyer concluded that "no association of women would knowingly compromise with unscrupulous methods" used by their male allies in working to defeat the amendment. Boyer underscored that foes had engaged in voting frauds, including the fact that prominent Portland politicians and a leading businessman "induced a number of young boys . . . to vote against the Amendment."

Portlander Sarah Evans' history of the Oregon suffrage movement published in 1922 reiterated the explanations given by the women of the national organization. Evans concluded:

> The impetus given the cause by the national convention the previous summer and the activity of the national workers in the present campaign aroused the corrupt influences in politics

> and the upper and lower classes of antisuffragists as never before and they jointly employed Ferdinand Reed, an experienced politician, at a high salary, as manager of a skillfully organized effort to defeat the amendment.[70]

Many years after the election, Carrie Chapman Catt wrote about the frustrating Oregon fight. (She and others seemed to rehash it as often as the painful 1896 California failure.) A solid student of politics, Catt judged that in 1906 "all the vicious elements of the population," including the liquor industry, fought the amendment.[71] She and others no longer blamed corporations for attempting to limit the size of the Oregon electorate in 1906, but it should be emphasized that in the Progressive period Portland businessmen, for reasons of self-interest, did contribute money and votes against the reform. Perhaps Catt, who had demonstrated her political and organizational skills in the successful Colorado and Idaho suffrage fights, might have found ways to have reduced the influence of these negative Portland businessmen. Her biographer relates that many reformers encouraged Catt to manage the key 1906 Oregon campaign. She refused for a personal reason: "I should dearly love to undertake the work in Oregon, but my husband needs me now, and is going to need me more, and more, and I will not leave him."[72] Her friends understood her decision but reasoned that she would have been far more resourceful as a commander of the Oregon battle than Shaw. Some attributed the defeat to the NAWSA president herself because she lacked administrative skills and the ability to work with allies, especially those who questioned her decisions.

Duniway, of course, voiced her own interpretations of the 1906 election. Soon after learning the results she informed her son that it was "a splendid campaign of its kind. But it was of the kind that never wins anywhere."[73] She also admitted that she felt less upset by the 1906 failure than the failed one in 1900 because she had observed that "fool friends were leading us to defeat and was prepared for it." A month after the election she wrote a favorable resolution: "That our late brilliant and dignified campaign, with the rapidly growing vote in favor of our cause, is to us an irresistible inspiration to increased effort."[74] At about the same time she told Alice Blackwell "that the chief gain of the whole [1905-1906] struggle was the opportunity it afforded our National officers to see for themselves the standing I have before the voters here, which alone made the campaign possible."[75] Duniway denounced the "freaks and parasites" who took state control and misled the campaigners.

In the summer of 1906 she had harsh words to say about the state suffrage leaders who, in the previous winter, had sought to cooperate with the WCTU, making "the equal suffrage movement a tail to the Prohibition kite."[76] Duniway again insisted that many men voted no because suffrage workers simultaneously pushed the suffrage and local option initiatives. For the moment the old reformer also denounced the "Hobo elements, or floating population who have no homes or families, but who now hold the balance of power at all elections, against the home-making women of Oregon."[77] Privately, however, Duniway was advancing another reason for the frustrating loss: the NAWSA's old and ineffective open campaign managed by outsiders. Duniway confided to friends that she was "for the fourth time, resurrecting the ship"; in other words, she was campaigning to become reelected president of the OSESA. The politician promised to direct a different type of campaign; there would not be a repeat of the Anthony-type because "voters will not listen to women speakers, unless they are already with us."[78] Duniway assured that when she was in charge that both the prohibitionists and Portland businessmen would be supportive. By excluding the WCTU she predicted an early victory.

In the fall Duniway and some of her allies and a few NAWSA officers openly denounced each other for the election's outcome. Tactics, personalities, and prohibition were at the heart of the dispute. The tension of the arduous campaign could no longer be restrained; several leaders wrote accusations about responsibility for the failure. Duniway said, "I am in a row with Annie Shaw et al which greatly pleases me. We would have won beyond a reasonable doubt if they had remained away."[79]

Undoubtedly Abigail asked her brother to write his opinions about the 1906 election and related matters. In August, Harvey stated in his *Oregonian* that he would not speculate about why equal suffrage had been rejected, but he did praise his sister for long and devoted service to her cause. But in a second, lengthy editorial Scott ruled that easterners had incorrectly interpreted the election by overemphasizing the role played by "liquor men, the corporations and the politicians."[80] Scott conceded that these groups and wealthy women enjoying "perfumed ease" had all contributed to the election outcome. But he judged that the suffragists "having succeeded in arousing general public attention . . .

were defeated, largely for that reason." Thus, in his opinion, the NAWSA, as Duniway and others had long argued, employed the wrong tactics. Abigail and Harvey were for once in agreement on a suffrage topic.

Because of the bitter controversy in the suffrage ranks, the meeting of their state organization in November 1906 received considerable newspaper publicity. The fact that the NAWSA had taken control of the OSESA in 1905 and ran the 1906 campaign was a major issue; furthermore, the WCTU members supporting suffrage expressed irritation with Duniway and sought to win the association's presidency. Duniway defeated her prohibitionist foe by a vote of 41-28. After being elected, she heatedly spoke against the appointments of Clara Colby as her vice president and Dr. Mary Thompson as auditor; they had both aligned with the NAWSA against her leadership. In blocking the nomination of these two opponents, Duniway bluntly stated that "it was necessary to have a board of officers who would work in harmony."[81] Once again she was the state's suffrage leader. Apparently any hard feelings she had about her mentor soon evaporated; in fact, Duniway enjoyed to the end of her days the title, "The Susan B. Anthony of the West."

But the Portlander's relationship with Shaw and other officers of the NAWSA worsened as each side blamed the other for the 1906 failure. Anthony and Catt would have opposed these recriminations as a waste of energy. Shaw and Duniway made accusations against each other for years. For example, the Portlander complained to the national leader: "It is indeed strange that you cannot see the necessity for a change in the National method, after so many failures." The aging agitator concluded that the "National Association is composed chiefly of *hot air*."[82] In late 1906 Shaw confessed that "I consider the election of Mrs. Duneway [*sic*] to the presidency the greatest disaster that has befallen the state for many years. The real defeat of woman suffrage in Oregon was not at the polls last spring, but by women themselves in their state convention this fall." The president fussed, "I feel as if I had given two of the best years of my life to [Oregon] and I regret that there is so little to show for it."[83] However, President Shaw's ineffective leadership of the national organization and her hostility to Duniway meant that some suffragists, including DeVoe, defended the Portlander. Undoubtedly this support increased over time because Shaw, who lacked political and personal leadership skills, became involved in controversy with several state associations. Historian Robert Booth Fowler has recently concluded: "The fact is that the national suffrage movement fell into a serious and deepening crisis in the years 1910-1915, and the finger of blame pointed to Shaw."

Her chilly relationship with the Shaw-directed NAWSA influenced Duniway's interpretation of the 1906 election. In her autobiography she denounced Shaw and her allies, blaming them for the campaign's failure. Ruth Moynihan, Duniway's most recent biographer, fully agrees with these assessments, calling the 1906 campaign "disastrous and expensive." Moynihan's sympathetic account, however, erroneously concludes: "After Susan B. Anthony's death . . . Anna Howard Shaw and others hurried to Oregon to make their work a symbolic tribute to Anthony. Mrs. Duniway was ignored and slandered, her methods ridiculed."[84] Actually the Oregon fight, including Shaw's part in it, had been arranged months before the leader's death. It should be emphasized that Mary Anthony, Alice Blackwell and the majority of the NAWSA leadership made a long rail journey to win a victory, not provide a "symbolic tribute." Moynihan correctly states that the Portlander did not play the role she had in 1900, that she was criticized (especially by Shaw), and that her co-workers treated her still hunt tactic with contempt. Anthony, Shaw, Catt, Cooper, and others concluded that they must set Duniway aside. But the seasoned leader was not ignored; she played a reduced but significant role in the 1906 battle. She appeared on campaign platforms, sometimes lectured with national leaders, and wrote numerous private and public letters. The leadership, especially Alice Blackwell, gave the rejected veteran attention. In summary, Duniway could do anything she wanted—except to manage the campaign—and suffrage editors made certain that she received recognition.

As stated earlier, many Oregonians agreed with the national officers that Duniway, despite her dedicated service, could not lead them to victory. While many admired her wit, dedication, energy, and ability to write and speak, they disliked her denunciations of the national organization, her provocative assertions, her name calling, her still hunt campaign tactic (which had failed in 1900), and her independent manner. While these insiders appreciated that the Oregon reformer was deeply hurt by the political action employed against her, they must also have resented her assertion that the national leaders looted the suffragist treasury. Everyone was aware that some of the national leaders worked without any compensation at all and that there was little money to misappropriate.

Duniway's autobiography fervently and mistakenly blames the national leadership for the 1906 defeat. The reasons for failure were many. The liquor interest provided money and an unknown number of votes; the business community donated funds, considerable political literature, and the organization of Portland "antis"; and indifferent, hostile, or conservative men cast the rejecting votes. Many voted no because they feared that it would lead to the prohibition of alcoholic liquors. During the long campaign the WCTU actually subordinated leadership to the NAWSA, whose officers did not fault prohibitionist women for the political failure. Duniway, however, scolded the WCTU for its role in this and other referenda contests.

Another factor that contributed to defeat was female apathy, as was reported to headquarters by Clay and other workers. Shaw recognized this problem late in the contest and responded by sending large quantities of circulars to Oregonians. "It certainly is needed," she wrote in exasperation, "for of all the apathetic lot of people on earth nothing surpasses the people of this state."[85] She thought it would take another year to educate Oregonians, but she and other like-minded politicians kept the nagging problem of female apathy out of the newspapers. Their assessments of the readiness of individual communities were also kept from reporters. Shaw, for example, praised Eugeneans but denounced Astoria for its foreign-born residents, whom she called "not at all an intellectual lot of people."

Colonel Wood, Editor Scott, and Portland "antis" before and during the campaign had correctly played up the fact that many women took little interest in the franchise. Two days after the election Scott gave a simple interpretation of the result: "It would seem that Oregon is not for woman suffrage." State president Coe agreed and thus insisted upon a new educative campaign; the reform would not be realized until many more Oregonians understood the need for it. Obviously it would take a great effort to make suffrage an important public issue. During the 1906 election Oregon newspapers thoroughly debated the qualifications of candidates seeking either national or state offices. They paid much less attention to the suffrage amendment. In other words, in 1906 as in 1871 Oregon journalists considered the reform to be a secondary concern. These molders of public opinion had become much less critical of the issue but partisan politics continued to be much more important.

Traditional male hostility to equal suffrage was much deeper than the feminists acknowledged in their lengthy and varied explanations for the 1906 defeat. A Salem *Statesman* editorial, employing old arguments, probably spoke for many antisuffragists in evaluating the state's rejection of the amendment. The editor reminded that many men went to the polling stations irritated by the fact that they had to compete with female workers. "Man was born to be woman's admirer," the writer explained, "but when woman is brought too close, comes into competition with man, the spirit of admiration gives way to the spirit of commercial relation. . . . Man likes to be close to one woman but not to all womankind."[86] It was his opinion that men had voted no primarily because they did not want women to leave their homes and become involved in turbulent politics. The editor concluded by rejecting the popular suffragist assertion that if women voted it would improve Oregon: few men "were heard to express either a fear or a hope that the extension of the ballot privilege to women would make a material change in conditions in this state or that it would affect party alignments or materially change the character of legislation."

Although feminists suffered a bitter disappointment in 1906, the open campaign advanced by Anthony, U'Ren, Colby, Evans, Coe, and many others was an appropriate tactic for Progressive America. Even in reform-minded Oregon, however, the idea of equal suffrage could not overcome traditional resistance, much of which was identical to that aroused by Anthony in her 1871 tour. In 1906 as in 1871 there was still great concern about "woman's sphere."

The still hunt tactic proved troublesome in several Oregon referenda votes. In 1900 Duniway had utilized this method and had garnered about 48 percent of the vote; the favorable vote won by the still hunt dropped to about 39 percent in 1908 and 36 percent in 1910. This evidence helped support Sarah Evans, a participant in all these efforts, in her pronouncement that those led by Duniway in 1908 and 1910 were "disastrous."[87]

Probably Ida Harper's evaluation of the 1906 contest was considered to be the official one. Although she fully understood the internal bickering and the apathy problems, she ignored them. Instead, Harper hailed the effort that Anthony had helped organize, and concluded, "Never, unless perhaps in that of California in 1896, was there as large an amount of splendid work done, never as much money spent in speakers, literature, etc.; and never was there such a combination in opposition."[88] She repeated the assertion made by some politicians that suffragists had actually been cheated out of a 1906 victory by corporations, liquor interests, and organized antisuffragist women.

Thus for many years after 1906, Harper, Duniway, and others, have attempted to explain the defeat through a discussion of the tactics employed by both sides. But the tactics of reformers were of less importance to the outcome than the controversial nature of the issue they advocated. Neither national nor local leaders would have been successful in 1906. Oregon well deserved its reputation as being one of the most progressive states, but it was not yet ready to enact an equal suffrage law. While voters rejected the amendment backed by the NAWSA, they approved five reform initiative measures pushed by William U'Ren. It was necessary for reformers—in and out of the state—to make suffrage as vital as it had been in Colorado (1893) and in Idaho (1896). Surely the NAWSA and Duniway wasted too much time faulting each other after the 1906 campaign, but suffragists, like other groups, could engage in hurtful internal politics. In summary, all interpretations of the twentieth century suffrage elections in Oregon must be tentative until scholars carefully detail them in the same way that Professor T.A. Larson studied the fights in Idaho and Washington. Furthermore, Professor Norman H. Clark's explanation for the rejection of female suffrage in Washington in the 1880s considered factors that also played a part in the 1906 defeat in Oregon. He summarized that suffrage and the equally controversial issue of prohibition "were both inextricably enmeshed in the conflicts between capital and labor, between lower and middle class, [and] between 'the interests' and 'the people.'"[89] Those seeking to understand the Oregon and Washington referenda campaigns of the twentieth century must consider Clark's interpretation.

A comparison of the Oregon rejection in 1910 with the success in Washington that same year will shed light on the personalities, tactics, arguments, and problems of Pacific Northwest suffragists. Emma Smith DeVoe led Washington to a victory by overcoming a variety of political, geographic, and personality problems. A follower of Anthony and Catt and a veteran of several suffrage campaigns, including those in Idaho in 1896 and Oregon ten years later, she worked closely with members of the

Washington legislature so that they would permit an election to decide on the enfranchisement of her sex. DeVoe accepted Anthony's tactic of organizing at all levels. In fact, she maintained that in 1896 she herself—not Duniway—had organized Idaho, and that she had discovered that Duniway's leadership in Washington had not resulted in adequate organizations. DeVoe, unlike her Oregon colleague, worked harmoniously with Shaw, taking her in as "a partner and a confidante." The Washington leader assured the national president that there would not be "such wicked stuff published in the papers about eastern women as was published in the Oregon campaign."[90] The NAWSA cooperated with its long time field representative; it sent DeVoe money, held a national convention in Seattle in 1909, including Catt, and considerable encouragement. The NAWSA stressed to DeVoe, who won its esteem because she had been a steadfast soldier in various western state battles, that she now commanded a vital campaign—given the discouragement of women at the fact they had not won a state since Idaho in 1896—and reminded her to be inspired by Anthony's career.

Duniway provided different advice. "If the NAWSA won't send supplies to your beleaguered garrison unless they send along their army of suckers to consume the supplies faster than they can be gathered . . . for sweet Liberty's sake, keep them away." And indeed, in 1909 and 1910 Devoe clashed with some national leaders over financial matters and their influence in the state suffrage organization. But the real challenge to DeVoe's generalship of the fight came not from President Shaw but from May Arkwright Hutton, president of the Spokane suffrage club and a local Democratic leader. Their differences produced frustration and consumed energy as Hutton challenged DeVoe but proved no more harmful to the outcome than had the squabbles between Shaw and Duniway in the Oregon campaign.

A pragmatic politician, DeVoe began with the still hunt method and then utilized the Anthony-type open campaign practiced in Oregon in 1906 and recommended by Catt in 1910. DeVoe evaluated these tactics: "The national officers believe in an all-speaking campaign, and Mrs. Dunneway [*sic*] believes exclusively in a still hunt. . . . Now I believe in working on our plan with a campaign of partly speech making and partly still hunting."[91] She also insisted that most volunteers should be state residents and that there should not be "too much speaking, there is danger of tiring our friends out on the one hand, and arousing our enemies to action on the other."

DeVoe's calm approach and careful planning were more effective than Duniway's confused 1910 Oregon effort. Biographer Harper called the Washington campaign "the ablest campaign for the suffrage ever known"; historian Larson correctly concludes that "Mrs. DeVoe ran a smoother, better organized campaign than Mrs. Duniway ever did."[92] His interpretation of the Washington victory includes the assumption that the liquor interests "were lulled into a feeling of security" because Oregon had rejected suffrage in 1906 and 1908; furthermore, the scholar notes that "DeVoe managed to persuade the prohibitionists to support the amendment actively but quietly." On the other hand, Larson maintains that some Oregon prohibitionists had not pushed for suffrage in their state because Duniway denounced them. Norman Clark found that the 1910 fight for local option in Washington attracted considerable attention and that "the suffrage pitch was by comparison soft and subtle."[93] This shrewd tactic reflected the experience and leadership of DeVoe, not Duniway. Surely the difference in character, tactics, and leadership is one of the reasons why in 1910 Washington suffragists won by about 22,000 votes while those south of the Columbia failed by about the same margin.

Duniway accurately anticipated that "Washington's victory spells success for Oregon."[94] Suffragists everywhere, in fact, took heart. By 1914 six additional states and Alaska Territory had adopted the reform. This string of accomplishments—stemming in part from a single West Coast victory—was what Anthony had predicted and sought through her work in California in 1896 and in Oregon in 1896 and 1905.

The other western coastal states immediately followed Washington's example. California adopted the reform in 1911. The fact that Oregon was now surrounded by suffrage states contributed to its 1912 victory. The still hunt tactic was set aside and an open campaign, one that was more like that waged in Oregon in 1906 than that of 1908 or 1910, was adopted. Duniway, her allies, and outsiders (including Shaw) participated. Duniway, who had employed the initiative law, became seriously ill and would be infirm during much of this long battle. Allies organized committees, worked at the precinct level, distributed literature, held rallies, and coordinated parades.[95] In the successful California campaign suffragists rejected Duniway's still hunt and "adopted the methods of mass marketing and advertising" to arouse public attention.[96] This new tactic proved to be equally effective in Oregon.

Before that crucial 1912 Oregon vote, Duniway, Shaw, Evans and others continued to bicker over political power within the state movement. The old hostilities consumed energies but again made little difference to voters. Despite solid organization, great publicity (including the sentimental appeal of the ailing, dedicated Duniway), and her participation, Oregon adopted suffrage by only 52 percent of the vote—a much lower margin of victory than the 64 percent of the vote won two years earlier in Washington. It is very likely that many men in 1912 actually voted against the controversial Duniway. In fact, opposition to her and her politics was one reason why it took six referenda contests to win equal suffrage; no other state took as many votes as Oregon. Duniway offered a different explanation: the state victory was delayed because it took six years "to clear the wreckage" resulting from the 1906 NAWSA-directed campaign. An observer explained that from 1907 to 1912 the OSESA officers had insisted that the NAWSA representatives stay out of Oregon because they "gotta quit kickin' their dog around."[97]

In her own time and long since, Duniway has been called the mother of Idaho, Washington and Oregon suffrage. Obviously she played an important regional role, especially in Oregon. Anthony's work, prestige, character, followers, and tactics also advanced suffrage in these states. It is time to further investigate the contributions of the various leaders who helped enfranchise Northwest women. Surely such research of the role played by famous and forgotten females, especially DeVoe, will enrich our understanding of one of the region's great reform movements. Such scholarship will demonstrate that political squabbling among suffragists was common. All national reform movements—for abolition, temperance, and education—included political infighting. Disputes in the reform ranks are similar to those within political parties. In each, strong-willed and disappointed individuals fault those within as well as without their groups. Thus the woman suffrage movement at both national and state levels, including Oregon and Washington, endured disagreements over tactics, objectives, and the personalities of its leaders. Strains within the early twentieth century woman's movement over how best to bring about political change are similar to those in the contemporary feminist movement. Militants and moderates continue to differ over leadership, organization, and tactics. The proponents of the Equal Rights Amendment, for example, have various explanations for the failure to carry the required thirty-eight states despite the fact that public opinion polls demonstrated that a strong majority approved the measure. Equal Rights Amendment supporters, including historians, disagree whether the defeat was owing to complacency, controversial sit-in tactics, the inability of woman's groups to coordinate strategy, the relationship to the political parties, or the actions of opponents.

Eighty years earlier advocates of equality also disagreed over such matters, including strategy. Anthony's insistence that NAWSA representatives be given control of state referenda campaigns was, as Duniway argued, a dubious undertaking—NAWSA directed battles won in Colorado and Idaho and failed in South Dakota, California, and Oregon. This control, of course, led to charges of "outside professional agitators" or as one journalist wrote: paid "feminine Colonels from the effete East" created mischief in California society by battling for additional rights for women.[98] More importantly, it led to hard feelings between local and national participants. The best approach appears to have been the one adopted by DeVoe in 1910. She mixed the still hunt with the open tactic, demanded that skilled state officers manage the campaign, and used national women as allies, not as directors.

Additional research will most likely sustain Anthony's opinion of Duniway. It is obvious that Abigail, like her brother Harvey, was a better editor and publicist than a politician and organizer. Duniway recruited many women and men to the suffragist ranks and sustained a regional reform movement for decades, but her personal shortcomings, her disinterest in establishing and nurturing suffrage organizations, her enthusiasm for the still hunt tactic, and her inability to win equal suffrage in a progressive state all shaped Anthony's political evaluation of Duniway and her region. No matter what one thinks of Duniway's bluntness and political tactics, all would agree with Alice Blackwell, who, in 1943, described the *New Northwest* as having been "the most picturesque" suffrage newspaper and called its editor "a character."[99]

For about thirty-five years Anthony had tried to make this "character" into an effective regional suffrage leader. In 1871 the New Yorker chose the Oregonian and gave her a practical education in reform tactics and followed this up with supportive correspondence and friendship. Disappointed with the results, Anthony had taken different actions in

1896 and 1905. While Duniway was important to her, success in the region was even more significant.

Duniway, for her part, was among those who disapproved of Anthony's powerful control of the NAWSA; surprisingly, the Duniway collection does not contain criticisms of her mentor or correspondence from disaffected state and national leaders. Although Anthony restricted her and eventually played politics against Duniway in her own state, this lack of evidence indicates that Abigail threw shafts at easier targets, including Colby, Shaw, and their Portland allies.

From the time Anthony came to the Pacific Northwest as a middle-aged woman in 1871 to initiate the reform movement until her death in 1906, she sought ways to enfranchise its females. The Easterner labored to attain her life's work in many places across the nation, but none were more important to her in her last years than the Pacific Northwest. Anthony's personal efforts and those of her talented followers, including Catt, DeVoe, and Duniway, were major reasons why the region's women at last attained a basic right of citizenship. Both the ideals and the politics of the regional suffragist movement and its leaders are still relevant as a broader fight for full equality continues. Like Susan B. Anthony, contemporary feminists, advocating economic, social, and political change, have included the Pacific Northwest in their plans. They are seeking a harvest from the reform seed first scattered under the careful direction of Anthony almost one hundred twenty years ago.

# *Notes*

FOREWORD

1. Isabella Hooker Collection, Stowe-Day Collection, Hartford, Connecticut.
2. Olympia Brown Papers, 3 September 1890. Schlesinger Library, Radcliffe College.

INTRODUCTION

1. Boston *Woman's Journal*, 17 March 1906.
2. *The Ladies Home Journal*, (March 1933): 24.
3. Quotes from DAR and NOW. DAR 14, NOW 12 of Hearing Committee on Banking, Housing, 95th Congress, 1978. Susan B. Anthony Dollar Coin Act of 1978, 14.
4. Portland *Oregonian*, 3 August 1978.
5. Ellen Carol DuBois, "Outgrowing the Compact of the Fathers: Equal Rights, Woman Suffrage, and the United States Constitution, 1820-1878." *Journal of American History*, 74 (1987): 842.
6. *Congressional Quarterly Almanac*, 92nd Congress, 2nd session, 1972. Washington, D.C. 1972, 202.
7. Susan B. Anthony, "Woman's Half-Century of Evolution," *North American Review*, 175 (December 1902): 800.
8. *Life*, 4 September 1970, 21.
9. McKenzie, Midge, *Shoulder to Shoulder*, (New York: Alfred A. Knopf, 1975), ix.
10. Portland *Oregonian*, 19 August 1987.

1 A PEACEFUL WARRIOR

1. Diary of Susan B. Anthony, 26 August 1871, Susan B. Anthony Papers, Library of Congress. Hereinafter SBA Diary.

2. Elizabeth Cady Stanton, *Eighty Years & More: Reminiscences 1815-1897*, (New York: Schocken Books, 1971), 162.
3. Stanton, *Eighty Years & More*, 166.
4. Kathleen Barry, *Susan B. Anthony: A Biography of a Singular Feminist*, (New York: New York University Press, 1988), 37.
5. Stanton, *Eighty Years & More*, 157.
6. Quoted in Ellen Carol DuBois, *Feminism and Suffrage: The Emergence of an Independent Woman's Movement in America, 1848-1869*, (Ithaca: Cornell University Press, 1978), 28.
7. Nancy Woloch, *Women and the American Experience*, (New York: Alfred A. Knopf, 1984), 194.
8. Ellen Carol DuBois, *Feminism and Suffrage*, 42.
9. Ellen Carol DuBois, (ed.), *Elizabeth Cady Stanton-Susan B. Anthony: Correspondence, Writings, Speeches*, (New York: Schocken Books, 1981), 91.
10. Stanton, *Eighty Years & More*, 185.
11. DuBois, *Elizabeth Cady Stanton-Susan B. Anthony*, 94.
12. SBA Diary, December 31, 1871.
13. Quoted in Ida Harper, *Life and Work of Susan B. Anthony*, (Indianapolis: Hollenbeck Press, 1898), 1: 391.
14. SBA Diary, 15 and 21 July 1871.
15. "After the sentiments this woman [Stanton] expressed concerning the murderess, Mrs. Fair, people claiming respectability ought to make it a point to avoid instead of inviting her." Portland *Oregonian*, 18 August 1871.
16. Duniway challenged other editors to explain why they opposed woman suffrage. "The editorial fraternity," she reasoned, "owe to humanity, to justice, to common sense, and common philanthropy, no more than to our humble, but nevertheless aspiring self, a cogent and satisfactory reason or reasons for their desire to withhold the ballot from the hand of women." She acknowledged the importance of ministers also in influencing public opinion and asked them to ponder her goals. "When the churches acknowledged themselves converted, we shall have little difficulty in converting the world." Portland *New Northwest*, 26 May, 2 June, 16 June, and 14 July 1871.
17. Portland *New Northwest*, 9 June 1871.
18. Portland *New Northwest*, 26 May 1871.
19. Like many other newspapers, the Portland *Oregonian* of 18 August 1871, denounced Fair. "What Mrs. Fair is and what her paramour was we do not need to say—he deserved the infamy

which her bullet gave him, and she deserves hanging as much as any murderer ever did." The Portland *Bulletin* 30 July 1871, was highly critical of Joaquin Miller: "there is no language strong enough to justly denounce the meanness, cowardice and villainy of the man who, with his pockets filled with gold, earned in part by the loving and self-sacrificing labors of his wife, will deliberately desert that wife and his own children, leaving them to poverty, beggary or destruction."

20. Olympia *Washington Standard*, 19 August 1871.
21. Harper, *The Life and Work of Susan B. Anthony*, 1: 395.
22. T.A. Larson, "Woman's Rights in Idaho," *Idaho Yesterdays*, Spring, 1972.
23. New York *Revolution*, 28 September 1871.

## 2 EDUCATING THE TEACHER

1. Portland *New Northwest*, 28 June 1872.
2. Sacramento *Union*, 20 November 1871.
3. Thomas W. Prosch Collection, Speeches and Writings, 1858-1889, University of Washington Archives, Seattle, Washington.
4. Ray A. Billington, *Westward Expansion*, 5th ed., (New York: Macmillan, 1982), 10.
5. *Settlers' Guide to Oregon and Washington Territory*, (New York: 1872) 32.
6. Portland *Oregonian*, 17 November 1871.
7. J. Orin Oliphant, *On the Cattle Ranges of the Oregon Country*, (Seattle: University of Washington Press, 1968), 109.
8. Frances Fuller Victor, *All Over Oregon, and Washington*, (San Francisco: John H. Carmany and Co., 1872), 368.
9. Portland *Herald*, 1 October 1871.
10. George S. Turnbull, *History of Oregon Newspapers*, (Portland: Binfords & Mort, 1939), 81.
11. G. Thomas Edwards, "The Politics of Railroads, 1869," *The Call Number*, 30 (Spring 1969): 22.
12. Kalama *Beacon*, 29 September 1871.
13. Kalama *Beacon*, 30 May 1871.
14. Seattle *Intelligencer*, 18 September 1871; Portland *Oregonian*, 24 November 1871.
15. Portland *Herald*, 28 November 1871.
16. DuBois, *Feminism and Suffrage*, 159-160.
17. DuBois, *Feminism and Suffrage*, 155.
18. Portland *New Northwest*, 15 and 29 December 1871.

19. Portland *New Northwest*, 26 May 1871.
20. Portland *Bulletin*, 30 September 1870.
21. *Puget Sound Business Directory and Guide to Washington*, (Olympia: Murphy & Harned, 1872), 64.
22. *Settlers' Guide to Oregon and Washington Territory*, 30.
23. The *Oregonian* had similarly provided a humorous description of Laura de Force Gordon: "She is still young, with a pleasant, intelligent face. . . . We can positively assure our readers that she does not wear spectacles, nor, as far as we could discover, false hair or false teeth. If the woman's advocates were all to come in such guise, we think it would not be at all a hardship to welcome them with, shall we say, open arms, and to endure for an hour or two their railing at the inhumanity of man to woman." Portland *Oregonian*, 2 August, 1 and 2 September 1871.
24. Portland *Herald*, 2 September 1871.
25. Harper, *Life and Work of Susan B. Anthony*, 1: 396.
26. Harper, *Life and Work of Susan B. Anthony*, 1: 396.
27. SBA Diary, 6 September 1871.
28. Portland *Bulletin*, 2 September 1871.

## 3 URBAN CAMPAIGNS

1. Portland *Herald*, 28 November 1871.
2. Harper, *Life and Work of Susan B. Anthony*, 1: 342.
3. Abigail Scott Duniway, *Path Breaking* (New York: Schocken Books, 1971), 44.
4. Portland *New Northwest*, 15 September 1871.
5. SBA Diary, 6 September 1871.
6. Harper, *Life and Work of Susan B. Anthony*, 1: 396-397.
7. Portland *Bulletin*, 7 September 1871.
8. Portland *Oregonian*, 7 September 1871.
9. Portland *Herald*, 7 September 1871.
10. Portland *Pacific Christian Advocate*, 9 September 1871.
11. Portland *New Northwest*, 8 September 1871.
12. Portland *Bulletin*, 9 September 1871.
13. Portland *Oregonian*, 9 September 1871.
14. Portland *Herald*, 9 September 1871.
15. Portland *New Northwest*, 15 September 1871.
16. SBA Diary, 9 September 1871.
17. Portland *Oregonian*, 11 September 1871.
18. Portland *Herald*, 10 September 1871.
19. Woloch, *Women and the American Experience*, 319.

20. Harper, *Life and Work of Susan B. Anthony*, 1: 398.
21. Portland *Oregonian*, 11 September 1871.
22. The most complete accounts appeared in the Portland *Oregonian*, 12 September 1871 and the Portland *New Northwest*, 15 September 1871.
23. Portland *Bulletin*, 12 September 1871.
24. Portland *Pacific Christian Advocate*, 16 September 1871.
25. Portland *Pacific Christian Advocate*, 23 September 1871.
26. Portland *Oregonian*, 16 September 1871.
27. Portland *New Northwest*, 22 September 1871.
28. Portland *Bulletin*, 17 September 1871.
29. Portland *Herald*, 13 September 1871.
30. SBA Diary, 12 September 1871.
31. Portland *New Northwest*, 15 September 1871.
32. Portland *New Northwest*, 7 July 1871.
33. Oregon City *Weekly Enterprise*, 15 September 1871.
34. Portland *New Northwest*, 22 September 1871.
35. Victor, *All Over Oregon and Washington*, 170.
36. Salem *Statesman*, 6 and 10 September 1871. In her response to Mrs. Frost's letter, Rose Greenleaf insisted that those working for the ballot were women of "intellect, broad culture and deep philanthropy." She complained that females were presently taught that "to make herself attractive is the only legitimate employment of a woman's mind." Duniway, of course, was also furious with Frost's letter. In an editorial entitled "J.B. Frost, Stand Up!" the editor angrily charged: "You are accused before Almighty God and these witnesses of perpetrating a libel upon your own sex." After a critical evaluation of the antisuffragist's ideas, Duniway concluded, "We can forgive an ignoramus of the genus masculine who reviles woman, but when a self-conceited upstart like yourself essays such wickedness she sins away her day of grace." Portland *New Northwest*, 8 Sept 1871. Her brother's newspaper criticized Frost's letter in more moderate tones. It failed "inasmuch as it is more a condemnation of free love than of the doctrine of suffrage for woman." Scott believed that only a few suffragists championed free love; moreover, most "are pure and exemplary in all the relations of life." Portland *Oregonian*, 5 September 1871.
37. Salem *Statesman*, 10 September 1871.
38. SBA Diary, 14 September 1871.
39. Portland *New Northwest*, 29 September 1871.

40. Portland *New Northwest*, 22 September 1871.
41. Salem *Weekly Mercury*, 3 June, 30 August, and 20 September 1871. Albany *Democrat*, 29 September 1871.
42. Salem *Statesman*, 20 September 1871.
43. Salem *Statesman*, 10 September 1871.
44. Cooke doubted that Anthony earned $5,000 in Oregon, and declared that whatever the actual cost to Oregonians it was "very small pay for the amount of light received and delight experienced." She insisted that the private lecture provided "more valuable information and more reasonable theories for the advancement and perfection of the human race than I ever heard in any political speech in my life" and denied that the visitor employed "improbable and low" anecdotes. Portland *New Northwest*, 29 September 1871.
45. SBA Diary, 16 and 17 September 1871.
46. Portland *Bulletin*, 11 August 1871. The newspaper's correspondent added: Mrs. Gordon "handled the subject very well, but the people here don't care much to listen to her again."

### 4 SCATTERING THE REFORM SEED

1. Portland *New Northwest*, 6 October 1871.
2. The Dalles *Weekly Mountaineer*, 2 and 16 September, 7 October 1871.
3. Portland *New Northwest*, 6 October 1871.
4. Duniway, *Path Breaking*, 46.
5. Portland *New Northwest*, 6 October 1871.
6. SBA Diary, 20 September 1871.
7. Walla Walla *Union*, 16 September 1871.
8. The two reformers praised the Pixley sisters. Anthony, who often ackowledeged female achievements, noted that the three beautiful sisters, Annie, Minnie, and Lucy aged eighteen, sixteen, and twelve "manage their own business and hire men to fill up plays." SBA Diary, 21 September 1871.
9. SBA Diary, 23 September 1871.
10. Portland *New Northwest*, 20 October 1871.
11. Walla Walla *Union*, 23 September 1871.
12. One editor found it hard to comprehend "How an editor with the experience and acknowledged ability of . . . Newell" could throw filth. Portland *Bulletin*, 26 July 1871.
13. Walla Walla *Statesman*, 23 September 1871.

14. Walla Walla *Statesman*, 30 September 1871.
15. Walla Walla *Statesman*, 30 September, and 7 October 1871.
16. Albany *Democrat*, 6 October 1871.
17. Walla Walla *Union*, 23 September 1871; Portland *New Northwest*, 20 October 1871.
18. Walla Walla *Statesman*, 30 September 1871.
19. Portland *New Northwest*, 20 October 1871.
20. *Oregonian*, 6 March 1871.
21. SBA Diary, 25 September 1871.
22. SBA Diary, 26 September 1871.
23. SBA Diary, 27 September 1871.
24. New York *Revolution*, 11 November 1871; SBA Diary, 28 and 30 September 1871.
25. SBA Diary, 28 September 1871.
26. SBA Diary, 28 September 1871. Duniway expressed fondness for the residents of her former hometown: "in no other city of its size upon the Pacific coast can be found so many intelligent, bright and agreeable women as are to be met in Albany. The men are also sensible, enterprising and gentlemanly." Portland *New Northwest*, 6 October 1871.
27. Albany *Democrat*, 29 September 1871.
28. Albany *Democrat*, 29 September 1871.
29. Portland *Herald*, 4 October 1871.
30. The Albany *Democrat* of 6 October 1871 published a story about hissing that was obviously aimed at Duniway. "Hissing is a poor substitute for argument and a certain indication of ill breeding or want of brains."
31. Frost referred to a letter from a Portland correspondent who chided Duniway for stumping the state and "leaving her two young boys to run around the streets without a mother's care, and as a consequence they have been figuring in our police court for stealing pumpkins." Albany *Democrat*, 29 September 1871. Duniway blamed others: "When all mothers find employment for their young and growing sons *as we have*, there will be no gangs of idle ruffians running loose in the streets to entrap children into mischief. Under man-made laws . . . Portland is so dirty and vile that children who have honorable employment cannot go into the street for a little needed exercise without being led into temptation by the children of mothers who 'have all the rights they want.'" She announced that her newspaper would fight to make it "a penal offense to bring up boys in idleness" and concluded: "Our fifteen-

year-old boy (not boys), who was thoughtlessly betrayed into the company of a bevy of man's rights offspring, is . . . mercilessly ashamed of himself." Portland *New Northwest*, 6 October 1871.

32. Albany *Democrat*, 13 October 1871; SBA Diary, 29 September 1871. Duniway blistered Frost: "A creature who represents herself as a historian—of whom nobody has ever heard only as she blows her own trumpet—has been endeavoring to earn a cheap and dirty notoriety by pandering to the vicious element of man's rights men in Albany." The angry editor called her the "prurient champion of masculine free-lovers" who delivered "inane sophistries." Portland *New Northwest*, 6 October 1871.
33. SBA Diary, 30 September 1871.
34. Albany *Good Templar*, 4 October 1871.
35. Portland *New Northwest*, 6 October 1871.
36. Albany *Democrat*, 15 September 1871.
37. Albany *Democrat*, 29 September 1871.
38. Albany *Democrat*, 13 October 1871. Portland *Bulletin*, 14 October 1871.
39. SBA Diary, 3 October 1871.
40. Corvallis *Benton Democrat*, 5 and 12 October 1871.
41. Corvallis *Benton Democrat*, 26 October 1871.
42. McMinnville *West Side*, 4 August 1871.
43. McMinnville *West Side*, 13 October 1871.
44. Portland *New Northwest*, 20 October 1871.
45. SBA Diary, 7 October 1871.
46. SBA Diary, 9 October 1871.
47. Seattle *Intelligencer*, 30 October 1871.
48. SBA Diary, 13 October 1871.
49. Sacramento *Union*, 24 October 1871.
50. Portland *New Northwest*, 20 October 1871.
51. Salem *Statesman*, 6 October 1871.
52. Salem *Statesman*, 14 October 1871.
53. Portland *Herald*, 17 October 1871. At the same time the *Herald* gave space to the antisuffragist visitors, Taggart and Frost, it continued to denounce Anthony and her sympathizers. It relished doggerel written by a Portlander aimed at the "Old Gal" and predicted that Anthony "will rave when she reads this piece of biting but just sarcasm." One stanza read:

    From near and far, throughout the land
    Progressive females swell'd her band;
    While lowly matrons left their Lords,

And struck for better beds and boards;
The higher joined the strange melee,
And struck for their affinity;
While shriller still her bugle rung,
To Salt Lake on! and Breed 'em Young—

54. Seattle *Intelligencer*, 30 October 1871.
55. Portland *Bulletin*, 14 October 1871.
56. Portland *New Northwest*, 20 October 1871.
57. SBA Diary, 12 October 1871.
58. Portland *New Northwest*, 20 October 1871.

## 5 NORTH TO PUGET SOUND AND VICTORIA

1. The Seattle *Intelligencer* of 21 August 1871 insisted that Laura de Force Gordon's "discourse wrought a visible change of opinion and elicited many comments in favor of a recognition of Woman's Rights; and, so far as her hearers are concerned, it is evident that they may be regarded as permanent converts to that cause—unless some other strong-minded woman, devoid of tact or charms, shall invade this field and mar her work."
2. In the spring of 1870 an unidentified woman, signing a public letter with the pseudonym "Equal Rights," made a remarkable legal argument similar to that advanced by Anthony in the fall of 1871, for the enfranchisement of Washington women. "Equal Rights" maintained that the territorial election law gave women the vote, concluding like Anthony that: "It therefore being admitted that women are persons, we certainly must be recognized as citizens, and if citizens then according to our laws we have the right to vote, and if the right, then devolves upon us the duty to make the best of our citizenship by coming out to the Polls at the coming election and casting our vote." Olympia *Washington Standard*, 4 June 1870.
3. SBA Diary, 17 October 1871.
4. Olympia *Tribune*, 6 October 1871. Prosch had been one of the first to encourage women to leave crowded eastern cities and come to Washington Territory. In the late 1860s he wrote: "Here is the market to bring your charms to, girls. Don't be backward, but come right along—all who want good husbands and comfortable homes in the most beautiful country and the finest climate in the world." *Puget Sound Herald* quoted in Clarence B. Bagley, *History of King County*, (Chicago: S.J. Clarke, Publishing Co., 1929), 1: 226.

5. Olympia *Echo*, 19 October 1871.
6. Olympia *Tribune*, quoted in Portland *New Northwest*, 27 October 1871.
7. Olympia *Washington Standard*, 21 October 1871.
8. As befitted a Harvard law school graduate, Daniel R. Bigelow had made his mark on Olympia since his arrival in 1851. A successful lawyer, an influential Republican, and an active Methodist, he was also superintendent of local schools at the time of Anthony's visit. His speech on behalf of woman's suffrage sought to explain why women did not have the vote and how women and the nation both would be served if she were enfranchised. He made several significant points; for example, "But it is said that woman may trust man to make laws for her. No class of men ever did make just and equal laws for another unrepresented class; and our whole system of laws demonstrate that man has never done so for woman. . . . The fall of nations has generally been preceded by the decay of public virtue and private worth. It is conceded by the best masculine minds of this nation . . . that woman surpasses man in developing the educational and moral faculties of mankind." *Speech of the Hon. D.R. Bigelow on Female Suferage (sic)*, 14 October 1871, Olympia, 1871, 9.
9. *Puget Sound Business Directory and Guide*, Olympia, 1872, 53.
10. *Puget Sound Business Directory and Guide*, Olympia, 1872, 50.
11. *Puget Sound Business Directory and Guide*, Olympia, 1872, 60.
12. Bigelow, *Speech on Female Suferage (sic)*, 11.
13. SBA Diary, 18 October 1871.
14. Murphy's account of the addresses delivered by Anthony and Duniway appeared in the Olympia *Washington Standard*, 21 October 1871, and was reprinted in the Portland *New Northwest*, 27 October 1871.
15. Olympia *Transcript*, 21 October 1871.
16. Portland *New Northwest*, 27 October 1871.
17. *Journal of the House of Representatives of the Territory of Washington*, Olympia, 1871, 61.
18. Portland *New Northwest*, 27 October 1871. Republican editor Edward Ross reported the vote and commented "So, notwithstanding all Miss Susan B's eloquence, female suffrage is 'busted.' But we hope the women will not all leave the Territory and go to Wyoming where they can vote." Walla Walla *Union*, 4 November 1871.
19. Olympia *Washington Standard*, 28 October 1871.

20. Olympia *Tribune*, 28 October 1871.
21. Olympia *Washington Standard*, 28 October 1871.
22. Portland *New Northwest*, 3 November 1871.
23. *Puget Sound Business Directory and Guide*, Olympia, 1872, 5.
24. Victoria *British Colonist*, 31 October 1871.
25. Elizabeth Cady Stanton, Susan B. Anthony, and Matilda Joslyn Gage, eds., *History of Woman Suffrage*, (Rochester, Privately printed, 1886), 3: 769.
26. Victoria *Standard*, 25 October 1871. A public letter from "Minnie" thought "that most men are of the opinion that it is useless to argue with a woman and that a gentleman would not contradict 'the fair sex.'" She furnished a solution: "should Miss Anthony meet with the opposition of an intelligent woman, I feel sure that most of her arguments would be upset." Victoria *British Colonist*, 26 October 1871.
27. Victoria *British Colonist*, 26 October 1871.
28. Victoria *British Colonist*, 27 October 1871.
29. SBA Diary, 26 October 1871.
30. Portland *New Northwest*, 3 November 1871.
31. Victoria *British Colonist*, 26 October 1871.
32. Victoria *British Colonist*, 27 October 1871.
33. SBA Diary, 27 October 1871.
34. Frances Fuller Victor, *All Over Oregon and Washington*, 250.
35. Port Townsend *Cyclop*, 19 October 1871, Susan B. Anthony Scrapbooks, Library of Congress. Hereinafter SBA scrapbooks.
36. Port Townsend *Cyclop*, 30 October 1871, SBA Scrapbooks.
37. Quoted in Portland *New Northwest*, 10 November 1871. Another Washington editor also gave opinions on voting. Mrs. M.L. Money, the only other woman editor in Washington Territory, paid only slight attention to woman's suffrage in her Kalama *Beacon*. She had heard Anthony lecture in Portland but refused to use her pen for the reform. Money, like Pettygrove, expressed negative views of universal suffrage. "If we could have our say so, there would be less voters than there are now. Who can deny the present corruption or abuse of the ballot? No one who cannot read and write, knows what he is voting for; but those who vote for gold or grog, do know what they are voting for; and so do those 'political rings' that corral and control the vile hordes to be found in large cities. . . . Now, if extending the right of suffrage to women will wipe out the rubbish, purify the ballot, have a tendency to eradicate the 'social evil,' intemperance, and make them more independent and

happy, as a class, we will work for it—might and main." To accomplish such change, she insisted, "women must all come up to the standard with these objects in view." Money concluded on a negative note: "a good acquaintance with the world has taught us not to expect too much from the 'fair sex.'" Kalama *Beacon*, 22 September 1871.

38. Quoted in Portland *New Northwest*, 24 November 1871. A bit later Pettygrove published a well-publicized piece of humor: "The woman question: what did she have on?" Port Townsend *Argus*, 11 January 1872.
39. SBA Diary, 30 October 1871.
40. An evaluation of conditions on Puget Sound in 1871 is in G. Thomas Edwards, "Terminus Disease," *Pacific Northwest Quarterly*, 70 (October 1979), 163-177.
41. Seattle *Intelligencer*, 2 October 1871.
42. Seattle *Intelligencer*, 6 November 1871.
43. Seattle *Intelligencer*, 16 October 1871.
44. Seattle *Territorial Dispatch*, 6 November 1871, SBA Scrapbook.
45. Seattle *Puget Sound Dispatch*, 11 December 1871. Brown's opposition to Anthony was a part of his defense of public morals. In Olympia he had supported the public library because he feared that the young might find a "morbid gratification in reading such flashy literature as is found in the *Police Gazette*" and similar publications. These publications, he warned, were a menace. "The libidinous postures of the women there pictorially exhibited, with the remarks following are a positive insult to our better nature. If it be true that man became what he contemplates, such gratification would naturally lead to sensual and licentious indulgence." He reminded that "In this age of general enlightenment, railways and telegraphs, to be equal to the period, the mind must be stored with very different knowledge." Olympia *Washington Standard*, 1 July 1871.
46. Harper, *Life and Work of Susan B. Anthony*, 1: 400.
47. SBA Diary, 4 November 1871.
48. SBA Diary, 6 November 1871.
49. Portland *New Northwest*, 17 November 1871.
50. Garfielde had surprised many constituents by suddenly appearing in the territory so as to mend political fences. Many scolded him for his political conduct, especially for leaving Congress when it was in session. Duniway joined the chorus of critics because Garfielde was unaware that woman's suffrage "commanded any

serious attention." She urged the voters to retire this "weathercock" so that he would "have time to study up the great question of suffrage." Olympia *Transcript* quoted in Portland *New Northwest*, 17 November 1871.

51. Portland *New Northwest*, 17 November 1871.
52. The official proceedings of the Woman Suffrage Campaign appeared in several newspapers, including the Olympia *Echo*, 16 November 1871.
53. W.D. Lyman, *An Illustrated History of Walla Walla County*, (n.p. W.H. Lever, 1901) 401.
54. In his refutation, Lasater boasted to his colleagues in the lower house that he had not drunk "half a gallon spirits in thirty-five years." Olympia *Transcript*, 28 October 1871.
55. Walla Walla *Statesman*, 28 November 1871. The editor of this newspaper, William H. Newell, quarreled with Lasater and explained the difficulty with his fellow Democrat: Lasater "plead in extenuation that the editor of the *Statesman* had called him the 'tail end' of the Legislature. We admit that we made a mistake, he was something just under the tail." Walla Walla *Statesman*, 27 January 1872.
56. Olympia *Washington Standard*, 11 November 1872.
57. Walla Walla *Statesman*, 18 November 1871.
58. Olympia *Transcript*, 11 November 1871.
59. Olympia *Washington Standard*, 11 November 1871.
60. Olympia *Tribune*, 11 November 1871.
61. SBA Diary, 9 November 1871.
62. SBA Diary, 10 and 11 November 1871.
63. Portland *New Northwest*, 17 November 1871.
64. Portland *New Northwest*, 1 December 1871.
65. Olympia *Tribune*, 18 November 1871. Prosch published another story about Anthony's influence: "A late issue of the *Boston Journal* contained the following gross libel upon the women of the Territory. 'Miss Anthony—Susanbe—is having wonderful success among the Flathead Indians of Oregon. She has converted them to the single bed faith, and thinks she has got them sure on woman suffrage. Susan is a tulip.' Of course, it confounds Oregon with Washington. We don't object, however, to an evidence of ignorance so common in the East; but we do object to the lovely white women of Puget Sound being called Flathead Indians. And that other slander upon the single bed faith. The nights are too cold and the women too sensible for that faith to succeed here."

66. Port Townsend *Argus*, 14 December 1872. According to O'Ragan, he wrote this letter in response to an incident that happened aboard a steamer. He maintained that about a dozen women expressed to him their displeasure with his opposition to the woman's suffrage convention. One woman, O'Ragan recalled, denounced him: "You ugly, hateful, wifeless, impertinent and motherless man, how dare you go around this Sound country making all manner of sport of the ladies who took a leading part in the woman's convention." O'Ragan was probably the author of 25 stanzas of verse denouncing the meeting. Olympia *Tribune*, 18 November 1871.
67. Portland, *New Northwest*, 15 December 1871.
68. There was a connection between the two controversial issues of woman's suffrage and prohibition. Representative Lasater said: "He had been opposed all his life to prohibition, but as it was apparent that the ladies would hold up the evils of intemperance as a means of advancing their cause, he would now vote to remove the club from their hands." By a close vote of 16-13 prohibition was rejected. Of the 25 men voting on both woman's suffrage and prohibition, 15 were consistent; they voted for or against both reforms. Olympia *Transcript*, 25 November 1871.
69. Olympia *Transcript*, 2 December 1871; Portland *New Northwest*, 8 December 1871.
70. Olympia *Tribune*, 2 December 1871. Edward E. Ross, editor of the Walla Walla *Union*, embellished the story: "right in the face of all those frowning females the incorrigible Noyes, with the scent of doughnuts and cookies in his nostrils, moved this amendment which took the very backbone out of the bill. . . . If Noyes is not already married, he had just as well leave the Territory when he goes a sparking; or else he must only pay his addresses to some damsel who is not sensible of her misery and does not wish to vote; or perhaps, find some forlorn creature whose motto is 'matrimony first and suffrage afterwards.'" Walla Walla *Union*, 9 December 1871.
71. *Statutes of the Territory of Washington*, Olympia, 1871, 175.
72. Mary Osburn Douthit, (ed.) *The Souvenir of Western Women* (Portland: Anderson & Duniway, 1905), 105. T.A. Larson, "The Woman's Suffrage Movement in Washington," *Pacific Northwest Quarterly*, 67 (1976): 50. Another historian ignored Miss Anthony's influence and explained that the legislators passed this law because "they became restive" under Duniway's attacks. Edmond

S. Meany, *History of the State of Washington*, (New York: Macmillan Co., 1927), 270.
73. Walla Walla *Union*, 9 December 1871.
74. Portland *New Northwest*, 15 December 1871.

## 6 FINAL OREGON EFFORTS

1. Portland *Bulletin*, 12 September 1871 and 20 October 1871, quoted in *New Northwest*, 27 October 1871. Another editor made the same charge against Miss Anthony and concluded: "Far-sighted philanthropistess! . . . Noble Susie! Vale!" Corvallis *Benton Democrat*, 26 October 1871.
2. Portland *New Northwest*, 27 October 1871.
3. Portland *Weekly Bulletin*, 28 October 1871.
4. Portland *Herald*, 29 October and 7 November 1871. The *Herald* said it could not call Duniway a lady. She responded with a story. "We feel something like the soldier did who was dying from the effects of a wound caused by the kick of a donkey. When it became known to him that the hour of his departure was near at hand he burst into tears. His comrades tried to cheer him, telling him not to fear death, but to meet it bravely like a man. 'I'm not afraid to die,' replied the despondent hero; 'that's not it; but after passing through so many battles, where death would have been honorable, to at last be kicked to death by a Government mule!'" Portland *New Northwest*, 17 November 1871.
5. Portland *Herald*, 25 October 1871.
6. Portland *Catholic Sentinel*, 28 October 1871. The *Herald* agreed: Mrs. Frost's "lectures will shake the faith of any converts that incline to the new doctrines as advocated by Susan B. Anthony, Mrs. Woodhull, and others." Portland *Herald*, 22 October 1871.
7. Portland *Herald*, 1 November 1871.
8. Portland *Oregonian*, 30 October 1871.
9. Kalama *Beacon*, 22 September 1871.
10. Portland *New Northwest*, 17 November 1871.
11. Portland *Oregonian*, 15 November 1871.
12. Portland *Herald*, 15 November 1871.
13. Portland *Herald*, 26 November 1871.
14. Portland *Oregonian*, 15 November 1871.
15. SBA Diary, 15 November 1871.
16. Harper, *Life and Work of Susan B. Anthony*, 1: 400.
17. Portland *Oregonian*, 16 November 1871.
18. Portland *New Northwest*, 17 November 1871.

19. Portland *Herald*, 18 November 1871.
20. Portland *New Northwest*, 24 November 1871.
21. Portland *Herald*, 24 November 1871.
22. Harper, *Life and Work of Susan B. Anthony*, 1: 400.
23. Portland *Oregonian*, 16 November 1871.
24. SBA Scrapbook, September 1871, 38.
25. "Hope" wrote that a nervous young man "with fear of future connubial disaster," asked Anthony ' . . . what would be done if the woman jurist was in possession of a helpless family, consisting of a husband and several small children, in case he'—the helpless creature first mentioned—'was from a pecuniary point of view, unable to hire help? Would'—horrible thought—'the husband be compelled to stay at home and mind the babies?' The reformer answered that a woman, like a man, could be excused from jury duty. "Hope" also thought that the young man should have been informed that his gender could mind babies. Portland *New Northwest*, 24 November 1871.
26. Oregon City *Weekly Enterprise*, 10 November 1871.
27. Oregon City *Weekly Enterprise*, 24 November 1871.
28. SBA Diary, 18 November 1871.
29. SBA Diary, 20 November 1871.
30. Portland *Oregonian*, 17 November 1871.
31. Eugene *Oregon State Journal*, 21 October and 25 November 1871.
32. Eugene *Oregon State Journal*, 18 November 1871.
33. Eugene *Oregon State Journal*, 2 December 1871.
34. Eugene City *Guard*, 14 October and 23 December 1871.
35. Eugene City *Guard*, 11 November 1871. Duniway accused Buys of culling "all manner of execrable offal from papers" and adding an editorial column "of still more filthy sewerage." Portland *New Northwest*, November 24, 1871.
36. Eugene City *Guard*, 25 November 1871.
37. SBA Diary, 22 November 1871.
38. Portland *New Northwest*, 1 December 1871.
39. SBA Diary, 21 November 1871.
40. Harper, *Life and Work of Susan B. Anthony*, 1: 403.
41. Dr. Bethenia Owens-Adair, *Dr. Owens-Adair, Some of Her Life Experiences*, (Portland: Mann & Beach, 1906), 476. Edward T. James (ed.), *Notable American Women*, 1607-1950, (Cambridge, Harvard University Press, 1971), 2: 659.
42. Portland *Pacific Empire*, 13 August 1896.

43. Roseburg *Plaindealer*, 24 November 1871.
44. SBA Diary, 25 November 1871.
45. Jacksonville *Sentinel*, 1 December 1871.
46. Jacksonville *Democratic Times*, 16 September and 2 December 1871.

### 7 RAMIFICATIONS AND ASSESSMENTS

1. San Francisco *Call*, 14 December 1871.
2. Portland *New Northwest*, 5 January 1872; New York *Revolution*, 30 December 1871.
3. Albany *Register*, 16 September 1871.
4. SBA Diary, 31 December 1871.
5. Eugene *Oregon State Journal*, 18 November 1871; Samuel Clarke Scrapbook, 226d, 198, Oregon Historical Society. Michael H. Cramer, "Public and Political: Documents of the Woman's Suffrage Campaign in British Columbia, 1871-1917: The View from Victoria," Barbara Latham (ed.), *In Her Own Right*, (Victoria: Camosun College, 1980), 79. Files in the British Columbia Provincial Archives in Victoria provide information about Anthony's impact. One writer generalized that Anthony "made little headway with her crusade, although perhaps the seeds she sowed eventually did bear fruit" because in the mid-1870s Victoria's women began to vote in municipal elections.
6. Portland *Oregonian*, 27 November 1871.
7. Stanton et al, *History of Woman's Suffrage*, 3: 769. Duniway elaborated on her indebtedness to Anthony for personally introducing her to a variety of famous reformers including William Lloyd Garrison, Wendell Phillips, Horace Greeley, and Elizabeth Cady Stanton. Duniway, "Eminent Women I Have Met," David C. Duniway Collection, Salem, Oregon. Hereafter referred to as Duniway Collection.
8. Portland *Oregonian*, 5 December 1871.
9. Eugene *Oregon State Journal*, 3 February 1872. Clarke Scrapbook, 198.
10. Duniway wrote from Laramie that she wished that the Oregon legislators could learn how equal suffrage in Wyoming had made the territory famous. If the politicians became informed then they "would decide en masse to bring our State into favorable public notice" by electing a woman to the Senate." This would mean that "the fair name of far off Oregon might thus become prominent in

history as a leader in the van of the inevitable." Portland *New Northwest*, 12 July 1872.

11. Duniway, *Pathbreaking*, 48.
12. Duniway, *Pathbreaking*, 52-53.
13. Walter M. Merrill (ed.), *Letters of William Lloyd Garrison*, (Cambridge, Harvard University Press, 1976), 4: 435.
14. Portland *Oregonian*, 19 March 1872.
15. New York *Revolution*, 6 October 1870.
16. Portland *New Northwest*, 19 April 1872.
17. Portland *Herald*, 8 October 1871.
18. Alma Lutz, *Susan B. Anthony: Rebel, Crusader, Humanitarian*. (Boston: Beacon Press, 1959), 189.
19. Lee Nash, "Harvey v. Abigail: Sibling Rivalry in the Oregon Campaign for Woman Suffrage," unpublished manuscript in the possession of Professor Nash, George Fox College, Newburg, Oregon, 15.
20. Biographer Lutz incorrectly judged that western men were more receptive to Anthony because "These men, looking upon women as partners who had shared with them the dangers and hardships of the frontier, recognized at once the justice of woman suffrage and its benefit to the country." Lutz, *Susan B. Anthony*, 191. Professor Larson, a leading authority on woman suffrage in the West, furnishes several credible explanations for why westerners granted women the vote and rejects the argument that western egalitarianism explains the political change. The evidence from Pacific Northwest sources of 1871 definitely support Larson over Lutz. T.A. Larson, "Woman Suffrage," *The Reader's Encyclopedia of the American West*, Howard R. Lamar (ed.), (New York: Thomas Y. Crowell, 1977), 1282-1285.
21. Portland *The Pacific Empire*, 18 June 1896.
22. Salem *Oregon Statesman*, 10 September 1871; Portland *Oregonian*, 7 October 1871.
23. Dalles *Republican*, 7 October 1871; Walla Walla *Union*, 2 December 1871; and Portland *Herald*, 28 November 1871.
24. According to a scholar, [Iowa] newspapers wherever Anthony went "were too busy lampooning her as the perfect caricature of the woman's right advocate to report what she had to say." Louise R. Noun, *Strong-Minded Women*, (Ames: Iowa State University Press, 1969), 160.
25. Albany *Democrat*, 6 October 1871.

26. Eugene *Guard*, 2 December 1871.
27. San Francisco *Pioneer*, 9 February 1871.
28. Portland *Oregonian*, 5 May 1871.
29. Portland *New Northwest*, 21 July 1871.
30. Scott's interpretation and his sister's rebuttal are in Portland *Oregonian*, 6 December 1871 and Portland *New Northwest*, 8 December 1871.
31. Portland *New Northwest*, 1 December 1871.
32. Portland *Oregonian*, 3 March 1871.
33. Portland *Oregonian*, 4 December 1871.
34. Portland *New Northwest*, 29 December 1871.
35. Lois Banner, *Elizabeth Cady Stanton*, (Boston: Little, Brown & Co., 1980), 118.
36. Portland *New Northwest*, 29 December 1871. Duniway was responding to the numerous denunciations of Woodhull that appeared in the regional press. One newspaperman summarized, "A beautiful structure, built on a rotten foundation, is short lived. We are sorry they are building on Woodhull." Albany *Register*, 9 December 1871. His competitor was vicious: the woman suffrage movement under Mrs. Woodhull's influence "is really a flank movement of the devil to secure a fresh footing." Albany *Democrat*, 15 December 1871.
37. Portland *Oregonian*, 7 December 1871.
38. T.A. Larson, "The Woman Suffrage Movement in Washington," *Pacific Northwest Quarterly*, 67 (April 1976): 62.
39. Portland *New Northwest*, 6 January 1887.
40. Portland *The Pacific Empire*, 10 October 1895.
41. Phoebe Goodell Judson, *A Pioneer's Search for an Ideal Home*, (Tacoma: Washington State Historical Society, 1966), 277.
42. Seattle *Post-Intelligencer*, 6 February 1887.
43. SBA Scrapbook, May 1871.
44. New York *Revolution*, 30 December 1871.
45. Portland *Oregonian*, 9 September 1871.
46. Portland *New Northwest* 15 September 1871.
47. Ellen Carol DuBois, *Feminism and Suffrage: The Emergence of an Independent Women's Movement in America*, 1848-1869, (Ithaca: Cornell University Press, 1978), 177-178, 187.
48. Banner, *Elizabeth Cady Stanton*, 105.
49. Telephone interview with Professor T.A. Larson, 25 July 1979.
50. Portland *New Northwest*, 22 November 1872.

51. Katherine Anthony, *Susan B. Anthony: Her Personal History and Her Era*, (New York: Doubleday, 1954), 267-68.
52. DuBois, *Feminism and Suffrage*, 202.
53. Her work in the region supports Professor DuBois's generalization: "The switch from agitation to organizing forced suffragists to make important changes in their political style and content. As Garrisonian ultraists, they had been trained to express their ideas in the most radical form possible. Yet this approach was rarely the best way to organize new women into active involvement in the suffrage movement. Instead, they learned that they were successful as organizers to the degree they communicated their ideas in terms that their audiences could understand and on which they could act." DuBois, *Feminism and Suffrage*, 183.
54. Stanton, *Eighty Years & More*, 170, 297.

## 8 A NEW WORLD OF ORGANIZED WOMEN

1. Susan B. Anthony to Henry B. Blackwell, 22 July 1872, Blackwell Family Papers, Reel 9, Library of Congress.
2. Anna Howard Shaw, "'Aunt Susan,' 1890," to be found in Ellen Carol DuBois, (ed.), *Elizabeth Cady Stanton-Susan B. Anthony: Correspondence, Writings, Speeches*, (New York: Schocken Books, 1981), 218. Cecilia M. Wittmayer, "The 1889-1890 Woman Suffrage Campaign: A Need to Organize," *South Dakota History*, 31 (1981): 199-225.
3. Anthony to Clara Colby, 12 March 1894.
4. Portland *Oregonian*, 29 May 1896.
5. Stanton, *Eighty Years & More*, 168.
6. Nancy Woloch, *Women and the American Experience*, (New York: Alfred A. Knopf, 1984), 333.
7. SBA Scrapbook, 1896, 5: 156.
8. Susan B. Anthony Letters, 7 September 1894; Susan B. Anthony Memorial Collection, Huntington Library; *Woman's Journal*, 30 May 1896.
9. Portland *New Northwest*, 5 June, 19 June 1884.
10. Harper, *Life and Work of Susan B. Anthony*, 2: 592.
11. Harper, *Life and Work of Susan B. Anthony*, 2: 593.
12. T.A. Larson, "The Woman Suffrage Movement in Washington," *Pacific Northwest Quarterly*, April 1976, 55.
13. Leslie Wheeler, ed., *Loving Wariors: Selected Letters of Lucy Stone and Henry B. Blackwell* (New York: The Dial Press, 1981),

326. Carrie Chapman Catt and Nettie Rogers Shuler, *Woman Suffrage and Politics*, (New York: Charles Scribner's Sons, 1926), 113.

14. Portland *New Northwest*, 2 June 1876, 12 February 1875, and 11 January 1878.
15. *Congressional Record*-Senate, 25 January 1887, 996.
16. Larson, "The Woman Suffrage Movement in Washington," 55.
17. Alma Lutz, "Susan B. Anthony", *Notable American Women*, 1: 55.
18. Melinda A. Schaffer, Presidents's Address, Western Washington WCTU, 8th Annual Convention, 1891, Tacoma 1891.16.
19. Quoted in Larson, "The Woman Suffrage Movement in Washington," 56.
20. T.A. Larson, "The Woman's Rights Movement in Idaho," *Idaho Yesterdays*, 16 (Spring 1972): 9.
21. Mary A. Livermore to Jeanne Carr, n.d., Carr Collection, Huntington Library; Robert Booth Fowler, *Carrie Catt: Feminist Politician*, (Boston: Northeastern University Press, 1986) 21-22.
22. Duniway, *Path Breaking*, 205.
23. Duniway, *Path Breaking*, 130.
24. Portland *The Pacific Empire*, 6 February 1896. Duniway complained that the *Pacific Empire* had only a few hundred subscribers and that it had less influence than she had anticipated. She thought, however, it was important to the cause "simply as a bulletin" and that it made the *Oregonian* treat suffragists fairly. Abigail to Clyde Duniway, 23 February 1896, Duniway Collection.
25. Portland *The Pacific Empire*, 31 October 1895.
26. Portland *The Pacific Empire*, 23 January 1896.

## 9 REVIVAL OF THE REGIONAL SUFFRAGE MOVEMENT

1. G. Thomas Edwards and Carlos A. Schwantes, (eds.), *Experiences in a Promised Land: Essays in Pacific Northwest History*, (Seattle: Univeristy of Washington Press, 1986), 81-82.
2. Harvey Scott, *History of Portland*, Oregon, 438.
3. Seattle *Post-Intelligencer*, June 4, 1896.
4. Scott, *History of Portland*, 451.
5. *Seattle City Directory*, 1895-1896, 29.
6. *Portland City Directory*, 1897, 35.
7. *Seattle City Directory*, 1896, 29; *Seattle City Directory*, 1897, 32.

8. *Pacific Empire*, 6 February 1896.
9. *The Pacific Northwest, Its Wealth and Resources, Oregon, Washington, Idaho, Portland*, (1896), 3.
10. Portland *Oregonian*, 29 May 1896.
11. Portland *Oregonian*, 27 May 1896.
12. Portland *Oregonian*, 4 June 1896.
13. Portland *Telegram*, 3 June 1896.
14. Seattle *Post-Intelligencer*, quoted in *Oregonian*, 4 June 1896.
15. Portland *Telegram*, 2 June 1896.
16. Anthony to Clara B. Colby, 8 September 1896, Colby Collection.
17. Portland *Oregonian*, 26 May 1896.
18. Portland *Oregonian*, 23, 25, and 26 May 1896.
19. Portland *Telegram*, 10 June 1896.
20. Harper, *Life and Work of Susan B. Anthony*, 2: 859.
21. Portland *Oregonian*, 5 June 1896.
22. Portland *Oregonian*, 2 June 1896.
23. Portland *Rural Northwest*, 15 July 1896.
24. Seattle *Post-Intelligencer*, 10 June 1896.
25. Portland *Oregonian*, 25 May 1896.
26. Even in the work that was relegated to them, women were not taken seriously as professionals. A male reporter observing "lady teachers" assembled in the superintendent's office, wrote that they "most favorably impressed the student of physiognomy. Their neat and tidy appearance, their genteel and cheerful demeanor, and their kind faces beaming with intelligence, made a living picture fascinating to the eye and exceedingly agreeable to the mind." Portland *Telegraph*, 20 June 1896.
27. Anthony to Colby, 26 July 1896, Colby Collection; Harper, *Life and Work of Susan B. Anthony*, 2: 871.
28. Carrie Chapman Catt to Abigail Scott Duniway, 14 March 1895, DeVoe Papers, Washington State Library, Olympia.
29. Carrie Chapman Catt to Emma Smith DeVoe, 9 February 1895, DeVoe Papers.
30. Catt to DeVoe, 3 January 1895, DeVoe Papers.
31. Catt to DeVoe, 16 July 1895, DeVoe Papers.
32. Larson, "The Woman's Rights Movement in Idaho," *Idaho Yesterdays*, 16 (Spring, 1972): 10.
33. Duniway to M.C. Athey, 6 January 1897, Duniway Papers. Although Duniway was hurt by Catt and Anthony for preventing her from playing a major role in the Idaho struggle, she did not hold a grudge. In 1901, she defended Catt in a public letter: "Mrs. Catt is

a handsome, cultivated and most womanly woman. She is the loyal and happy wife of a noble . . . and manly man, who aids her loyally in her work for equal rights. Her home life is beautiful—far more beautiful, I admit, than her name, which if women helped to make the laws would not be forced upon anybody." Duniway Scrapbook 2, Duniway Collection.

34. Duniway, *Path Breaking*, 210.
35. Portland *Pacific Empire*, June 11, 1896.
36. Moynihan, *Rebel for Rights*, 195.
37. Seattle *Times*, 30 May 1896.
38. *History of Woman's Century Club*, Seattle, 1892, n.p.; *The Year Book of the Woman's Century Club*, 1896 and 1897. Seattle.
39. Seattle *Post-Intelligencer*, 5 June 1896.
40. Seattle *Post-Intelligencer*, 6 June 1896.
41. Seattle *Times*, 1 June 1896.
42. Seattle *Post-Intelligencer*, 6 June 1896.
43. Seattle *Argus*, 30 May 1896.
44. Seattle *Post-Intelligencer*, 31 May 1896.
45. Seattle *Post-Intelligencer*, 6 June 1896.
46. Seattle *Post-Intelligencer*, 6 June 1896.
47. Seattle *Post-Intelligencer*, 7 June 1896.
48. San Francisco *Examiner*, 9 August 1896.
49. Seattle *Post-Intelligencer*, 7 June 1896.
50. Tacoma *Ledger*, 6 June 1896.
51. Portland *Oregonian*, 7 June 1896.
52. Portland *Oregonian*, 8 June 1896.
53. Portland *Oregonian*, 8 June 1896.
54. Portland *Telegram*, 8 June 1896.
55. Portland *Pacific Empires*, 11 June 1896.
56. Portland *Pacific Empires*, 1 June 1896.
57. Portland *Oregonian*, 10 June 1896.
58. Portland *Oregonian*, 10 June 1896.
59. Portland *Pacific Empire*, 11 June 1896.
60. Portland *Oregonian*, 11 June 1896.
61. James, *Notable American Women*, 1: 380-2.
62. Portland *Pacific Empire*, 11 June 1896.
63. Portland *Oregonian*, 11 June 1896.
64. Portland *Pacific Empire*, 11 June 1896.
65. Portland *Oregonian*, 10 June 1896.
66. Portland *Pacific Empire*, 25 June 1896.

67. Vancouver *Register*, 11 June 1896.
68. San Francisco *Examiner*, 28 June and 9 August 1896.
69. Carolyn Stefanco, "Networking on the Frontier: The Colorado Women's Suffrage Movement, 1876-1893," in Susan Armitage and Elizabeth Jameson (eds.), *The Women's West*, (Norman: University of Oklahoma Press, 1987), 273.
70. Portland *Oregonian*, 14 June 1896.
71. Portland *Pacific Empire*, 11 June 1896.
72. Portland *Oregonian*, 14 June 1896.
73. Portland *Oregonian*, 13 June 1896.
74. Boston *Woman's Journal*, 4 July 1896.
75. *Congressional Record*—Senate, Forty-Ninth Congress, Second Session, 25 January 1887, 984. Anthony noted name-calling in California: an antisuffragist, Dr. George L. Fitch, described her, Stanton, and Lucy Blackwell as "Those foul and midnight hags who go about the land screeching hag-fashion at the tyrant, man." Anthony to Alice Stone Blackwell, 3 October 1895, Blackwell Family Collection, Library of Congress.
76. Stanton, *Eighty Years and More*, 174-75.
77. San Francisco *Examiner*, 21 June 1906.
78. Portland *Oregonian*, 14 June 1896.
79. Midge Mackenzie, *Shoulder to Shoulder*, (New York: Alfred A. Knopf, 1975), 142.
80. Portland *Telegram*, 8 June 1896.
81. Portland *Oregonian*, 11 June 1896.
82. Portland Evening *Telegram*, 10 June 1896.
83. Portland, *Rural Northwest*, 1 July 1896.
84. Portland *Oregonian*, 9 June 1896.
85. Portland *Telegram*, 10 June 1896. The Methodist newspaper, the Portland *Pacific Christian Advocate*, had responded to Anthony's addresses in 1871, but ignored her in 1896. Its editor, who stressed the vital role of women in church work, as foreign missions, probably opposed Anthony's message.
86. Duniway, *Path Breaking*, 109-110.
87. Quoted in Kathleen Barry, *Susan B. Anthony: A Biography of a Singular Feminist*, (New York: New York University Press, 1988), 317.
88. Anthony's 1896 views of the Prohibition Party, temperance, and the WCTU are in Harper, *Life and Work of Susan B. Anthony*, 2: 872-887.

89. Boston *Woman's Journal*, 4 July 1896.

10 OREGON BECOMES CRUCIAL

1. Quoted in Elisabeth Griffith, *In Her Own Right: The Life of Elizabeth Cady Stanton*, (New York: Oxford University Press, 1984), 214.
2. Portland *Oregonian*, 16 February 1900.
3. Griffith, *In Her Own Right*, 213-214.
4. Anthony to Clara Colby, 20 January and 10 May 1898, Clara Colby Collection, Huntington Library.
5. Duniway, *Pathbreaking*, 178.
6. Portland *Oregonian*, 13 February 1900.
7. Duniway, *Pathbreaking*, 157.
8. Duniway, *Pathbreaking*, 163.
9. Moynihan, *Rebel for Rights*, 207.
10. Abigail Scott Duniway Scrapbook 2, Duniway Collection.
11. Duniway, *Pathbreaking*, 211.
12. Anthony to Clara B. Colby, 12 February 1897. Clara B. Colby Letters, Huntington Library.
13. Anthony to Rev. Thomas Lamb Eliot, Rev. Thomas Lamb Eliot Collection, Reed College, 5 January 1895.
14. Harper, *Life of Susan B. Anthony*, 2: 879.
15. Anthony to Clara B. Colby, Colby Letters, 20 January 1898.
16. Anthony to Clara B. Colby, 7 January 1898 and 19 May 1899, Colby Letters.
17. Boston *Woman's Journal*, 16 June 1900.
18. Boston *Woman's Journal*, 16 June 1900.
19. Portland *Oregonian*, 28 May 1900.
20. Portland *Oregonian*, 3 June 1900.
21. Portland *Oregonian*, 8 June 1900.
22. Portland *Oregonian*, 28 May 1900.
23. Boston *Woman's Journal*, 9 June and 7 July 1900.
24. Boston *Woman's Journal*, 16 June 1900.
25. Boston *Woman's Journal*, 14 July 1900.
26. Portland *Woman's Tribune*, 7 January 1905.
27. Duniway Scrapbook 1, Duniway Collection.
28. Duniway, *Pathbreaking*, 219.
29. Anthony to Clara Colby, 7 January 1898, Colby Letters.
30. Boston *Woman's Journal*, 17 June 1905.
31. Duniway, *Pathbreaking*, 224.

32. Portland *Woman's Tribune*, 13 May 1905.
33. Boston *Woman's Journal*, 17 June 1905.
34. Portland *Oregon Journal*, 27 June 1905.
35. Boston *Woman's Journal*, 1 July 1905.
36. Portland *Oregon Journal*, 27 June 1905.
37. Diary of Mary Anthony, 26 June 1905.
38. Diary of Mary Anthony, 27 June 1905.
39. Harper, *Life of Susan B. Anthony*, 3: 1362-63.

## 11 SYMBOLS AND POLITICS

1. Mary A. Anthony Diary, 27 June 1905.
2. Portland *Oregonian*, 28 June 1905.
3. Portland *Oregonian*, 28 June 1905.
4. Portland *Oregon Journal*, 28 June 1905.
5. Portland *Oregon Journal*, 27 June 1905.
6. Portland *Oregonian*, 28 June 1905.
7. Portland *Oregon Journal*, 29 June 1905.
8. Portland *Oregon Journal*, 27 June 1905.
9. Portland *Oregon Journal*, 27 June 1905.
10. Portland *Oregonian*, 28 June 1905.
11. Portland *Oregonian*, 28 June 1905.
12. Portland *Oregon Journal*, 27 June 1905.
13. Portland *Telegram*, 28 June 1905.
14. Portland *Oregon Journal*, 29 June 1905; Boston *Woman's Journal*, 8 July 1905.
15. Portland *Oregonian*, 30 June 1905.
16. Boston *Woman's Journal*, 19 August 1905.
17. Portland *Oregonian*, 30 June 1905.
18. Portland *Telegram*, 1 July 1905; Portland *Oregonian*, 30 June 1905.
19. Portland *Oregonian*, 30 June 1905.
20. Portland *Oregonian*, 30 June 1905.
21. Portland *Oregon Journal*, 30 June 1905; Boston *Woman's Journal*, 19 August 1905.
22. Abigail to Clyde Duniway, 2 and 13 July 1905, Duniway Collection. Biographer Moynihan has a different view: "The NAWSA convention deliberately snubbed Mrs. Duniway in the 1905 proceedings. Even though she was the Oregon Association's president she was not even included on the program." *Rebel for Rights*, 211. Duniway was honorary, not state president, her name appeared

twice on the program, and she advertised one of her books in it. Newspaper reports also indicate the Oregon leader's significant role in the various sessions.

23. Boston *Woman's Journal*, 15 July 1905.
24. Portland *Oregon Journal*, 30 June 1905; Abigail to Clyde Duniway, 2 July 1905, Duniway Collection.
25. Portland *Oregonian*, 1 July 1905.
26. Portland *Oregon Journal*, 1 July 1905; Portland *Oregonian*, 1 July 1905; Boston *Woman's Journal*, 19 August 1905; Portland *Woman's Tribune* 8 July 1905; History of Woman Suffrage, 5: 135.
27. Portland *Oregon Journal*, 1 July 1905.
28. Portland *Oregonian*, 1 July 1905; Portland *Telegram*, 30 June 1905.
29. Portland *Woman's Tribune*, 8 July 1905.
30. Portland *Oregonian*, 2 July 1905; Portland *Woman's Tribune*, 8 July 1905; Stanton et al, *History of Woman Suffrage*, 5: 138.
31. Boston *Woman's Journal*, 5 August 1905.
32. Portland *Oregonian*, 2 July 1905. Florence Kelley, an expert on the abuses of child labor and author of *Some Ethical Gains Through Legislation* (1905) explained how to get information into newspapers: "Write something in editorial style just about as you want it to appear and send it to the editor with the deprecatory note to the effect that it is only raw material but perhaps it would be whipped into an editorial by his able pen. The chances are that the first time he is hard up for one he will use it—probably beheaded or with the end off or the middle amputated to show that the editor is editing, but it will be published." Stanton et al, *History of Woman Suffrage*, 5: 132.
33. Boston *Woman's Journal*, 26 August 1905.
34. Portland *Oregonian*, 2 July 1905.
35. Portland *Oregonian*, 2 July 1905.
36. Portland *Oregon Journal*, 3 July 1905.
37. Portland *Oregon Journal*, 3 July 1905.
38. Boston *Woman's Journal*, 26 August 1905.
39. Boston *Woman's Journal*, 26 August 1905.
40. Diary of Mary Anthony 4 July 1905.
41. Boston *Woman's Journal*, 2 September 1905.
42. Portland *Woman's Tribune*, 22 July 1905.
43. Portland *Oregon Journal*, 4 July 1905.
44. Boston *Woman's Journal*, 2 September 1905.

45. Anna Howard Shaw, *The Story of a Pioneer*, (New York: Harper & Brothers, 1915), 288.
46. All quotations from politicians in Boston *Woman's Journal*, 2 September 1905.
47. Diary of Mary Anthony, 5 July 1905.
48. Portland *Oregonian*, 6 July 1905.
49. Portland *Oregonian*, 6 July 1905.
50. Portland *Oregon Journal*, 6 July 1905.
51. Portland *Telegram*, 6 July 1905.
52. Portland *Telegram*, 6 July 1905.
53. Portland *Oregon Journal*, 6 July; Portland *Telegram*, 6 July; Portland *Oregonian*, 7 July 1905.
54. Portland *Oregon Journal*, 6 July 1905.
55. Portland *Oregonian*, 7 July 1905.
56. Diary of Mary Anthony, 6 July 1905; Stanton et al, *History of Woman Suffrage*, 6: 540-541.
57. Shaw, *The Story of a Pioneer*, 289-290.
58. Taber writes, "'Did Sacagawea's name help Oregon woman suffrage over the top?' Inasmuch as it provided a rallying point and inspiration to the women who formed the Oregon Equal Suffrage association, it did." While women might have found Sacagawea an inspiring figure, they formed the OSESA for more important reasons. Ronald W. Taber, "Sacagawea and the Suffragettes: An Interpretation of a Myth," *Pacific Northwest Quarterly*, 58 (January 1967): 7-13.
59. Diary of Mary Anthony, 6 July 1905.
60. Portland *Oregonian*, 8 July 1905.
61. Portland *Telegram*, 10 July 1905; Portland *Oregonian*, 11 July 1905; and Portland *Woman's Tribune*, 14 April 1906.
62. Portland *Oregonian*, 10 July 1905.
63. Portland *Oregonian*, 26 June 1905.
64. Diary of Mary Anthony 7 July 1905; Stanton et al, *History of Woman Suffrage*, 5: 123.
65. Stanton et al, *History of Woman Suffrage*, 6: 541.
66. Portland *Oregon Journal*, 6 July 1905.
67. *Pacific Monthly*, August 1905, 199.
68. Boston *Woman's Journal*, 29 July 1905.
69. Boston *Woman's Journal*, 16 December 1905.
70. Diary of Mary Anthony, 13 July 1905.
71. Diary of Mary Anthony, 13 July 1905. 19 July 1905.

72. Harper, *Life and Work of Susan B. Anthony*, 3: 1371.
73. Diary of Mary Anthony, 3 August 1905.
74. Boston *Woman's Journal*, 6 December 1905.
75. Portland *Oregonian*, 9 November 1905.
76. Boston *Woman's Journal*, 9 December 1905.
77. Portland *Woman's Tribune*, 3 March 1906.
78. Boston *Woman's Journal*, 3 February 1906.
79. Portland *Woman's Tribune*, 3 February 1906.
80. Harper, *Life and Work of Susan B. Anthony*, 3: 1376.
81. Harper, *Life and Work of Susan B. Anthony*, 3: 1396.
82. Harper, *The History of Woman Suffrage*, 5: 161.
83. Portland *Woman's Tribune*, 17 February 1906.
84. Boston *Woman's Journal*, 9 December 1905.
85. Portland *Oregonian* quoted in Boston *Woman's Journal*, 31 March 1906. Duniway made much of the fact that some of the rich women opposed to the reform were "not following the convictions of their husbands and fathers in this matter." She insisted that W.S. Ladd, J.B. Montgomery, H.J. Corbett, and Henry Failing had been staunch suffragists. Portland *Oregonian*, 26 November 1905.
86. *Corvallis Times* quoted in Portland *Woman's Tribune*, 3 February 1906.
87. Portland *Telegram*, 27 June 1905.
88. Duniway, *Pathbreaking*, 227.
89. Abigail to Clyde Duniway, 4 November 1906, Duniway Collection.
90. Abigail to Clyde, 17 December 1905. Duniway Collection.
91. Abigail to Clyde, 9 January 1906, Duniway Collection.
92. Duniway to Colby, 22 January 1906, Colby Papers.
93. Portland *Oregon Journal*, 11 February 1906.
94. Portland *Telegram*, 6 July 1905.
95. Portland *Oregon Journal*, 11 February 1906.
96. Harper, *The Life and Work of Susan B. Anthony*, 3: 1405-1407.
97. Harper, *The Life and Work of Susan B. Anthony*, 3: 1409.
98. Harper, *The Life and Work of Susan B. Anthony*, 3: 1422.

## 12 THE THINNER THE POPULATION THE DEEPER THE SUPPORT

1. Rochester *Democrat and Chronicle*, 15 March 1906; NAWSA workers Gregg and Boyer wired Mary Anthony that they had "strong faith in Oregon's victory." Rochester *Democrat and Chron-*

icle, 14 March 1906. Boston *Women's Journal*, 17 March 1906. Many regional residents grieved over Anthony. Emma Edwards Green of Boise, for example, explained to Alice Blackwell that she "must write and tell some one of the sorrow in my heart for the death of so noble a woman as dear Miss Anthony; I regret I never knew her until I met her in Portland" in 1905. Emma Edwards Green to Alice Blackwell, 14 March 1906, Blackwell Family Papers, Library of Congress, Reel 9.

2. Quoted in Mary Gray Peck, *Carrie Chapman Catt: A Biography.* (New York: H.W. Wilson Co., 1944), 144-45.
3. Washington, D.C. *Progress*, March 1906, 3.
4. Portland *Oregonian*, 17 March 1906; Harper, *The Life and Work of Susan B. Anthony*, 3: 1503.
5. Washington, D.C. *Progress*, April 1906, 2. Rochester, New York newspapers of 14 March 1906 note that several organizations sent money for the Oregon fight rather than a floral offering.
6. Portland *Woman's Tribune*, 14 April 1906.
7. Lexington *Herald*, 22 July 1906.
8. Washington, D.C. *Progress*, March 1906, 4.
9. Boston *Woman's Journal*, 19 May 1906, 2 June 1906; Shaw to DeVoe, 24 April 1906, Emma Smith DeVoe Papers, Washington State Library, Olympia.
10. Boston *Woman's Journal*, 19 May 1906.
11. Boston *Woman's Journal*, 19 May 1906.
12. Eva Emery Dye to Professor Hawley, 20 February 1906, Dye Papers.
13. Duniway Scrapbook 1, Duniway Collection. In an open letter Duniway and others asked those who traveled the Oregon Trail in the 1840s and 1850s and who now had white hair and poor vision to grant woman "equal station." Duniway, et al., *To the Pioneer Voters of Oregon*, 1906, Duniway Collection.
14. Charles Erskine Scott Wood, Woman Suffrage," *Pacific Monthly*, 5 (May 1906): 578; Shaw to campaign committee 30 April 1906, Dye Papers.
15. Lucy Anthony to Eva Emery Dye, 5 May 1906, Dye Papers.
16. Boston *Woman's Journal*, 19 May 1906.
17. Stanton et al, *History of Woman Suffrage*, 6: 542.
18. Abigail to Clyde Duniway, Duniway Collection, 4 March 1906.
19. Abigail to Clyde Duniway, 3 May 1906.
20. Paul Fuller, *Laura Clay and the Woman's Rights Movement*, 99.
21. Marie Equi to Anna Shaw, 1912, Scrapbook 2, Duniway Collection.

22. Portland *Oregonian*, 31 May 1906.
23. Moynihan, *Rebel for Rights*, 211.
24. Portland *Oregonian*, 16 March 1906. Dye predicted victory in May; her papers provide vital information on how the campaign was waged at the local level.
25. Duniway, *Pathbreaking*, 225.
26. Duniway to Jefferson Myers, 20 February 1906. Duniway Collection, Scrapbook 1. Perhaps it rankled Abigail to work with some NAWSA lecturers who received salaries; she had never been paid for political work and had to write books and take in boarders to cover her living expenses.
27. Shaw, *The Story of a Pioneer*, 293. Anna Shaw to Emma Smith DeVoe, 18 April 1906, DeVoe Papers.
28. Boston *Woman's Journal*, 19 May 1906.
29. Portland *Oregonian*, 17 May 1906; Boston *Woman's Journal*, 19, 26 May 1906.
30. Boise *Idaho Daily Statesman* quoted in *Woman's Tribune*, 26 May 1906.
31. Boston *Woman's Journal*, 2 June 1906.
32. Pendleton *East Oregonian* quoted in Portland *Oregonian*, 30 May 1906.
33. Boston *Woman's Journal*, 2 June 1906.
34. Boston *Woman's Journal*, 26 May 1906.
35. Portland *Oregonian*, 30 May 1906.
36. Portland *Oregonian*, 1 June 1906; Eugene *Guard*, 2 June 1906.
37. Boston *Woman's Journal*, 9 June 1906.
38. Portland *Oregonian*, 29, 30, and 31 May 1906.
39. Portland *Oregonian*, 19 May 1906.
40. Portland *Woman's Tribune*, 26 May 1906.
41. Portland *Oregon Journal*, 27 May 1906.
42. Portland *Oregonian*, 3 June 1906. An assessment of the role of Oregon newspapers in the 1906 suffrage campaign is in Lauren Kessler, "The Fight for Woman Suffrage and the Oregon Press," Karen J. Blair (ed.), *Women in Pacific Northwest History* (Seattle: University of Washington Press, 1988), 43-58.
43. Portland *Oregonian*, 2 June 1906.
44. Portland *Oregonian*, 4 June 1906.
45. Portland *Oregonian*, 2 June 1906.
46. Portland *Oregonian*, 3 June 1906.
47. Boston *Woman's Journal*, 9 June 1905.
48. Portland *Oregonian*, 31 May 1906.

49. Boston *Woman's Journal*, 9 June 1906.
50. Port Orford *Tribune* quoted in Boston *Woman's Journal*, 9 June 1906.
51. Portland *Oregon Journal*, 3 June 1906.
52. Portland *Oregon Journal*, 3 June 1906.
53. Boston *Woman's Journal*, 16 June 1906.
54. Portland *Telegram*, 5 June 1906; Portland *Oregon Journal*, 4 June 1906.
55. Shaw, *The Story of a Pioneer*, 291-292.
56. Portland *Woman's Tribune*, 9 June 1906.
57. Anna H. Shaw to Chairman of the Campaign Committee, 1 June 1906, Dye Papers.
58. Portland *Telegram*, 5 June 1906.
59. Harper, *Life and Work of Susan B. Anthony*, 3: 1504.
60. Portland *Woman's Tribune*, 9 June 1906; Portland *Oregonian*, 9 June 1906. In a letter to those who had fought for the reform at the local level, Shaw thanked them for their support, praised the NAWSA methods, admitted to some mistakes, complained that some workers had worked in a half-hearted fashion, denounced liquor dealers and corporate interests, and criticized those women who attempted to work for other issues and for some candidates during the campaign. She warned, "It is a useless task to undertake to carry on two reforms at the same time." Anna H. Shaw to Chairman of the Campaign Committee, 7 June 1906, Dye Papers.
61. Eva Emery Dye to [Sam] Jackson and Eva Emery Dye to Harvey W. Scott, 6 June 1906. Dye Papers, Oregon Historical Society. The Portland *Oregonian*'s attitude was not changed by the election returns or by requests from suffragists. On 8 June it stated that women would seek another election in 1908 and concluded that by then "the men may be so rested from the annoyance of this last campaign that they will not feel resentment at another intrusion of the issue nor at bothersome women at the polls."
62. Portland *Oregon Journal*, 10 June 1906.
63. Anna H. Shaw to Chairman of the Campaign Committee, 7 June 1906, Dye Papers. In her autobiography, Shaw provided a further—and dubious—explanation for the 1906 failure. "I have always believed that we would have carried Oregon . . . if the disaster of the California earthquake had not occurred to divert the minds of Western men from interest in anything save that great catastrophe." Shaw, *The Story of a Pioneer*, 291-92.
64. Boston *Woman's Journal*, 16 June 1906.

65. Washington, D.C. *Progress*, October 1906, 2-3.
66. Boston *Woman's Journal*, 4 August 1906.
67. Fuller, *Laura Clay and the Woman's Rights Movement*, 99.
68. Harper, *Life and Work of Susan B. Anthony*, 3: 1504.
69. Washington, D.C. *Progress*, July 1906, 1.
70. Stanton et al, *History of Woman Suffrage*, 6: 543.
71. Carrie Chapman Catt and Nettie Rogers Shuler, *Woman Suffrage and Politics*, 124-125; 177.
72. Quoted in Peck, *Carrie Chapman Catt*, 143; Fowler, *Carrie Catt*, 25.
73. Abigail to Clyde Duniway, 14 June 1906. Willis Duniway wrote Clyde his assessment: "The campaign was an earnest one, and the liquor interests were very active, as were the wealthy members of the Society Opposed. My counsel, given some months ago to Eastern women who especially invited me to confer with them, was not taken. Instead of a campaign made unobtrusively through the country, and nothing in the cities, we had a very lively and aggressive contest, so the liquor interests became alarmed and put up a stubborn fight. . . . Mother was rather pushed to one side by the Eastern workers, and she is not suffering so much—not a tenth so much as six years ago." Willis to Clyde Duniway, 19 June 1906, Duniway Collection.
74. Boston *Woman's Journal*, 21 July 1906.
75. Duniway to Alice Blackwell, 28 July 1906, Duniway Collection, Scrapbook 2.
76. Duniway Collection, Scrapbook 1.
77. Duniway to Editors of the Boston *Woman's Journal*, 25 July 1906, Duniway Collection, Miscellaneous Scrapbooks.
78. Boston *Woman's Journal*, 17 November 1906; Portland *Oregonian*, 4 November 1906, and Duniway to Alice Blackwell, 28 July 1906, Duniway Collection Miscellaneous Scrapbooks.
79. Abigail to Clyde Duniway, 5 October 1906.
80. Duniway Collection, Scrapbook 1.
81. Boston *Woman's Journal*, 17 November 1906.
82. Duniway to National President, 27 May 1907, Eva Emery Dye Papers, Oregon Historical Society.
83. Anna H. Shaw to Eva Emery Dye, 19 November 1906, Dye Papers. Shaw also maintained that the defeat led to criticism of her and then explained, "There never has been a campaign conducted anywhere, when after it was over Miss Anthony has not had to

endure the same abuse and misrépresentation as I am enduring from Oregon."

84. Moynihan, *Rebel for Rights*, 212.
85. Anna Shaw to Emma DeVoe, 4 May 1906, DeVoe Papers.
86. Salem, *Oregon Statesman*, 10 June 1906.
87. Stanton et al, *History of Woman Suffrage*, 6: 544. For a sympathetic view of Duniway and a critical interpretation of Sarah Evans, see Moynihan, *Rebel for Rights*, 214-217.
88. Harper, *Life and Work of Susan B. Anthony*, 3, 1504.
89. Norman H. Clark, *The Dry Years: Prohibition & Social Change in Washington* (Seattle: University of Washington Press, rev. ed., 1988) 38.
90. Devoe to Shaw, 14 December 1907 and DeVoe to Shaw, 30 March 1909. DeVoe Papers.
91. Duniway to DeVoe, 23 February 1909; DeVoe to Catt, 23 November 1909, DeVoe Papers.
92. Ida Husted Harper, *How Six States Won Woman Suffrage*, New York City, n.d., 13; T.A. Larson, "The Woman Suffrage Movement in Washington," *Pacific Northwest Quarterly*, 62.
93. Clark, *The Dry Years*, 94.
94. T.A. Larson, "The Woman Suffrage Movement in Washington," *Pacific Northwest Quarterly*, 62.
95. Ruth Moynihan, *Rebel for Rights*, 215.
96. Steven M. Buechler, *The Transformation of the Woman Suffrage Movement: The Case of Illinois*, 1850-1920 (New Brunswick, Rutgers University Press, 1986), 14.
97. Duniway Miscellaneous Scrapbooks, Duniway Collection.
98. Santa Cruz *Surf* quoted in Sacramento *Record-Union*, 20 May 1896.
99. Alice Stone Blackwell to Edna L. Stantial, 21 February 1943, NAWSA Records, Box 10, Library of Congress.

# *Sources*

*Books*

Adair, Bethenia Angelina (Owens). *Dr. Owens-Adair. Some of Her Life Experiences*. Portland: Mann & Beach, printers, 1906

Additon, Lucia H. Faxon. *Twenty Eventful Years of the Oregon Woman's Christian Temperance Union, 1880-1900*. Portland: Gotschall Printing Co., 1904.

Anthony, Katherine. *Susan B. Anthony: Her Personal History and Her Era*. New York: Doubleday, 1954.

Bagley, Clarence B. *History of King County*. 4 vols. Chicago: S. J. Clarke Publishing Co., 1929.

Banner, Lois. *Elizabeth Cady Stanton*. Boston: Little, Brown, 1980.

Barry, Kathleen. *Susan B. Anthony: A Biography of A Singular Feminist*. New York: New York University Press, 1988.

Billington, Ray A., *Westward Expansion*. 5th ed. New York: MacMillan, 1982.

Blair, Karen J., ed. *Women in Pacific Northwest History: An Anthology*. Seattle: University of Washington Press, 1988.

Buechler, Steven M. *The Transformation of the Woman Suffrage Movement: The Case of Illinois, 1850-1920*. New Brunswick: Rutgers University Press, 1986.

Catt, Carrie Chapman, and Nettie Rogers Shuler. *Woman Suffrage and Politics*. New York: Charles Scribner's Sons, 1926.

Clark, Norman H. *The Dry Years: Prohibition and Social Change in Washington*. Rev. ed. Seattle: University of Washington Press, 1988.

Cleverdon, Catherine L. *The Woman Suffrage Movement in Canada*. Toronto: University of Toronto Press, 1974.

Douthit, Mary Osborn, ed. *Souvenir of Western Women*. Portland: Anderson & Duniway Co., 1905.

Downs, Winfeld Scott, ed. *Encyclopedia of Northwest Biography*. New York: The American Historical Co., 1943.

DuBois, Ellen Carol. *Feminism and Suffrage: The Emergence of an Independent Women's Movement in America, 1848-1869*. Ithaca: Cornell University Press, 1978.

DuBois, Ellen Carol, ed. *Elizabeth Cady Stanton-Susan B. Anthony: Correspondence, Writings, Speeches*. New York: Schocken Books, 1981.

Duniway, Abigail Scott. *Path Breaking*. 2nd ed. New York: Schocken Books, 1971.

Edwards, G. Thomas and Carlos A. Schwantes, eds. *Experiences in a Promised Land: Essays in Pacific Northwest History*. Seattle: University of Washington Press, 1986.

Flexner, Eleanor. *Century of Struggle: The Woman's Rights Movement in the United States*. New York: Atheneum, 1974.

Fowler, Robert Booth. *Carrie Catt: Feminist Politician*. Boston: Northeastern University Press, 1986.

Fuller, Paul. *Laura Clay and the Woman's Right Movement*. Lexington: The University Press of Kentucky, 1975.

Gilbert, Frank T. *Historic Sketches of Walla Walla County*. Portland: A.G. Walling, 1882.

Gilman, Charlotte Perkins. *The Living of Charlotte Perkins Gilman: An Autobiography*. New York: Arno Press, 1972.

Griffith, Elisabeth. *In Her Own Right: The Life of Elizabeth Cady Stanton*. New York: Oxford University Press, 1984.

Harper, Ida. *How Six States Won Women Suffrage*. New York City: National American Woman Suffrage Association, 1912.

Harper, Ida. *The Life and Work of Susan B. Anthony*. 3 vols. Indianapolis: The Hollenbeck Press, 1898, 1908.

Hersch, Blanche Glassman. *The Slavery of Sex: Feminist-Abolitionists in America*. Urbana: University of Illinois Press, 1978.

James, Edward T., ed. *Notable American Women, 1607-1950*. 3 vols. Cambridge: The Belknap Press of Harvard University Press, 1971.

Johansen, Dorothy O. *Empire of the Columbia*. 2nd ed. New York: Harper & Row, 1967.

Judson, Phoebe Goodell, *A Pioneer's Search for an Ideal Home: A Book of Personal Memoirs*. Tacoma: Washington State Historical Society, 1966.

Kelley, Florence. *Some Ethical Gains Through Legislation*. New York:

The Macmillan Co., London, Macmillan and Co., Ltd., 1905.

Kraditor, Aileen S. *The Ideas of the Woman Suffrage Movement, 1890-1920*. New York: W. W. Norton, 1981.

Latham, Barbara, ed. *In Her Own Right: Selected Essays on Women's History in British Columbia*. Victoria: Camosun College, 1980.

Lutz, Alma. *Susan B. Anthony: Rebel, Crusader, Humanitarian*. Boston: Beacon Press, 1959.

Meany, Edmond S. *History of the State of Washington*. New York: The Macmillan Co., 1927.

Merrill, Walter M., ed. *Letters of William Lloyd Garrison*. vol. 4. Cambridge: Belknap Press of Harvard University Press, 1971-1981.

McKenzie, Midge. *Shoulder to Shoulder*. New York: Alfred A. Knopf, 1975.

Moynihan, Ruth Barnes. *Rebel for Rights: Abigail Scott Duniway*. New Haven: Yale University Press, 1983.

Noun, Louise R. *Strong-Minded Women: The Emergence of the Woman Suffrage Movement in Iowa*. Ames: Iowa State University Press, 1959.

Oliphant, J. Orin. *On the Cattle Ranges of the Oregon Country*. Seattle: University of Washington Press, 1968.

Peck, Mary Gray. *Carrie Chapman Catt: A Biography*. New York: H.W. Wilson Co., 1944

Scott, Harvey. *History of Portland, Oregon*. Syracuse: D. Mason, 1890.

Shaw, Anna Howard. *The Story of A Pioneer*. New York: Harper & Brothers, 1915.

Smith, Helen Krebs. *The Presumptuous Dreamers, A Sociological History of the Life and Times of Abigail Scott Duniway*. vol. 1. Lake Oswego: Smith, Smith and Smith Publishing Co., 1974.

Stanton, Elizabeth Cady. *Eighty Years & More: Reminiscences 1815-1897*. New York: Schocken Books, 1971.

Stanton, Elizabeth Cady, Susan B. Anthony, and Matilda Joslyn Gage, eds. *History of Woman Suffrage*. Rochester, New York: privately published by Susan B. Anthony and National American Woman Suffrage Association. 6 vols. 1881-1922.

Turnbull, George S. *History of Oregon Newspapers*. Portland: Binfords & Mort, 1939.

Tyler, Helen E. *Where Prayer and Purpose Meet*. Evanston: The Signal Press, 1949.

Victor, Frances Fuller. *All Over Oregon and Washington: Observations on the Country, Its Scenery, Soil, Climate, Resources, and Improvements.* San Francisco: John H. Carmany & Co., 1872.
Wheeler, Leslie, ed. *Loving Warriors: Selected Letters of Lucy Stone and Henry B. Blackwell, 1853-1893.* New York: The Dial Press, 1981.
Woloch, Nancy. *Women and the American Experience.* New York: Alfred A. Knopf, 1984.

*Newspapers*

Albany *Democrat.* 1871.
Albany *Good Templar.* 1871.
Albany *Register.* 1871.
Boston *Woman's Journal.* 1900, 1905, 1906.
Corvallis *Times.* 1906.
Corvallis *Benton Democrat.* 1871.
The Dalles *Republican.* 1871.
Eugene City *Guard,* 1871.
Eugene *Oregon State Journal,* 1871.
Jacksonville *Democratic Times.* 1871.
Jacksonville *Sentinel.* 1871.
Kalama *Beacon.* 1871.
Lexington, Kentucky *Herald.* 1906.
McMinnville *West Side.* 1871.
New York *Revolution.* 1871.
Olympia *Echo.* 1871.
Olympia *Washington Standard.* 1871.
Olympia *Transcript.* 1871.
Olympia *Tribune.* 1871.
Oregon City *Weekly Enterprise.* 1871.
Philadelphia *Press.* 1871.
Port Townsend *Argus.* 1872.
Port Townsend *Cyclop.* 1871.
Portland *Bulletin.* 1870, 1871.
Portland *Catholic Sentinel.* 1871.
Portland *Herald.* 1871.
Portland *New Northwest.* 1871, 1872, 1875, 1884.
Portland *Oregon Journal.* 1905, 1906.
Portland *Oregonian.* 1871, 1896, 1900, 1905, 1906.
Portland *Pacific Christian Advocate.* 1871, 1896.
Portland *The Pacific Empire.* 1896.

Portland *The Rural Northwest*. 1896.
Portland *Telegram*. 1896, 1905, 1906.
Rochester, New York *Democrat and Chronicle*, 1906.
Rochester, New York *Democrat and Herald*, 1906.
Rochester, New York *Union and Advertiser*, 1906.
Roseburg *Plaindealer*. 1871.
Sacramento *Union*. 1871.
Salem *Statesman*. 1871, 1906.
Salem *Weekly Mercury*. 1871.
San Francisco *Call*. 1871.
San Francisco *Examiner*. 1896.
San Francisco *Pioneer*. February 9, 1871.
Seattle *Argus*, 1896.
Seattle *Intelligencer*, 1871
Seattle *Post-Intelligencer*, 1887, 1896.
Seattle *Puget Sound Dispatch*. 1871.
Seattle *Territorial Dispatch*. 1871.
Seattle *Times*, 1896, 1906.
Tacoma *Ledger*. 1896.
The Dalles *Weekly Mountaineer*, 1871.
Vancouver *Register*. 1896.
Victoria *British Colonist*. 1871.
Victoria *Standard*. 1871.
Walla Walla *Statesman*. 1871, 1872.
Walla Walla *Union*. 1871.
Washington, D.C., and Portland, Oregon *The Woman's Tribune*. 1905-1906.

*Manuscripts*

Anthony Family Papers. The Huntington Library.
Anthony, Diary of Mary S., 1905. Schlesinger Library, Radcliffe College, Cambridge, Massachusetts.
Anthony, Diary of Susan B., Scrapbook, Susan B. Anthony Papers. Library of Congress.
Anthony, Susan B. Memorial Collection. The Huntington Library.
Blackwell Family Collection. Library of Congress.
Blackwell Family Papers. Reel 9, Library of Congress.
Carr, Jeanne Collection. Huntington Library.
Clarke, Samuel, Scrapbooks. Oregon Historical Society.
Colby, Clara Dorothy Papers. The Huntington Library.

DeVoe, Emma Smith Collection. Washington State Library, Olympia.
Duniway, Abigail Scott Letters and Scrapbooks. David Duniway Collection, Salem, Oregon.
Dye, Eva Emery Papers, 1906. Oregon Historical Society.
Grant, Marie File. Provincial Archives of British Columbia, Victoria.
Harbert, Elizabeth Morrison Papers. The Huntington Library.
Harper, Ida A. Papers. The Huntington Library.
National American Woman Suffrage Association Collection. Library of Congress.
Prosch, Thomas W. Collection. University of Washington Archives, Seattle, Washington.
Severance, Caroline Maria Papers. The Huntington Library.
Woman Suffrage File. Provincial Archives of British Columbia, Victoria.

*Government Documents*

*Abstract of Votes Cast at the General Election in Oregon on 4 June 1906*. Oregon Archives, Salem.
*Congressional Record*, 1887. Vol. 18-19. Washington, D.C.: Government Printing Office, 1887.
*Congressional Record* - Senate, 49th Congress, 2nd Session. #70.
*Journal of the House of Representatives of the Territory of Washington*. Olympia, 1874.
*Statutes of Territory of Washington*. Olympia: Prosch & McElroy, 1871.

*Articles*

Beeton, Beverly and G. Thomas Edwards, "Susan B. Anthony's Woman Suffrage Crusade in the American West," in Glenda Riley (ed.) *Women in the West*. Manhattan, Kansas: Sunflower University Press, 1982.
Edwards, G. Thomas. "The Politics of Railroads, 1869," *The Call Number*. 30 (Spring 1969): 6-24.
Edwards, G. Thomas. "Terminus Disease," *Pacific Northwest Quarterly*. 70 (October 1979): 163-77.
Larson, T. A. "Idaho's Role in America's Woman Suffrage Crusade," *Idaho Yesterdays*. 18 (Spring 1974): 2-15.
Larson, T. A. "Woman's Rights in Idaho," *Idaho Yesterdays*. 16 (Spring 1972): 2-15.

Larson, T. A. "Woman Suffrage," *The Reader's Encyclopedia of the American West*, edited by Howard R. Lamar. New York: Thomas Y. Crowell, 1977.

Larson, T. A. "The Woman Suffrage Movement in Washington," *Pacific Northwest Quarterly*. 67 (1976): 49-62.

Nash, Lee. "Harvey v. Abigail: Sibling Rivalry in the Oregon Campaign for Woman Suffrage," in Possession of Professor Nash.

Stefanco, Carolyn. "Networking on the Frontier: The Colorado Women's Suffrage Movement, 1876-1893," in Susan Armitage and Elizabeth Jameson (eds.) *The Women's West*, Norman: University of Oklahoma Press, 1987.

Taber, Ronald W., "Sacagawea and the Suffragettes: An Interpretation of a Myth," *Pacific Northwest Quarterly*, 58 (January 1967): 7-13.

Wittmayer, Cecilia M. "The 1889-1890 Woman Suffrage Campaign: A Need to Organize," *South Dakota History* 31 (Summer 1981): 199-225.

*Miscellaneous*

*Annual Meeting: Woman's Christian Temperance Union of Western Washington*, n.p., 1903.

*Pacific Monthly*, 1905, 1906.

*The Pacific Northwest, Its Wealth and Resources, Oregon, Washington, Idaho*. Portland. Oregon Immigration Board, (1891?).

*Portland City Directory*. 1897.

*Progress*. Published by the National American Woman Suffrage Association at Warren, Ohio, 1905, 1906.

*Puget Sound Business Directory and Guide to Washington*. 1872.
Olympia: Murphy & Harned, 1972.

Shaffer, Melinda A. "President's Address." Western Washington WCTU, 8th Annual Convention, 1891, Tacoma.

*Seattle City Directory*. 1895, 1896, 1897.

*Settlers' Guide to Oregon and Washington Territory*. New York: 1872.

*Speech of the Hon. D. R. Bigelow on Female Suferage* [sic.], 14 October 1871. Olympia: R. H. Hewitt Printer, 1871.

*The Yearbook of the Woman's Century Club*, 1896-1897, Seattle, 1897.

# Index

# *Colophon*

THE TYPEFACE used for both text and display in *Sowing Good Seeds* is Sabon. The last typeface designed by one of the twentieth century's foremost designers, Jan Tschichold, Sabon was created in the early 1960s. Sabon was intended to meet specific pre-photocomposition era technical requirements. A group of German master printers commissioned Tschichold to execute the nearly impossible task of creating a "harmonized" typeface with identical forms for mechanical (Monotype and Linotype) and foundry composition. The resultant typeface, Sabon, is highly readable and pleasing to the eye.

*Sowing Good Seeds* is printed on 60 lb. Glatfelter paper. It is bound in Holliston Kingston Natural Finish (35438), with green/white headbands and Holliston Silver (M809B) stamping on its spine. Endpapers are Rainbow Antique (Teal-B). The colors on the jacket are PMS 5483 and 473, along with black.

The production of *Sowing Good Seeds* was accomplished through the cooperation and professional skill of the following persons and firms:

TYPESETTING: Focus Typographers, St. Louis, Missouri
PAPER, PRINTING & BINDING: Thomson-Shore, Inc., Dexter, Michigan
CHAPTER OPENING ORNAMENT: Rachael R. Resch
MAPS: Christine Rains
COVER ILLUSTRATION: Chris Michel

This book was designed and produced by the Oregon Historical Society Press.